Travel Discount Coupon

This coupon entitles yo◼◼
when you book you◼◼

◼ TRAVEL NE◼WO◼◼
RESERVATION SERVICE

Hotels ◆ Airlines ◆ Car Rentals ◆ Cruises
All Your Travel Needs

Here's what you get: *

A discount of $50 on a booking of $1,000** or more for two or more people!

A discount of $25 on a booking of $500** or more for one person!

Free membership for three years, and 1,000 free miles on enrollment in the unique Miles-to-Go™ frequent-traveler program. Earn one mile for every dollar spent through the program. Earn free hotel stays starting at 5,000 miles. Earn free roundtrip airline tickets starting at 25,000 miles.

Personal help in planning your own, customized trip.

Fast, confirmed reservations at any property recommended in this guide, subject to availability.***

Special discounts on bookings in the U.S. and around the world.

Low-cost visa and passport service.

Reduced-rate cruise packages.

Call us toll-free in the U.S. at 1-888-940-5000, or fax us at 201-567-1832. In Canada, call us toll-free at 1-800-883-9959, or fax us at 416-922-6053.

---

* To qualify for these travel discounts, at least a portion of your trip must include destinations covered in this guide. No more than one coupon discount may be used in any 12-month period, for destinations covered in this guide. Cannot be combined with any other discount or program.
**These are U.S. dollars spent on commissionable bookings.
***A $10 fee, plus fax and/or phone charges, will be added to the cost of bookings at each hotel not linked to the reservation service. Customers must approve these fees in advance.

Valid until December 31, 1997. Terms and conditions of the Miles-to-Go™ program are available on request by calling 201-567-8500, ext 55.

MIA123

Frommer's

4th Edition

Miami & the Keys

by Victoria Pesce Elliott

Macmillan • USA

ABOUT THE AUTHOR

Victoria Pesce Elliott is a freelance journalist who contributes to many local and national newspapers and magazines, including the *New York Times*. A native of Miami, she returned there after nearly a decade in New York City, where she graduated from the Columbia University Graduate School of Journalism. She is a co-author of *Frommer's Florida '97*.

MACMILLAN TRAVEL

A Simon & Schuster Macmillan Company
1633 Broadway
New York, NY 10019

Find us online at **http://www.mcp.com/mgr/travel** or
on America Online at Keyword: **Frommer's.**

ISBN: 0-02-860912-3
ISSN:1047-790X

Editor: Robin Michaelson
Production Editor: Charles Bowles
Design by Michele Laseau
Digital Cartography by TK

SPECIAL SALES

Bulk purchases (10+ copies) of Frommer's travel guides are available to corporations at special discounts. The Special Sales Department can produce custom editions to be used as premiums and/or for sales promotion to suit individual needs. Existing editions can be produced with custom cover imprints such as a corporate logos. For more information write to Special Sales, Simon & Schuster, 1633 Broadway, New York, NY 10019.

Manufactured in the United States of America

Contents

1   Introducing Miami   1

1 Frommer's Favorite Miami Experiences   2

2 The City Today   3

3 A Look at the Past: A Century of Change   6

★ *Dateline*   6

4 Famous Miamians   8

5 Architecture 101   9

6 Miami's Bill of Fare   10

2   Planning a Trip to Miami   12

1 Visitor Information & Money   12

★ *What Things Cost in Miami*   13

2 When to Go   14

★ *Miami Calendar of Events*   15

3 Insurance & Safety Concerns   18

4 Tips for Travelers with Special Needs   19

5 Getting There   20

3   For Foreign Visitors   24

1 Preparing for Your Trip   24

2 Getting to the U.S.   26

3 Getting Around the U.S.   27

★ *Fast Facts: For the Foreign Traveler*   28

4   Getting to Know Miami   32

1 Orientation   32

2 Getting Around   37

★ *Fast Facts: Miami*   39

5   Accommodations   43

1 Best Bets   45

2 South Beach   45

3 Miami Beach: Surfside, Bal Harbour & Sunny Isles   54

4 Key Biscayne 62

★ *Family-Friendly Hotels* 63

5 Downtown 63

6 West Miami 66

7 North Dade 68

8 Coral Gables 68

9 Coconut Grove 72

10 Camping & Hostels 74

11 Long-Term Stays 75

6 Dining 77

1 Best Bets 78

2 Restaurants by Cuisine 80

3 South Beach 82

4 Miami Beach: Surfside, Bal Harbour & Sunny Isles 95

5 Key Biscayne 99

6. Downtown 101

7 Little Havana 104

★ *From Ceviche to Picadillo: Spanish Cuisine at a Glance* 105

8 West Dade 107

9 North Dade 107

★ *Family-Friendly Restaurants* 109

10 Coral Gables & Environs 111

11 Coconut Grove 116

12 South Miami 118

7 What to See & Do 121

★ *Suggested Itineraries* 121

1 Miami's Beaches 122

2 The Art Deco District 126

3 Animal Parks 127

4 Miami's Museum & Art Scene 128

5 More Attractions 132

6 Nature Preserves, Parks & Gardens 134

7 Especially for Kids 136

8 Organized Tours 136

9 Water Sports 139

10 More Places to Play, Both Indoors & Out 142

★ *Seasonal Pleasures: Pick Your Own Produce* 143

11 Spectator Sports 147

8 Driving and Walking Around Miami 150

1 Driving Tour 1—Miami Panorama 150

2 Driving Tour 2—Downtown, Coconut Grove & Coral Gables 153

3 A Walking Tour—South Beach: The Deco District 157

★ *A Deco District Glossary* 158

9 Shopping 161

1 The Shopping Scene 161

★ *Best Buys* 163

2 Shopping A to Z 164

★ *A Taste of Old Florida* 171

10 Miami After Dark 176

1 The Performing Arts 177

2 The Club & Music Scene 180

★ *Roots, Rhythms & Rituals: A Secret Beach Party* 182

3 The Gay & Lesbian Scene 183

4 The Latin Scene 184

★ *Where to Learn to Salsa* 185

5 Movies & More 186

6 Late-Night Bites 186

11 Side Trips from Miami 187

1 Biscayne National Park 187

★ *Robert Is Here Selling Fruit* 190

2 Everglades National Park 190

3 Quick Getaways to the Bahamas 202

12 The Keys 204

1 Exploring the Keys by Car 206

2 The Great Outdoors 208

3 The Upper Keys: Key Largo to Marathon 210

4 The Lower Keys: Big Pine Key to Coppitt Key 223

5 Key West 229
★ *The 10 Keymanments* 232
6 The Dry Tortugas 246

Appendix 249

Index 251

Map List

Florida   4

Miami at a Glance   35

South Beach
  Accommodations   49

Miami Beach
  Accommodations   55

Accommodations in Coral
  Gables, Coconut Grove
  & Downtown   69

South Beach Dining   83

Miami Beach Dining   97

Dining in Coral Gables,
  Coconut Grove &
  Downtown   113

Miami Area Attractions &
  Beaches   124

South Beach Attractions   129

Attractions in Greater Miami,
  South   135

**Miami Driving/Walking
Tours**

Driving Tour—Miami
  Panorama   151

Driving Tour—Downtown,
  Coconut Grove & Coral
  Gables   155

Walking Tour—South
  Beach: The Deco
  District   159

Side Trips from Miami

Everglades National Park   193

The Keys   207

Key West   231

ACKNOWLEDGMENTS

The author wishes to thank her entire family—Dr. Paul Pesce, Eleanor Pesce, Christopher and P.J. Pesce, and especially her husband/pilot/chauffeur, Eric Robinson Elliott—for their generous support and input. Special thanks to Laura Brancella for her dedication, ability to work under pressure, and her mustard. I am also grateful to Robin Michaelson for her friendship, insight, and humor. Additional acknowledgment must go to Lourdes Alvares, Michael Aller, Nancy Domeyer, Natalie Morales, The Greater Miami Convention and Visitor's Bureau, and the entire Miami staff of the *New York Times*, including Kerry Gruson, Mia Navarro, and John Steinman.

AN INVITATION TO THE READER

In researching this book, I discovered many wonderful places. I'm sure you'll find others. Please tell me about them, so I can share the information with your fellow travelers in upcoming editions. If you were disappointed with a recommendation, I'd love to know that, too. Please write to:

Victoria Elliott
Frommer's Miami & the Keys, 4th Edition
Macmillan Travel
1633 Broadway
New York, NY 10019

AN ADDITIONAL NOTE

Please be advised that travel information is subject to change at any time—and this is especially true of prices. We therefore suggest that you write or call ahead for confirmation when making your travel plans. The author, editors, and publisher cannot be held responsible for the experiences of readers while traveling. Your safety is important to us, however, so we encourage you to stay alert and be aware of your surroundings. Keep a close eye on cameras, purses, and wallets, all favorite targets of thieves and pickpockets.

WHAT THE SYMBOLS MEAN

✪ Frommer's Favorites

Hotels, restaurants, attractions, and entertainment you shouldn't miss.

⑤ Super-Special Values

Hotels and restaurants that offer great value for your money.

The following abbreviations are used for credit and charge cards:

AE	American Express	EURO	Eurocard
CB	Carte Blanche	JCB	Japan Credit Bank
DC	Diners Club	MC	MasterCard
DISC	Discover	V	Visa
ER	enRoute		

Introducing Miami

It is hard to know in which language to introduce yourself to this polyglot mini-nation. When you land at Miami International Airport, the nation's second-largest hub for international travelers, you'll hear Spanish, Portuguese, Creole, French, and Italian as a matter of course. Once in Miami, you'll find a curious mix of Caribbean immigrants, orthodox Jews, retirees seeking easier winters, models, actors, artists, wealthy real-estate moguls, and movie executives, as well as an already diverse crowd of longtime Floridians, black ancestors of Bahamian railroad workers, Native Americans, and Hispanics. The city is a virtual mosaic of colors, sounds, and scents.

Although some residents say disdainfully, "It's just not like it used to be," the truth is Miami has always been a magnet for the masses. In fact, since 1980, Dade County's population, with Miami as its largest municipality, has grown nearly 33 percent.

Since the Spanish first colonized the area in the 16th century, Miami has been a home to runaways, castaways, and dreamers. Through its many incarnations, two Miami characteristics have remained constant—its predictable year-round warmth and its location, a peninsula pointing emphatically toward so many other nations. These traits have attracted newcomers year after year. Now Miami, known as "The Capital of the Americas," serves as Latin American and International headquarters for hundreds of multinational corporations. It's also the second-largest banking center in the United States.

Encompassing both the mainland and the barrier islands of Miami Beach, Greater Miami boasts about 2 million residents and hosts more than 9 million visitors annually. They come for different reasons. Some are drawn by the unadulterated sea and surf; some for the outrageous nightlife; others for the business opportunities; still others can't get enough of the natural wilderness right in the city's backyard.

Fortunately, the evolution of America's southernmost metropolitan region—from a simple playground to a vibrant cosmopolitan city—has not been achieved at the expense of the area's celebrated surf and sand. Despite Miami's quick transformation, the almost complete absence of heavy industry has left the air and water as clear, clean, and inviting as ever. But Miami is no longer just a beach vacation—you'll also find high-quality hotels, distinctive restaurants, unusual attractions, and top shopping. Relaxing days on the water are now complemented by nights that include choice theater and opera, restaurants serving exotic and delicious food, a hopping club scene, and a lively cafe culture.

1 Frommer's Favorite Miami Experiences

- **Boating off the Coast of Miami Beach:** Miami Beach bills itself as the sun and surf capital of the world—find out why! A high-speed boat ride off the coast of Miami Beach is a must, especially if you've never been here before.
- **Cruising with the Top Down:** Driving over the causeways onto any of Miami's wonderful islands, especially Key Biscayne, with the roof down is one of my favorite things to do. Tune the radio to a hokey country station, catch a nice tan on your bare shoulders, and watch the water glimmer around you.
- **Lunching in Little Havana:** Miami's Cuban center is the city's most important ethnic enclave. Located just west of Downtown, Little Havana is centered around "Calle Ocho," SW 8th Street. Car-repair shops, tailors, electronics stores, and restaurants all hang signs in Spanish; salsa rhythms thump from the radios of passersby; and old men in guayaberas chain-smoke cigars over their daily games of dominoes. Stop for a big filling lunch, and top it off with a Cuban coffee to really get the day going.
- **Swimming at Midnight:** At any time of day the ocean is beautiful and fun to swim in. However, there's nothing more exciting than going down to the shore with a friend in the middle of the night and taking a late-night dip. Most people can't help invoking the scary warning music from the movie Jaws, but don't worry: Sharks don't usually mistake people for food, even in the dark.
- **Waking up to the Sound of the Surf:** Sometimes when I am staying in a Miami oceanfront hotel, I'll hear what sounds like pouring rain against the windows. Still sleepy, I'll pull the shades open and see a cloudless blue sky and realize it's just the pounding of the waves against the shore. It's a nice sound to wake up to.
- **Biking, Blading, or Walking Through the Art Deco District on Ocean Drive:** The beauty of South Beach's celebrated Art Deco District culminates on the 15-block beachfront strip known as Ocean Drive. Most of the buildings on this stretch are hotels built in the late 1930s and early 1940s. You'll appreciate the architecture as you go down this colorful street—by bike, by in-line skates, or by foot.
- **Tanning on Miami's Beaches:** You can choose your spot on dozens of miles of white-sand beaches, edged with coconut palms on one side and a clear turquoise ocean on the other. Each of Miami's many beach areas boasts its own distinctive character. While Europeans and naturalists enjoy a popular nude beach in North Dade, families barbecue on remote stretches of beach in Key Biscayne.
- **Dancing Until Dawn:** Choose your dance floor: From full-moon drumming sessions on the beach or salsa at the Latin clubs to wading through "foam parties" at European-style discos and jamming at outdoor reggae bars.
- **Enjoying New World Cuisine:** World-class chefs have discovered the richness of locally harvested ingredients, including tropical fruits and seafood. This culling of techniques and ingredients from the Cuban, Haitian, and Asian communities has created the now-famous "New World Cuisine."
- **Doing Whatever on, in, or Above the Water:** One of the best ways to appreciate Miami is from the water—on it, in it, or above it. Options include parasailing, jetskiing, kayaking, sailing, scuba diving, snorkeling, and windsurfing. Of course, you can always swim or ride the waves.

- **Snorkeling in Biscayne National Park:** The thriving reef system at Biscayne National Park, a unique ecological preserve that's mostly underwater, attracts thousands of scuba divers and snorkelers every year.

2 The City Today

Miami today is a unique American polyglot. There are more than 2 million residents in Dade County, of which 25% are non-Latin white, 21% black, and 55% Hispanic, according to estimates from the Dade County Planning Department. The city's heterogeneous mix includes more than 560,000 Cubans, 40,000 Jamaicans and Bahamians, 72,000 Puerto Ricans, 23,000 Dominicans, and perhaps as many as 100,000 Haitians. Add to this a 1995 total of 9.4 million visitors from all around the world, and it's easy to understand why this is truly an international city.

In recent years, Miami has had a spate of publicity—some bad and some good. In the early 1990s, a spurt of freeway shootings persuaded several European governments to issue advisories against travel to Florida, resulting in a sharp drop in the number of international visitors coming to the city and the state overall. In 1992, America's most destructive hurricane demolished billions of dollars worth of local real estate.

More recently, Miami has made the news for more positive reasons. The Summit of the Americas, held in 1994, brought together more than 30 heads of state from throughout the Western Hemisphere. In 1995, the city hosted tens of thousands of sports fans for the Superbowl. In 1996, extravagant celebrations, including an 850-pound cake, helped mark the city's Centennial. On the sports front, a new celebrity coach, Pat Riley, joined the Miami basketball team, the Heat, while the former Cowboy's maverick, Jimmy Johnson, took over Don Shula's team, the Dolphin's. And in 1996, MTV put together another "Real World" episode on South Beach. After passing through the city during film shoots, many celebrities, such as Sylvester Stallone, Madonna, Cher, Sophia Loren, and Whitney Houston, now call Miami their home.

Thanks to the increased vigilance of Miami police and the harsh sentences meted out to the perpetrators of the much-publicized murders, both the rates of violence against tourists and overall crime have dropped to an all-time low. The city, like many other large metropolises, still suffers from random muggings and the like, but in the more-touristed areas, visitors are relatively safe.

If we could isolate a single principle that has kept Miami afloat over its short but tumultuous lifetime, it would be resiliency. Problems are nothing new to Miami, and the city always seems to rebound. Over the years, hurricanes, riots, and waves of immigration have altered the city's physical and cultural landscape. But with each cataclysm, a new stability has emerged, creating a city that is both more complex and more dynamic than the one that preceded it.

Impressions

In so many ways, Miami represents the promise of hemispheric integration. I have been deeply moved over the last few years when I've had the opportunity to go to Miami and see the heroic efforts that people have made to build a genuine, multicultural, multiracial society that would be at the crossroads of the Americas, and therefore at the forefront of the future.

—U.S. President William Clinton, at the Summit of the Americas, 1994

Florida

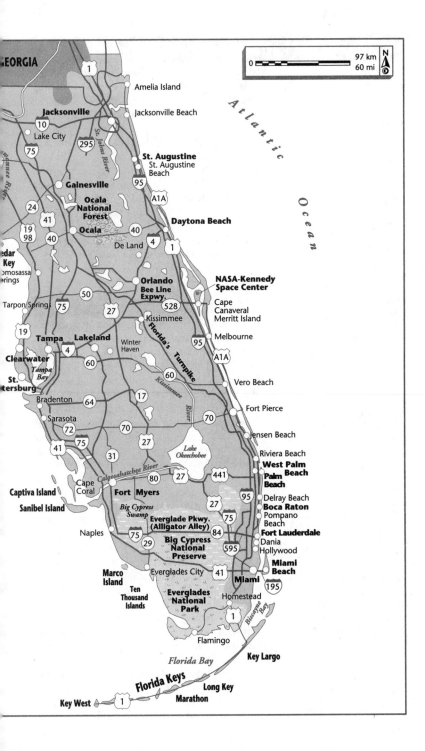

GEORGIA

Amelia Island

Jacksonville
Jacksonville Beach
10
Lake City
295
St. Johns River
75
St. Augustine
St. Augustine Beach
Gainesville
95
Ocala National Forest
24
41
Ocala
40
19
98
40
De Land
Daytona Beach
4
1
edar Key
omosassa rings
Tarpon Springs
50
Orlando
Bee Line Expwy.
NASA-Kennedy Space Center
75
27
528
Kissimmee
Cape Canaveral Merritt Island
19
Tampa **Lakeland**
Winter Haven
Florida's Turnpike
Melbourne
95
4
A1A
Clearwater
60
St. tersburg
Tampa Bay
60
Kissimmee River
Vero Beach
Bradenton
64
17
Fort Pierce
Sarasota
70
70
Jensen Beach
72
Lake Okeechobee
41
75
31
27
Riviera Beach
West Palm Beach
Caloosahatchee River
80
27
441
Palm Beach
Cape Coral
Fort Myers
95
Delray Beach
Captiva Island
Big Cypress Swamp
27
Boca Raton
Pompano Beach
Sanibel Island
Everglade Pkwy. (Alligator Alley)
75
84
Fort Lauderdale
Naples
75
29
Big Cypress National Preserve
595
Dania
Hollywood
Marco Island
Everglades City
41
Miami
Miami Beach
195
Ten Thousand Islands
Everglades National Park
Homestead
Biscayne Bay
1
Flamingo
Key Largo
Florida Bay
Florida Keys
Long Key
Key West
1
Marathon

Atlantic Ocean

0   97 km
          60 mi
N

5

3   A Look at the Past: A Century of Change

Dateline

- **1513** Juan Ponce de Leon is first European to land in Florida.
- **1600** Spanish colonization continues.
- **1763** England trades Havana for Florida. British plantations established.
- **1776** Florida fights on England's side during American Revolution.
- **1783** England returns Florida to Spain in exchange for the Bahamas and Gibraltar.
- **1785** Border disputes between Spain and America.
- **1821** U.S. acquires Florida. Andrew Jackson appointed first governor.
- **1835–42** Seminole War; some 300 remaining natives deported to reservations.
- **1845** Florida becomes the 27th U.S. state.
- **1881** Philadelphia industrialist, Hamilton Disston, buys 1 million acres of Everglades, paving the way for South Florida's development.
- **1896** Henry M. Flagler extends railroad to Miami.
- **1898** Spanish-American War; army camps based in Miami.
- **1900** Florida's population is 530,000.
- **1915** Carl Fisher dredges Biscayne Bay to build Miami Beach.
- **1921** President-elect Warren Harding spends winter in Miami.
- **1925** Freedom Tower built in downtown Miami.
- **1926** Hurricane swamps Miami; the Biltmore Hotel completed in Coral Gables.

continues

Miami, a city that just celebrated its 100th birthday, only now is defining itself as a cultural, historical, and financial capital of the Americas.

Not so long ago, it was an uninhabitable wilderness plagued by mosquitoes and warring natives. Until the final years of the 19th century, much of the Florida peninsula remained unsurveyed, inhabited by only a few remaining Native American Seminoles. To most Americans, southern Florida was arduously remote, visited by only enterprising explorers and hunters. Some adventurers attempted the journey south on horseback, following ancient Native American trails; others went by sea on one of the open sloops that carried the coastal trade. Either way, the voyage down Florida's east coast was both long and dangerous.

Even though in 1891 an unescorted woman traveling alone was considered nothing short of scandalous, Julia Tuttle, the widow of a wealthy Cleveland industrialist, arrived in a small southeast Florida town with determination and a dream. At that time, the town consisted of little more than a few plantations, a small trading post, and the ruins of a U.S. Army camp once known as Fort Dallas. Sensing the economic and social potential of America's most tropical land, Tuttle set out to transform it into a full-blown town. Realization of her dream depended on easier access to the area, but the northern railroad magnates were less than enthusiastic. Fate intervened, however, in the winter of 1895, when a gripping freeze practically destroyed the state's northern citrus crop. With a shipment of fresh orange blossoms as evidence of both southern Florida's ability to rebound quickly from severe cold and its agricultural prospects, Tuttle again courted America's rail barons. The following year, Henry Flagler's first train steamed into town; Tuttle had gifted him half of her 600-acre prime riverfront property. Thus Tuttle became the only woman in American history to start a major city.

It wasn't long before Miami's irresistible combination of surf, sun, and sand prompted wealthy Americans to build elaborate winter retreats overlooking Biscayne Bay. (One of these mansions, Villa Vizcaya, remains and is open to the public—see Chapter 7.) Miami became a chic place to be, and, following World War I, widespread middle-class interest in the region prompted spectacular growth.

The newcomers discovered that hefty windfalls could be made in real-estate speculation, and tales of million-dollar profits drove the population of Miami up from 30,000 to 100,000 in just five years. More than 300,000 vacationers visited Miami in the winter of 1924–25 alone.

The building boom of the Roaring Twenties was directly responsible for the city's distinctive neighborhoods of today. Coral Gables, the single largest real-estate venture of the time, became one of the most beautiful and exclusive residential areas in Miami. The towns of Hialeah, Miami Springs, and Opa-Locka were planned and built by entrepreneur Glenn H. Curtiss as winter homesites for upper-middle-class northerners. Opa-Locka, his most celebrated development, was designed around an Arabian Nights theme, complete with domes, parapets, and minarets. Another fanciful developer, Carl Fisher, dredged Biscayne Bay and built up the islands of Miami Beach for his opulent hotels, tennis courts, golf courses, and polo fields.

The Great Depression slowed Miami's boom and changed the nature of the city's buildings, exemplified primarily by the art deco styles of South Beach. The buildings are at the same time austere and whimsical, reflecting both a stark reality and the promise of better times. Regarded as architectural masterpieces today, these pastel structures offer budget-minded visitors an attractive alternative to the luxurious accommodations up the beach.

Miami's belt-tightening days were short-lived. The end of World War II brought a second boom and another development frenzy. Again entire communities were built and sold wholesale. Miami Beach's communities were redesigned and rebuilt as resorts, and some television shows, like Arthur Godfrey's in the 1950s and Jackie Gleason's in the 1960s, began to be telecast coast-to-coast from Miami.

Tourism waned again in the 1960s, but, at the same time, Miami began welcoming a new wave of dreamers. With a desire for a better life and a steadfast belief in the American Dream, Cuban refugees and other sunbelt settlers started Miami's transformation from a resort community to a city of international stature. Most of the original 265,000 Cuban freedom-seekers came with little more than their entrepreneurial skills and a desire to build new lives. Their overwhelming accomplishments in constructing a strong educational, economic, and

- **1930s** Hundreds of art deco hotels built in South Beach.
- **1947** Everglades National Park dedicated by President Harry S Truman.
- **1950** Frozen citrus concentrate becomes a major industry.
- **1954** Fontainebleau Hotel opens on Miami Beach.
- **1958** First jet passenger service between Miami and New York.
- **1959** Fidel Castro assumes power in Cuba; a mass exodus to South Florida follows.
- **1968** Richard Nixon nominated for president at the Republican National Convention in Miami Beach.
- **1973** Miami Dolphins win Super Bowl VII, boasting the only undefeated season in NFL history.
- **1977** Orange juice spokesperson Anita Bryant leads fight against equal rights ordinance for gays; Dade County rejects rights bill.
- **1980** Four ex-Miami policemen acquitted of killing black insurance executive, Arthur McDuffie; riots leave 6 dead, 370 wounded. Some 140,000 Cubans enter South Florida when Castro opens port of Mariel.
- **1984** Miami's $1-billion Metrorail opens.
- **1991** Greater Miami's population reaches 1.9 million.
- **1992** Hurricane Andrew sweeps through Dade and Monroe Counties, causing an estimated $30 billion in damage.
- **1994** Miami hosts the Summit of the Americas, in which heads of 34

continues

countries from South, Central, and North America, and the Caribbean meet in the first such hemispheric conference in 28 years.

■ **1996** Miami celebrates its centennial with festivals and events throughout the year.

■ **1997** The Everglades National Park marks its 50th year.

cultural base is one of America's greatest success stories.

In the early 1980s, Miami underwent its biggest building boom yet. Fantastically beautiful and unique skyscrapers sprang up downtown and along the boulevards flanking Biscayne Bay; the city's harbor became the biggest cruise-ship port in the world; and Miami International Airport grew to be America's second-busiest international gateway. Hundreds of multinational corporations, banks, and insurance firms opened offices, and a billion-dollar, futuristic Metrorail system whisked its way into the city.

The 1988 reopening of the Miami Beach Convention Center, with its high-tech "new deco" facade, marked the rebirth of South Florida conventioneering.

Suddenly Miami wasn't just blooming; it was stylish. The hit television series, "Miami Vice," spotlighted the quirky and colorful city. Filmmakers found it hard to resist the rich texture and year-round accessibility of Miami as a backdrop. The show also put the city on the fashion map, with the world's top models and photographers seduced by the region's climate and colors. As the city became more sophisticated it began catering to the needs of commercial and artistic film crews with full-capacity studios, rental houses, film labs, and production equipment. In 1985, the Miami Office of Film, Television, and Print issued a total of about 350 permits. Ten years later, they issued nearly 5,000 permits, and moviegoers across the country got a memorable glimpse of South Beach in the 1996 film *The Birdcage*.

4 Famous Miamians

Muhammad Ali (b.1942)   Like many other boxers who hit the big time, Muhammad Ali (born Cassius Clay) lived in Miami and trained in South Beach's Fifth Street Gym, demolished in the 1990s to make room for the spectacular growth in South Beach.

Al Capone (1899–1947)   In the late 1920s, Chicago's most infamous gangster moved his operations to Miami and settled into a white-stucco mansion on Palm Island.

Roy Cohn (1927–1986)   Disbarred just before he died, Roy Cohn is best known as the chief counsel for the "red-baiting witch hunts" organized by Senator Joseph McCarthy in the 1950s. Cohn was raised in Miami Beach, where he was a childhood friend of television journalist Barbara Walters.

Amelia Earhart (1897–1937)   The world's most famous aviatrix began her ill-fated flight around the world from Miami. A city park is named in her honor.

Gloria Estefan (b.1957)   She's come a long way from the Miami Sound Machine. Estefan sang for Pope John Paul and composed the theme song for the 1996 Olympic Games in Atlanta. She is frequently spotted at one of her restaurants in town.

Impressions

They say Miami Beach will make a comeback, and who knows, maybe it will . . . for me, Miami Beach is still one of the most beautiful places in the world.

—Isaac Bashevis Singer, *My Love Affair with Miami Beach* (1986)

She and her husband, record producer Emilio Estefan, keep a palatial mansion on Miami Beach's Star Island.

Perry Farrel (b. 1960 Perry Bernstein)   The lead singer of alternative L.A. rock bands Jane's Addiction and Porno for Pyros grew up in North Miami Beach, where he spent most of his time surfing and performing until he hit the West Coast big.

Don Johnson (b.1950)   New episodes of "Miami Vice" are no longer being produced, but Don Johnson, one of the show's stars, still likes to kick around the city that made him famous. Johnson bought a home on Star Island, a fancy parcel in the middle of Biscayne Bay.

Madonna (b. 1958)   Since purchasing her $4.9 million mansion in Coconut Grove, the platinum record singer has become a fixture on the Miami nightclub scene. She has also done many photo shoots here for her albums and books, including *Bedtime Stories* and *Sex*.

Bob Marley (1945–1981)   Perhaps one of the most influential figures in Jamaican history, Bob Marley was more than just a reggae musician. He was a spokesman for his people, a cultural leader of millions. Marley spent a lot of time in Miami and eventually died in a Miami hospital.

Richard M. Nixon (1913–1994)   Richard Nixon made Key Biscayne his "Winter White House" during his years as President of the United States. Subsequent owners have remodeled the property extensively, making it unrecognizable as the ex-president's ex-residence.

Mickey Rourke (b.1956)   The actor/biker has started several restaurants and clubs in South Beach, his hometown, and often shows up at smoky bars throughout the city.

Sylvester Stallone (b. 1946)   A movie star, director, and producer, Stallone attended the University of Miami in the late 1960s, and then returned to Miami to purchase an $8-million bayfront estate that's next door to Madonna and near the famed Vizcaya. He is now very active in the community's cultural affairs and is part owner of the South Beach nightclub, Bar None.

Barbara Walters (b. 1931)   The renowned television interviewer grew up in Miami Beach and went to Beach High. Other notable Beach High alums are actor Andy Garcia and Roy Firestone, a sports commentator for ESPN.

5   Architecture 101

Miami's flamboyant, surprising, and fanciful architecture is one of the city's greatest treasures. This young city's various building styles occurred too close together in time to classify them in "eras," but three distinct forms, indigenous to specific periods, are clearly in evidence.

The best of the "old" buildings were constructed between 1914 and 1925 by Miami's first developers. Designed primarily in an Italian Renaissance style are such structures as Villa Vizcaya, the Biltmore Hotel, and the Venetian Pool. The many Mediterranean Revival homes built in the late 1920s and 1930s use antique Spanish tiles, arched doorways, and open courtyards. Other monuments in and around Coral Gables and Coconut Grove, including George Merrick's wonderful plazas and fountains, are timeless examples of tasteful wealth and beauty. See "Driving Tour 2" in Chapter 8 for more in-depth descriptions.

Miami's second distinct building style is its most famous. The celebrated Art Deco District in South Beach is a remarkable dreamlike foray into fashion and art on a

Impressions

The first time I saw Miami, I experienced a series of emotions and was able to relive certain atmospheres, and breathe in the same imagination and creativity that was alive in the streets of Capri and St. Tropez' golden years. That is how I began my love affair with this city—with its people, its colors and its surprisingly contagious vitality . . . Miami is an oasis where one can be regenerated, with a tremendous feeling of freedom.

—Designer and Miami resident, Gianni Versace, 1995

grand scale. For the casual observer, the best buildings are the recently rehabilitated ones fronting the Atlantic on Ocean Drive. Until recently, South Beach, as the area is also called, had fallen into massive decay. But, thanks to strong community involvement and support, the district is now protected by a 1979 listing on the National Register of Historic Places. Continuously undergoing intensive revitalization, South Beach's hotels are now some of the hippest in Miami. See "A Walking Tour" in Chapter 8 for more in-depth information.

The sleek 21st-century skyline of downtown Miami represents the city's newest building wave. Almost every structure in the small bayfront cluster is a gem. Designed with independence, creativity, and a flamboyant flair, the skyscrapers in and around Brickell Avenue stand sharp and proud, like exotic entrants in a futuristic design competition. From across the bay, the cluster of shining buildings creates one of the most awesome cityscapes in the world. See "Driving Tour 2" in Chapter 8.

Other innovative architecture includes internationally acclaimed designs by Arquitectonica in downtown Miami and Miami Beach. The critics have come up with a profusion of monikers for the brash designs that forever altered the Miami skyline: surrealistic, exuberant, Romantic Modernism, and Beach Blanket Bauhaus.

6 Miami's Bill of Fare

Miami is an exciting place to eat. What's on the menu? Everything from exotic fruits and vegetables to stone crab and fresh fish, from foreign cooking to delicious inventions. You can taste it all not only in the city's many restaurants but in the kiosks and grocery stores where locals buy their groceries.

Miami's regional cooking, coined "New World Cuisine," stems from the city's unique location, climate, and ethnic composition. Miami cuisine is based on the California model, exemplified by creatively prepared dishes using fresh local ingredients. Many of the presentations are health-oriented fish and vegetable dishes, highlighted by delicate dashes of color. Fruity sauces topping succulent seafood are common, as are jazzed-up versions of traditional meat and poultry dishes. Local citrus fruits are widely used as garnishes in sauces, and as the primary ingredient in such recipes as Key lime pie.

Miami's ethnic edibles are as rich and diverse as the city's brilliant blend of cultures. In addition to the many straightforward rice-and-beans dishes served in traditional South and Central American restaurants (see "Little Havana" in Chapter 6 for details), you'll find Latin and Caribbean influences on even the most conservative menus. Cuban fried yucca, Bahamian conch fritters, tropical Caribbean preserves, Creole-style blackened fish, Spanish arroz con pollo, and all kinds of tapas are available all over town.

Here's a short list of readily available local specialties:

Alligator, usually farm-raised, provides a smooth meat which is extremely lean and therefore likely to become tough if not cooked carefully. Usually it's battered and fried and very tasty. In some spots you may find alligator stew, an Old Florida specialty.

Conch, pronounced "conk," is a chewy shellfish that comes in those huge shells you can blow like horns or put next to your ear to "hear" the ocean. This Bahamian specialty is usually served as an appetizer, either in a marinated *ceviche* or salad, in chowder, or battered and fried as "fritters."

Dolphin is a popular fish that has nothing to do with "Flipper" or his marine mammal relatives. This Florida specialty is a plump, white-meat saltwater fish that is great blackened or skewered or just plain grilled.

Key lime pie is the region's most famous dessert. The citrus fruit that flavors the filling is small and yellow and indigenous to South Florida and the Florida Keys. The most authentic pie is sweetened with condensed milk and has a yellow pudding-like filling and a graham-cracker crust.

Florida **lobster** is smaller and somewhat sweeter than the Maine shellfish of the same name. But the spiny Florida variety has no claws, so look for a big meaty tail or a variety of pasta dishes that use the meat for filling or sauces.

Florida **mangos** only grow for a few short months, from roughly May to August, although they are used in sauces and chutneys throughout the year. From the Sanskrit word *ama* (meaning "of the people"), mangos are a truly unifying force in this city. During the season hundreds of varieties grow in yards and roadsides and are so plentiful that neighbors gift each other bags of the luscious fruits and help each other cut, peel, and process them.

Floridians wait for **stone crab** season the way the French wait for the new Beaujolais. The crab's claws are the only part of the animal you eat. Crabbers clip one or two claws, then toss the crustacean back in the water so it can grow more.

Citrus fruits are the area's largest legal cash crop, accounting for the lion's share of Florida's $12-billion agricultural industry. The state produces more than 80% of the nation's limes, 50% of the world's grapefruits, and 25% of the world's oranges. Needless to say, citrus juice is the drink of choice in these parts. Try starting your day with a cool glass of the freshest orange or grapefruit juice you've ever had. At night, get a sense of the city's close Caribbean connections by mixing that juice with rum from one of the nearby islands.

A variety of ✪ **smoked fishes,** especially marlin, amberjack, and dolphin, appear on bar and restaurant menus and are sold at smokehouses throughout the city. The tender meat has a rough, smoky taste and is often served as a dip mixed with mayonnaise and spices.

2

Planning a Trip to Miami

Although it is possible to land in Miami without an itinerary or reservations, your trip will be much more rewarding with a little bit of advance planning.

Of the many special events scheduled throughout the year, the bulk are staged from October through May. This reflects the close relationship between tourism and festivals, but in no way means that Miami's special events are canned tourist traps. In fact, these events are just the opposite; Miamians have a talent for creating popular outdoor festivals. Although the success of city festivals often relies on tourist dollars, the inspiration and creativity that goes into them is 100% homegrown.

1 Visitor Information & Money

VISITOR INFORMATION

The best source for any kind of specialized information about the city is the **Greater Miami Convention and Visitors Bureau,** 701 Brickell Ave., Miami, FL 33131 (☎ 305/539-3063, or 800/283-2707, or gmcvb@aol.com or http:www.Miamiandbeaches.com). Even if you don't have a specific question, call ahead to request their free magazine, *Destination Miami,* which includes several good, easy-to-use maps. The office is open weekdays from 9am to 5pm.

For information on traveling in Florida, contact the **Florida Division of Tourism (FDT),** 126 W. Van Buren St., Tallahassee, FL 32399 (☎ 904/487-1462). The office is open weekdays from 8am to 5pm. Europeans should note that FDT maintains an office in Great Britain at 18/24 Westbourne Grove, 4th floor, London W2 5RH (☎ 071/727-1661).

In addition to information on some of South Beach's better hotels, the **Miami Design Preservation League,** 1001 Ocean Dr. (P.O. Bin L), Miami Beach, FL 33119 (☎ 305/672-2014), offers an informative free guide to the Art Deco District and several books on the subject. It's open Monday through Saturday from 10am to 7pm.

Greater Miami's various chambers of commerce also send maps and information about their particular neighborhoods. These include:

- **Coconut Grove Chamber of Commerce,** 2820 McFarlane Rd., Miami, FL 33133 (☎ 305/444-7270).
- **Coral Gables Chamber of Commerce,** 50 Aragon Ave., Coral Gables, FL 33134 (☎ 305/446-1657).
- **Florida Gold Coast Chamber of Commerce,** 1100 Kane Concourse (Bay Harbor Islands), Miami, FL 33154 (☎ 305/866-6020)—this office represents Bal Harbour, Sunny Isles, Surfside, and other North Dade waterfront communities.
- **Greater Miami Chamber of Commerce,** Omni International, 1601 Biscayne Blvd., Miami, FL 33132 (☎ 305/539-3063, or 800/283-2707).
- **Miami Beach Chamber of Commerce,** 1920 Meridian Ave., Miami Beach, FL 33139 (☎ 305/672-1270).

The following organizations represent dues-paying hotels, restaurants, and attractions in their specific areas. These associations can arrange accommodations and tours as well as provide discount coupons to area sights: **Miami Beach Resort Hotel Association,** 407 Lincoln Rd., Miami Beach, FL 33139 (☎ 305/531-3553, or 800/531-3553); and **Sunny Isles Beach Resort Association,** 3909 Sunny Isles Blvd., Suite 307, Sunny Isles, FL 33160 (☎ 305/947-5826, or 800/327-6366).

MONEY

You never have to carry a lot of cash in Miami. Automated teller machines (ATMs) are located at virtually every bank in the city, and credit cards are accepted by the vast majority of Miami's hotels, restaurants, attractions, shops, and nightspots. U.S.-dollar traveler's checks are also widely accepted for goods and services, and can be exchanged for cash at banks and check-issuing offices.

1st Nationwide Bank, 517 Arthur Godfrey Rd., accepts cards on Cirrus, Honor, and Metroteller networks. For the location of the nearest ATM, call **800/424-7787**

What Things Cost in Miami	U.S. $
Taxi from Miami Airport to a Downtown hotel	22–26
Local telephone call	.25
Double room at the Grand Bay Hotel (Expensive)	285.00
Double room at the Indian Creek Hotel (Moderate)	120.00
Double room at the Suez Motel (Inexpensive)	70.00
Lunch for one at the Centro Vasco (Moderate)	13.00
Lunch for one at Mrs. Mendoza's (Inexpensive)	6.00
Dinner for one, without wine, at Chef Allen's (Very Expensive)	49.00
Dinner for one, without wine, at Versailles (Inexpensive)	13.00
Pint of beer	2.75
Coca-Cola in a restaurant	1.50
Cup of coffee	1.25
Roll of ASA 100 film, 36 exposures	6.50
Admission to Miami Metrozoo	6.00
Movie ticket	7.50

for the Cirrus network or **800/843-7587** for the Plus system. Banks making cash advances against MasterCard and Visa cards include Barnett Bank (☎ 800/342-8472) and NationsBank (☎ 800/367-6262). American Express cardholders can write a personal check, guaranteed against the card, for up to $1,000 in cash at any American Express office (see "Fast Facts: Miami" in Chapter 4 for locations).

2 When to Go

Miami's tourist season, from December through April, is more reflective of the weather up north than it is of climatic changes in South Florida. It's always warm in Miami. No matter what time of year you visit, you'll find that indoor spaces are always air-conditioned, cafes always have tables out on the sidewalk, and the beaches are always full.

Terrific weather has always been Miami's main appeal and is a particular delight during the winter, when the rest of the country is shivering. When it's winter in Wisconsin it's still summer in the Sunshine State. The period from November to mid-May is considered the high season; many hotels tend to raise prices by the first week of November and lower them by the end of May.

Don't overlook traveling to Miami during the "off " seasons, when vacationing can be every bit as rewarding. The weather is still great, and hotel prices are significantly lower than at other times of the year. In addition, restaurants, stores, and highways are less crowded.

South Florida's unique climate is extremely tropical. Hot, sometimes muggy summers are counterbalanced by wonderfully warm winters. Winds are strong and clouds move fast across the sky. It's not uncommon for a sudden shower to be followed by several hours of intense sunshine. For most natives, "winter" is too cold for swimming; for the rest of us, however, 70-degree January afternoons are welcome miracles of nature. But don't be misled: There are occasional cold snaps, and even one short tropical rain shower can ruin a day at the beach.

Finally, a word about Florida's tropical storms and hurricanes: Most occur between August and November. For local property owners, the tumultuous winds that sweep in from the Atlantic Ocean can be devastating. In August 1992, for example, Hurricane Andrew—one of the fiercest storms ever recorded in Florida—caused about $30 billion in damage to residential and business districts in Dade and Monroe Counties. More than 250,000 people were left homeless.

For visitors, the high winds and incessant rains *usually* mean little more than a delayed vacation. Visitors to Miami who stayed through Hurricane Andrew found that most hotels and major tourist attractions suffered relatively little damage and all have since reopened.

Meteorologists know far in advance when a storm is brewing off the Atlantic Coast and can determine pretty accurately what force it will have; the information is then broadcast nationwide. With respect to Andrew, the National Hurricane Center, located in Coral Gables, gave due warning of the storm and tracked it closely as it approached Florida, though they were unable to predict the exact spot where the storm would make landfall, causing many of the inland residents in Homestead and

Miami's Average Temperatures & Rainfall

	Jan	Feb	Mar	Apr	May	June	July	Aug	Sept	Oct	Nov	Dec
Avg. High (°F)	75	76	79	82	85	87	89	90	88	84	80	76
Avg. Low (°F)	59	60	64	68	72	75	76	77	76	72	66	61
Avg. Rain (In.)	2.0	2.0	2.3	3.6	6.3	8.6	6.7	7.2	8.6	6.9	2.9	1.9

beyond to be unprepared for the hit. But, if there are reports of an impending storm before you leave for Florida, you may want to postpone your trip.

MIAMI CALENDAR OF EVENTS

January

- ✪ **The Orange Bowl.** Featuring two of the year's toughest college teams, this football game at Joe Robbie Stadium kicks off New Year's Day. Tickets are available, starting March 1 of the previous year, through the Orange Bowl Committee, Box 350748, Miami, FL 33135 (☎ 305/371-4600).

- **The Three Kings Parade.** Since Fidel Castro outlawed this religious celebration more than 25 years ago, the Cuban-Americans in Little Havana have staged this Bacchnalian parade in Miami. Paraders dress in native costumes and march down Calle Ocho from Fourth Avenue to 27th Avenue, accompanied by horse-drawn carriages and marching bands. The parade is held during the first week of January; call 305/447-1140 for the exact date.

- **Art Miami.** This fine art fair features more than a hundred galleries from all over the world. The annual event, particularly noted for its impressive collection of Latin American work, attracts thousands of visitors and buyers to the Miami Beach Convention Center in early January. For information and ticket prices, call 407/220-2690.

- ✪ **Art Deco Weekend.** Held along the beach between 5th and 15th Streets, this festival—with bands, food stands, antique vendors, tours, and other festivities—celebrates the whimsical architecture that has made South Beach one of America's most unique neighborhoods. The event is usually held mid-month; call 305/672-2014 for details.

- **Annual Redlands Natural Arts Festival.** This unusual event for lovers of exotic vegetation and food features experts from around the globe who demonstrate cooking techniques and offer free tastings. One weekend in mid-January, hundreds of locals gather at the Fruit and Spice Park, 24801 SW 187th Ave., in Homestead. Call 305/247-5727 for the dirt.

- **Taste of the Grove Food and Music Festival.** During this festival, visitors can sample menu items from some of the city's top restaurants. The party is held in the Grove's Peacock Park in a mid-month weekend. For details, call 305/444-7270.

- **International Kwanzaa Celebrations.** Miami honors its African heritage by hosting many events to welcome the year's harvest. For details and event locations, call 305/939-5805.

- **Miami International Boat Show.** This yearly event draws almost a quarter of a million boat enthusiasts to the Miami Beach Convention Center to see the megayachts, sailboats, dinghies, and boating accessories. It's the biggest show of its kind. For information and ticket prices, call 305/531-8410.

- **Martin Luther King Day Parade.** This parade along NW 62nd Avenue, north of Downtown, honors Dr. King. For information, call 305/636-1924.

- **The Key Biscayne Art Festival.** This art festival, held in Cape Florida State Park, brings more than 200 artists together in late January for a high-quality, adjudicated show—all for charity. Call 305/361-2531 for more information.

- **Annual South Florida International Wine and Food Festival.** Hard-core foodies and wine-lovers flock to this weekend-long round of tastings, lectures, and demonstrations. Here you can learn how to pair French wines with cheeses, bid on ancient magnums, and sample the dishes from some of the country's best restaurants. The festival is usually held on Super Bowl weekend. The cost depends on which activities you choose. Call The Doral Resort (☎ 305/531-4851 or 800/20-EVENT) for more information.

- **The Royal Caribbean Classic.** World-renowned golfers compete for more than $1 million in prize money at The Links golf course on Key Biscayne. Lee Trevino is a two-time winner of this championship tournament. For details, call 305/365-0365.

February

✪ **Miami Film Festival.** This festival, running for ten days in mid-February, is an important screening opportunity for Latin American cinema and American independent filmmakers. Fashioned after San Francisco's film festival, this annual event is relatively small, well-priced, and easily accessible to the general public. Contact the Film Society of Miami, 7600 Red Rd., Miami, FL 33157 (☎ 305/377-FILM).

- **Coconut Grove Art Festival.** Many locals say their favorite annual event is this one—the state's largest art festival held mid-month. More than 300 artists are selected from thousands to show their works at this prestigious show. Almost every medium is represented, including the culinary arts. For details call 305/447-0401.

- **The Lipton Championships.** One of the world's most watched tennis events is hosted mid-month at the lush International Tennis Center of Key Biscayne. See the biggest names in tennis, like Andre Agassi and Pete Sampras, compete for more than $4 million in prize money. For further information, call 305/446-2200.

- **Doral Ryder Golf Open.** One of the county's most prestigious tournaments, held in late February or early March, attracts the big names, like Jack Nicklaus and Payne Stewart. Call 305/477-GOLF for more information.

March

- **The Grand Prix of Miami.** An auto race that rivals the big ones in Daytona, this high-purse, high-profile event attracts the top Indy car drivers and large crowds to the 344-acre Homestead Motorsports Complex. For information and tickets, contact the Homestead Motorsports Complex, One Speedway Blvd., Homestead (☎ 305/230-5200).

- **Calle Ocho Festival.** This is Miami's answer to Carnival. More than 1 million people attend this salsa-filled blowout held along 23 blocks of Little Havana's SW 8th Street. For more information, call 305/644-8888.

- **The Italian Renaissance Festival.** Stage plays, music, and period costumes complement Villa Vizcaya's neo-Italian architectural style. Call 305/250-9133 for more information.

- **The Italian Film Festival.** This recently inaugurated event drew hundreds of film buffs from out of their casas. It should get bigger and better as it matures. Call 305/532-4986 to see where and when it's rolling.

- **Dade County Youth Fair and Exposition.** This huge two-week carnival-style romp held in late March features dozens of rides, at least 100 food booths, and more than 350 shows, including dancers, magicians, and clowns. For more information, call 305/223-7060.

April

- **Arabian Knight's Festival.** This yearly event commemorates the distinctive Moorish architecture in the heart of Opa-Locka. Historical tours, street festivals, and food booths are part of the fun. For details, call 305/953-2821.

May

- **The Great Sunrise Balloon Race & Festival.** Every Memorial Day weekend, dozens of multicolored balloons rise up over Harris Field in Homestead as sky divers fall from the sky. The race is celebrated on the ground with a variety of food, music, arts, and crafts. For information, call 305/275-3317.

June

○ **Coconut Grove Goombay Festival.** Celebrating Miami's Caribbean connection, this bash is billed as the largest Black-heritage festival in America. You can dance in the streets and enjoy the sounds of the Royal Bahamian Police marching band. For festival details, call 305/372-9966.

• **Queer Flickering Light Film Festival.** A weekend of whimsy, exotica, and erotica is on the big screen of the Colony Theater on Lincoln Road. Call 305/375-5191.

July

• **Independence Day.** Celebrate July 4th on the beach, where parties, barbecues, and fireworks flare all day and night. For a weekend's worth of events on Key Biscayne, call 305/361-5207. You can also find fireworks and festivities at **Bayfront Park,** 301 N. Biscayne Blvd. For more on these free events, call 305/358-7550.

• **Miccosukee Everglades Music and Crafts Festival.** Native American rock, razz (reservation jazz), and folk bands perform down south while visitors gorge themselves on exotic treats like pumpkin bread and fritters. Watch the hulking old gators wrestle with Native Americans. Call 305/223-8380 for prices and details.

August

• **Miami Reggae Festival.** Jamaica's best dancehall and reggae artists turn out for this two-day festival, scheduled the first Sunday in August. Participants in previous years included Burning Spear, Steel Pulse, Spragga Benz, and Juggsy King. For information, contact Jamaica Awareness (☎ 305/891-2944).

September

• **Fontainebleu Hilton Annual Chocolate Festival & Fair.** Do you like it rich and gooey or crisp and toasty? You can find chocolate and cocoa in a thousand guises at this chocoholic's convention. Try cookies, cakes, ice creams, drinks, and more at this annual gorge-fest. Call 305/535-3240.

• **Festival Miami.** Sponsored by the University of Miami, this three-week program of performing and visual arts is centered in and around Coral Gables. For a schedule of events contact the University of Miami's School of Music, Box 248165, Coral Gables, FL 33146 (☎ 305/284-3941).

October

○ **The Columbus Day Regatta.** Find anything that can float from an inner-tube to a 100-foot yacht and you'll fit right in. Yes, there actually is a race, but who can keep track when you are partying with a bunch of semi-naked psychos in the middle of Biscayne Bay. It's free and it's wild. You may want to consider renting a boat, jetski, or sailboard to check out this event up close. Be sure to book early though; everyone wants to be there.

• **Oktoberfest.** They close the streets for this German beer and food festival thrown by the Mozart Stub Restaurant in Coral Gables. You'll find loads of great music and dancing at this wild party. For further details, call Harald Neuweg at 305/446-1600.

November

• **Miami Book Fair International.** You can attend some great lectures and readings by respected authors during this show, which draws publishers and authors from around the world. For more information, call 305/754-4931.

• **The Jiffy Lube Miami 300 weekend of NASCAR.** Here's more world-class racing at the newly constructed 344-acre motorsports complex. For information and tickets contact Homestead Motorsports Complex, One Speedway Blvd., Homestead (☎ 305/230-5200).

December

- **The Ramble.** Old-time Floridians love this yearly event at the Fairchild Tropical Gardens, usually the first weekend in December. Here you can buy antiques, exotic orchids, or vintage clothes. If you're not shopping, it's still worth strolling around the lush park where you can learn about various botanical miracles. For more information, call 305/667-1651.
- **The Fair of Seville.** Eat from a giant pot of paella, watch hundreds of flamenco performers, see the Andalusian horse show, and dance the Macarena at this non-stop weekend fair. For details, call 305/442-1586.
- **The Indian Arts Festival.** Sometime between Christmas and New Year's the Miccosukees host an arts festival with native dances and foods that kids and adults will enjoy. Call the village (☎ 305/223-8380) for more information.
- **The King Mango Strut.** On December 30, this fun-filled parade goes from Commodore Plaza to Peacock Park in Coconut Grove. Everyone is encouraged to wear wacky costumes and join the floats in a spoof on the King Orange Jamboree Parade, held the following night. After the parade, comedians and musicians perform in Peacock Park. For more information, call the Coconut Grove Chamber of Commerce (☎ 305/444-7270).
- ✪ **The King Orange Jamboree Parade.** Ending the year, this special New Year's Eve event may be the world's largest nighttime parade and is followed by a long night of festivities. The parade marches along Biscayne Boulevard. For information and tickets (which cost $7.50 to $13), contact the Greater Miami Convention and Visitors Bureau (☎ 305/539-3063, or 800/283-2707).

3 Insurance & Safety Concerns

INSURANCE

Many travelers are covered by their hometown health-insurance policies in the event of an accident or sudden illness while away on vacation. Make sure that your Health Maintenance Organization (HMO) or insurance carrier can provide services for you while you're in Florida. If there's any doubt, a health-insurance policy that specifically covers your trip is advisable.

You can also protect yourself with insurance against lost or damaged baggage and trip-cancellation or interruption costs. These coverages are often combined into a single comprehensive plan, sold through travel agents, credit- and charge-card companies, and automobile and other clubs.

Most travel agents can sell low-cost health, loss, and trip-cancellation insurance to their vacationing clients. Compare these rates and services with those offered by local banks as well as by your personal insurance carrier.

PERSONAL SAFETY

Reacting to several highly publicized crimes against tourists, both local and state governments have taken steps to help protect visitors. These include special, highly visible police units patrolling the airport and surrounding neighborhoods, and better signs on the state's most-touristed routes.

When driving around Miami, always have a good map, and know where you are going. Never stop on a highway—if you get a flat tire, drive to the nearest well-lighted, populated place. Keep car doors locked and stay alert. If you are arriving in Miami at night and plan to rent a car, I suggest taking a taxi from the airport to your hotel and arranging to have a rental car delivered to your hotel. Opt for any additional safety features in the car such as cellular telephones or electronic maps. For short stays or trips that will be centered in one area of the city, such as South Beach, you could dispense with a rental car altogether, and just rely on taxis, which are generally safe and relatively inexpensive.

Don't walk alone at night, and be extra wary when walking or driving though Little Haiti and Downtown.

During the hurricane season, listen to radio and television broadcasts, which will describe evacuation routes. Better hotels will arrange transportation for their guests to safe areas.

4 Tips for Travelers with Special Needs

FOR TRAVELERS WITH DISABILITIES   Several hotels offer special accommodations and services for wheelchair-bound visitors and travelers with disabilities. These include large bathrooms, ramps, and telecommunication devices for the deaf. The Greater Miami Convention and Visitors Bureau (see "Visitor Information") has the most up-to-date information.

The City of Miami Department of Parks and Recreation, 2600 S. Bayshore Dr. (Coconut Grove), Miami, FL 33133 (☎ 305/579-3431; TTY 305/579-3436), maintains many programs for people with disabilities at parks and beaches throughout the city. Call or write for a listing of special services. The office is open weekdays from 8am to 5pm. The Metro-Dade County Parks & Recreation Department also runs hundreds of programs from swimming to sailing for visitors with disabilities. For a complete listing, call the department (☎ 305/857-3350) weekdays from 9am to 5pm. Primarily a referral service, the Deaf Services Bureau, 4800 W. Flagler St., Suite 213, Miami, FL 33134 (☎ 305/668-DEAF) may be contacted for any special concerns you have about traveling in and around Miami. Hours are weekdays from 9am to 5pm. The Division of Blind Services, 401 NW 2nd Ave., Suite 700, Miami, FL 33128 (☎ 305/377-5339), offers similar services as the Deaf Services Bureau, above, but to those with visual impairments. The office is open weekdays from 8am to 5pm.

FOR GAY & LESBIAN TRAVELERS   Miami, particularly South Beach, has a significant gay community, supported by a wide range of services. There are many gay-oriented publications with information, up-to-date calendars, and listings of gay-friendly businesses and services. *TWN* is the only local gay newspaper in town; you'll find it in lavender boxes throughout the city and at bookstores and gay bars. Other local publications include *WIRE*, *Hot Shots*, *LIPS* for women, *Out Pages*, and *Pride*.

The **Gay and Lesbian Community Hotline** (☎ 305/759-3661), an interactive recording that can be reached with a push-button phone, lists fourteen categories of information of interest to the gay community. These include political issues, gay bars, special events, support groups, businesses serving the gay community, doctors and lawyers, help wanted, and others.

The **Lambda Passages/Gay Community Bookstore**, 7545 Biscayne Blvd. (☎ 305/754-6900), features quality literature, newspapers, videos, music, cards, and more. It's open Monday to Saturday from 11am to 9pm and Sunday from noon to 6pm.

Also, on South Beach, **GW The Gay Emporium**, known as the Queer Woolworth's, 720 Lincoln Rd. (☎ 305/534-4763), sells T-shirts, underwear, rainbow paraphernalia, sex toys, leather, and periodicals. It's open Sunday to Thursday from 11am to 10pm and Friday from 11am to 11pm.

FOR SENIORS   Miami is well versed when it comes to catering to seniors. Ask for discounts everywhere—at hotels, movie theaters, museums, restaurants, and attractions—you may be surprised how often you'll be offered reduced rates. You'll find numerous early-bird specials at restaurants and that most places honor AARP membership.

FOR STUDENTS   A valid high school or college ID often entitles you to discounts at attractions (particularly at museums), and sometimes to reduced rates at bars during "college nights." You're most likely to find these discounts at places near the local colleges, in downtown Miami and Coral Gables.

You'll find lots of fellow students at the large main campus of the University of Miami, located in south Coral Gables. This campus encompasses dozens of classrooms, a huge athletic field, a large lake, a museum, a hospital, and more. For general information, call the university (☎ 305/284-2211). The school's main student building is the Whitten University Center, 1306 Stanford Dr. (☎ 305/284-2318). Social events are often scheduled here, and important information on area activities is always posted. The building houses a recreation area, a pool, a snack shop, and a Ticketmaster outlet.

The Jerry Herman Ring Theatre, on the University of Miami campus, 1380 Miller Dr. (☎ 305/284-3355), is the main stage for the Department of Theater Arts' advanced-student productions. Faculty and guest actors are regularly featured, as are contemporary works by local playwrights. See Chapter 10 for more information.

The Gusman Concert Hall, 1314 Miller Dr. (☎ 305/284-2438 voice, 305/284-6477 recording), features performances by faculty and students of the university's School of Music, as well as concerts by special guests. See Chapter 10 for more information, and call for schedules and tickets.

For tickets to Miami Hurricanes basketball, football, and baseball home games, call the U of M Athletic Department (☎ 305/284-4861, or 800/GO-CANES in Florida). See "Spectator Sports" in Chapter 7 for more information.

The University's Bill Cosford Cinema (☎ 305/284-4861) is named after the deceased Miami Herald's film critic and features new and classic films. Call for ticket prices and screening schedules. The theater closes during school holidays, including a month over Christmas.

5 Getting There

One hundred years ago, Miami, basically a swampy jungle, was a hard place to reach—but no more. Today, transportation companies, most notably airlines, fight perpetual price wars to woo tourists to the Sunshine State. In fact, airfares are so competitive that, unless you are visiting from an adjacent state, flying to Miami will almost always be your most economical option. However, take a look at your alternatives, too. An overland journey to Florida's Gold Coast is both a more scenic and a more flexible way to travel. Greyhound/Trailways offers several types of bus passes, and Amtrak offers a host of rail services to the South.

BY PLANE

More than 80 scheduled airlines service Miami International Airport, including almost every major domestic and foreign carrier. The city is so well connected that the problem isn't getting there, but rather deciding what service and fare to select.

Major American carriers offering regular flights to Miami include **American Airlines,** 150 Alhambra Plaza, Coral Gables (☎ 800/433-7300 or 305/358-6800); **Continental,** 38 Biscayne Blvd., Downtown (☎ 800/525-0280 or 305/871-1400); **Delta Airlines,** 201 Alhambra Circle, Suite 516, Coral Gables (☎ 800/221-1212 or 305/448-7000); **Northwest** Airlines, 150 Alhambra Plaza, Coral Gables (☎ 800/447-4747); and **United Airlines,** Miami International Airport (☎ 800/521-4041).

Florida destinations are often at the heart of "fare wars" that airlines wage; flights to the city are usually pretty reasonable, if not downright cheap. The lowest round-trip airfares from New York usually fluctuate below $200, around $300 from Chicago, and around $400 from Los Angeles. Sometimes you can do better, especially by calling the airlines directly.

You might be able to get a great deal on airfare by calling a consolidator, such as **Travac,** 989 Ave. of the Americas, New York, NY 10018 (☎ 212/563-3303 or 800/TRAV-800); and **Unitravel,** 1117 N. Warson Rd. (P.O. Box 12485), St. Louis, MO 63132 (☎ 314/569-0900 or 800/325-2222).

MIAMI INTERNATIONAL AIRPORT

Originally carved out of scrubland in 1928 by Pan American Airlines, Miami International Airport (MIA) has emerged as one of the busiest airports in the world. Unfortunately, as it undergoes major reconstruction to expand its capacity, the airport can feel like a maze with inadequate signage and surly employees. Plus if you have a lot of bags, note that it's one of the few airports in the country *without* luggage-cart rentals.

The route down to the baggage-claim area is clearly marked. You can change money or use your Honor or Plus System ATM card at Barnett Bank of South Florida, located near the exit.

Like most good international airports, MIA has its fair share of boutiques, shops, and eateries. Unless you are starving or forgot to get a gift for the person picking you up, bypass these overpriced establishments. The airport is literally surrounded by restaurants and shops; if you can wait to get to them, you will save a lot of money. If you are exiting Miami on an international flight, don't miss the excellent duty-free selection in the departure lounge.

Visitor information is available at the Miami International Airport Main Visitor Counter, Concourse E, 2nd floor (☎ 305/876-7000). Open 24 hours a day.

RELAXING AT THE AIRPORT HOTEL   If you find yourself waiting in the airport with time to kill, consider going up to the Miami International Airport Hotel to catch a few rays. For a $5 fee, the Top of the Port Health Club allows anyone to use their facilities, which include a sundeck, weights, sauna, showers, and a pool.

Although the hotel is literally in the airport, finding it is a little tricky. From the 2nd level of the airport at Concourse E, take the elevator to the 7th floor where you will turn right and find another elevator which will take you to the 8th floor. Exit and you'll see the health club right in front of you.

GETTING INTO TOWN   The airport is located about six miles west of Downtown and about twelve miles from the beaches, so it's likely that you can get from the plane to your hotel room in less than an hour. Of course, if you're arriving from an international destination, it will take added time to go through Customs and Immigration.

By Car   All the major car-rental firms operate off-site branches that are reached via shuttle from the terminals. See "Getting Around" in Chapter 4 for a list of major rental companies. Signs at the airport's exit clearly point the way to various parts of the city. But if you're arriving at night, I suggest taking a taxi to your hotel and having the car-rental firm deliver a car to your hotel the next day.

By Taxi   Taxis line up in front of a dispatcher's desk outside the airport's arrivals terminals. Cabs are metered and will cost about $14 to Coral Gables, $22 to Downtown, and $24 to South Beach. Tip 10% to 15%. Depending on traffic, the ride to Coral Gables or Downtown takes about 15 to 20 minutes, and to South Beach, 20 to 25 minutes.

By Limo or Van   Group limousines (multipassenger vans) circle the arrivals area looking for fares. Destinations are posted on the front of each van, and a flat rate is charged for door-to-door service to the area marked.

    SuperShuttle (☎ 305/871-2000) is one of the largest airport operators, charging between $10 and $20 per person for a ride within Dade County. Its vans operate 24 hours a day and accept American Express, MasterCard, and Visa.

    Private limousine arrangements can be made in advance through your local travel agent. A one-way meet-and-greet service should cost about $50.

By Public Transportation   I do not recommend taking public transportation to get from the airport to your hotel. Buses heading Downtown leave the airport only once per hour (from the arrivals level), and connections are spotty at best. Including waiting time, the trip takes about 45 minutes to Coral Gables; 50 minutes to an hour to Downtown; and about an hour and a half to South Beach. The fare is $1.25, plus an additional 25 cents for a South Beach transfer.

BY CAR

No matter where you start your journey, chances are you'll reach Miami by way of I-95. This north-south interstate is the city's lifeline and an integral part of the region. The highway connects all of Miami's different neighborhoods, the airport, and the beach; and it connects all of South Florida to the rest of America. Unfortunately, many of Miami's road signs are completely confusing and notably absent when you need them. Take time out to study I-95's placement on the map. You will use it as a reference point time and again.

    Other major highways include I-10, which originates in Los Angeles and terminates in Jacksonville; and I-75, which begins in North Michigan and runs through the center of Florida.

    Before you set out on a long car trip, you might want to join the **American Automobile Association** (AAA) (☎ 800/336-4357), which has hundreds of offices nationwide. Members receive excellent maps (they'll even help you plan an exact itinerary) and emergency road service. Other auto clubs include the **Allstate Motor Club,** 1500 Shure Dr., Arlington Heights, IL 60004 (☎ 708/253-4800); and the **Amoco Motor Club,** P.O. Box 9046, Des Moines, IA 50369 (☎ 800/334-3300).

BY TRAIN

Amtrak (☎ 800/USA-RAIL) may be a good option. Two trains leave daily from New York—the *Silver Meteor* at 8:40am and the *Silver Star* at 4:30pm—and take 26½ hours to complete the journey. At press time, the lowest-priced round-trip ticket from New York to Miami cost $152, climbing to a whopping $417 for a sleeper (based on double occupancy).

    If you are planning to stay in South Florida for some time, you might consider taking your car on Amtrak's East Coast Auto Train. The 16½-hour ride, connecting Lorton, Virginia (near Washington, D.C.), with Sanford, Florida (near Orlando), has a glass-domed viewing car and includes breakfast and dinner in the ticket price. Round-trip fares are only a few dollars higher than one-way—about $170 for adults, $85 for children under 12, and $300 for your car. One-way fares are discounted as much as 50% when most traffic is going in the opposite direction.

You'll pull into Amtrak's Miami terminal at 8303 NW 37th Ave. (☎ 305/835-1205). Unfortunately, none of the major car-rental companies has an office at the train station; you'll have to go to the airport to rent a car. Hertz (☎ 800/654-3131) will reimburse your cab fare from the train station (up to $10) to the airport provided you rent one of their cars.

Taxis meet each Amtrak arrival. The fare to Downtown will cost about $22; the ride takes less than 20 minutes.

BY BUS

Bus travel is often an inexpensive and flexible option. **Greyhound/Trailways** (☎ 800/231-2222) can get you to Miami from anywhere, and it offers several money-saving multiday bus passes. Round-trip fares vary depending on your point of origin, but few, if any, exceed $200.

Greyhound/Trailways buses pull into a number of stations around the city, including 99 NE 4th St. (Downtown); 16250 Biscayne Blvd., North Miami Beach; and 7101 Harding Ave., Miami Beach.

3 For Foreign Visitors

This chapter provides specific suggestions about getting to the United States as economically and effortlessly as possible, plus some helpful information about how things are done in Miami—from receiving mail to making a local or long-distance telephone call.

1 Preparing for Your Trip

ENTRY REQUIREMENTS

DOCUMENT REGULATIONS   Canadian citizens may enter the United States without visas; they need only proof of residence.

Citizens of the United Kingdom, New Zealand, Japan, and most Western European countries traveling on valid passports may not need a visa for fewer than 90 days of holiday or business travel to the United States, providing they hold a round-trip or return ticket and enter the United States on an airline or cruise line participating in the visa-waiver program.

Note: Citizens of these visa-exempt countries who first enter the United States may then visit Mexico, Canada, Bermuda, and/or the Caribbean islands and then reenter the United States, by any mode of transportation, without needing a visa. Further information is available from any U.S. embassy or consulate.

Citizens of countries other than those stipulated above, including citizens of Australia, must have two documents: a valid passport, with an expiration date at least six months later than the scheduled end of the visit to the United States; and a tourist visa, available without charge from the nearest U.S. consulate. To obtain a visa, the traveler must submit a completed application form (either in person or by mail) with a 1 1/2-inch-square photo and demonstrate binding ties to a residence abroad.

Usually you can obtain a visa at once or within 24 hours, but it may take longer during the summer rush from June to August. If you cannot go in person, contact the nearest U.S. embassy or consulate for directions on applying by mail. Your travel agent or airline office may also be able to provide you with visa applications and instructions. The U.S. consulate or embassy that issues your visa will determine whether you will be issued a multiple- or single-entry visa and whether there will be any restrictions regarding the length of your stay.

MEDICAL REQUIREMENTS No inoculations are needed to enter the United States unless you are coming from, or have stopped over in, areas known to be suffering from epidemics, particularly cholera or yellow fever.

If you have a condition requiring treatment with medications containing narcotics or drugs requiring a syringe, carry a valid signed prescription from your physician to allay any suspicions that you are smuggling drugs.

CUSTOMS REQUIREMENTS Every adult visitor may bring in free of duty: 1 liter of hard liquor; 200 cigarettes or 100 cigars (but no cigars from Cuba) or 3 pounds of smoking tobacco; $100 worth of gifts. These exemptions are offered to travelers who spend at least 72 hours in the United States and who have not claimed them within the preceding 6 months. It is altogether forbidden to bring foodstuffs (particularly cheese, fruit, and cooked meats) and plants (vegetables, seeds, tropical plants, and so on) into the country. Foreign tourists may bring in or take out up to $10,000.00 in U.S. or foreign currency with no formalities; larger sums must be declared to Customs on entering or leaving.

INSURANCE

There is no national health system in the United States. Because the cost of medical care is extremely high, we strongly advise all travelers to secure health coverage before setting out.

You may want to take out a comprehensive travel policy that covers (for a relatively low premium) sickness or injury costs (medical, surgical, and hospital); loss or theft of your baggage; trip-cancellation costs; guarantee of bail in case you are arrested; and costs of accident, repatriation, or death. Automobile clubs sell packages (for example, "Europe Assistance" in Europe) at attractive rates; packages are also offered by insurance companies and travel agencies.

MONEY

CURRENCY The U.S. monetary system has a decimal base: one American dollar ($1) = 100 cents (100¢). Dollar bills commonly come in $1 ("a buck"), $5, $10, $20, $50, and $100 denominations (the last two are not welcome when paying for small purchases and are not always accepted in taxis).

There are six coin denominations: 1¢ (one cent or "penny"), 5¢ (five cents or "nickel"), 10¢ (ten cents or "dime"), 25¢ (twenty-five cents or "quarter"), 50¢ (fifty cents or "half dollar"), and the $1 pieces (both the older, large silver dollar and the newer, small Susan B. Anthony coin).

TRAVELER'S CHECKS Traveler's checks in U.S. dollars are accepted at most hotels, motels, restaurants, and large stores. Sometimes picture identification is required to cash or change a traveler's check. American Express, Thomas Cook, and Barclay's Bank traveler's checks are readily accepted in the United States.

CREDIT CARDS The most widely used method of payment is the credit card: Visa (BarclayCard in Britain), MasterCard (EuroCard in Europe, Access in Britain, Diamond in Japan), American Express, Discover, Diners Club, enRoute, JCB, and Carte Blanche, in descending order of acceptance.

You can save yourself trouble by using "plastic" rather than cash or traveler's checks in 95% of all hotels, motels, restaurants, and retail stores. A credit card can also serve as a deposit for renting a car, as proof of identity, or as a "cash card," enabling you to draw money from automated teller machines (ATMs) that accept them.

You can telegraph money or have it wired to you very quickly using the Western Union system (☎ 800/325-6000).

SAFETY

While tourist areas are generally safe, crime is a persistent problem everywhere, and U.S. urban areas tend to be less safe than those in Europe or Japan. Visitors should always stay alert. This is particularly true of large U.S. cities. It is wise to ask the city's or area's tourist office if you're in doubt about which neighborhoods are safe. Avoid deserted areas, especially at night. Don't go into any city park at night unless there is an event that attracts crowds.

Remember also that hotels are open to the public, and in a large hotel, security may not be able to screen everyone entering. Always lock your room door—don't assume that once inside your hotel, you are automatically safe and no longer need to be aware of your surroundings.

DRIVING   Safety while driving is particularly important. Question your rental agency about personal safety or ask for a brochure of traveler safety tips. Obtain written directions, or a map with the route marked in red, from the agency showing how to get to your destination. Opt for any additional safety features in the car such as cellular telephones or electronic maps. And, if possible, arrive and depart during daylight hours. If you are arriving at night, consider taking a taxi from the airport to your hotel and then having your rental car delivered.

Recently, more and more crime has involved cars and drivers. If you drive off a highway into a doubtful neighborhood, leave the area as quickly as possible. If you have an accident, even on the highway, stay in your car with the doors locked until you assess the situation or until the police arrive. If you are bumped from behind on the street or are involved in a minor accident with no injuries and the situation appears to be suspicious, motion to the other driver to follow you. Never get out of your car in such situations. Go directly to the nearest police precinct, well-lighted service station, or all-night store.

If you see someone on the road who indicates a need for help, do not stop. Take note of the location, drive into a well-lighted area, and telephone the police by dialing 911.

Park in well-lighted, well-traveled areas if possible. Always keep your car doors locked, whether attended or unattended. Look around you before you get out of your car and never leave any packages or valuables in sight. If someone attempts to rob you or steal your car, do not try to resist the thief/carjacker—report the incident to the police department immediately.

Reacting to several highly publicized crimes against tourists in Florida, both the local and state governments have taken steps to help protect visitors. These include special, highly visible police units patrolling the airport and surrounding neighborhoods and better signs on the state's most-touristed routes. Still, especially in Miami, the signs can be extremely confusing. Make sure to chart your course before leaving an area. If you are staying on South Beach, you may want to consider skipping a car rental altogether, or at least for the time you are on the island. Taxis are plentiful and relatively inexpensive (see Chapter 4, "Getting Around").

2 Getting to the U.S.

Travelers from overseas can take advantage of the APEX (Advance Purchase Excursion) fares offered by all the major U.S. and European carriers. **British Airways** (☎ 081/897-4000 from within the U.K.) offers direct flights from London to Miami and Orlando, as does **Virgin Atlantic** (☎ 02/937-47747 from within the U.K.). Canadian readers might book flights with **Air Canada** (☎ 800/776-3000), which offers service from Toronto and Montreal to Miami and Tampa.

As we rode over the causeway, I could hardly believe my eyes. It was almost unimaginable that in Miami Beach it was 80 degrees while in New York it was 20. Everything—the buildings, the water, the pavement—had an indescribable glow to it. The palm trees especially made a great impression on me.

—Isaac Bashevis Singer, describing his first visit to Miami in 1948

Miami International Airport is a hub for flights to and from Latin America. Carriers include Aerolineas Argentinas, Aeroméxico, American Airlines, Avianca, Lan Chile Airlines, and Varig Brazilian Airlines.

The visitor arriving by air, no matter what the port of entry, should cultivate patience and resignation before setting foot on U.S. soil. Getting through Immigration control may take as long as two hours on some days, especially summer weekends, so have your guidebook or something else to read handy. Add the time it takes to clear Customs and you will see you should make a very generous allowance for delay in planning connections between international and domestic flights—figure on two to three hours at least.

In contrast, for the traveler arriving by car or by rail from Canada, the border-crossing formalities have been streamlined to the vanishing point. And for the traveler by air from Canada, Bermuda, and some places in the Caribbean, you can sometimes go through Customs and Immigration at the point of departure, which is much quicker and less painful.

3 Getting Around the U.S.

On their transatlantic or transpacific flights, some large U.S. airlines offer special discount tickets for any of their U.S. destinations (American Airline's **Visit USA** program and Delta's **Discover America** program, for example). The tickets or coupons are not on sale in the United States and must be purchased before you leave your point of departure. This system is the best, easiest, and fastest way to see the United States at low cost. You should obtain information well in advance from your travel agent or the office of the airline concerned, since the conditions attached to these discount tickets can be changed without advance notice.

International visitors can also buy a **USA Railpass,** good for 15 or 30 days of unlimited travel on Amtrak. The pass is available through many foreign travel agents. Prices in 1996 for a 15-day pass are $245 off-peak, $355 peak; a 30-day pass costs $350 off-peak, $440 peak (peak is June 17 to August 21). (With a foreign passport, you can also buy passes at some Amtrak offices in the United States including locations in San Francisco, Los Angeles, Chicago, New York, Miami, Boston, and Washington, D.C.) Reservations are generally required and should be made for each part of your trip as early as possible.

Visitors should also be aware of the limitations of long-distance rail travel in the United States. With a few notable exceptions (for instance, the Northeast Corridor line between Boston and Washington, D.C.), service is rarely up to European standards: delays are common, routes are limited and often infrequently served, and fares are rarely significantly lower than discount airfares. Thus, cross-country train travel should be approached with caution.

Although ticket prices for short bus trips between cities are often the most economical form of public transit, at this writing, bus passes are priced slightly higher than similar train passes. **Greyhound,** the nationwide bus line, offers an **Ameripass** for unlimited travel for 7 days (for $179), 15 days (for $289), and 30 days (for $399). Bus travel in the United States can be both slow and uncomfortable, so this option is not for everyone. In addition, bus stations are often located in undesirable neighborhoods.

See "Getting There" in Chapter 2 for more information about travel to Miami.

FAST FACTS: For the Foreign Traveler

Automobile Organizations   Auto clubs will supply maps, suggested routes, guide-books, accident and bail-bond insurance, and emergency road service. The major auto club in the United States, with 983 offices nationwide, is the **American Automobile Association** (AAA). Members of some foreign auto clubs have recip-rocal arrangements with the AAA and enjoy its services at no charge—inquire about AAA reciprocity before you leave. The AAA can provide you with an International Driving Permit validating your foreign license, although drivers with valid licenses from most home countries don't really need this permit. You may be able to join the AAA even if you are not a member of a reciprocal club. To inquire, call 619/233-1000 or 800/222-4357. In addition, some car-rental agencies now provide these services, so ask when you rent your car.

Business Hours   Banks are open weekdays from 9am to 3pm or later and some-times Saturday morning, although there's 24-hour access to the automatic tellers (ATMs) at most banks and other outlets. Offices are usually open weekdays from 9am to 5pm. Shops, especially department stores and those in shopping complexes, tend to stay open late—until about 9pm weekdays and until 6pm weekends.

Climate   See "When to Go" in Chapter 2.

Currency   See "Preparing for Your Trip" earlier in this chapter.

Currency Exchange   The "foreign-exchange bureaus" so common in Europe are rare in the United States. You'll find one in Concourse E of the Miami Inter-national Airport—**BankAmerica International** (☎ 305/377-6000; open 24 hours). **Thomas Cook Currency Services** offers a wide variety of services: more than 100 currencies, commission-free traveler's checks, drafts and wire transfers, and check collections. Rates are competitive and service is excellent. The Miami office is downtown at 155 SE Third Ave. (☎ 305/381-9252); it's open weekdays from 9am to 5pm. Another downtown money-changing office is **Abbot Foreign Exchange,** 255 E. Flagler St. (☎ 305/374-2336); it's open weekdays from 8am to 5pm and Saturday from 8am to 2pm.

Drinking Laws   The legal age to drink alcohol is 21.

Electricity   The United States uses 110–120 volts, 60 cycles, compared to 220–240 volts, 50 cycles, as in most of Europe. Besides a 100-volt converter, small appliances of non-American manufacture, such as hairdryers or shavers, will require a plug adapter, with two flat, parallel pins. The easiest solution is to purchase dual-voltage appliances that operate on both 110 and 220 volts; then all that is required is a U.S. adapter plug.

Embassies/Consulates   All embassies are located in the national capital, Wash-ington, D.C.; some consulates are located in Miami. Travelers from other countries can get telephone numbers for their embassies and consulates by calling "Information" in Washington, D.C. (☎ 202/555-1212).

Brazil's Consulate General is located in Coconut Grove at 2601 S. Bayshore Dr., Suite 800, Miami, FL 33133 (☎ 305/285-6200); the British Consulate is also located in Coconut Grove at the Brickell Bay Tower, Suite 2110, 1001 S. Bayshore Dr., Miami, FL 33131 (☎ 305/374-1522); a Canadian Consulate is located at 200 S. Biscayne Blvd., Suite 1600, Miami, FL 33132 (☎ 305/579-1600); Germany's Consulate General is located at 100 N. Biscayne Blvd., Miami, FL 33132 (☎ 305/358-0290); and the Portugese consulate is in Coral Gables at 1901 Ponce de Leon Blvd., Miami, FL (☎ 305/444-6311).

Emergencies   Call **911** for fire, police, and ambulance. If you encounter such traveler's problems as sickness, accident, or lost or stolen baggage, call **Traveler's Aid,** an organization that specializes in helping distressed travelers. The Jewish Family Service of Greater Miami operates a traveler's aid center at the downtown Howard Johnson, 100 Biscayne Blvd. (☎ 305/448-8228) provides general travel assistance for travelers in need around the clock.

U.S. hospitals have emergency rooms, with a special entrance where you will be admitted for quick attention. **Health South Doctors' Hospital,** 5000 University Dr., Coral Gables (☎ 305/666-2111), is a 285-bed acute-care hospital with a 24-hour physician-staffed emergency department.

Gasoline (Petrol)   One U.S. gallon equals 3.75 liters, while 1.2 U.S. gallons equals one Imperial gallon. A gallon of unleaded gas (short for gasoline), which most rental cars accept, costs about $1.30 if you fill your own tanks (it's called "self-serve"); 10¢ more if the station attendant does it (called "full-service"). Most Miami gas stations are self-serve, with credit card processors right on the pump.

Holidays   On the following legal national holidays, banks, government offices, post offices, and many stores, restaurants, and museums are closed: January 1 (New Year's Day); third Monday in January (Martin Luther King Day); third Monday in February (Presidents' Day, Washington's Birthday); last Monday in May (Memorial Day); July 4 (Independence Day); first Monday in September (Labor Day); second Monday in October (Columbus Day); November 11 (Veterans Day/Armistice Day); fourth Thursday in November (Thanksgiving); and December 25 (Christmas). The Tuesday following the first Monday in November is Election Day.

Languages   Major hotels may have multilingual employees. Unless your language is very obscure, they can usually supply a translator on request. Because more than half of Miami residents fluently speak Spanish, most signs and brochures are printed in both English and Spanish. In addition, since a large number of French, Canadian, Italian, and German tourists visit Miami, most visitor information is available in these respective languages.

Legal Aid   If you are stopped for a minor infraction (for example, of the highway code, such as speeding), never attempt to pay the fine directly to a police officer; you may be arrested on the much more serious charge of attempted bribery. Pay fines by mail, or directly into the hands of the clerk of the court. If accused of a more serious offense, it is best to say and do nothing before consulting a lawyer. Under U.S. law, an arrested person is allowed one telephone call to a party of his or her choice. Call your embassy or consulate.

Mail   The Main Post Office, 2200 Milam Dairy Rd., Miami, FL 33152 (☎ 305/639-4280), is located west of Miami International Airport. Letters addressed to you and marked "c/o General Delivery" can be picked up at 500 NW 2nd Ave., Miami, FL 33101. The addressee must pick it up in person and produce proof of identity (driver's license, credit card, passport, or the like). Mailboxes are blue with a red-and-white logo, and carry the inscription U.S MAIL.

Within the United States, it costs 20¢ to mail a standard-size postcard and 32¢ to send an oversize postcard (larger than 4¹/₄-by-6 inches, or 10.8-by-15.4 centimeters). Letters that weigh up to 1 ounce (that's about five pages, 8-by-11 inch, or 20.5-by-28.2 centimeters) cost 32¢, plus 23¢ for each additional ounce. A postcard to Mexico costs 35¢, a ¹/₂-ounce letter 40¢; a postcard to Canada costs 40¢, a ¹/₂-ounce letter 46¢. A postcard to Europe, Australia, New Zealand, the Far East, South America, and elsewhere costs 50¢, while a ¹/₂-ounce letter is 60¢, and a 1-ounce letter is $1.

Medical Emergencies   See "Emergencies," above.

Newspapers/Magazines   The *Miami Herald* and the magazines *Newsweek* and *Time* cover world news and are available at newsstands. Most magazine racks at drugstores, airports, and hotels include a good selection of foreign periodicals, such as *Stern*, *The Economist*, and *Le Monde*. *El Herald* and *Diarios Las Americas* are Spanish-language newspapers. Spanish-language magazines are particularly abundant.

Post   See "Mail," above.

Safety   See "Safety" in "Preparing for Your Trip," above.

Taxes   In the United States, there is no VAT (value-added tax), or other indirect tax at a national level. There is a $10 Customs tax, payable on entry to the United States, and a $6 departure tax.

A 6% state sales tax (plus .5% local tax, for a total of 6.5% in Miami) is added on at the register for all goods and services purchased in Florida. These taxes are not refundable. In addition, most municipalities levy special taxes on restaurants and hotels. In Surfside, hotel taxes total 10.5%; in Bal Harbour, 9.5%; in Miami Beach (including South Beach), 11.5%; and in the rest of Dade County, a whopping 12.5%. In Miami Beach, Surfside, and Bal Harbour, the resort (hotel) tax also applies to hotel restaurants and restaurants with liquor licenses.

Telephone and Fax   Pay phones can be found on street corners, as well as in bars, restaurants, public buildings, stores, and at service stations. A call costs 25¢.

For local directory assistance ("information"), dial **411;** for long-distance information, dial **1**, then the appropriate area code and **555-1212.**

In the past few years, many American companies have installed "voice-mail" systems. Listen carefully to the instructions (you'll probably be asked to dial 1, 2, or 3 or wait for an operator to pick up); if you can't understand, sometimes dialing zero will put you in touch with a company operator. It's frustrating even for locals!

For long-distance or international calls, it's most economical to charge the call to a telephone charge card or a credit card; or you can use a lot of change. The pay phone will instruct you how much to deposit and when to deposit it into the slot on the top of the telephone box.

For long-distance calls in the United States, dial **1** followed by the area code and number you want. For direct overseas calls, first dial **011,** followed by the country code (Australia, 61; Republic of Ireland, 353; New Zealand, 64; United Kingdom, 44), and then by the city code (for example, 71 or 81 for London, 21 for Birmingham, 1 for Dublin) and the number of the person you wish to call.

Before calling from a hotel room, always ask the hotel phone operator if there are any telephone surcharges. There almost always are, often as much as 75¢ or $1, even for a local call. Avoid these charges by using a public phone, calling collect, or using a telephone charge card.

For reversed-charge or collect calls and for person-to-person calls, dial **0** (zero, not the letter "O") followed by the area code and number you want; an operator will then come on the line, and you should specify that you are calling collect, or person-to-person, or both. If your operator-assisted call is international, immediately ask to speak with an overseas operator.

Most hotels have fax machines available for their customers and usually charge to send or receive a facsimile. You will also see signs for public faxes in the windows of small shops.

Telephone Directory   The local phone company provides two kinds of telephone directories. The general directory, called the "white pages," lists businesses and personal residences separately, in alphabetical order. The first few pages are devoted to community-service numbers, including a guide to long-distance and international calling, complete with country codes and area codes.

The second directory, the "yellow pages," lists all local services, businesses, and industries by type, with an index at the back. The listings cover not only such obvious items as automobile repairs by make of car, or drugstores (pharmacies), often by geographical location, but also restaurants by type of cuisine and geographical location, bookstores by special subject and/or language, places of worship by religious denomination, and other information that a visitor might otherwise not readily find. The yellow pages also include city plans or detailed area maps, often showing postal ZIP codes and public transportation.

Time   Miami, like New York, is in the eastern standard time zone; the United States is divided into six time zones. Between April and October, eastern daylight saving time is adopted, and clocks are set one hour ahead. America's eastern seaboard is five hours ahead of Greenwich mean time. To find out what time it is, call 305/324-8811.

Tipping   Waiters and bartenders expect a 15% tip, as do taxi drivers and hairdressers. Porters should be tipped 50¢ to $1 per bag, and parking valets should be given $1. It's nice to leave a few dollars on your pillow for the hotel maid, and lavatory attendants will appreciate whatever change you have.

Toilets   Visitors can usually find a restroom in a bar, restaurant, hotel, museum, department store, or service station—and it will probably be clean (although the last-mentioned sometimes leaves much to be desired). The cleanliness of toilets at railroad stations and bus depots may be more questionable. You'll also find toilets at many public beaches and large parks. Some public places are equipped with pay toilets, which require you to insert one or more coins into a slot on the door before it will open. Restrooms in cafes and restaurants usually are for patrons only, but in an emergency you can just order a cup of coffee or simply ask to use the pay phone, usually conveniently positioned beside the restrooms.

4 Getting to Know Miami

Miami is not a complicated city to negotiate, but, like all unfamiliar territories, this metropolis will take a little time to master.

1 Orientation

VISITOR INFORMATION

The best up-to-date, specialized information is provided by the **Greater Miami Convention and Visitors Bureau,** 701 Brickell Ave., Miami, FL 33131 (☎ 305/539-3063, or 800/283-2707, or e-mail: gmcvb@aol.com or web site: http://www.Miamiandbeaches.com). Chambers of commerce in Greater Miami also send out information regarding their particular neighborhoods; for a complete list of tourist boards and other information sources, please refer to the "Visitor Information" section in Chapter 2.

When you arrive at the Miami International Airport, you can pick up visitor information at the airport's main visitor counter, located on the second floor of Concourse E. It's open 24 hours a day.

You can also get more maps and brochures from your hotel concierge or from the following visitor information offices:

- The **Miami Beach Chamber of Commerce,** 1920 Meridian Ave. (☎ 305/672-1270); open Monday through Friday from 8:30am to 6pm, Saturday 10am to 4pm.
- The **Jewish Family Service of Greater Miami** in the South Miami/ Coral Gables area, 1790 SW 27 Ave. (☎ 305/445-0555). It also operates a traveler's aid center at the downtown Howard Johnson, 1100 Biscayne Blvd., (☎ 305/448-8228), providing travel assistance for travelers in need.
- The **Greater Homestead/Florida City Chamber of Commerce,** 160 US Hwy. 1 (☎ 305/245-9180); open daily 8am to 6pm.
- The **Sunny Isles Beach Resort Association Visitor Information Center,** 17100 Collins Ave., Suite 208 (☎ 305/947-5826); open Monday through Friday from 9am to 2pm.

Always check local newspapers for special things to do during your visit. The city's only daily, the *Miami Herald,* is an especially good source for current-events listings, particularly the "Weekend" section in Friday's edition.

CITY LAYOUT

Miami may seem confusing at first, but it quickly becomes easy to negotiate. The small cluster of buildings that make up the Downtown area is at the geographical heart of the city. You can see these sharp stalagmites from most anywhere, making them a good reference point. In relation to Miami's downtown, the airport is northwest, the beaches are east, Coconut Grove is south, Coral Gables is west, and the rest of the country is north.

FINDING AN ADDRESS   Miami is divided into dozens of areas with official and unofficial boundaries. To make map reading easier, each address listed in this book is followed by an area listing, indicating which part of the city it is in.

Street numbering in the city of Miami is fairly straightforward, but you must first be familiar with the numbering system. The mainland is divided into four sections—NE, NW, SE, and SW—by the intersection of Flagler Street and Miami Avenue. First Street and First Avenue begin near this corner, and, along with Places, Courts, Terraces, and Lanes, the numbers increase from this point. Hialeah streets are the exceptions to this pattern; they are listed separately in map indexes.

Establishment addresses are often descriptive; 12301 Biscayne Boulevard is located at 123rd Street. It's also helpful to remember that avenues generally run north-south, while streets go east-west.

Getting around the barrier islands that make up Miami Beach is somewhat easier than moving around the mainland. Street numbering starts with First Street, near Miami Beach's southern tip, and increases to 192nd Street, in the northern part of Sunny Isles. Collins Avenue makes the entire journey from head to toe. As in the city of Miami, some streets in Miami Beach have numbers as well as names. When they are part of listings in this book, both names and numbers are given.

You should know that the numbered streets in Miami Beach are not the geographical equivalents of those on the mainland, but they are close. For example, the 79th Street Causeway runs into 71st Street on Miami Beach.

STREET MAPS   It's easy to get lost in sprawling Miami, so a reliable map is essential. If you are not planning on moving around too much, the tourist board's maps, located inside their free publication *Destination Miami*, may be adequate. If you really want to get to know the city, it pays to invest in one of the large accordion-fold maps, available at most gas stations and bookstores. The Trakker Map of Miami ($2.50) is a four-color accordion map that encompasses all of Dade County; it's handy if you plan on visiting the many attractions in Greater Miami South.

Some maps of Miami list streets according to area, so you'll have to know which part of the city you are looking for before the street can be found. All the listings in this book include area information for just this reason.

NEIGHBORHOODS IN BRIEF

Much of Miami is sprawling suburbia. But every city has its charm, and aside from a fantastic tropical climate and the vast stretch of beach that lies just across its glistening Biscayne Bay, Miami's unique identity comes from extremely interesting cultural pockets within various residential communities. Here's a brief rundown of the characteristics of its diverse neighborhoods.

South Beach—The Art Deco District   In the last several years, South Beach has been the hottest area of Miami. While technically it's just 15 blocks at the southern tip of Miami Beach, South Beach has a style all its own. The thriving Deco District within South Beach contains the largest concentration of art deco architecture in the world. In Chapter 8, there's an in-depth walking tour of Miami's most fascinating area.

Young investors, artists, handsome model-types, and the usual Miami smattering of Cubans, African-Americans, and Caribbeans populate this vibrant community. Hip clubs and cafes are filled with vacationing Europeans, working models, photographers, musicians, and writers who enjoy the exciting and sophisticated atmosphere.

Miami Beach—the Mid and Central Areas, Including Surfside, Bal Harbour, and Sunny Isles   To tourists in the 1950s, Miami Beach was Miami. Its huge self-contained resort hotels were vacations unto themselves, providing a full day's worth of meals, activities, and entertainment. Then, in the 1960s and 1970s, people who fell in love with Miami began to buy apartments rather than rent hotel rooms. Tourism declined, and many area hotels fell into disrepair.

However, since the late 1980s, Miami Beach has experienced a tide of revitalization. Huge beach hotels are finding their niche with new, international tourist markets and are attracting large convention crowds. The Miami Beach Convention Center, 1901 Convention Center Dr., Miami Beach, FL 33139 (☎ 305/673-7311), has more than 1 million square feet of exhibition space. New generations of Americans have discovered the special qualities that originally made Miami Beach so popular, and they are finding out that the beach now comes with a thriving, international, exciting city.

The north part of "The Beach"—Surfside, Bal Harbour, and Sunny Isles, plus other neighborhoods a few blocks big—are, for the most part, an extension of the beach community below it. Collins Avenue crosses town lines with hardly a sign, while hotels, motels, restaurants, and beaches continue to line the strip.

In exclusive Bal Harbour, fancy homes, tucked away on the bay, hide behind walls, gates, and security cameras. For visitors, it seems that—with some outstanding exceptions—the farther north one goes, the cheaper lodging becomes. All told, excellent prices, location, and facilities make Surfside, Bal Harbour, and Sunny Isles attractive places to stay. To keep up with demand for beachfront property, many of the area's moderately priced hotels have been converted to condominiums, leaving fewer and fewer kitschy and affordable places to stay.

Note that North Miami Beach, a residential area near the Dade–Broward county line, is a misnomer. It is actually northwest of Miami Beach on the mainland and has no beaches. North Miami Beach is part of North Dade County and has some of Miami's better restaurants and shops.

Key Biscayne   Technically one of the first islands in the Florida Key chain is Miami's forested and fancy Key Biscayne. However, this luxurious island is nothing like its southern neighbors. Located south of Miami Beach, off the shores of Coconut Grove, Key Biscayne is protected from the troubles of the mainland by the long Rickenbacker Causeway and a $1 toll. Key Biscayne is largely an exclusive residential community with million-dollar homes and sweeping water views. For visitors, this key offers great beaches, some top resort hotels, and several good restaurants. Hobie Beach, adjacent to the causeway, is the city's premier spot for sailboarding and jetskiing (see "Water Sports" in Chapter 7). On the island's southern tip is Bill Baggs State Park, offering great beaches, bike paths, and dense forests for picnicking and partying.

Downtown   Miami's downtown boasts one of the world's most beautiful cityscapes. If you do nothing else in Miami, make sure you take your time studying the area's inspired architectural designs. During the day, a vibrant community of students, businesspeople, and merchants make their way through the bustling streets. Vendors sell fresh cut pineapples and mangos while young Latin American consumers lug bags and boxes through the streets on shopping sprees. The Downtown area does have its mall (Bayside Marketplace) where many cruise passengers come to browse, its culture (Metro-Dade Cultural Center), and a number of good restaurants (listed in Chapter 6).

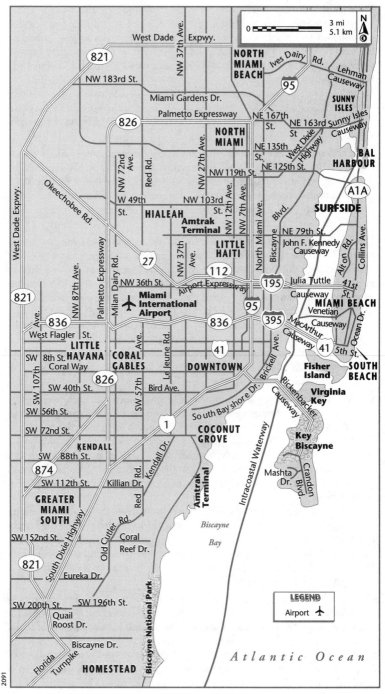

Little Haiti   During a brief period in the late 1970s and early 1980s, almost 35,000 Haitians arrived in Miami. Most of the new refugees settled in a decaying 200-square-block area north of Downtown. Extending from 41st to 83rd streets and bordered by I-95 and Biscayne Boulevard, Little Haiti, as it is known, is a relatively depressed neighborhood with at least 60,000 residents, more than half of whom were born in Haiti.

On Northeast Second Avenue, Little Haiti's main thoroughfare, is the now-closed, once-colorful Caribbean Marketplace, located at the corner of 60th Street. Previously filled with bustling shops, it stands as a sad reminder of the neighborhood's economic distress.

Little Havana   Miami's Cuban center is the city's most important ethnic enclave. Referred to locally as "Calle Ocho" (pronounced *Ka-yey O-choh*), SW Eighth Street, located just west of Downtown, is the region's main thoroughfare. Car-repair shops, tailors, electronics stores, and inexpensive restaurants all hang signs in Spanish. Salsa rhythms thump from the radios of passersby, while old men in guayaberas chain-smoke cigars over their daily game of dominoes.

Coral Gables   Just over 70 years old, Coral Gables is the closest thing to "historical" that Miami has. It's also one of the prettiest parcels in the city. Created by George Merrick in the early 1920s, the Gables was one of Miami's first planned developments. The houses here were built in a "Mediterranean style" along lush tree-lined streets that open onto beautifully carved plazas, many with centerpiece fountains. The best architectural examples of the era have Spanish-style tiled roofs and are built from Miami oolite, a native limestone commonly called "coral rock." Coral Gables is a stunning example of "boom" architecture on a grand scale—plus it's a great area to explore. Some of the city's best restaurants are located here, as are top hotels and good shopping. See the appropriate chapters for listings and "Driving Tour 2," in Chapter 8, for details.

Coconut Grove   There was a time when Coconut Grove was inhabited by artists, intellectuals, hippies, and radicals. But times have changed. Gentrification has pushed most alternative types out, leaving in their place a multitude of cafes, boutiques, and nightspots. The intersection of Grand Avenue, Main Highway, and McFarlane Road pierces the area's heart, which sizzles with dozens of interesting shops and eateries. Sidewalks here are often crowded with businesspeople, high school students, and loads of foreign visitors—especially at night, when it becomes a great place to people-watch.

Coconut Grove's link to the Bahamas dates from before the turn of the century, when islanders came to the area to work in a newly opened hotel called the Peacock Inn. Bahamian-style wooden homes, built by these early settlers, still stand on Charles Street. Goombay, the lively annual Bahamian festival, celebrates the Grove's Caribbean link and has become one of the largest Black-heritage street festivals in America (see "Miami Calendar of Events" in Chapter 2).

Greater Miami South   To locals, South Miami is both a specific area, southwest of Coral Gables, and a general region that encompasses all of southern Dade County and includes Kendall, Perrine, Cutler Ridge, and Homestead. For the purposes of clarity, this book has grouped all these southern suburbs under the rubric "Greater Miami South." Similar attributes unite the communities: They are heavily residential, and all are packed with condominiums and shopping malls as well as acres upon acres of farmland. Tourists don't stay in these parts, as there are no beaches and few cultural offerings. But Greater Miami South does contain many of the city's top attractions (see Chapter 7), making it likely that you'll spend some time during the day here.

2 Getting Around

Officially, Dade County has opted for a "unified, multimodal transportation network," which basically means you can get around the city by train, bus, and taxi. However, in practice, the network doesn't work too well. In most cases, unless you are going from downtown Miami to a not-too-distant spot, you are better off in a rented car or a taxi.

With the exception of downtown Coconut Grove and South Beach, Miami is not a walker's city. Because it is so spread out, most attractions are too far apart to make walking to them feasible. In fact, most Miamians are so used to driving that they drive even when going just a few blocks.

BY PUBLIC TRANSPORTATION

BY RAIL   Two rail lines, operated by the Metro-Dade Transit Agency (information ☎ 305/638-6700), run in concert with each other.

Metrorail, the city's modern high-speed commuter train, is a 21-mile elevated line that travels north-south, between downtown Miami and the southern suburbs. If you are staying in Coral Gables or Coconut Grove, you can park your car at a nearby station and ride the rails Downtown. Unfortunately for visitors, the line's usefulness is limited. There are plans to extend the system to service Miami International Airport, but until those tracks are built, these trains don't go most places tourists go. Metrorail operates daily from about 6am to midnight. Fare is $1.25.

Metromover, a 4.4-mile elevated line, connects with Metrorail at the Government Center stop and circles Downtown. Riding on rubber tires, the single-train car winds past many of the area's most important attractions and shopping and business districts. Metromover offers a fun, futuristic ride that you might want to take to complement your Downtown tour. You get a beautiful perspective from the towering height of the suspended rails. System hours are daily from about 6am to midnight. Fare is 25¢.

BY BUS   Miami's suburban layout is not conducive to getting around by bus. Lines operate, and maps can be had, but instead of getting to know the city, you'll find that relying on bus transportation will acquaint you only with how it feels to wait at bus stops. You can get a bus map by mail, either from the Greater Miami Convention and Visitors Bureau (see "Visitor Information" in Chapter 2) or by writing the Metro-Dade Transit System, 3300 NW 32nd Ave., Miami, FL 33142. In Miami call 305/638-6700 for public-transit information. Fare is $1.25.

BY CAR

Tales circulate about vacationers who have visited Miami without a car, but they are very few indeed. If you are counting on exploring the city, even to a modest degree, a car will be essential. Miami's restaurants, attractions, and sights are far from one another, so any other form of transportation is impractical. You won't need a car, however, if you are spending your entire vacation at a resort, are traveling directly to the Port of Miami for a cruise, or are here for a short stay centered in one area of the city, such as South Beach.

When driving across a causeway or through Downtown, allow extra time to reach your destination due to frequent drawbridge openings. Some bridges open about every half hour for large sailing vessels that make their way through the wide bays and canals that criss-cross the city, stalling traffic for several minutes. Don't get frustrated by the wait. It's all part of the easy pace of South Florida life.

RENTALS   It seems as though every car-rental company, big and small, has at least one office in Miami. Consequently, the city is one of the cheapest places in the world to rent a car. Many firms regularly advertise prices in the neighborhood of $100 per week for their bottom-of-the-line tin can—not an unreasonable sum for seven days of sun and fun.

A minimum age, generally 25, is usually required of renters. Some rental agencies have also set maximum ages. A national car-rental broker, A Car Rental Referral Service (☎ 800/404-4482), can often find companies willing to rent to drivers over the age of 21 and also are able to obtain discounts from major companies as well as some regional ones.

National car-rental companies with toll-free numbers include: **Alamo** (☎ 800/327-9633), **Avis** (☎ 800/331-1212), **Budget** (☎ 800/527-0700), **Dollar** (☎ 800/800-4000 or 800/327-7607), **Hertz** (☎ 800/654-3131), **National** (☎ 800/328-4567), and **Thrifty** (☎ 800/367-2277). Literally dozens of other regional companies —some offering lower rates—can be found in the Miami yellow pages under "Automobile Renting & Leasing." One excellent local company that has offices in every conceivable part of town and offers extremely competitive rates is **Enterprise** (☎ 800/325-8007).

Many companies offer cellular phone or electric map rental. It might be wise to open for these additional safety features, although the cost can be exorbitant: You may want to consider at least the phone option for times when you may get disoriented. There is nothing worse than being lost in a foreign city in a questionable area with no one to turn to.

Finally, think about splurging on a convertible. Few things in life can match the feeling of cruising along warm Florida highways with the sun smiling on your shoulders and the wind whipping through your hair. At most companies, the price is only about 20% more.

PARKING   Always keep plenty of quarters on hand in order to feed hungry meters. Parking is usually plentiful (except on South Beach and Coconut Grove), but when it's not, be careful: Fines for illegal parking can be stiff, up to $18.

In addition to parking garages, valet services are commonplace and often used. Expect to pay from $3 to $10 for parking in Coconut Grove and on South Beach's Ocean Drive on busy weekend nights.

LOCAL DRIVING RULES   Florida law allows drivers to make a right turn on a red light after a complete stop, unless otherwise indicated. In addition, all passengers are required to wear seat belts, and children under 3 must be securely fastened in government-approved car seats.

BY TAXI

If you're not planning on traveling much within the city, an occasional taxi is a good alternative to renting a car. If you plan on spending your holiday within the confines of South Beach's Art Deco District, you may also wish to avoid the parking hassles that come with renting your own car. The taxi meter starts at $1.10, and ticks up another $1.75 each mile and 25¢ for each additional minute. There are standard flat-rate charges for frequently traveled routes—for example, Miami Beach's Convention Center to Coconut Grove would cost about $16.

Major cab companies include **Metro** (☎ 305/888-8888), **Yellow** (☎ 305/444-4444), and on Miami Beach, **Central** (☎ 305/532-5555).

BY BICYCLE

Miami has several interesting areas to bike, including most of Miami Beach where the hard-packed sand and boardwalks make it an easy and scenic route. However, unless you are a former New York City bicycle messenger, you won't want to use a bicycle as your main means of transportation.

For more information on bicycles, including where to rent the best ones, see Chapter 7.

FAST FACTS: Miami

Airport   See "Getting There," in Chapter 2.

American Express   You'll find American Express offices in downtown Miami at 330 Biscayne Blvd. (☎ 305/358-7350); 9700 Collins Ave., Bal Harbour (☎ 305/865-5959); and 32 Miracle Mile, Coral Gables (☎ 305/446-3381). Offices are open weekdays from 9am to 5pm and Saturday from 10am to 4pm. The Bal Harbour office is also open on Sunday from noon to 6pm. To report lost or stolen traveler's checks, call 800/221-7282.

Area Code   The area code for Miami and all of Dade County is 305. Even though areas in the Keys still share the Dade County area code, calls are considered long distance and must be preceded by 1-305. When calling Miami from within the city, simply dial the seven-digit code.

Baby-Sitters   Hotels can often recommend a baby-sitter or child-care service. If yours can't, try **Central Sitting Agency,** 1764 SW 24th St. (☎ 305/856-0550).

Business Hours   Banking hours vary, but most banks are open weekdays from 9am to 3pm. Several stay open until 5pm or so at least one day during the week, and many banks feature automated-teller machines (ATMs) for 24-hour banking. Most stores are open daily from 10am to 6pm; however, there are many exceptions. Shops in the Bayside Marketplace are usually open until 9 or 10pm, as are the boutiques in Coconut Grove. Stores in Bal Harbour and other malls are usually open an extra hour one night during the week (usually Thursday). As far as business offices are concerned, Miami is generally a 9am-to-5pm town.

Car Rentals   See "Getting Around," above.

Climate   See "When to Go" in Chapter 2.

Dentists   The East Coast District Dental Society staffs an **Emergency Dental Referral Service** (☎ 305/285-5470). **A&E Dental,** 11400 N. Kendall Dr., Mega Bank Building (☎ 305/271-7777), also offers round-the-clock care and accepts MasterCard and Visa.

Doctors   In an emergency, call an ambulance by dialing 911 from any phone. The Dade County Medical Association sponsors a **Physician Referral Service** (☎ 305/324-8717) weekdays from 9am to 5pm. Health South Doctors' Hospital, 5000 University Dr., Coral Gables (☎ 305/666-2111), is a 285-bed acute-care hospital with a 24-hour physician-staffed emergency department.

Driving Rules   See "Getting Around," above.

Drugstores   See "Pharmacies," below.

Embassies/Consulates   See Chapter 3, "For Foreign Visitors."

Emergencies   To reach the police, ambulance, or fire department, dial **911** from any phone. No coins are needed. Emergency hotlines include Crisis Intervention (☎ 305/358-4357 or 305/358-HELP); Poison Information Center (☎ 800/282-3171); and Rape Hotline (☎ 305/585-6949).

Eyeglasses   Pearle Vision Center, 7901 Biscayne Blvd. (☎ 305/754-5144), in Miami, can usually fill prescriptions in about an hour.

Hospitals   See "Doctors," above.

Information   See "Visitor Information," above.

Laundry/Dry Cleaning   All Laundry Service, 5701 NW 7th St. (west of Downtown, ☎ 305/261-8175), does dry cleaning and offers a wash-and-fold service by the pound in addition to self-service machines; it's open daily from 7am to 10pm. **Clean Machine Laundry,** 226 12th St., South Beach (☎ 305/534-9429), is convenient to South Beach's art deco hotels; it's open 24 hours. **Coral Gables Laundry & Dry Cleaning,** 250 Minorca Ave., Coral Gables (☎ 305/446-6458), has been dry cleaning, altering, and laundering since 1930. It offers a lifesaving same-day service and is open weekdays from 7am to 7pm and Saturday from 8am to 3pm.

Libraries   The Main Library in the Dade County system is located Downtown at 101 W. Flagler St. (☎ 305/375-2665). It's open Monday to Wednesday, Friday, and Saturday from 9am to 6pm; Thursday from 9am to 9pm; and Sunday from 1pm to 5pm during the school year.

Liquor Laws   Only adults 21 or older may legally purchase or consume alcohol in the state of Florida. Minors are usually permitted in bars that serve food. Liquor laws are strictly enforced; if you look young, carry identification. Beer and wine are also sold in most supermarkets and convenience stores. The city of Miami's liquor stores are closed on Sunday. Liquor stores in the city of Miami Beach are open all week.

Lost Property   If you lost it at the airport, call the Airport Lost and Found office (☎ 305/876-7377). If you lost it on the bus, Metrorail, or Metromover, call Metro-Dade Transit Agency (☎ 305/638-6700). If you lost it somewhere else, phone the Dade County Police Lost and Found (☎ 305/375-3366). You may also wish to fill out a police report for insurance purposes.

Luggage Storage/Lockers   In addition to the baggage check at Miami International Airport, most hotels offer luggage-storage facilities. If you are taking a cruise from the Port of Miami (see Chapter 11), bags can be stored in your ship's departure terminal.

Maps   See "City Layout" earlier in this chapter.

Newspapers/Magazines   The well-respected *Miami Herald* is the city's only English-language daily. It is especially known for its Latin American coverage and its excellent Friday "Weekend" entertainment guide. There are literally dozens of specialized Miami magazines geared toward tourists and natives alike. Many are free and can be picked up at hotels, at restaurants, and in vending machines all around town. The most respected alternative weekly is the well-respected tabloid *New Times.* You can pick up *Ocean Drive,* a gorgeous over-sized glossy magazine, at most South Beach establishments. *South Florida*, on sale at newsstands, is the area's trendy glossy magazine with up-to-date listings.

For a large selection of foreign-language newspapers and magazines, check out Al's News, 8219 SW 124th St., South Miami (☎ 305/253-1762); Bus Terminal News, 2320 Salzedo St., Coral Gables (☎ 305/443-7979); Eddie's Normandy, 1096 Normandy Dr., Miami Beach (☎ 305/866-2026); Plaza News, 7900 Biscayne Blvd., Miami (☎ 305/751-NEWS); and Worldwide News, 1629 NE 163rd St., North Miami Beach (☎ 305/940-4090).

Pharmacies   Walgreens Pharmacies are all over town, including 8550 Coral Way (☎ 305/221-9271), in Coral Gables; 1845 Alton Rd. (☎ 305/531-8868), in South Beach; and 6700 Collins Ave. (☎ 305/861-6742), in Miami Beach. Their branch at 5731 Bird Rd. (SW 40th Street, ☎ 305/666-0757) is open 24 hours, as is **Eckerd Drugs,** 1825 Miami Gardens Dr. NE (185th Street), North Miami Beach (☎ 305/ 932-5740).

Photographic Needs   One Hour Photo in the Bayside Marketplace (☎ 305/ 377-FOTO) is one of the more expensive places to have your film developed. They charge $17 to develop and print a roll of 36 pictures; it's open Monday to Saturday from 10am to 10pm and Sunday from noon to 8pm. **Coconut Grove Camera,** 3317 Virginia St. (☎ 305/445-0521), features 30-minute color processing and maintains a huge selection of cameras and equipment. It rents, too. Walgreens or Eckerd's will develop film for the next day for about $6 or $7.

Police   For emergencies, dial 911 from any phone. No coins are needed. For other matters, call 305/595-6263.

Post Office   The Main Post Office, 2200 Milam Dairy Rd., Miami, FL 33152 (☎ 305/639-4280), is located west of Miami International Airport. Letters addressed to you and marked "c/o General Delivery" can be picked up at 500 NW 2nd Ave. Conveniently located post offices include 1300 Washington Ave. (☎ 305/ 531-7306), in South Beach, and 3191 Grand Ave. (☎ 305/443-0030), in Coconut Grove.

Radio   About five dozen radio stations can be heard in the Greater Miami area. On the AM dial, 610 (WIOD), 790 (WNWS), 1230 (WJNO), and 1340 (WPBR) are all talk. The only all-news station in town is 940 (WINZ). WDBF (1420) is a good Big Band station and WPBG (1290) features golden oldies. The best rock stations on the FM dial include WZTA (94.9), WGTR (97.3), and the progressive-rock station WVUM (90.5). WKIS (99.9) is the top country station, and public radio can be heard either on WXEL (90.7) or WLRN (91.3). WDNA (88.9) has the best Latin jazz and multiethnic sounds.

Religious Services   Miami houses of worship are as varied as the city's population and include St. Patrick Catholic Church, 3716 Garden Ave., Miami Beach (☎ 305/531-1124); Temple Judea, 5500 Granada Blvd., Coral Gables (☎ 305/ 667-5657); Coconut Grove United Methodist, 3713 Main Hwy. (☎ 305/ 443-0880); Christ Episcopal Church, 3481 Hibiscus St. (☎ 305/442-8542); and Plymouth Congregational Church, 3400 Devon Rd., at Main Highway (☎ 305/ 444-6521).

Restrooms   Stores rarely let customers use the restrooms, and many restaurants offer their facilities for customers only. Most malls have bathrooms, as do many of the ubiquitous fast-food restaurants. Many public beaches and large parks provide toilets; in some places you have to pay or tip an attendant. Most large hotels have clean restrooms in their lobbies.

Safety   Don't walk alone at night, and be extra wary when walking or driving though Little Haiti and Downtown. It's always a good idea to stay aware of your surroundings when you're in any unfamiliar city, even in the most heavily touristed areas. When driving around Miami, always have a good map, and know where you are going. Never stop on a highway—if you get a flat tire, drive to the nearest well-lighted, populated place. Keep car doors locked and stay alert.

Taxes   A 6% state sales tax (plus .5% local tax, for a total of 6.5% in Miami) is added on at the register for all goods and services purchased in Florida. In addition, most municipalities levy special taxes on restaurants and hotels. In Surfside, hotel taxes total 10.5%; in Bal Harbour, 9.5%; in Miami Beach (including South Beach), 11.5%; and in the rest of Dade County, a whopping 12.5%. In Miami Beach, Surfside, and Bal Harbour, the resort (hotel) tax also applies to hotel restaurants and restaurants with liquor licenses.

Taxis   See "Getting Around" earlier in this chapter.

Television   The local stations are Channel 6, WTVJ (NBC); Channel 4, WCIX (CBS); Channel 7, WSVN (Fox); Channel 10, WPLG (ABC); Channel 17, WLRN (PBS); Channel 23, WLTV (independent); and Channel 33, WBFS (independent).

Time Zone   Miami, like New York, is in the eastern standard time zone. Between April and October, eastern daylight saving time is adopted, and clocks are set one hour ahead. America's eastern seaboard is five hours ahead of Greenwich mean time. To find out what time it is, call 305/324-8811.

Transit Information   For Metrorail or Metromover schedule information, phone 305/638-6700.

Weather   For an up-to-date recording of current weather conditions and forecast reports, call 305/229-4522.

Accommodations 5

There is no shortage of places to stay in Miami. However, the prices and quality of the city's hotels vary dramatically. During the winter months, after Thanksgiving until March or April, the beach hotels fill up with travelers seeking refuge from the cold, the international jet-set crowd on their way to the Caribbean, and even locals from inland who want a weekend getaway. Since so much of the beach action is geared towards visitors, you'll find deals if you are flexible and willing to come mid-week and off-season, especially during the summer. You'll also find less expensive rates in hotels that have not been renovated recently.

Many of the old hotels from the 1930s, 1940s, and 1950s (when the bulk of Miami resorts were constructed) have been totally rehauled from the ground up, while others have survived with occasional coats of paint and new carpeting, which owners like to call renovation. Ask about what work has been done, since, especially on the ocean, sea air and years of tourist-wear can result in musty, paint-peeled rooms. It's just as important to ask if renovations will be going on when you are visiting, because I know I don't enjoy the sounds of jackhammers over breakfast. In the listings below, I've ignored the more worn hotels and included those that have been fully upgraded in the past few years. Exceptions are noted.

You may already know that South Florida's tourist season is well defined, beginning in mid-November and lasting until Easter. From the season's commencement, hotel prices escalate until about February, after which they again begin to decline. During the off-season, hotel rates are typically 30% to 50% lower than their winter highs. Oceanfront rooms are also easier to get between Easter and November, and shops, roads, and restaurants will be less crowded.

But timing isn't everything. In many cases, rates will also depend on your hotel's proximity to the beach and how much ocean you can see from your window. Small motels, a block or two from the water, can be up to 40% cheaper than similar properties right on the sand. When a hotel *is* right on the beach, it's probable that its oceanfront rooms will be significantly more expensive than similar accommodations in the rear. Still, despite their higher prices, oceanfront rooms can often be hard to get; if you want one, I definitely recommend making a reservation in advance.

If, after inquiring about room availability at the hotels listed in this guide, you still come up empty-handed (an extremely unlikely prospect), you can always try to find a room along Miami Beach's Collins Avenue. Dozens of hotels and motels line this strip, and a room—in all price categories—is bound to be available.

The hotels listed in this chapter are categorized first by area, then by price. I've used the following guide for per-night prices: **Very Expensive,** more than $200; **Expensive,** $130 to $200; **Moderate,** $80 to $130; and **Inexpensive,** less than $80.

Prices are based on published rates for a standard double room during the high season; you can often do better. The rates are broken down into two broad categories: Winter (usually between November and March or April), and off-season (usually May through August). The rates for the months in between—the shoulder season—should fall somewhere in between the high and lows. The prices given do not include state and city taxes, which, in some parts of Miami are as high as 12.5%. (See "Fast Facts: Miami" in Chapter 4.)

Also note that many hotels have additional parking charges and levy heavy surcharges for telephone use. Some places, especially those in South Beach, also tack on an additional service charge. These listings should be read as a guideline, not as a guarantee.

Toll-free numbers operated by the chain hotels can also help you in your search for accommodations. These "800" numbers will save you time and money when inquiring about rates and availability. Some of the larger hotel chains with properties in the Miami area include **Best Western** (☎ 800/528-1234), **Days Inn** (☎ 800/325-2525), **Holiday Inn** (☎ 800/327-5476), **Howard Johnson** (☎ 800/446-4656), **Hyatt** (☎ 800/236-1234), **Quality Inn** (☎ 800/228-5151), **Ramada Inn** (☎ 800/272-6232), and **TraveLodge** (☎ 800/255-3050).

Another good choice are the art deco hotels run by **Island Outpost** group (☎ 800/OUTPOST). I've reviewed several—the Casa Grande, The Kent, and Cavalier—but also worth considering for both location and price are the Marlin Hotel, 1200 Collins Ave., and the Leslie, 1244 Ocean Drive.

RESERVE IN ADVANCE Although there are many hotels in Miami in every price range, it makes sense to call in advance to get the best available rates. You're not going to be stuck on the street if you don't reserve in advance; even during the height of the tourist season, you can usually drive right into the city and find decent accommodations fairly quickly. But be careful. If you have your sights set on one particular hotel, if you have to have an oceanfront room, or if you want to stay in an area where accommodations are not particularly plentiful, you should reserve your room at least a few weeks in advance of your arrival.

RESERVATION SERVICES A centralized reservation service, Central Reservations (☎ 800/950-0232 or 305/274-6832 or on the internet: http://www.reservation-services.com or e-mail: rooms@america.com), works with many of Miami's hotels and can often secure discounts of up to 40% off published room rates. The service also offers advice on where to stay in specific locations, especially in Miami Beach and Downtown.

The **South Florida Hotel Network** (☎ 800/538-3616 or 305/538-3616) lists more than 300 hotels throughout the area, from Palm Beach to Miami and down to the Keys.

1 Best Bets

- **Best Historical Hotel:** The **Biltmore Hotel Coral Gables** (☎ 305/445-1926 or 800/228-3000) just celebrated its 70th birthday. The founder of Coral Gables, George Merrick, built this grand old hotel in a Mediterranean style with a huge bell tower based on the Giralda tower in Seville. It's now restored to its original 1926 splendor, and rooms are large and luxurious.
- **Best for Business Travelers:** The **Hotel Inter-Continental Miami** (☎ 305/577-1000 or 800/332-4246) wins for its location and amenities. Near the Metrorail and only a 10-minute drive from Miami International Airport, this hotel features an extensive variety of well-appointed meeting rooms and every imaginable executive service on sight. The dining options are also superb.
- **Best for a Romantic Getaway:** The ivy-covered **Hotel Place St. Michel** (☎ 305/444-1666 or 800/848-HOTEL) in Coral Gables is a small old-world style hotel. Warm architectural details like arched doorways and teak floors covered by Oriental rugs make visitors feel like they are staying in a well-run Italian mansion.
- **Best Trendy Hotel:** With its Alice-in-Wonderlandesque interior designed by Philip Starck, the recently reinvented **Delano Hotel** (☎ 305/672-2000 or 800/555-5001), on South Beach, easily wins the vote for Miami's trendiest spot.
- **Best Hotel Lobby for Pretending That You're Rich:** Lounge around one of the tapestried divans in the **Fisher Island Club** (☎ 305/535-6026) long enough, and you'll find yourself calling for Jeeves in a heavily affected accent. You can't help it in this magnificent marbled palace.
- **Best for Families:** The **Sonesta Beach Resort Hotel Key Biscayne** (☎ 305/361-2021 or 800/SONESTA) has family-friendly everything: restaurants, game rooms, gym, tennis courts, and a pool. Add to that the educational and entertaining programs, and you'll find your children will be coming back with their children. It's the perfect place for the entire family.
- **Best Moderately Priced Hotel:** The **Bay Harbor Inn** (☎ 405/868-4141) is so popular with discriminating budget-conscious travelers that it is booked a year in advance in season. Nothing beats the impeccable service and style at this antique-laden inn, located in the exclusive Bal Harbour area.
- **Best Hotel Pool:** The **Fontainebleau Hilton's** (☎ 305/538-2000 or 800/HILTONS) dramatic grotto and waterfall make its pool one of the most interesting and fun pools to swim in. On the other hand, the pool at the **Biltmore** is the nation's largest, graced with Italian statues and columns beneath a huge Gothic tower.
- **Best Spa:** When you want to relax or be pampered, there's no better place to go than the world-famous **The Spa at the Doral,** at the **Doral Golf Resort and Spa,** (☎ 305/592-2000, 800/22-DORAL, or 800/71-DORAL). And **Fisher Island Club's** (☎ 305/535-6026) exclusive facilities are the most luxurious I've ever seen.

2 South Beach

In South Beach—the southern tip of Miami Beach—hotels were mostly built in the 1930s, just after the Great Depression. Since the area was originally built as an affordable destination for middle-class folks from the Northeast, none of the hotels were built to be particularly luxurious. However, these hotels just happened to be situated on one of the most beautiful strips of beach in the United States. It was the large resorts north of South Beach that were built in later years, like the Fontainebleau, that attracted celebrities and a jet-set crowd.

But after many transitional years, South Beach gained national recognition for its art deco architecture. What the hotels lacked in real luxury they made up for in innovative design details. Now this neighborhood is the number one tourist destination in South Florida. In addition, the bulk of the city's best restaurants and nightclubs are located in South Beach.

The most expensive rooms are on Ocean Drive, just across the street from the beach. Thanks to zoning, for at least most of South Beach, buildings cannot be built directly on the sand and cannot exceed three stories.

Collins Avenue, just one block west, runs parallel to Ocean Drive. This pretty stretch of the street is not on the water, but staying here usually means lower room rates and a quieter night's sleep.

Under construction at press time was the 800-room **Loew's Miami Beach Hotel,** the first convention hotel to be built in Miami Beach in 30 years. Although the $135-million project will not be completed until at least 1998, the 16-story new structure should be a premiere property. Plans also call for a complete renovation of the St. Moritz, a 10-story classic art deco hotel built in 1939. The mammoth resort will feature a pool, health spa, tennis courts, eighteen meeting rooms, and four restaurants.

VERY EXPENSIVE

✪ **Casa Grande Suite Hotel.** 834 Ocean Dr., Miami Beach, FL 33139. ☎ **305/672-7003** or 800/OUT-POST. Fax 305/673-3669. 38 suites. A/C TV MINIBAR TEL. Winter $185 studio, $240–$325 one-bedroom suite, $425 two-bedroom suite, $1,000 three-bedroom suite. Off-season $150 studio, $200–$250 one-bedroom suite, $325 two-bedroom suite, $700 three-bedroom suite. Children under 12 stay free. Additional person $15. No-smoking rooms available. AE, DISC, MC, V. Parking $14.

The Casa Grande is South Beach's most luxurious yet low-key property. As you stand in the lobby, you'll notice a subtle, earthy scent of fresh wood and flowers. It's not incense nor potpourri, but the natural smell of mahogany and teak furnishings. This epitomizes the warmth and hominess you'll experience at this all-suite hotel.

Europeans and vacationing stars who want privacy enjoy the casual elegance and thoughtful service of this superior property. You'll feel like you are in a very stylish apartment, not a cookie-cutter hotel room. Every room here is outfitted in a slightly different style with beautifully tiled baths, reed rugs, mahogany beds, handmade batik prints, and antiques from all over the world, especially Indonesia. Add to the equation ocean views, a fridge you can stock, and every amenity to enjoy, and you'll know why this is the most desirable hotel on South Beach.

Dining/Entertainment: An adjacent restaurant, Mezzaluna, serves great pastas and Italian fare.

Services: Concierge and room service, overnight laundry and dry-cleaning service, complimentary newspaper and evening turndown with chocolates, in-room massage, twice-daily maid service, baby-sitting arrangements available, express checkout.

Facilities: Fully equipped kitchenettes, VCRs available, HBO, videos from an extensive library delivered ($7), access to a nearby health club, conference rooms, car rental, activities desk.

✪ **Delano.** 1685 Collins Ave., Miami Beach, FL 33139. ☎ **305/672-2000** or 800/555-5001. Fax 305/532-0099. 238 rms, lofts, suites, bungalows, and penthouses. A/C TV MINIBAR TEL. Winter $200–$300 double, $400 loft, $550 suite, $600 bungalow, $1,500 penthouse. Off-season $150–$200 double, $275 loft, $300 suite, $350 bungalow, $1,500 penthouse.

Additional person $20. Children under 18 stay free. No-smoking rooms available. AE, CB, DISC, MC, V. Parking $12.

Here's the hippest place to stay in South Beach. The recently revamped Delano has graced the cover of nearly every architecture and style magazine with its whimsical and elegant design. If you still don't recognize the hotel, there's no sign, so look for a huge hedge with a simple blue arched door in its center. In case you miss that, a futuristic finned rocketlike tower (an original 1947 detail) sprouts from the top of the 12-story building.

New York's Ian Shrager of Studio 54 and The Paramount fame brought in designer Philip Starck, who went wild with an impossible decor of Adirondack chairs placed near full-size fur-draped beds in the lobby.

All the fabulous people stay here in the all-white rooms that boast only one dose of color: a perfectly crisp Granny Smith apple green. It sounds antiseptic, but it's not. It's incredibly sexy, like a perfume ad. Somehow, if you can get over the trendiness, you'll find the model-gorgeous staff gracious and even thoughtful.

The location couldn't be more ideal. Although the Delano is at the northernmost end of the Art Deco District, it is still walking distance to Lincoln Road, right on the beach and smack in the middle of cool. Even if you don't stay here, do stop in for a drink and sit at the marble-top eat-in kitchen that is an exaggerated reminiscence of an old farm house kitchen counter.

The cabanas poolside are the most desirable rooms because of their huge size and deluxe amenities, but I say opt for the ocean view up high where you will really appreciate the privileged vantage point.

Dining/Entertainment: Every night, the elegant bar attracts tons of curious beautiful people. The Blue Door serves an impressive but inconsistent menu (see the review in Chapter 6). The thatched Beach Bar restaurant serves fantastic sandwiches and salads. Every manner of other in-house food and beverage facilities keep any patron sated at all hours.

Services: Full concierge services, 24-hour room service, same-day laundry and dry-cleaning services, newspaper delivery, evening turndown, in-room massage, executive business services, express checkout, valet parking.

Facilities: HBO, video on demand, a large outdoor heated pool, 24-hour state-of-the-art gym, extensive water-sports recreation, children's movie theater and child activity programs, extensive business center, conference rooms, car rental, tour desks, boutique.

Fisher Island Club. One Fisher Island Dr., Fisher Island, FL 33190. ☎ **305/535-6026.** Fax 305/535-6037. 60 rms, suites, cottages, seaside villas. A/C TV TEL. Winter $350 double, $525 suite, $575–$1,165 cottage, $625–$1,260 villa. Off-season $300 double, $375 suite, $445–$820 cottage, $475–$990 villa. Golf, tennis, and spa packages available seasonally. 20% gratuity added to food and beverages. No-smoking rooms available. AE, DC, MC, V.

Nothing beats the luxury of this secluded island, which technically is not on South Beach but rather floats in the middle of the bay just offshore. There are no bridges or roadways to Fisher Island, just a ferry that operates every 15 minutes around the clock. Attendants rinse each Mercedes and Rolls with fresh water as it glides off the ferry. Not to worry, however, if you are car-less, since on this exclusive island golf carts get you anywhere you need to go.

As for location, you are only minutes from the airport, South Beach, Coral Gables, or The Grove (not counting ferry time). Still, considering the pampering you'll receive in this former Vanderbilt mansion turned resort extraordinaire, you probably won't want to leave the island. Most of the other buildings are million-dollar condos owned by seasonal visitors. This is where the stars stay, including Pavarotti, who has performed for the residents and guests. A world-class spa and club offer anything you could possibly imagine. Ask and you shall receive.

Dining/Entertainment: The elegant Vanderbilt Club offers continental cuisine. The Beach Club and Golfer's Grill serve basic but expensive sandwiches and salads, including a great club sandwich. An Italian Cafe prepares exceptional pastas and seafood. A dinner theater features live music.

Services: Concierge, room service (7am–10pm), dry cleaning, laundry, national newspaper delivery, nightly turndown, twice-daily maid service, baby-sitting, secretarial service, valet parking, courtesy airport transportation.

Facilities: The Spa Internazionale, P.B. Dye Golf Course, 18 tennis courts, 2 deep-water marinas, boutiques, huge corporate board room, a helipad, seaplane ramp, auto-ferry system.

EXPENSIVE

Astor Hotel. 956 Washington Ave., Miami Beach, FL 33139. ☎ **305/531-8081** or 800/270-4981. Fax 305/531-3193. 42 rms, including 24 suites. A/C MINIBAR TV TEL. Winter $105–$160 double, $190–$450 suite. Off-season $85–$145 double, $175–$375 suite. Rates include continental breakfast. No children under 10. AE, MC, V. Parking $14.

Completed last year, the Astor is a well-placed property in the heart of South Beach. Its streamlined look incorporates many original details of the 1936 facade. Inside and out you'll find incredible attention to detail.

You'll also notice inside that no expense was spared. Everything from the thick Belgian linens to the marble bathrooms are tasteful and elegant. But one drawback is the rooms are small.

The clean, sleek look attracts a trendy, young crowd, especially from the fashion world. The hotel is convenient to shopping and nightlife, but the ocean is a two-block walk away. You can swim on the premises in a pretty small pool, where a wall of water rushes down a stone wall in a continuous sheet of shimmering gold.

The Astor's big draw is the personal attention of the staff. No request is too small. They pride themselves on not balking at any request, from running down the street for a pack of Marlboros to scheduling a photo shoot in your room. As one of the newest luxury renovations on the beach, the Astor should excel.

Dining/Entertainment: Well-known restaurateur Dennis Max created yet another hit with his Astor Place Restaurant, which serves American cuisine from breakfast until dinner in an atriumlike setting overlooking the pool. The Sunday gospel brunch is popular.

Services: Full concierge services, room service (6pm–midnight), dry cleaning, same and next-day laundry service, nightly turndown, in-room massage, twice-daily maid service, baby-sitting can be arranged, valet parking.

Facilities: 30-foot pool, daily membership to a nearby gym for a minimal fee, front desk business center.

Ocean Front Hotel. 1230–38 Ocean Dr., Miami Beach, FL 33139. ☎ **305/672-2579.** Fax 305/672-7665. 27 rms, suites, apts, and penthouses. A/C TV TEL. Winter $180–$190 double, $225–$290 suite, $275–$365 apt, $425 penthouse. Off-season $175–$180 double, $205–$275 suite, $245–$335 apt, $385 penthouse. Additional person/bed $45, pets $15. Rates include continental breakfast. AE, DC, JCB, MC, V. Self-parking $4 weekdays, $6 weekends and holidays.

Even though the hotel does not receive much media attention, it is, overall, a fine setting for a typically upscale South Beach experience. The service and ambience is very French. The rooms are pleasant, decorated with period furnishings and all modern amenities. Most rooms face Ocean Drive, with an ocean view; a complete gut renovation over the past two years included sound-proofing, so that noise is minimal except when windows are open in the evening. The bathrooms are well laid

South Beach Accommodations

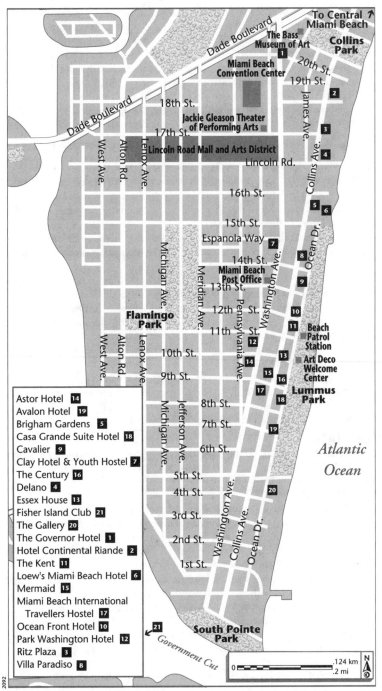

To Central ↑
Miami Beach

Dade Boulevard

The Bass
Museum of Art **1**

Collins
Park

Miami Beach
Convention Center

20th St.
19th St. **2**

18th St.

James Ave.

Dade Boulevard

Jackie Gleason Theater
of Performing Arts **3**

17th St.

4

West Ave.

Alton Rd.

Lenox Ave.

Lincoln Road Mall and Arts District

Collins Ave.

Lincoln Rd.

16th St.

5 **6**

15th St.

Ocean Dr.

Espanola Way **7**

14th St. **8**

Michigan Ave.

Miami Beach
Post Office **9**

Meridian Ave.

13th St.

Washington Ave.

12th St. **10**

Flamingo
Park

11th St. **11**

Beach
Patrol
Station

12

Pennsylvania Ave.

West Ave.

Alton Rd.

Lenox Ave.

10th St.

13

Art Deco
Welcome
Center

14

9th St.

15 **16**

Jefferson Ave.

17

Lummus
Park

8th St.

18

7th St.

19

6th St.

*Atlantic
Ocean*

Astor Hotel **14**
Avalon Hotel **19**
Brigham Gardens **5**
Casa Grande Suite Hotel **18**
Cavalier **9**
Clay Hotel & Youth Hostel **7**
The Century **16**
Delano **4**
Essex House **13**
Fisher Island Club **21**
The Gallery **20**
The Governor Hotel **1**
Hotel Continental Riande **2**
The Kent **11**
Loew's Miami Beach Hotel **6**
Mermaid **15**
Miami Beach International
  Travellers Hostel **17**
Ocean Front Hotel **10**
Park Washington Hotel **12**
Ritz Plaza **3**
Villa Paradiso **8**

Michigan Ave.

5th St.

4th St.

Washington Ave.

20

3rd St.

Collins Ave.

Ocean Dr.

2nd St.

1st St.

21

South Pointe
Park

Government Cut

0   .124 km
     .2 mi

N

2092

out with pale marble flooring and accents as well as thoughtful additions such as a magnifying mirror on a swivel arm and a separate bath and shower in most rooms.

Dining/Entertainment: Les Deux Fontaines serves good French food (see the review in Chapter 6) in three different areas: The Patio, Le Bistro, and La Brasserie.

Services: Concierge services, room service, same-day laundry and dry cleaning, evening turndown, twice-daily maid service.

Facilities: In-room VCR, video library ($5), access to nearby gym for reduced rates, Jacuzzi in some suites, 6 rooms with sundeck, large conference room, small gift shop.

The Ritz Plaza. 1701 Collins Ave., Miami Beach, FL 33139. ☎ **305/534-3500** or 800/ 522-6400. Fax 305/531-6928. 132 rms and suites. A/C TV TEL. Winter $145–$185 double, $275–$450 suite. Off-season $125–$165 double, $250–$425 suite. Children under 18 stay free. Packages available. 15% gratuity added. Rates include coffee service. AE, DC, MC, V. Parking $6.

The Ritz Plaza is another of the taller buildings on South Beach, slightly north of the Art Deco District's historic area. Its larger size—11 stories—allows for such amenities as a pool and room service that are so often not available in the smaller hotels down the street. Also, here you are directly on the ocean, and you can enjoy majestic views from the rooms higher up.

Originally built in 1940 in the art moderne style, the hotel underwent a complete renovation in 1990 (the renovation won an award from the Miami Design Preservation League). While there is nothing overwhelming about the place, the Ritz Plaza is extremely comfortable and well-run. It also features all the elements of the best deco hotels; the lobby, for example, has beautifully restored terrazzo floors, high ceilings, and striking lighting fixtures. A mix of visitors stay here, from business-types to families to fashion models.

Dining/Entertainment: There's the Ritz Cafe, plus Harry's Bar.

Services: Room service, daily dry-cleaning service, in-house baby-sitting services.

Facilities: Olympic-size outdoor swimming pool, small fitness room, large conference room, laundry facilities on property, car-rental desk.

MODERATE

Avalon Hotel. 700 Ocean Dr., Miami Beach, FL 33139. ☎ **305/538-0133** or 800/933-3306. Fax 305/534-0258. 106 rms. A/C TV TEL. Winter $115–$175 double. Off-season $65–$145 double. Rates include breakfast. Children under 12 stay free. Additional person $10. A 10% discount for stays of seven days or more. AE, DC, DISC, MC, V. Parking $14.

The Avalon is an excellent example of classic art deco digs right on the beach. Occupying a pretty parcel that wraps around the corner of 7th Street, the hotel is striking both inside and out. Rooms are well decorated in traditional 1930s style. The hotel's modest lobby is occupied by a casual restaurant, best for sandwiches at lunch either inside or on the breezy outdoor patio.

The experienced management, known for its excellent inns in Newport, Rhode Island, runs this hotel with an even hand. If the Avalon is full, don't hesitate to accept a room in its other property, the Majestic, located across the street.

Dining/Entertainment: The lobby restaurant, A Fish Called Avalon, is a popular seafood/American place for an informal lunch or a relaxing snack. By night, the menu gets fancier, prices get higher, and the cozy bar becomes a romantic place to pass the time.

Services: Full concierge services, room service (6:30am–11pm), same-day dry-cleaning and laundry service, nightly turndown, in-room massage available, valet parking and free shuttle to the convention center for large groups.

Facilities: VCRs, video rentals in lobby ($7), access to a nearby health club, nearby golf course, large meeting room, car rental, tour desk.

Cavalier. 1320 Ocean Dr., Miami Beach, FL 33139. ☎ **305/534-2135** or 800/OUTPOST. Fax 305/531-5543. 46 rms, including 3 suites. A/C TV MINIBAR TEL. Winter $135–$165 double, $250–$350 suite. Off-season $95–$135 double, $190–$240 suite. Children under 12 stay free. Additional person $15. No-smoking rooms available. AE, DC, DISC, MC, V. Valet parking $14, self-parking $6.

Like all the properties owned by music mogul Chris Blackwell as part of Island Outpost, the Cavalier is kept in shape by yearly refurbishments. Here palm trees brush the ceilings of the modest lobby where young trendy guests make their way to their bright-colored rooms. Funky prints cover the Tequila sunrise–colored walls.

You can't beat this oceanfront location with shops and restaurants adjacent to the hip, well-priced hotel. A young and competent staff waits on guests with lots of good advice for which clubs and restaurants to visit, as well as help in planning haircuts, massages, or shopping excursions. For an Ocean Drive hotel, most rooms are pretty quiet.

Services: Front-desk services, room service, same-day laundry and dry-cleaning services, evening turndown, in-room massage, twice-daily maid service, baby-sitting arrangements available, express checkout, valet parking.

Facilities: VCR, video rentals delivered to the room ($7), access to a nearby health club, conference rooms, car-rental and tour-desk services.

The Century. 140 Ocean Dr., Miami Beach, FL 33139. ☎ **305/674-8855.** Fax 305/538-5733. 36 rms, including 11 suites. A/C TV TEL. Winter $140 double, $220–$295 suite. Off-season $90 double, $140–$195 suite. Rates include breakfast. Additional person $5. Children under 5 stay free. AE, DC, MC, V.

The Century, considered off-the-beaten path a few years ago, is suddenly in the middle of things as the area below 5th Street is just now becoming popular. More and more clubs and restaurants are opening down there, which is both good and bad for The Century. The good news is more people are aware of the little deco rehab and the area has gotten safer. On the negative side, the noise from neighboring clubs can be deafening. Ask for a room in the newly refurbished Century Beach Club right on the ocean. The rooms are adequate in size and decorated in an eclectic beachy style. Many fashion-types stay here and enjoy the cozy private bar and beach area behind the hotel.

However, be sure to check that construction has not started on the vacant lot next door. Developers have been planning something there for a while now.

Dining/Entertainment: The Century Restaurant serves an interesting and varied menu and full liquor beach-club bar.

Services: Customer-service desk, room service (9am–11pm), express checkout.

Facilities: Access to nearby health clubs at reduced rates (Delano and Club Body Tech), water-sports arrangements, nature trails, car-rental arrangements, small gift shop.

✪ Essex House. 1001 Collins Ave., Miami Beach, FL 33139. ☎ **305/534-2700** or 800/55-ESSEX. Fax 305/532-3827. 50 rms, including 12 suites. A/C TV TEL. Winter $125–$145 double. Off-season $75–$96 double. Rates include breakfast. A 10% service charge is additional. Weekend minimum of 2 nights; holidays, 3 nights. Additional person $20. AE, DC, MC, V. Nearby parking available $4 weekdays, $6 weekends and holidays.

This art deco landmark is one of South Beach's finest gems. Now a TraveLodge affiliate, the pretty Essex House is a textbook example of the famous "Streamline Moderne" style, complete with large porthole windows, original etched glasswork, ziggurat arches, and detailed crown moldings. The solid oak bedroom furnishings are also original and, like many other details in this special hotel, were painstakingly restored.

The homey, personal touches include teddy bears on the beds and "touch-sensitive" lamps. The Essex also features 24-hour reception, a high-tech piano in the lobby/lounge, and a state-of-the-art security system.

Located one block from the ocean, this hotel is spick-and-span clean, almost too much like a chain. But the staff is extremely pleasant and helpful. Smoking is not permitted in any of the rooms. In general, you won't find families staying at the Essex, since, according to the hotel staff, children are "inappropriate" here.

Dining/Entertainment: The hotel's lobby/lounge acts as an all-purpose room serving light lunches, afternoon tea, and evening cocktails. Pianists sometimes entertain.

Services: Front-desk services.

Facilities: In-room massage available.

The Governor Hotel. 35 21st St., Miami Beach, FL 33139. ☎ **305/532-2100** or 800/542-0444. Fax 305/532-9139. 125 rms. A/C TV TEL. Winter $85–$125 double. Off-season $55–$85 double. Children under 18 stay free. No-smoking rooms available. AE, DC, DISC, MC, V. Free parking.

This inexpensive hotel on the northernmost border of South Beach is frequented by conventioneers who until recently had no real hotel to stay in. The Governor is nothing special, but the rooms are decent enough and the rates are pretty cheap.

As an example of art deco architecture this hotel is one of the most stylish in the area. It has streamlined details from the checkerboard floor tiles to the steel marquee and looming flagstaffs. But don't expect too much inside. A recent revamping improved the slightly tacky decor and introduced some more service-oriented staff to the place. You'll want to drive to the beach since it's a few long blocks through a not-so-scenic neighborhood of mostly unrenovated hotels serving as residences to a pretty seedy set.

Dining/Entertainment: A small cafe and piano bar serve decent snacks. Go elsewhere for your meals.

Services: Dry-cleaning and laundry services, secretarial services, valet parking.

Facilities: Medium outdoor pool, discounted access to nearby gym, nearby golf and tennis, car-rental arrangements.

⑤ The Kent. 1131 Collins Ave., Miami Beach, FL 33139. ☎ **305/531-6771** or 800/OUTPOST. Fax 305/531-0720. 54 rms including 2 suites. A/C TV MINIBAR TEL. Winter $95–$135 double, $175 suite. Off-season $65–$95 double, $125 suite. Rates include breakfast. Children under 12 stay free. Additional person $15. No-smoking rooms available. AE, DC, DISC, MC, V. Valet parking $14, self-parking $6.

One of the larger buildings on South Beach, this moderately priced hotel is one of the most recent additions to the superbly maintained Island-Outpost group's Art Deco Hotels. For the price, this is an excellent value right in South Beach's active center.

The staff includes a young hip bunch of Caribbeans who cater primarily to the fashion industry. Frequent photo shoots are coordinated in the lobby and conference room, where full office services are available. Thanks to a vacant lot in the backyard, some rooms in the rear offer nice views of the ocean. The decor is modest but tasteful.

Services: Front-desk services, same-day dry-cleaning and laundry service, nightly turndown and in-room massage, twice-daily maid-service upon request, baby-sitting arrangements available, express checkout, valet parking.

Facilities: VCRs available, video rental available and delivered ($7), reduced rates to nearby gym, conference room, car-rental and tour-activity desks.

The Mermaid. 9309 Collins Ave., Miami Beach, FL 33140. ☎ and fax **305/538-5324.** 9 rms, 1 suite. A/C MINIBAR TEL. Winter $85–$95 double, $200 suite. Off-season $65–$85 double, $175 suite. Rates include breakfast. Small children stay free. Additional person $10. AE, MC, V.

There is something magical about this little hideaway tucked behind tropical gardens in the very heart of South Beach. You won't find the amenities of the larger hotels, but this one-story guesthouse offers charm and hospitality that keeps drawing visitors back. You'll frequently find a young set of travelers from Europe and Uruguay (where the owners are from) who hang out in the garden drinking and playing music in the evenings. It's sort of like summer camp, where you get to meet new and interesting people as part of the package.

In 1996, new owners cleaned the place thoroughly, added brightly colored fretwork around the doors and windows, and installed phones in each room. Also, the wood floors have been stripped or covered in straw matting, one of the many Caribbean touches that make this place so cheery. Unfortunately, the success of a nearby club makes a few rooms noisy, so request a room in the main building for a good night's sleep.

Dining/Entertainment: There is a bar, late-night jazz, and a Caribbean band on the patio, plus occasional free impromptu dinners.

Services: Room/bar service, taxi service to and from airport ($15).

Hotel Continental Riande. 1825 Collins Ave., Miami Beach, FL 33139. ☎ **305/531-3503** or 800/RIANDE-1. Fax 305/531-2803. 250 rms. A/C TV MINIBAR TEL. Winter $125–$155 double. Off-season $105–$135 double. Special discount rates available. Children under 12 stay free. Additional person $25. No-smoking rooms available. AE, DC, DISC, MC, V. Parking $7.

Catering to a largely Latin clientele, The Riande has become quite well-known with its simple formula for success. The rooms and lobby areas are clean and well cared for but not too fussy. The hotel overlooks the ocean and is just two blocks from the Delano Hotel and all of South Beach. Sort of like a Spanish-flavored Howard Johnson, the Riande is the ticket if you want value and convenience.

Dining/Entertainment: Restaurant/coffee shop with buffet and menu.

Services: Concierge, room, laundry and valet services, twice-daily maid service.

Facilities: Large outdoor pool, water-sports arrangements available, banquet and meeting rooms, boutique.

INEXPENSIVE

Brigham Gardens. 1411 Collins Ave., Miami Beach, FL 33139. ☎ **305/531-1331.** Fax 305/538-9898. 18 rms and suites. A/C TV TEL. Winter $75–$125 double and suites nightly, $375–$775 weekly. Off-season $50–$95 double and suites nightly, $295–$575 weekly. Rates include breakfast. Pets stay for $6 a night and young children stay free. Additional person $5. AE, MC, V.

You'll feel like you're in a rainforest or a zoo at the Brigham Gardens. And I mean that in the nicest of all possible ways. When you enter the tropically landscaped garden, you'll hear macaws and parrots chirping, and see cats and lizards running through lawns covered with bougainvillea. The lush grounds are framed by quaint Mediterranean buildings that are pleasant, though in need of some sprucing up.

Ask for a listing of the exotic plants that give the gardens its lush tropical feel. There are literally hundreds of indigenous plants on display, which makes the property seem even more secluded and special. Since many rooms have kitchens, many people stay here for longer than a weekend. You may too, once you've settled into this happy spot. The mother and daughter who run Brigham Gardens go out of their way to make sure that you, as well as their little menagerie, are thriving.

Services: In-room coffee service.

Facilities: Privileges to local fitness club, laundry facilities.

⊙ Park Washington Hotel. 1020 Washington Ave., Miami Beach, FL 33139. ☎ **305/ 532-1930.** Fax 305/672-6706. 50 rms, including 15 suites. A/C TV TEL. Winter $69–$99 double. Off-season $49–$69 double. Rates include breakfast. Additional person $10. Children stay free in parents' room. AE, MC, V.

The Park Washington offers some of the best values in South Beach. Located two blocks from the ocean, this hotel has made a name for itself by offering good-quality accommodations at incredible prices. Designed in the 1930s by Henry Hohauser, one of the beach's most famous architects, the Park Washington reopened in 1989. Most rooms have original furnishings and well-kept interiors.

The Park Washington also runs the adjacent art deco Taft House and Kenmore hotels; these two properties attract a large gay clientele. All three hotels offer consistent quality and value, and are connected by a geometric wall for privacy and lush landscaping.

Services: In-room massage available, express checkout, free coffee and danish in lobby.

Facilities: Fully equipped kitchenettes in 16 rooms, medium outdoor heated pool, access to a nearby health club, bicycle rental, car rental and tour services.

Villa Paradiso. 1415 Collins Ave., Miami Beach, FL 33139. ☎ **305/532-0616.** Fax 305/ 667-0074. 17 apts. A/C TV TEL. Winter $85–$135 double nightly, $495–$750 weekly. Off-season $55–$95 double nightly, $350–$550 weekly. Additional person $10. AE, DC, MC, V.

This guesthouse, like the Mermaid or Brigham Gardens, is more like a cozy apartment house than a hotel. Instead of an elegant lobby or restaurant, you'll find a friendly host who is happy to give you a room key and advice on what to do. Villa Paradiso is located smack in the middle of the bustling area, a few blocks from Lincoln Road and all of the beach's best clubs.

Rooms are simple, and most have Murphy beds or fold-out couches for extra friends. One big advantage is that most rooms have a full kitchen, which can save you lots of money. The rooms overlook a lushly landscaped courtyard and are quiet considering their location. There are also laundry facilities.

3 Miami Beach: Surfside, Bal Harbour & Sunny Isles

The section of Miami Beach, known as Mid-Beach and North-Beach, described here runs from 21st Street to 192nd Street. This large area varies slightly from end-to-end; at its center are Bal and Bay Harbour, neighborhoods that are exclusive and full of character. The neighborhoods north and south of here, like Surfside and Sunny Isles, have nice beaches and some shops, but mostly need severe rehabilitation.

This area just above South Beach is also known as "Condo Canyon." Zoning codes did not restrict growth from the 1950s to the 1970s, so builders continually constructed bigger and more brazen structures that blocked out the ocean views for passersby but maximized oceanfront space for those who could afford to buy in. The result is a glut in the medium-quality condo market and a few scattered hold-outs of older hotels and motels that front the ocean.

Miami Beach Accommodations

BAL
HARBOUR

0 0.6 mi
   1 km

N

NE 125th St.   Miami Blvd.

Broad
Causeway

96th St.

Biscayne
Park

1

NE 103rd St.

SURFSIDE

North Shore Dr.

77th St.

Southshore Dr.

71st St.

Normandy Dr.

Harbor
Island

Allison
Island

John F. Kennedy Causeway   934   Normandy Isle

North Bay
Island

Treasure
Island

La Gorce Island

NE 79th St.

N. Bay
Rd.   W. 63rd St.

907

MIAMI
BEACH

W. 51st St.

Biscayne
Bay

W. 47th St.

Johns Island

Collins Island

Arthur Godfrey Rd.

44th St.

←To Miami

Julia Tuttle
Causeway

907

Sunset
Isles

Bay Rd.

30th
24th
St.

Rivo Alto
Island

Belle
Isle

W. 20th St. Dade Blvd.

23rd St.

City
Park

Collins
Park

Lincoln   Rd. Mall

Flamingo
Park

14th   St.

11th St.

Star
Island

Alton Rd.

9th St.

7th St.

Lummus
Park

41

1st St.

Biscayne
St.

Pier
Park

Sams
Island

Atlantic
Ocean

ACCOMMODATIONS:
Alexander All-Suite Luxury Hotel 8
Bay Harbor Inn 2
Baymar Ocean Resort 4
Compostela Motel 5
Dezerland Surfside Beach Hotel 6
Doral Ocean Beach Resort 9
Eden Roc Hotel and Marina 10
Fontainebleau Hilton 11
Indian Creek Hotel 12
Sheraton Bal Harbour
  Beach Resort 3
Suez Oceanfront Resort 1
The Inn on the Bay 7

VERY EXPENSIVE

The Alexander All-Suite Luxury Hotel. 5225 Collins Ave., Miami Beach, FL 33140. ☎ **305/865-6500** or 800/327-6121. Fax 305/864-8525. Telex 808172. 150 suites. A/C TV TEL. Winter $310 one-bedroom suite, $420 two-bedroom suite. Off-season $225 one-bedroom suite, $324 two-bedroom suite. Additional person $35. Children under 18 stay free in parents' room. Packages available. AE, CB, DC, MC, V. Parking $8.50.

This hotel is a good choice if you want to be off the beaten path but in the lap of luxury. One of the most exclusive offerings on Miami Beach, the Alexander is an all-suite hotel, featuring spacious one- and two-bedroom mini-apartments. Each suite contains a living room, a fully equipped kitchen, two baths, and a balcony. The rooms are elegant without being pretentious and offer every convenience you could want.

The hotel itself is well decorated with fine sculptures, paintings, antiques, and tapestries, most of which were garnered from the Cornelius Vanderbilt mansion. Lush vegetation surrounds two oceanfront pools; one of the "lagoons" is also fed by a cascading waterfall.

There is a certain elegance about this pretty hotel, and you'll feel like you are truly being pampered. Of course you pay a lot for the service and attention you receive, but it's worth it. The attentive staff is available at all hours for any request.

Dining/Entertainment: Dominique's is a gourmet restaurant, serving excellent French cuisine, including seafood, rack of lamb, rattlesnake, and Everglades alligator (see the review in Chapter 6). There are also a piano lounge and a pool bar.

Services: Full concierge service, room service (7am–10pm), dry-cleaning and laundry service, newspaper delivery, evening turndown upon request, in-room massage upon request, twice-daily maid service, baby-sitting service, valet parking.

Facilities: Some in-suite fully equipped kitchenettes, VCRs upon request, Spectravision with eight channels, two large outdoor heated pools, small state-of-the-art health club, four Jacuzzis, sauna, bicycle rental, nature trails, adequate business center, car rental and tour desk, small gift shop.

Doral Ocean Beach Resort. 4833 Collins Ave., Miami Beach, FL 33140. ☎ **305/532-3600** or 800/223-6725. Fax 305/534-7409. 420 rms, including 127 suites. A/C MINIBAR TV TEL. Winter $200–$325 double, $350–$2,000 suite. Off-season $110–$200 double, $240–$1,500 suite. Children under 17 stay free. Additional person $40. Weekend and other packages available. No-smoking floor available. AE, CB, DC, DISC, MC, V. Parking $12.

The Doral is one of Miami Beach's old grand hotels that still attracts conventioneers and fun-seeking visitors who remember the resort in its glory days of the 1960s. Today the eighteen-story monolith has become something of a relic, surrounded almost exclusively by converted condominiums. The current management says they plan a much-needed rehaul of the rooms and lobby areas, which are spacious but a bit tired.

Still, the hotel features all the activities you'd expect from a top waterfront resort, including sailing, waterskiing, jetskiing, and windsurfing. The biggest benefit of staying here, however, is that guests are entitled to use the facilities of the Doral's affiliated hotels (see "West Miami" below), which include six golf courses and one of the best health spas in America. A free shuttle bus connects this beach resort with the others.

In addition, considering the location, just a few miles from South Beach and near an entrance to I-95, you can get some good deals on rooms with sweeping views of the ocean and intracoastal.

Dining/Entertainment: The Seabreeze Restaurant, specializing in stir-fries, gourmet pizzas, and health-oriented edibles, sits adjacent to the pool. The Doral Resort also offers two other restaurants, a nightclub, two lounges, and a pool bar.

Services: Concierge services, 24-hour room service, laundry service, baby-sitting available, complimentary transportation to Doral Golf Resort and Spa, valet parking.

Facilities: VCRs upon request, eight-channel Spectravision, video rental ($6.95), outdoor Olympic-size pool, fitness center, two Jacuzzis, water-sports rentals, two lighted tennis courts, child activity center and game room, car rental, activities services.

Fontainebleau Hilton. 4441 Collins Ave., Miami Beach, FL 33140. ☎ **305/538-2000** or 800/HILTONS. Fax 305/531-9274. Telex 519362. 1,206 rms, including 60 suites. A/C TV TEL. Winter $290–$350 double, $420–$700 suite. Off-season $170–$255 double, $410–$700 suite. Additional person $25. Children stay free in parents' room. Weekend and other packages available. No-smoking rooms available. AE, CB, DC, DISC, MC, V. Parking $10.

Far and away the most famous hotel in Miami, the Fontainebleau (pronounced "fountain-blue") has built its reputation on garishness and excess. For most visitors, this spectacle is more tourist attraction than hotel; its massive structure, with an incredible lagoon-style pool and waterfall, really shouldn't be missed.

Since opening its doors in 1954, the hotel has hosted presidents, pageants, and movie productions—including the James Bond thriller *Goldfinger.* The sheer size of the Fontainebleau, with its full complement of restaurants, stores, and recreational facilities, plus over 1,100 employees, makes this a perfect place for conventioneers. Unfortunately, the same recommendation cannot be extended to individual travelers. It's easy to get lost here, both physically and personally. The lobby is terminally crowded, the staff is overworked, and lines are always long. Still, this is the one and only Fontainebleau, and in many ways it's the quintessential Miami hotel. Despite its shortcomings, this is one place you'll never forget.

Dining/Entertainment: Seven different eateries are located throughout the property. The Steak House is open for dinner only and reservations are required. The Dining Galleries, a continental restaurant, is open for Sunday buffet brunch only from 10am to 3pm. The Trop-Art Café serves meals from 7am to 2am. Additionally, there are four other cafes and coffee shops (including two by the pool), as well as a number of cocktail lounges, including the Poodle Lounge, which offers live entertainment and dancing nightly. Club Tropigala, just off the lobby, features a Las Vegas–style floor show with dozens of performers and two orchestras.

Services: Full concierge services, room service (6am–1:30am), laundry and dry-cleaning service, newspaper delivery, nightly turndown upon request, in-room massage, large state-of-the-art health club, baby-sitting arrangements available, express checkout, valet parking, free morning coffee in lobby (4:30am–6:30am).

Facilities: Movie channels, two large outdoor pools, award-winning spa, three whirlpool baths, sauna, sundeck, seven lighted tennis courts, water-sports equipment rental, bicycle rental, nearby golf course, game rooms, special year-round activities for children and adults, elaborate business center, conference rooms, car-rental and tour desks, beauty salon, boutique and shopping arcade with 28 stores.

Sheraton Bal Harbour Beach Resort. 9701 Collins Ave., Bal Harbour, FL 33154. ☎ **305/865-7511** or 800/325-3535. Fax 305/864-2601. Telex 519355. 655 rms, including 52 suites. A/C MINIBAR TV TEL. Winter $255–$355 double, $450 suite. Off-season $150–$230 double, $300 suite. Children under 18 stay free in parents' room. Additional person $25. Weekend and other packages and senior discounts available. No-smoking rooms available. AE, CB, DC, DISC, JCB, MC, V. Parking $9.

This hotel has the best location in Bal Harbour, on the ocean and just across from the swanky Bal Harbour Shops. Bill and Hillary Clinton stay here when in town, and Bill even jogged along the beach with the local fitness enthusiasts. It's one of the nicest Sheratons I've seen, with large, well-decorated rooms and a glass-enclosed two-story atrium lobby. A spectacular staircase wraps itself around a cascading fountain full of wished-on pennies.

One side of the hotel caters to corporations, complete with ballrooms and meeting facilities, but the main sections are relatively uncongested and removed from the convention crowd. A full complement of aquatic playthings can be rented on the beach, including sailboats and jetskis.

Dining/Entertainment: Guests have their choice of four restaurants and lounges. Al Carbon, an Argentinian steakhouse, serves good heavy meals with live Latin American music nightly. The other less formal spots serve Mediterranean beach food. A lounge blends good tropical drinks.

Services: Concierge services, room service (6:30am–12pm), laundry and drycleaning services, newspaper delivery, nightly turndown and in-room massage upon request, twice-daily maid service upon request, baby-sitting, secretarial services, express checkout, valet parking, free coffee and refreshments in the lobby.

Facilities: Fully equipped kitchenette in penthouse, eight-channel Spectravision service, Waterscape Fantasy aquatic facilities, large state-of-the-art fitness center and spa with aerobics, Jacuzzi, sauna, sundeck, two outdoor tennis courts, water-sports concession, jogging track, nearby golf course, game room, children's programs, large business center, conference rooms, tour desk, arrangement for beauty salon visit at adjacent Bal Harbour Shops, gift shop and shopping arcade.

EXPENSIVE

Eden Roc Hotel and Marina. 4525 Collins Ave., Miami Beach, FL 33140. ☎ **305/531-0000** or 800/327-8337. Fax 305/531-6955. Telex 807120. 351 rms, including 45 suites. A/C TV TEL. Winter $195–$350 double, $275–$1,500 suite. Off-season $120–$250 double, $175–$1,000 suite. Additional person $15. Children under 17 stay free. Weekend and spa packages available. AE, CB, DC, DISC, MC, V. Parking $8.50.

The Eden Roc is one of those big hotels that help give Miami Beach its flamboyant image. A recent $30 million restoration upgraded the resort for its 40th anniversary in 1996. Because of the hotel's size, unless there is a big event going on (which frequently occurs), you should be able to negotiate a good rate.

Accommodations here are more than a bit showy, but the amenities by far make up for the ostentatious display. The refurbished rooms, decorated in bright tropical shades of teal, lime, and violet and funky furniture, are unusually spacious, and each has an Italian marble bathroom.

Plus the hotel has one of the area's most complete spas with every imaginable amenity and equipment and very good aerobics classes. The glass-enclosed weight room overlooks the pool and ocean. The indoor sports club has a rock climbing wall, plus basketball, squash, and racquetball courts. There is even a separate woman's facility for the ultra-conservative Jewish patrons who frequent the hotel in season.

Dining/Entertainment: Fresco Mediterranean Cafe serves exceptionally good food, from carved meats to a full selection of tapas and a delicious brunch. Jimmy Johnson's, a sports bar, serves snack food, including good salads and burgers. An informal deli also provides good picnic fare.

Services: Concierge services, room service (7am–10:30pm), laundry and drycleaning services, newspaper delivery, nightly turndown, in-room massage, twice-daily maid service, baby-sitting upon request, secretarial services, express checkout, valet parking, free coffee in the lobby.

Facilities: Two outdoor pools, water-sports concession, game room, spa, racquetball, squash, conference facilities, car-rental desk, beauty salon, shopping arcade.

MODERATE

Ⓢ Bay Harbor Inn. 9660 E. Bay Harbor Dr., Bay Harbor Island, FL 33154. ☎ **305/868-4141.** Fax 305/868-4141 ext. 602. 38 rms, 10 suites. A/C TV TEL. Winter $85–$120 suite, $150–$235 penthouse suite. Off-season $70–$80 suite, $90–$150 penthouse suite. Rates include breakfast. Additional person $25. Children under 16 stay free. AE, CB, DC, MC, V. Free parking.

This quaint little inn looks like it ought to be in Vermont or somewhere woodsy and remote. It's not. The Bay Harbor Inn is moments from the beach, some fine restaurants, and some of the city's best shopping.

The inn actually has two parts. The more modern section sits squarely on a little river—known as "the creek"— and overlooks a kidney-shaped pool and a boat named the "Celeste" where patrons eat breakfast in the mornings. On the other side of the street is the cozier, antique-filled portion where glass-covered bookshelves hold good beach reading. You'll also find an eclectic array of Victorian desks and chairs scattered among modern oak side tables.

The rooms, too, have a hodgepodge of wood furnishings, like oak-framed mirrors, canopied beds, Victorian chairs, and modern vanities all comfortably arranged over a commercial brown carpeting. Some rooms are slightly larger, like nos. 301, 305, 308, and 311, and boast an extra half-bath at no extra cost. Request room 302 for a corner view of a quaint street. If you stay in a suite, you'll want to invite your friends over for drinks. You do at times smell the aroma of cooking from the restaurant below, but it only adds to the charm of this homey inn.

Call ahead of time to reserve a room, because this little find is a favorite among those in the know. Some guests book the same room season after season, so you may have a hard time finding anything here unless you call months in advance.

Dining/Entertainment: The Palm, a steak and lobster house, serves big portions (see the review in Chapter 6).

Services: Complimentary local paper, some secretarial services.

Facilities: Heated outdoor pool, conference room.

Dezerland Surfside Beach Hotel. 8701 Collins Ave., Miami Beach, FL 33154. ☎ **305/865-6661** or 800/331-9346 (800/331-9347 in Canada). Fax 305/866-2630. Telex 4973649. 225 rms. A/C TV TEL. Winter $85–$115 double. Off-season $60–$75 double. Additional person $8. Children under 19 stay free in parents' room. Special packages and group rates available. No-smoking rooms available. AE, CB, DISC, MC, V. Free parking.

Designed by car enthusiast Michael Dezer, Dezerland is a unique place—part hotel and part 1950s automobile wonderland. Visitors, who include many German tourists, are welcomed by a 1959 Cadillac stationed by the front door, and a 1955 Thunderbird hard-top sits in the lobby. A dozen other mint-condition classics are scattered about the floors, while the walls are decorated with related 1950s and 1960s memorabilia.

Billed as "America's largest '50s extravaganza," this Quality Inn member features rooms named after some of Detroit's most famous models, like the "Dodge Deluxe" or "The Belvedere." While the place isn't pristine, it's clean, and constant renovations improve it every year. Dezerland is located directly on the beach and features a mosaic of a pink Cadillac at the bottom of its surfside pool.

Dining/Entertainment: A restaurant and lobby lounge offer all-you-can-eat buffets and nightly entertainment.

Services: Concierge services, laundry, baby-sitting upon request.

Facilities: Some rooms contain fully equipped kitchenettes, outdoor heated pool, access to nearby health club, Jacuzzi, windsurf and jetski rental available, adjacent tennis courts, Laundromat, car rental and tour services, antique gift shop featuring 1950s memorabilia.

🌑 **Indian Creek Hotel.** 2727 Indian Creek Dr., Miami Beach, FL, 33140. ☎ **305/531-2727** or 800/207-2727. 61 rms including 6 suites. Winter $110 double, $190 suite. Off-season $90 double, $150 suite. Additional person $10. Group packages available. 18% gratuity added to room service, 15% added to restaurant check. No-smoking rooms available. DC, DISC, MC, V. Limited street parking.

Slightly north of South Beach sits this small hotel, where every detail of the 1936 Pan Coast–style building has been meticulously restored, from one of the beach's first operating elevators to the period steamer trunk in the lobby. It has a perfect location, just one short block from the beach, and within easy walking distance of the hectic South Beach scene. There's also easy access to the airport and the mainland.

The modest rooms are outfitted in deco furnishings with pretty tropical prints and modern amenities. New this year are large bungalow-style suites that overlook the palm-lined landscaped pool. The guests in this little treasure range from international travelers to business types looking for good value. That's just what you'll find here.

Dining/Entertainment: A tiny, cozy Pan Caribbean restaurant with a bar serves wonderfully innovative meals all day.

Services: Concierge and room service, laundry service, baby-sitting arrangements available, complimentary afternoon coffee in lobby.

Facilities: Pool, small fitness center, access to nearby health club, business center, two conference rooms, car-rental arrangements available.

INEXPENSIVE

🌑 **Baymar Ocean Resort.** 9401 Collins Ave., Miami Beach, FL 33154. ☎ **305/866-5446** or 800/8-BAYMAR. Fax 305/866-8053. 93 units, including 20 suites and 35 efficiencies. A/C TV TEL. Winter $75–$95 double, $115–$185 suite, $85–$105 efficiency. Off-season $60–$80 double, $95–$185 suite, $70–$90 efficiency. Children under 12 stay free. Additional person $10. AE, DC, DISC, MC, V. Free parking.

A recent renovation did wonders for this little hotel on the strip just south of Bal Harbour. It is owned by first-time hoteliers, the Martayan family from Belgium and New York. Depending upon what you're looking for, this could be one of the beach's best buys, if prices hold at this level.

The hotel is right on the ocean and has a pool. It also offers all the modern conveniences, including some kitchenettes and large closets. You won't flip over the decor, but it is pleasant and brand new. Oceanfront rooms tend to be smaller than others, but those on the first floor have a nice shared balcony space. The beach here is low-key with few other tourists.

Many families and conservative religious groups seemed comfortable in the new digs as construction was concluding on the lobby bar and restaurant. A really out-going staff seem eager to please. It helps to have a car here, because there's not much within walking distance; the surrounding area is run-down or converted into condos.

Dining/Entertainment: Locals and guests like the small restaurant serving basic American fare and the Tiki Bar.

Services: Front-desk services, room service (7am–10pm).

Facilities: Fully equipped kitchens in the efficiencies, Olympic-size heated outdoor pool, laundry facilities.

Compostela Motel. 9040 Collins Ave., Miami Beach, FL 33154. ☎ **305/861-3083.** Fax 305/865-2845. 20 suites, apts, and efficiencies. A/C TV TEL. Winter $60–$75 one-bedroom suite, $75 apartment, $55 efficiency. Off-season $50–$55 one-bedroom suite, $40 apartment, $40 efficiency. Children under 18 stay free. Additional person $5. AE, MC, V. Free parking.

The owners of the Compostela have recently set to renovating their three buildings, all within walking distance to the exclusive Bal Harbour Shops and many good shopping and dining areas. Although the buildings were run-down efficiencies for many years, the new interiors are really quite nice. All are carpeted, and most have full kitchenettes, a bonus when you are on a budget in a town full of expensive eateries.

What you get here is a lot of space and a great location for a low price. There is no fancy lobby, no doorman, and no amenities to speak of. But the staff is courteous, the area safe, and you're across the street from a great beach.

Services: Front-desk service, baby-sitting available.

Facilities: Full kitchenettes in the one-bedroom suites and the efficiencies, outdoor pool, laundry facilities.

The Inn on the Bay. 1819 79th St. Causeway, Miami, FL 33141. ☎ **305/865-7100** or 800/624-3961. Fax 305/868-3483. 122 rms. Winter $65–$95 double. Off-season $54–$84 double. Children under 14 stay free. Additional person $5. AE, DC, MC, V. Free parking.

Although this inn is not technically on Miami Beach, it is literally steps over the bridge that connects to the mainland. The recently renovated inn offers comfortable, large rooms. The decor is tropical and pleasant, yet a little like the interior of a dentist's office. The rooms with views overlook the beautiful bay and marina.

For the price, you can't beat this new addition to the Miami hotel scene. Although there's not much in the neighborhood, except a good Italian restaurant across the street, the area is relatively safe and quiet. You'll have to drive to the beaches (about five minutes over the bridge), or you can choose to sun and swim in the spacious pool on the premises.

You'll share the hotel with mostly a boating crowd, who stay for the large and relatively cheap boat slips; thus, when the boat show is in town during February, the rates at this otherwise budget hotel triple. In the well-known bar in the adjacent premises, you may run into some local anchors from the Channel 7 news station, which is just down the street. In the back you'll find a volleyball court and a pleasant breeze year-round.

⑤Suez Oceanfront Resort. 18215 Collins Ave., Sunny Isles, FL 33160. ☎ **305/932-0661** or 800/327-5278. Fax 305/937-0058. 150 rms and suites. A/C TV TEL. Winter $65–$88 double, $175 suite. Off-season $39–$67 double, $125 suite. Kitchenettes $10–$15 extra. Additional person $15. 15% gratuity added to food. AE, DC, MC, V. Free parking.

Guarded by an undersize replica of Egypt's famed Sphinx, the campy Suez offers decent rooms on the beach where most of the other old hotels have turned condo. This motel, on the ocean, is technically located in Miami Beach, but in a northern neighborhood called Sunny Isles that's closer to Hallandale in Broward County than to South Beach.

Following a fairly strict orange-and-yellow motif, the Suez is reminiscent more of a fast-food restaurant than anything in ancient Egypt. The thatch umbrellas over beach lounges and the Spanish Mediterranean–style fountains in the courtyard add to the confused decor. A kitschy but pleasant lounge offers good prices and a palm-lined area reminding you that you are indeed in a tropical paradise. For the price, it's not a bad place, and you can say you saw the pyramids.

Dining/Entertainment: The Oasis dining room offers a buffet dinner, children's menu, and a breakfast plan. You can get drinks or cappuccino at a poolside bar, where there's also live entertainment.

Services: Full concierge services, evening turndown services.

Facilities: Fully equipped kitchenettes in some rooms, large heated outdoor pool, kiddie pool, exercise room with saunas, lighted tennis courts, and free Laundromat.

4 Key Biscayne

Palms sway over busy beaches while windsurfers, jetskiers, and sailboats ply the waters just off shore. There are only a handful of hotels in Key Biscayne, though several more, including a super-luxurious Grand Bay, are planned. All are on the beach, and room rates are uniformly high. If you can afford it, Key Biscayne is a great place to stay. The island is far enough from the mainland to make it feel like a secluded tropical paradise yet close enough to Downtown to take advantage of everything Miami has to offer.

Silver Sands Oceanfront Motel. 301 Ocean Dr., Key Biscayne, FL 33149. ☎ **305/ 361-5441.** 50 mini-suites, 4 cottages. A/C TV TEL. Winter $149–$179 mini-suite, $275 cottage. Off-season $109–$129 mini-suite, $175 cottage. Weekly rates available. Additional person $30. Children under 14 stay free. AE, MC, V. Free parking.

If Key Biscayne is your destination of choice and you don't want to pay the prices of the Sonesta next door, consider this quaint one-story motel where everything is crisp and clean. The well-appointed rooms are very beachy, sporting a tropical motif and simple furnishings, including a microwave, sink, and refrigerator.

You'll sit poolside with an unpretentious set of Latin American families and Europeans who have come for long and simple vacations and get it. A pleasant staff will help with anything you may need.

Dining/Entertainment: The Sandbar Restaurant, a popular local hang-out, was destroyed during Hurricane Andrew and as of late 1996 was not fully restored.

Services: Front-desk services, baby-sitting.

Facilities: VCR and cable movie channels, Olympic-size heated pool, access to tennis courts ($10), water sports available, Laundromat.

✪ **Sonesta Beach Resort Hotel Key Biscayne.** 350 Ocean Dr., Key Biscayne, FL 33149. ☎ **305/361-2021** or 800/SONESTA. Fax 305/365-2096. 300 rms, including 15 suites. A/C MINIBAR TV TEL. Winter $195–$435 double. Off-season $145–$225 double. Year-round $500–$1,350 suite, $650–$1,300 vacation home. Special packages available. Up to two children under 12 stay free. 15% gratuity added to food and beverage. AE, DC, DISC, EURO, JCB, MC, V. Valet parking $9.25.

From the moment the tropical-print-clad valets park your car, you know you have entered a world of no worries. The Sonesta Beach is the ultimate in resort luxury. After a thorough renovation following the devastation of Hurricane Andrew, the hotel has come back better than before.

Everything is taken care of for you here. If you like sports, play tennis or golf or go jetskiing or whatever you want. Children are well cared for with supervised day and night field trips and activities. The restaurants regularly host locals, who have few dining options on "The Key." You may not want to leave the resort, but it's near many natural wonders like the Bill Baggs State Park, the area's best beaches, and sports. You're also about 15 minutes from Miami Beach and even closer to the Mainland and Coconut Grove.

Dining/Entertainment: Eight restaurants and bars, including Two Dragons restaurant featuring fine Chinese cuisine, an excellent seafood restaurant with a terrace, and several lounges and bars.

Services: Full concierge services, 24-hour room service, laundry and dry-cleaning services, newspaper delivery, nightly turndown, in-room massage, twice-daily maid service, in-house baby-sitting, secretarial services, express checkout, valet parking, complimentary transportation to and from Miami's shopping districts, free coffee in the lobby.

👪 Family-Friendly Hotels

Doral Ocean Beach Resort *(see page 56)* provides child care and a complimentary children's activity center.

Fontainebleau Hilton *(see page 57)* offers play groups and child care during holiday periods. The hotel's waterfall swimming pool is a child's dream come true.

Sonesta Beach Hotel *(see page 62)* offers a "Just Us Kids" program and a free, supervised play group for children 5 to 13. Experienced counselors lead morning field trips as well as daily beach games and evening activities.

Facilities: Fully equipped kitchenettes in the vacation homes, VCR rental available, 30-channel Spectravision, video rental available from neighboring shop, Olympic-size pool, large state-of-the-art fitness center, Jacuzzi, sauna, sundeck, nine tennis courts including three lit for night play, access to The Links championship golf course, racquetball courts, water-sports equipment rental, jogging track, bicycle rental, nature trail, game room, children's programs, elaborate business center, conference rooms, Laundromat, car-rental desk, tour desk, boutique and shopping arcade.

5 Downtown

As you would expect, most Downtown hotels cater primarily to business travelers. However, this hardly means tourists should overlook these well-located, good-quality accommodations. Miami's Downtown is small, so getting around is relatively easy. Staying here means being between the beaches and the Grove and within minutes of the Bayside Marketplace and the Port of Miami.

Although business-hotel prices are often high and less prone to seasonal markdowns, you'll get high-quality staff and service for those rates. Look for weekend discounts, when offices are closed and rooms often go empty. After dark, there's little to do outside of the hotels; the streets tend to be deserted, and crime can be a problem.

VERY EXPENSIVE

Hotel Inter-Continental Miami. 100 Chopin Plaza, Miami, FL 33131. ☎ **305/577-1000** or 800/332-4246. Fax 305/577-0384. Telex 153127. 646 rms, including 34 suites. A/C MINIBAR TV TEL. Winter $209–$289 double, $329–$450 suite. Off-season $189–$249 double, $329–$450 suite. Additional person $20 extra. Weekend and other packages available. No-smoking floors available. AE, CB, DC, MC, V. Parking $11.

The Hotel Inter-Continental Miami is an architectural masterpiece and, arguably, the financial district's swankiest hotel. Both inside and out, the hotel boasts more marble than a mausoleum. But the hard stone is often warmed by colorful, homey touches. The five-story lobby features a marble centerpiece sculpture by Henry Moore and is topped by a pleasing skylight. Plenty of plants, palm trees, and brightly colored wicker chairs also add charm and enliven the otherwise stark space. Brilliant building and bay views add luster to already posh rooms that are outfitted with every convenience known to hoteldom.

Dining/Entertainment: Three restaurants cover all price ranges and are complemented by two full-service lounges. Le Pavillon serves gourmet French, an American restaurant serves simple and elegant cuisine, plus there's Le Royal Palm Court and Le Pool Bar.

Services: Full concierge services, 24-hour room service, laundry and dry-cleaning service, newspaper delivery, nightly turndown, in-room massage available, twice-daily maid service, baby-sitting services available, express checkout, valet parking, free refreshments in the lobby.

Facilities: Fully equipped kitchenettes in some suites, VCRs, eight-channel Spectravision, Olympic-size heated outdoor pool, health spa under construction at press time, laundry room, access to nearby health club, sundeck, jogging track, bicycle-rental arrangements, nearby golf course, large business center, 15 conference rooms, Laundromat, car-rental desk, travel agency/tour desk, beauty and barber shop, gift shop and shopping arcade.

EXPENSIVE

Crowne Plaza Hotel. 1601 Biscayne Blvd., Miami, FL 33132. ☎ **305/374-0000,** 800/HOLIDAY, or 800/2-CROWN. Fax 305/374-0020. Telex 515005. 528 rms, including 57 suites. A/C MINIBAR TV TEL. Winter $165–$185 double, $650–$1,250 suite. Off-season $155–$175 double, $225–$1,250 suite. Extra person $20. Children under 12 stay free. Senior discounts and weekend and other packages available. No-smoking rooms available. AE, CB, DC, DISC, MC, V. Parking $10.

Formerly the Omni Hotel, this glass-and-chrome megastructure was recently purchased by the Crowne Plaza group. Really an upscale Holiday Inn, this full-service, contemporary hotel overlooks the beautiful Venetian Causeway and Biscayne Bay. Built in 1977 atop a large multistory shopping mall, the hotel has undergone several renovations and is still one of the luxury leaders in Miami's ever-growing hotel marketplace.

Rooms are traditionally decorated with modest but comfortable furnishings and deluxe fittings like bathroom telephones. However, the Crowne Plaza sits on top of a 150-plus shopping complex, a convenience that includes a popular multiplex cinema. Unfortunately, the area has been plagued by crime in recent years, though plans to improve the neighborhood, which include the building of a multimillion-dollar arts complex, are underway.

Dining/Entertainment: The Fish Market is an excellent, elegant place for seafood (see the review in Chapter 6). A coffee shop offers simpler meals and snacks. There are also lobby and poolside lounges.

Services: Concierge services, room service (6:30am–12:30pm), laundry and dry-cleaning services, newspaper delivery, nightly turndown upon request, in-room massage, baby-sitting upon request, express checkout, valet parking, courtesy car.

Facilities: Eight-channel Spectravision, large outdoor heated pool, small health club, access to nearby health club, sauna, sundeck, large business center, conference rooms, car-rental and tour desks.

Sheraton Brickell Point Miami. 495 Brickell Ave., Miami, FL 33131. ☎ **305/373-6000** or 800/325-3535. Fax 305/374-2279. Telex 6811701. 598 rms, including 14 suites. A/C TV TEL. Winter $129–$159 double, $305–$375 suite. Off-season $129–$159 double, $275–$375 suite. Additional person $10. Children under 18 stay free in parents' room. Senior discounts and weekend and other packages available. No-smoking rooms available. AE, CB, DC, DISC, MC, V. Parking $11.

This Downtown hotel's waterfront location is its greatest asset. Nestled between Brickell Park and Biscayne Bay, the Sheraton is set back from the main road and surrounded by a pleasant bayfront walkway.

Just as clean and reliable as other hotels in the Sheraton chain, Brickell Point has a pretty location and good water views from most of the rooms, as well as all the amenities you'd expect from a hostelry in this class. Its identical rooms are well furnished and comfortable. There isn't much to do in the area but you are within a short drive to anything Miami has to offer.

Dining/Entertainment: Ashley's serves continental and American cuisine overlooking Biscayne Bay. The Coco Loco Club serves indoor and out.

Services: Concierge services, room service (6am–2pm), laundry and dry-cleaning services, newspaper delivery, nightly turndown, in-room massage, twice-daily maid service upon request, baby-sitting, express checkout, valet parking, free refreshments in the lobby.

Facilities: Eight-channel Spectravision, large heated outdoor pool, state-of-the-art health club, access to nearby health club, sundeck, nearby golf course, game room, adequate business center, conference rooms, car-rental and tour desk, small gift shop.

MODERATE

Riande Continental Bayside. 146 Biscayne Blvd., Miami, FL 33132. ☎ **305/358-4555** or 800/RIANDE-1. Fax 305/371-5253. 250 rms. A/C MINIBAR TV TEL. Winter $105–$115 double. Off-season $85–$95 double. Children stay free. AE, DC, MC, V. Parking $7, limited to 35 spaces.

Like its sister hotel in South Beach, this Riande caters to a Latin American crowd who descend on Downtown in droves to load up on cheap electronics and clothes. The location is ideal, since it is steps away from Bayside, a multitude of great ethnic restaurants, and a Metrorail stop. The reasonable prices and helpful staff are reason enough to consider staying here if you want to be in downtown Miami.

Dining/Entertainment: International cuisine is served in the lobby restaurant with a bar.

Services: Room service (6–10am and 7–10pm), laundry and dry-cleaning services.

Facilities: Ten-channel Spectravision, access to a nearby gym, conference rooms, car-rental desk.

INEXPENSIVE

Everglades Hotel. 244 Biscayne Blvd., Miami, FL 33136. ☎ **305/379-5461** or 800/327-5700. Fax 305/577-8445. 371 rms, including 60 suites. A/C TV TEL. Year-round $80 double, $115 suite. Additional person $10. Children under 5 stay free. AE, DC, DISC, MC, V. Parking $7.

Bordering on dive quality, this hotel has been around about forever on Downtown's most active Biscayne Boulevard. And it shows: The lobby and rooms are in sore need of renovation. But the Everglades has a great location that's safe. Many traveling business types and Latin American families stay here because of its convenient location, low rates, and many services, which include a bank in the building. Also, it is one of the only Downtown properties with a pool. The hotel is near the highways and Metrorail, and there's great shopping across the street at Bayside Marketplace.

Dining/Entertainment: Coffee shop, bar.

Services: Customer-service desk and room service (7am–11pm), dry-cleaning services, twice-daily maid service, baby-sitting services arranged, secretarial services, valet parking.

Facilities: Medium rooftop swimming pool, access to nearby health club, game room, conference room, car-rental and tour desk, small sundry shop.

Miami River Inn. 118 SW South River Dr., Miami, FL 33130. ☎ **305/325-0045.** Fax 305/325-9227. A/C TV TEL. 40 rms, 38 with private bath. Winter $89–$109 double. Off-season $69–$89 double. Rates include breakfast. Additional person $15. Children under 12 stay free. No-smoking rooms available. AE, CB, DC, DISC, MC, V. Free parking.

Five buildings make up this compound of Historic Florida on the trade-laden Miami River. Some of the buildings date from as early as 1910 and have since been restored by careful and loving hands. The low year-round rates make this an attractive option for those who appreciate old things.

The rooms are nicely furnished with a mix of antiques from all eras and gentle wallpaper prints. Nice touches like a bough of flowers grace the walls. In the common area you'll find a collection of historical books about old Miami with histories of this land's former owners—Julia Tuttle, William Brickell, and Henry Flagler.

Many Downtown eateries and museums are within walking distance, but you'll want to drive or take the nearby Metrorail to stops like Bayside Marketplace. Some consider the area dicey, but actually working-class immigrants and tradespeople live in the immediate vicinity. Yet don't venture too far out of the enclave unless you want to see the ugly underside of Miami.

Services: Laundry and dry-cleaning services, some secretarial services.

Facilities: Movie channels, small outdoor pool, access to nearby YMCA, Jacuzzi, small conference facilities, Laundromat.

6 West Miami

As Miami continues to grow at its rapid pace, expansion has begun in earnest westward, where land is plentiful and much cheaper than the already developed oceanfront. With room to spare, several resorts have taken advantage of the space to build world-class tennis and golf courses that attract active visitors. You won't have a sea to swim in, but the plethora of amenities, including pools and health equipment, more than makes up for the lack of an ocean view.

VERY EXPENSIVE

Doral Golf Resort and Spa. 4400 NW 87th Ave., Miami, FL 33178. ☎ **305/592-2000,** 800/ 22-DORAL, or 800/71-DORAL. Fax 305/594-4682. 622 rms, including 45 suites and an additional 58 suites at the famous Spa. A/C MINIBAR TV TEL. Winter $175–$370 double, $315–$945 suite, $350–$1,280 Spa suite. Off-season $95–$275 double, $175–$645 suite, $275–$825 Spa suite. Several golf and spa packages available. Up to two children under 16 stay free. Additional person $35. 18% service charge added. AE, CB, DC, DISC, JCB, MC, V. Valet parking $9, self-parking free.

The Doral epitomizes the luxury resort in Florida and is one of the state's best sports resorts. While the decadent pamperings in the exclusive The Spa at Doral attract world-wide attention, the next-door golf resort hosts world-class tournaments. The season is booked well in advance by those who have been here before or have read about this resort's fantastic offerings.

The 650-acre resort is surrounded by warehouses and office buildings, just moments from the Miami airport. The spacious lobbies and dining areas shimmer with polished marble, mirrors, and gold. The rooms are also luxuriously large and decorated in tasteful sand colors; large windows overlook the tropical gardens or golf courses.

This is the home of the Blue Monster and three other killer championship courses, plus the Jim McLean Golf Learning Center. For tennis, the Arthur Ashe, Jr., Tennis Center features 15 courts and a 400-seat stadium. Doral offers great spa/golf, spa/tennis, and golf/tennis packages.

Dining/Entertainment: The Spa restaurant serves delicious low-fat cuisine, including "diet" desserts, such as reduced-calorie Key lime eclairs and chocolate mousses. Various other options include a cafe with super Italian sandwiches, salads, and pasta. The golf club sports bar has excellent club fare and grilled sandwiches.

Services: Full concierge services, 24-hour room service during winter season, laundry and dry-cleaning services, evening turndown, on-site baby-sitting, secretarial services, shuttle to the Doral Ocean Resort, valet parking.

Facilities: VCRs, eight-channel Spectravision, Olympic-size outdoor heated pool, three pools at the spa (1 indoor, 2 outdoor), state of the art full service spa, Jacuzzi, sauna, 15 tennis courts at the Arthur Ashe, Jr., Tennis Center and school, jogging track, bicycle rental, extensive golf facilities (Blue Monster Course—Top 25 in the country), game rooms, children's programs (Camp Doral) during the holidays or special functions, conference wing, car-rental and activities services, beauty salon, boutiques.

Don Shula's Hotel and Golf Club. Main Street, Miami Lakes, FL 33014. ☎ **305/821-1150** or 800/24SHULA. Fax 305/819-8298. 210 rms, including 5 suites. A/C TV TEL. Winter $209 double, $229–$259 suite. Off-season $129 double, $149–$159 suite. Additional person $10. Children stay free. Business packages available. No-smoking rooms available. AE, DC, MC, V.

Guests come for the golf. But there is more here for everyone's tastes. In addition to the plain-but-pretty rooms in the main building or surrounding the well-known golf course, the hotel offers an athletic club with cybex equipment and trainers who assist all exercisers.

Opened in 1992 to much fanfare from the sports and business community, Shula's world is an all encompassing little oasis in the middle of a highly planned residential neighborhood complete with a Main Street and nearby shopping facilities. The site is more than a 20-minute drive from anything. The award-winning steakhouse is reviewed in Chapter 6.

Dining/Entertainment: Shula's Steak House serves huge and tasty steaks as well as seafood. You may run into some big-name sports stars at the very popular Don Shula's All-Star Cafe. Another restaurant on the premises serves health food.

Services: Concierge service and room service (7am–10:30pm), laundry and dry-cleaning services, newspaper delivery, nightly turndown upon request, in-room massage, twice-daily maid service upon request, baby-sitting arrangements available, secretarial services, express checkout, valet parking, free morning coffee in the lobby.

Facilities: Kitchen facilities in some suites, VCRs upon request, 10-channel Spectravision, large outdoor swimming pool, Don Shula's state-of-the-art athletic club with aerobics, Jacuzzi, sauna, sundeck, 16 outdoor tennis courts, racquetball courts, water-sports equipment rental arrangements possible, two golf courses including one championship golf course, 22 conference and banquet rooms, car-rental and tour desks, boutique and shopping arcade.

EXPENSIVE

Miami International Airport Hotel. P.O. Box 997510. NW 20th St. and LeJeune Rd., Airport Terminal Concourse E., Miami, FL 33299-7510. ☎ **305/871-4100** or 800/327-1276. Fax 305/871-0800. 260 rms, including 7 suites. A/C TV TEL. Winter $135–$185 double, $250–$650 suite. Off-season $150–$170 double, $250–$265 suite. Additional person $10. Up to two children under 12 stay free. No-smoking rooms available. AE, CB, DC, EURO, JCB, MC, V. Parking $9.

I don't know of a nicer airport hotel and this one couldn't be more convenient—it is actually *in* the airport at Concourse E. The hotel also has every amenity of a first-class tourist destination. You'd think you'd be deaf from the roar of the planes, but all of the rooms have been sound-proofed and allow in very little noise. In addition, the hotel is extremely safe with modern security systems.

The rooms are modern and spacious with industrial-grade carpeting and non-descript furnishings, but if you need to be at the airport and want excellent services, including a top health spa, sauna, and racquetball courts, stay here. If you don't want the smell of smoke lingering in your room, request a no-smoking room.

Dining/Entertainment: Top of the Port Restaurant and lounge serves decent continental cuisine. The Poolside Snack Bar brings sandwiches and salads to the sun deck. The lobby bar provides good service and variety at a high price.

Services: Room service (7am–1pm), same-day laundry and dry-cleaning service, courtesy van in airport.

Facilities: VCR upon request, eight-channel Spectravision, large outdoor pool, rooftop health club, Jacuzzi, sauna, sundeck, racquetball courts, jogging track, small business center, conference room, Laundromat, tour desk.

7 North Dade

VERY EXPENSIVE

Turnberry Isle Resort and Club. 19999 West Country Club Dr., Aventura, FL 33180. ☎ **305/932-6200** or 800/327-7028. Fax 305/933-6550 270 rms and suites. A/C MINIBAR TV TEL. Winter $375–$405 at the resort, $295–$335 at the yacht club. Off-season $195–$245 at the resort, $150–$175 at the yacht club. AE, DC, DISC, MC, V. Valet parking $8, free self-parking.

The new Turnberry resort is one of Florida's finest, attracting a variety of domestic and international pleasure seekers. Visitors can only praise the gorgeous 300-acre compound that has every possible facility for active guests. The impeccable service from check-in to check-out brings loyal fans back for more. Unless you are into boating, the resort is the place to stay, with perfect spa facilities and the renowned Veranda restaurant.

The well-proportioned rooms are gorgeously tiled to match the Mediterranean-style architecture. The bathrooms even have a color TV mounted near each of the whirlpool bathtubs. The resort, conveniently located about halfway between Fort Lauderdale and Miami, is right in North Miami Beach, where you'll find some of Miami's best dining and excellent shopping surrounding the hotel. You'll pay a lot to stay at this luxurious destination, but it's worth it.

Dining/Entertainment: There are six restaurants, including The Veranda, which serves healthful and tropical New World cuisine in an elegant dining room. The several bars and lounges, including a popular disco, also have enough entertainment and local flavor to keep anyone busy for weeks.

Services: Concierge and (24-hour) room service, same-day laundry services, newspaper delivery, nightly turndown, valet parking, complimentary shuttle to and from Aventura Mall.

Facilities: Video rental, large swimming pool, complete state-of-the-art health spa, 24 outdoor tennis courts including 16 lit ones, two golf courses, large business center, four large meeting and conference centers, limousine and car-rental desks, helipad.

8 Coral Gables

Coconut Grove eases into Coral Gables, which extends north toward Miami International Airport. The Gables, as it's affectionately known, was one of Miami's original planned communities, and it's still one of the city's prettiest. In fact, it earned the name "The Beautiful City" because of its Spanish- and Mediterranean-style architecture, gushing fountains, and pretty plazas.

Accommodations in Coral Gables, Coconut Grove & Downtown

The Biltmore Hotel Coral Gables **10**
Crowne Plaza Hotel at Coconut Grove **13**
Doubletree Hotel at Coconut Grove **12**
Everglades Hotel **2**
Grand Bay Hotel **8**
Grove Isle Club & Resort **14**
Hotel Inter-Continental Miami **4**
Hotel Place St. Michel **7**
Hyatt Regency Coral Gables **8**
Mayfair House Hotel **11**
Miami River Inn **6**
Omni Colonnade **9**
Riande Continental Bayside **3**
Sheraton Brickell Point Miami **5**

KEY BISCAYNE
Key Colony for Guests **15**
Silver Sands Oceanfront Motel **17**
Sonesta Beach Resort Hotel **16**

2094

If you stay here, you'll experience Miami as many monied locals do. You'll be close to the shops along Miracle Mile and near some of Miami's nicest homes. Land in Coral Gables goes for top dollar, and houses in the area reflect this value. Like other wealthy communities, Coral Gables doesn't offer much in the way of inexpensive accommodations, but if you can afford it, the following hotels are great places to stay.

VERY EXPENSIVE

✪ **The Biltmore Hotel Coral Gables.** 1200 Anastasia Ave., Coral Gables, FL 33134. ☎ **305/ 445-1926** or 800/228-3000. Fax 305/442-9496. 275 rms, including 35 suites. A/C TV TEL. Winter $249 double, $349–$369 suite. Off-season $179 double, $299 suite. Additional person $20. Children under 18 stay free in parents' room. Special packages available. AE, DC, DISC, MC, V. Valet parking $9; free self-parking.

In 1996, The Biltmore celebrated its 70th birthday, making it the oldest hotel in Coral Gables and a landmark in the city. Rising above the Spanish Mediterranean–style estate is a majestic 300-foot copper-clad tower, modeled after the original Giralda bell tower in Seville. The tower is visible from throughout the city and draws thousands of luxury-seeking visitors every year.

The Biltmore has undergone many incarnations—after World War II it was used as a VA hospital—but it's now back to its original 1926 splendor. It was the site of the 1994 Summit of the Americas, and since then has attracted more foreign dignitaries than ever. They, like the presidents and gangsters of years past, appreciate the beauty of the rambling grounds and the hotel's majestic interior.

Now under the management of the Westin Hotel group, the hotel boasts large rooms decorated with tasteful period reproductions as well as all high-tech amenities. The enormous lobby with its 45-foot ceilings serves as an entry point for hundreds of weddings and business meetings each year.

Behind the hotel is an enormous 21,000-square-foot swimming pool, which holds more than 600,000 gallons of water. Arched walkways and Italian-style sculptures surround the pool. Beyond that, a romantic terrace is a popular wedding site. A rolling 18-hole golf course is as challenging as it is beautiful.

The Biltmore is just five minutes from the airport and five minutes from excellent dining and shopping selections; it's about 20 minutes from Miami Beach. This hotel is a great place to stay.

Dining/Entertainment: Il Ristorante serves French/Italian cuisine nightly and a champagne brunch on Sunday. An impressive wine cellar and cigar room make the hotel popular with local connoisseurs. The more casual Courtyard Cafeé and Poolside Grille serve three meals daily. There's also a lounge and piano bar where drinks are accompanied by live music nightly.

Services: Full concierge services, 24-hour room service, laundry and dry-cleaning services, newspaper delivery, nightly turndown upon request, baby-sitting, secretarial services, express checkout, valet parking, courtesy car to and from airport.

Facilities: VCR upon request, movie channels, 600,000-gallon swimming pool, state-of-the-art health club and full service spa, sauna, 10 lighted tennis courts, 18-hole golf course on property, children's program, elaborate business center, conference rooms, Laundromat, car-rental and tour desks, beauty salon, boutiques.

The Omni Colonnade Hotel. 180 Aragon Ave., Coral Gables, FL 33134. ☎ **305/ 441-2600** or 800/533-1337. Fax 305/445-3929. 157 rms, including 17 bi-level suites. A/C MINIBAR TV TEL. Winter $265–$305 double, $445 suite. Off-season $215–$245 double, $445 suite. Packages available. No-smoking rooms available. AE, CB, DC, DISC, MC, V. Parking $9.50.

The Colonnade occupies part of a large historic building, originally built by Coral Gables' founder George Merrick. Faithful to its original style, the hotel is a successful amalgam of new and old, with emphasis on the modern. An escalator brings guests from street level to the hotel's grand rotunda entrance. The lobby is just down the hall, but pause for a moment and admire the pink-and-black-marble floor, domed roof, and stylish column supports. This is the most eye-catching feature of the original building.

Guest rooms are outfitted with historic photographs, marble counters, gold-finished faucets, and understated furnishings worthy of the hotel's rates. Many business travelers enjoy the thoughtful extras like complimentary shoe shines and champagne upon arrival.

Dining/Entertainment: Doc Dammers Saloon is probably the best happy hour for the 30-something crowd. There is frequent live entertainment.

Services: 24-hour concierge and room services, same-day laundry and dry-cleaning service, newspaper delivery, evening turndown upon request, in-room massage, twice-daily maid service upon request, baby-sitting, express checkout, valet parking, free morning coffee and tea in the lobby.

Facilities: Eight-channel Spectravision, heated outdoor pool, small up-to-date rooftop fitness center, Jacuzzi, sundeck, large conference centers, Laundromat, car-rental and tour desks, gift shop and shopping arcade.

EXPENSIVE

Hyatt Regency Coral Gables. 50 Alhambra Plaza, Coral Gables, FL 33134. ☎ **305/ 441-1234** or 800/233-1234. Fax 305/442-0520. Telex 529706. 242 rms, including 50 suites A/C MINIBAR TV TEL. Winter $159–$280 double, $275–$1,800 suite. Off-season $129–$200 double, $275–$1,800 suite. Additional person $25. Packages and senior discounts available. No-smoking rooms available. AE, CB, DC, DISC, MC, V. Valet parking $10; self-parking $9.

High on style, comfort, and price, this Hyatt is part of Coral Gables' Alhambra, an office-hotel complex with a Mediterranean motif. The building itself is gorgeous, designed with pink stone, arched entrances, grand courtyards, and tile roofs. Inside you'll find overstuffed chairs on marble floors, surrounded by opulent antiques and chandeliers. The hotel opened in 1987, but, like many historical buildings in the neighborhood, the Alhambra attempts to mimic something much older and much farther away.

The good-size rooms are well appointed, outfitted with everything you'd expect from a top hotel—terry robes and all. Most furnishings are antique.

Dining/Entertainment: A good World Cuisine restaurant serves a varied and good menu with many local specialties. Alcazaba is a fun Latin-style dance spot (see "The Latin Scene" in Chapter 10).

Services: Full concierge services, room service (6am–midnight), same-day laundry and dry-cleaning services, newspaper delivery, nightly turndown upon request, in-room massage, baby-sitting arrangements available, secretarial services, express check-out, valet parking.

Facilities: Eight-channel Spectravision, large outdoor heated pool, health club with Nautilus equipment, Jacuzzi, two saunas, nearby golf course, basic business center, conference rooms, small gift shop.

MODERATE

✪ **Hotel Place St. Michel.** 162 Alcazar Ave., Coral Gables, FL 33134. ☎ **305/444-1666** or 800/848-HOTEL. Fax 305/529-0074. 27 rms, including 3 suites. A/C TV TEL. Winter $125 double, $165 suite. Off-season $95–$125 double, $135–$165 suite. Rates include breakfast. Children under 12 stay free in parents' room. Additional person $10. Senior discounts available. AE, CB, DC, MC, V. Parking $7.

It's always a pleasure to stay in this unusual cultured gem in the heart of Coral Gables. The accommodations and hospitality are straight out of old-world Europe, complete with dark wood-paneled walls, cozy beds, beautiful antiques, and a quiet elegance that seems startlingly out of place in hip, future-oriented Miami.

Everything here is charming, from the parquet floors to the paddle fans; one-of-a-kind furnishings make each room special. Guests are treated to fresh fruit baskets upon arrival and every imaginable service throughout their stay. Many international visitors come back over and over again to this romantic spot.

Dining/Entertainment: Restaurant St. Michel is a very romantic and elegant dining choice. A lounge and deli complete the hotel options.

Services: Front-desk services, room service (7am–10:30pm), laundry and dry-cleaning services, newspaper delivery, evening turndown, twice-daily maid service, express checkout.

Facilities: Access to nearby gym for Bally's members.

9 Coconut Grove

This intimate enclave hugs the shores of Biscayne Bay just south of U.S. 1. The Grove is a great place to stay, offering ample nightlife, excellent restaurants, and beautiful surroundings. Unfortunately, all the hotels are expensive. But, even if you don't stay here, you'll want to spend a night or two exploring the area.

VERY EXPENSIVE

✪ **Grand Bay Hotel.** 2669 S. Bayshore Dr., Coconut Grove, FL 33133. ☎ **305/858-9600** or 800/327-2788. Fax 305/858-1532. Telex 441370. 178 rms, including 47 suites. A/C MINIBAR TV TEL. Winter $255–$295 double. Off-season $205–$255 double. Year-round $350–$1,400 suite. Additional person $20. Packages available. No-smoking floors available. AE, CB, DC, MC, V. Parking $11.

When the Grand Bay opened in 1983, it immediately won praise as one of the fanciest hotels in the world. Designed by The Nichols Partnership, a local architectural firm, and outfitted with the highest-quality interiors, this stunning pyramid-shaped hotel is a masterpiece both inside and out.

The luxurious rooms feature comfortable overstuffed love seats and chairs; a large writing desk; and all the amenities you would expect in deluxe accommodations. Original art and armfuls of fresh flowers are generously displayed throughout.

There is no check-in counter; guests are escorted to a goldleaf-trimmed antique desk and encouraged to relax with a glass of champagne while they fill out the forms. The Grand Bay consistently attracts wealthy, high-profile people; it's a rendezvous spot for socialites and superstars. Guests come here to be pampered and to see and be seen.

Dining/Entertainment: The hotel's Grand Cafeé is one of Miami's top-rated restaurants. Drinks are served in the Ciga Bar and the lobby lounge, where a traditional afternoon tea is served from 3 to 6pm.

Services: 24-hour concierge and room service, same-day laundry and dry-cleaning services, newspaper delivery, evening turndown, masseuse on call, twice-daily maid service, baby-sitting, secretarial services, express checkout, valet parking, courtesy limousine service to Cocowalk, free refreshments in the lobby.

Facilities: VCRs, movie channels, video rental delivered to room ($8), heated outdoor pool, small health club, access to nearby health club, Jacuzzi, sauna, sundeck, water-sports equipment rental arrangement, bicycle rental, nearby golf course, good-sized business center, conference rooms, car-rental and activities desks, beauty salon, small gift shop.

Grove Isle Club and Resort. Four Grove Isle Drive, Coconut Grove, FL 33133. ☎ **305/ 858-8300** or 800/88-GROVE. Fax 305/854-6702. 49 rms, including 5 suites. A/C TV TEL. Winter $255–$275 double, $420–$550 suite. Off-season $220 double, $300–$400 suite. Rates include breakfast. Children under 14 stay free. Additional person $20. AE, DC, MC, V. Free valet parking.

A 1994 renovation has turned Grove Isle into one of the nicest spots to stay in Coconut Grove. Plus its location is stunning. From the lobby and many rooms, guests look out onto glimmering Biscayne Bay where sailboats drift lazily about and dolphins sometimes leap circles into the clear blue water. You'd almost think the property is on an island; actually, it is only a few minutes from Coconut Grove's business district.

Grove Isle feels like a country club, where everyone dresses in white and pastel, and if they are not on their way to a set of tennis they're not in a rush to anywhere. Rooms are nicely furnished as is the elegant but uncluttered lobby.

Dining/Entertainment: Mark of Mark's Place (see the review on page 108) oversees this relaxed menu of New World Cuisine.

Services: Concierge service, room service (6:30am–10pm), laundry and dry-cleaning services, newspaper delivery, nightly turndown, in-room massage, twice-daily maid service, baby-sitting, secretarial services, express checkout, valet parking, free coffee in the lobby.

Facilities: VCRs, movie channels, video rental delivered to room ($5), large heated outdoor pool, deluxe fitness facilities, 12 outdoor tennis courts, water-sports equipment rental available, jogging track, nature trails, conference rooms, beauty salon.

☉ Mayfair House Hotel. 3000 Florida Ave., Coconut Grove, FL 33133. ☎ **305/441-0000** or 800/433-4555. Fax 305/441-1647. 182 suites, including 6 penthouses. A/C MINIBAR TV TEL. Winter $235–$450 double, $450 penthouse. Off-season $205–$440 double, $450 penthouse. Packages available. No-smoking rooms available. AE, DC, DISC, MC, V. Valet parking $11; self-parking $6.

Situated inside Coconut Grove's posh Mayfair Shops complex, the all-suite Mayfair House is about as centrally located as you can get. Each guest room has been individually designed. All are extremely comfortable, and some suites are even opulent. Most of the more expensive accommodations include a private, outdoor, Japanese-style hot tub. Top-floor terraces offer good views, and all are hidden from the street by leaves and latticework.

The hotel contains several no-smoking suites and about 50 rooms with antique pianos. Since the lobby is in a shopping mall, recreation is confined to the roof, where a small pool, a sauna, and a snack bar are located. If you must be in the Grove, this is a good choice.

Dining/Entertainment: The Mayfair Grill serves a varied menu with particularly good steaks and seafood. There is also a rooftop snack bar for poolside snacks and a private nightclub open late.

Services: 24-hour concierge and room services, laundry and dry-cleaning services, newspaper delivery, nightly turndown, in-room massage, twice-daily maid service, baby-sitting, secretarial services, express checkout, valet parking, free coffee in the lobby.

Facilities: VCRs, 16-channel Lodgenet, video-rental delivery from neighborhood shop, individual Jacuzzis in each room, sundeck, elaborate business center, conference rooms, beauty salon.

EXPENSIVE

Doubletree Hotel at Coconut Grove. 2649 S. Bayshore Dr., Coconut Grove, FL 33133. ☎ **305/858-2500** or 800/222-8733. Fax 305/858-5776. 190 rms, including 18 suites. A/C TV TEL. Winter $139–$189 double, $209 suite. Off-season $129–$139 double, $149 suite. Additional person $10. AARP and AAA discounts as well as weekend and other packages available. No-smoking rooms available. AE, CB, DC, DISC, MC, V. Parking $9.

Doubletree hotels are known as business hotels, and this property is a good choice for working travelers. But its good location and relatively reasonable rates make it an excellent choice for vacationers as well. You'll be welcomed with hospitality uncommon in this area.

Standard rooms are not particularly fancy, but they are more than adequate. Suites are large and pretty and feature floor-to-ceiling windows. On higher floors, guests are treated to sweeping views of Biscayne Bay and Coconut Grove.

Dining/Entertainment: Café Brasserie, just off the lobby, offers a breakfast buffet and relaxed all-day dining. There are bars both inside and poolside.

Services: Full concierge services, room service (6:30am–11pm), laundry and dry-cleaning services, nightly turndown upon request, in-room massage, twice-daily maid service upon request, baby-sitting if staff available, express checkout, valet parking, complimentary van service to local shops, free morning coffee in the lobby.

Facilities: Some kitchenettes in a few rooms, On-Command video system, outdoor heated Olympic-size pool, access to nearby health club, two lighted tennis courts, bicycle rental, golf course on property, small business center, car-rental and tour desk.

10 Camping & Hostels

CAMPING

If you want to camp, try the **Larry and Penny Thompson Park,** 12451 SW 184th St., Miami, FL 33177 (☎ **305/232-1049**). This inland park encompasses more than 270 acres and includes a large freshwater lake for swimming and fishing. Laundry facilities and a convenience store are also on the premises. The tent area is huge and not separated into tiny sites. Sites cost from $14 to $20 (up to four people). The park is open year-round. From Downtown, take U.S. 1 south to SW 184th Street. Turn right and follow signs for about 4 miles. The park entrance is at 125th Avenue.

HOSTELS IN MIAMI BEACH

Clay Hotel & Youth Hostel. 438 Washington Ave., Miami Beach, FL 33139. ☎ **305/534-2988.** Fax 305/673-0346. 200 beds in singles, doubles, and multishares. $29–$35 double, $10–$14 per person in a multishare. Sheets $2 extra. Weekly rates available. JCB, MC, V.

A member of the International Youth Hostel Federation (IYHF), the Clay occupies a beautiful 1920s-style Spanish Mediterranean building at the corner of historic Española Way. Like other IYHF members, this hostel is open to all ages and is a great place to meet like-minded travelers. The usual smattering of Australians, Europeans, and other budget travelers makes this place Miami's best clearinghouse of "inside" travel information. Even if you don't stay here, you might want to check out the ride board and meet people.

Understandably, rooms here are bare-bones. Don't expect nightly turndown service or chocolates. Reservations are essential for private rooms year-round and recommended from December through April for all accommodations. Ask for a room with air conditioning in the summer months.

Miami Beach International Travellers Hostel. 236 9th St., Miami Beach, FL 33139. ☎ **305/534-0268** or 800/978-6787. Fax 305/534-5862. 28 rms, including 12 private rms and

16 hostel rms with 3 or 4 bed bunks. A/C. $36.80 for private room; $12 bed for members, $14 bed for non-members. MC, V.

This family-run addition to the hostel scene on Miami Beach couldn't be in a better spot. Only two blocks from the beach, the old building has been tidied up for the droves of young backpackers and explorers who find their way here to stay in simple rooms, some with wooden-planked bunk beds and others with plain but adequate single beds. For the price you can't beat this warm and friendly little South Beach crash pad. Plus there are private baths. And the young, helpful staff are always available to help plan trips and give tips on what's happening in town. As in other hostels, be particularly careful with your valuables.

On premises are a beer and wine bar and a small cafe. Services available include booking services for tours and car rentals. Facilities include a communal kitchen, laundry facilities, pool tables and soccer games, TV room with free nightly movies, international phone cards, and long-term storage.

11 Long-Term Stays

If you plan on visiting Miami for a month, a season, or more, think about renting a room in a long-term hotel in South Beach or a condominium apartment in Miami Beach, Surfside, Bal Harbour, or Sunny Isles. Rents can be extremely reasonable, especially during the off-season. And there's no comparison to a tourist hotel in terms of the amount of space you get for the same money. A short note to the chamber of commerce in the area in which you are looking will be answered with a list of availabilities (see "Visitor Information" in Chapter 2).

Long-term accommodations exist in every price category from budget to deluxe. Another good way to find out about seasonal opportunities is to read the *New York Times* classified section and alumni magazines from Ivy league colleges. It also pays to check with some of the inexpensive hotels listed in this chapter that often offer discounted weekly or monthly rates.

Some area real-estate agents also handle short-term rentals, including **Marco Corporate Housing,** 490 NW 165th St., Miami, FL 33169 (☎ 305/947-5668).

Listed below are two properties that offer good rates for stays longer than a week.

The Gallery. 436 Ocean Dr., Miami Beach, FL 33139. ☎ **305/532-7093** or 800/987-9867. Fax 305/532-2620. 62 studios. A/C TV TEL. Winter $41–$67 double nightly, $275–$295 weekly, $540 monthly. Off-season $35–$51 double nightly, $195–$215 weekly, $535 monthly. Additional person $6; additional bed $12. AE, MC, V. Parking $5 nightly, $20 weekly, and $40 monthly.

As if frozen in time, The Gallery still houses some families and retirees who live amidst the South Beach renaissance in happy oblivion. The rates at this somewhat rundown, under-renovated hotel reflect the condition of the building but not the area. Across the street is one of South Beach's most exclusive accommodations, La Voile Rouge, and all around the neighborhood has made the transition to fabulous. Still, the rooms are decent enough and services are plentiful. If you are on a budget, consider this rambling old apartment house as a place to call home and spend your time at the beautiful beach across the street—while it lasts.

Facilities include kitchenettes; a small gym with sauna, free weights, and aerobics; and laundry facilities. A restaurant/bar plans to serve pizzas and pasta.

Key Colony for Guests. 121 Crandon Blvd., Suite 146, Bromelia Lobby. Key Biscayne, FL 33149. ☎ **305/361-2170.** Fax 305/361-7420 or 305/361-0095. 40 two- or three-bedroom, two-bath condos. Winter $1,300–2,400 weekly, $3,800–$4,700 monthly. AE, MC, V.

There are plenty of houses to rent seasonally on Key Biscayne, but the prices are probably double what you'd pay to have a simple and elegant apartment with every imaginable convenience at your doorstep. For a week or two, this modern building is an excellent choice for the ultimate getaway. Many South Americans call Key Biscayne their winter residence and utilize the tennis, swimming, and dining facilities on site.

The Key Colony has 24-hour security service and bi-weekly maid service. Facilities include three pools, a fitness center, a beauty salon, a children's playground, jogging and walking trails, 12 tennis courts, and a Key Colony convenience center. There's also a pool bar and cafe.

Dining 6

During the last decade, Miami has developed a reputation in the culinary world rivaling, if not far surpassing, that of California in the 1970s. Along with some locals who have made it big, many classically trained northern chefs have opted to join the innovative food renaissance still blossoming in South Florida.

These chefs, like so many visitors, are attracted to this slightly slower and easier lifestyle where fresh produce grows in the backyards of some of the finest restaurants. No longer do people get their start here and hope to move on to New York or Los Angeles. Quite the contrary. There are literally hundreds of successful establishments that have opened first in the Northeast and then have opted to join the other successful outlets in sunny South Florida, bringing with them recipes and distinctive ideas about food that add even more variety to this hodgepodge of regional cuisine.

Most restaurateurs soon learn that things are different in Miami, from the pace to the clientele to the availability of goods. This is why the best learn to adapt—to include spices and recipes borrowed from the neighboring Caribbean islands and to blend tastes from the world while keeping the presentation value of a meal a priority. In the mecca for food lovers that is South Beach, models, actors, and photographers bask in the perfect glow of the sunset over the sea; it is, after all, still about appearances.

Regional cuisine in Miami is hard to define. It encompasses the varied tastes of the Caribbean, especially Cuba as well as an old–Floridian influence. The chefs who pioneered what's been dubbed "New World" cuisine have fused many influences into an ever-changing style that is limited only by the imagination of those preparing or eating the food. Chefs such as Norman Van Aken, Allen Susser, Mark Militello, and others have settled here and planted their roots deep. They have changed forever the landscape of southern Florida's food scene.

It is a blend of Caribbean and American fare accented with a dash of the old California nouvelle. In general, it works well, though at times it can be overambitious and pretentious. Think of mango-infused oils dotted on tuna tartar with jicama slaw served in a cracked coconut. Welcome to the new world.

In addition to the exciting inventions of native chefs, you can always find the exotic foods of almost every ethnicity—from Cuban to Haitian to Jamaican to Vietnamese. I've tried to present a good cross-section of these often-overlapping boundaries to make some of the city's more obscure options accessible.

To help you choose where to eat, restaurants below are divided first by neighborhood, then by price, using the following guide: **Very Expensive** (more than $40 per person), **Expensive** ($30 to $40 per person), **Moderate** ($20 to $30 per person), and **Inexpensive** ($6 to $20 per person). These categories reflect the price of an average meal, including a main course, an appetizer, coffee, and shared dessert, but do not include tax, tip, or beverages. Look for special lunch prices in the listings.

If you want to picnic on the beach or pick up some dessert, check out the gourmet food shops, greenmarkets, and bakeries listed in Chapter 9.

1 Best Bets

- **Best Spot for a Romantic Dinner:** The newly revitalized **The Forge Restaurant,** 432 Arthur Godfrey Rd. (at 41st Street), Miami Beach (☎ 305/538-8533), is where everyone's parents went in the 1950s for a really elegant meal. It is still the most romantic spot in town for black-tie service, stupendous meals, and private conversation. For a truly intimate experience, reserve a booth in "The Library," where some people have been known to pop the question.
- **Best Spot for a Celebration:** When you feel like splurging, **Dominique's,** 5225 Collins Ave., Miami Beach (☎ 305/865-0705), is the place to do it. Though the food and service is oh so French, this beautifully appointed dining room is neither stuffy nor intimidating. Feel free to sing "Happy Birthday."
- **Best View:** There are downtown skyscrapers with sweeping views of the city, but somehow the ground-level vista from the **South Pointe Seafood House,** 1 Washington Ave., on South Beach (☎ 305/673-5942), is my favorite for a breathtaking perspective on the city's active waterways. See cruise ships and tugboats wind their way through the channels as you dine on fresh seafood.
- **Best Wine List:** Without question, **The Forge Restaurant,** 432 Arthur Godfrey Rd. (at 41st Street), Miami Beach (☎ 305/538-8533), beats other Miami restaurants hands-down. Their wine list, a tome really, encompasses more than 3,000 vintages and 250,000 bottles from all over the world. If you are interested you can choose one of the only known bottles of 1822 Chateau Laffite Rothschild. It's priced at $100,000.
- **Best Value for Kids:** It's not a theme restaurant and there aren't any fun video games in the entryway, but **The Beverly Hills Cafe,** 17850 West Dixie Hwy, North Miami Beach (☎ 305/935-3660) offers simple and delicious kids meals for less than you'd pay at McDonald's. You can't complain about fresh pasta Marinara, turkey or chicken sandwiches, grilled cheese, or burgers all served with fries and a choice of beverages for less than $4.
- **Best Chinese Cuisine:** If fortune is with you, you will go to **The Red Lantern,** 3176 Commodore Plaza (at Grand Avenue), Coconut Grove (☎ 305/529-9998), where you will encounter superior Cantonese cooking.
- **Best Continental Cuisine:** The **Crystal Café,** 726 41st St., Miami Beach (☎ 305/673-8266), has been dubbed "New Continental" by local food reviewers who rightfully consider it a shame to waste the pedestrian-sounding title of plain old "continental" on this fantastic little spot.
- **Best Cuban Cuisine:** From diners, cafeterias, take-out windows, and elegant Cuban restaurants, there are so many different styles of Cuban food, it is hard to choose a "best." So if you're looking for a classic and filling Cuban meal, **Versailles,** 3555 SW 8th St., in Little Havana (☎ 305/444-0240), is it. If you want a lighter,

more expensive, nouvelle experience, **Yuca** is *el más sabroso*, the most delicious. You can find it in South Beach at 501 Lincoln Rd. (☎ 305/532-9822).

- **Best French Cuisine:** There are plenty of places to enjoy French fare in Miami, but the best is **The Bistro,** 2611 Ponce de Leon Blvd., Coral Gables (☎ 305/ 754-1707), where typical fare is livened up with uncommon spices and a ccoutrements.
- **Best Italian Cuisine:** With so many good pasta places, it's great to know Miami also knows how to enjoy elegant Italian like they have at **Osteria del Teatro,** 1443 Washington Ave., South Beach (☎ 305/538-7850).
- **Best Seafood:** For all around good seafood, including tasty stews, ceviches, and shellfish, the **Fishbone Grille,** 650 S. Miami Ave., Downtown (☎ 305/ 530-1915), is the place to go. The bonus is the price is down-right cheap.
- **Best Steakhouse: Shula's,** 7601 NW 154th St., Miami Lakes (☎ 305/820-8102), is a steak-lovers heaven. Other steakhouses offer big portions. Shula's are bigger.
- **Best Late-Night Dining:** You'll find dozens of good 24-hour spots especially on South Beach, but I say, go to Little Havana where **Casa Juancho,** 2436 SW 8th St. (☎ 305/642-2452), serves hearty good meals 'til all hours.
- **Best People-Watching:** The food looks good, but the people look better at **Bicé** (pronounced Bee-che), 455 Ocean Dr., South Beach (☎ 305/535-0099), where long-legged Europeans and pastel-suited gents vie for the attention of even better-looking waiters.
- **Best Afternoon Tea:** Somehow the formality of tea and the ease of Miami seem anachronistic. Yet, **The Tea Room,** 12310 SW 224th St., at Cauley Square (☎ 305/446-9976), manages to do afternoon finger sandwiches quite nicely, thank you. Another choice is on South Beach where **Les Deux Fontaines,** 1230-1238 Ocean Dr., in the Ocean Front Hotel (☎ 305/672-7878), serves lovely pastries, scones, and smoked salmon snacks in their chintz and lace tea room.
- **Best Brunch: Fresco Mediterranean Café,** at the Eden Roc hotel (☎ 305/ 674-5570), serves an excellent all-you-can-eat brunch for about $18. Carving tables, homemade pastas, eggs, and breads are too much at the newly remodeled and elegant cafe with comfortable sofa seating.
- **Best Pre-Theater Dinner: Kaleidoscope's** menu is so reasonable all the time that they need no special fixed-price pre-theater meal. It's a popular spot for those on their way to the Coconut Grove theater; it's located at 3112 Commodore Plaza (☎ 305/446-5010). For an even more elegant experience, try the $28-special at **Norman's,** 21 Almera Ave., in the Gables (☎ 305/446-6767), between 5pm and 7pm. Even if you don't have tickets to a show, it's a great way to eat cheap at this otherwise exorbitantly priced hotspot.
- **Best Fast Food: Mrs. Mendoza's,** 1040 Alton Rd., South Beach (☎ 305/ 535-0808), is the best fast food and the best Mexican in Miami. Time after time, they turn out the tastiest burritos, tacos, and enchiladas with a super-zingy salsa for the brave. They are also located at Doral Plaza, 9739 NW 41 St. **Pollo Tropical** ranks a close second with its superior rice and beans and roast chicken. Plus, they've got drive-thru windows at most locations for unbeatable speed and convenience. Locations include: 1454 Alton Rd., Miami Beach (☎ 305/ 672-8888); 11806 Biscayne Blvd. North Miami (☎ 305/895-0274); 18710 S. Dixie Hwy. (at 186th Street), South Miami. Check the phone book for others.
- **Best Brunch:** Michael Schwartz goes all out on Sundays with an endless brunch buffet at his terminally hip restaurant on South Beach, **Nemo's** (☎ 305/ 532-4550). For $19, the fare includes fresh juices, heaps of homemade salads and smoked fishes, and pancakes, eggs, and pastries. Also, **Dominique's** in the

Alexander Hotel (☎ 305/861-5252), serves a renowned feast of pastas, meats, salads, eggs, and hot entrees. All you can eat costs about $27. It's worth it.

- **Best Picnic Fare:** Stop by **Lyon Freres,** 600 Lincoln Rd., South Beach (☎ 305/534-0600), for a gourmet picnic that's as good as your best indoor meal. Eat your sandwiches and salads under a palm tree to make them taste even better.
- **Best Happy Hour:** The food at **John Martin's,** 253 Miracle Mile, in Coral Gables (☎ 305/445-3777), tastes even better when you've had one of their single-malt scotches or a pint of ale. Professionals and Irish nationals complete the scene at this week-day gala with trays of hot pizza, chicken wings, cheeses, and fruits.
- **Best Ice Cream:** Nothing's better than a cool cone in the middle of a hot day at the beach. Surprisingly, there aren't a lot of places making fresh ice cream worth getting excited about. One notable exception is the **Freize** with two locations at 1626 Michigan Ave., South Beach (☎ 305/538-0207); and 231 NE 2nd Ave., Downtown. (☎ 305/358-9106). They do mango, banana, guanabana, mamey, coconut, and anything else in season, plus all the usual chocolatey specialties.

2 Restaurants by Cuisine

AMERICAN
Beverly Hills Cafe (North Dade, *I*)
Biscayne Miracle Mile Cafeteria (Coral Gables, *I*)
Blue Door (South Beach, *VE*)
Christy's (Coral Gables, *VE*)
Curry's (Miami Beach, *I*)
The Forge Restaurant (Miami Beach, *E*)
Here Comes the Sun (North Dade, *I*)
Kaleidoscope (Coconut Grove, *E*)
Mercury (South Beach, *M*)
News Café (South Beach, *I*)
Sergio's (Coral Gables, *I*)
Sheldon's Drugs (Miami Beach, *I*)
The Strand (South Beach, *M*)
Sundays on the Bay (Key Biscayne, *E*)
Van Dyke Cafe (South Beach, *I*)

ASIAN
Pacific Time (South Beach, *E*)

BARBECUE
Shorty's (South Miami, *I*)
Tony Roma's (West Dade, *I*)

BISTRO
Jeffrey's (South Beach, *M*)

CANTONESE
The Red Lantern (Coconut Grove, *M*)

CONTINENTAL
Cafe Hammock (South Miami, *M*)
Crystal Cafe (Miami Beach, *M*)
Dominique's (Miami Beach, *VE*)
Green Street Cafe (Coconut Grove, *M*)
Jeffrey's (South Beach, *M*)
The Lagoon (North Dade, *M*)
The Palm (Miami Beach, *E*)
Rusty Pelican (Key Biscayne, *E*)

CREPES
The Crepe Maker (Downtown, *I*)

CUBAN
La Carreta (Little Havana, *I*)
Casa Juancho (Little Havana, *M*)
Centro Vasco (Little Havana, *M*)
Larios on the Beach (South Beach, *M*)
The Oasis (Key Biscayne, *I*)
Pollo Tropical (South Miami, *I*)
Puerto Sagua (South Beach, *I*)
Sergio's (Coral Gables, *I*)
Uva Wine Bar & Eatery (Coral Gables, *M*)
Versailles (Little Havana, *I*)

Key to Abbreviations: *E*= Expensive; *I*= Inexpensive; *M*= Moderate; *VE*= Very Expensive

Victor's Cafe (Little Havana, *E*)
Yuca (South Beach, *E*)

DELI

Bagel Factory (South Beach, *I*)
Lyon Freres (South Beach, *I*)
Stephan's Gourmet Market & Cafe
(South Beach, *I*)
Wolfie Cohen's Rascal House
(Miami Beach, *I*)

DINER FARE

S & S Restaurant (Downtown, *I*)

ENGLISH TEA

The Tea Room (South Miami, *I*)

EUROPEAN/AMERICAN

The Estate Wines & Gourmet Foods
(Coral Gables, *I*)

FAST FOOD

Irie Isle (North Dade, *I*)
Mrs. Mendoza's Tacos al Carbon
(South Beach, *I*)
Pollo Tropical (South Miami, *I*)
Raja's (Downtown, *I*)

FONDUE

The Melting Pot (North
Dade, *M*)

FRENCH

The Bistro (Coral Gables, *E*)
La Boulangerie (Key Biscayne, *I*)
Les Deux Fontaines (South
Beach, *M*)
Dominique's (Miami Beach, *VE*)
L'Entrecote de Paris (South
Beach, *M*)
Le Festival (Coral Gables, *E*)
The Gourmet Diner (North
Dade, *M*)
Norma's (South Beach, *E*)
La Sandwicherie (South Beach, *I*)

HAITIAN

Tap Tap (South Beach, *M*)

HEALTH FOOD

Here Comes the Sun (North
Dade, *I*)
The Juice Bar (North Dade, *I*)

INDIAN

House of India (Coral Gables, *I*)
New Delhi Restaurant
(North Dade, *M*)
Raja's (Downtown, *I*)

INTERNATIONAL

Cafe Tu Tu Tango (Coconut
Grove, *I*)

IRISH PUB

John Martin's (Coral Gables, *M*)

ITALIAN

Anacapri (South Miami, *M*)
Bicé Ristorante (South Beach, *E*)
Cafe Prima Pasta (Miami Beach, *M*)
Cafe Ragazzi (Miami Beach, *M*)
Cafe Sci Sci (Coconut Grove, *E*)
Caffe Abracci (Coral Gables, *E*)
Greenwich Village (Downtown, *M*)
Laurenzo's Cafe (North Dade, *I*)
Miami Beach Place (Miami Beach, *I*)
Oggi Caffe (Miami Beach, *M*)
Osteria del Teatro (South Beach, *E*)
Sport Cafe (South Beach, *I*)
Stefano's (Key Biscayne, *E*)
Stephan's Gourmet Market & Cafe
(South Beach, *I*)
Tula (Coconut Grove, *M*)
Uva Wine Bar & Eatery
(Coral Gables, *M*)

JAMAICAN

Caribbean Delite (Downtown, *I*)
Irie Isle (North Dade, *I*)
Norma's (South Beach, *E*)

JAPANESE

Toni's (South Beach, *M*)

MEXICAN

Mrs. Mendoza's Tacos al Carbon
(South Beach, *I*)
Señor Frogs (Coconut Grove, *M*)

NEW WORLD CUISINE

Aragon Café (Coral Gables, *E*)
Chef Allen's (North Dade, *VE*)
China Grill (South Beach, *VE*)
Mark's Place (North Dade, *E*)

The Nemo Restaurant
(South Beach, *E*)
Norman's (Coral Gables, *VE*)
Le Pavillon (Downtown, *VE*)

NOUVELLE

Blue Door (South Beach, *VE*)
Crystal Cafe (Miami Beach, *M*)
Mercury (South Beach, *M*)
Pacific Time (South Beach, *E*)

PIZZA

Miami Beach Place (Miami Beach, *I*)

SEAFOOD

Bayside Seafood Restaurant and
Hidden Cove Bar (Key
Biscayne, *I*)
East Coast Fisheries (Downtown, *M*)
Fishbone Grille (Downtown, *M*)
The Fish Market (Downtown, *E*)
Grillfish (South Beach, *M*)
Joe's Stone Crab Restaurant (South
Beach, *E*)
The Lagoon (North Dade, *M*)
Monty's Bayshore Restaurant
(Coconut Grove, *M*)
Monty's Stone Crab/Seafood House
(South Beach, *E*)

South Pointe Seafood House (South
Beach, *E*)

SPANISH

Cafe Tu Tu Tango (Coconut
Grove, *I*)
Casa Juancho (Little Havana, *M*)
Centro Vasco (Little Havana, *M*)
Las Tapas (Downtown, *M*)
Puerto Sagua (South Beach, *I*)

STEAKHOUSE

Shula's Steak House (West Dade, *E*)

SUSHI

Toni's (South Beach, *M*)
World Resources (South Beach, *I*)

SZECHUAN/PEKINESE

Chrysanthemum (South Beach, *M*)

THAI

Thai House South Beach (South
Beach, *M*)
World Resources (South Beach, *I*)

VIETNAMESE

Hy-Vong (Little Havana, *I*)

3 South Beach

The renaissance of South Beach has spawned dozens of first-rate restaurants. In fact, long-established eateries based elsewhere in the city have decided to capitalize on the location's international appeal and have begun to open branches in South Beach with great success. A few old standbys remain from the Miami Vice days, but a flock of newcomers dominate the scene, with places going in and out of style as quickly as the tides. The listings below represent the restaurants that have quickly gained national attention or should.

In addition, you'll find many places with good food and great atmosphere in the Lincoln Road area. Since it is impossible to list all of them, I recommend you go and browse. Most restaurants post a copy of their menu and staff are happy to chat with curious passersby.

With very few exceptions, the eateries on Ocean Drive are crowded with tourists and priced accordingly. Venture a little further into the pedestrian-friendly streets just west of Ocean Drive and enjoy.

VERY EXPENSIVE

Blue Door. 1685 Collins Ave. (at the Delano hotel), South Beach. ☎ **305/674-6400.** Reservations recommended for dinner. Main courses $19–$34; soups and salads $6–$12; lunch entrees $10–$16. AE, DC, MC, V. Daily 7am–11:30pm. AMERICAN NOUVELLE.

South Beach Dining

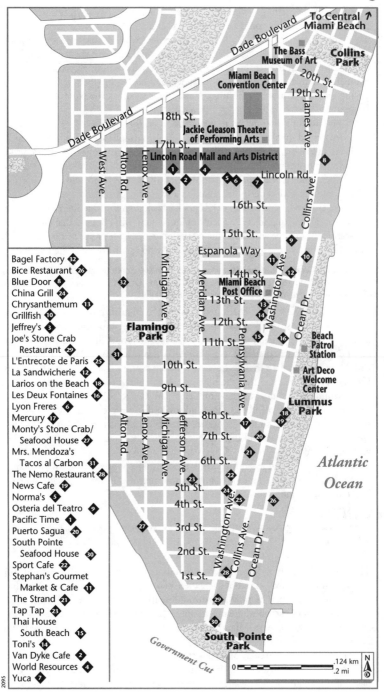

To Central Miami Beach

Dade Boulevard

The Bass Museum of Art

Collins Park

Miami Beach Convention Center

20th St.
19th St.

18th St.

Jackie Gleason Theater of Performing Arts

17th St.

Lincoln Road Mall and Arts District

Lincoln Rd.

West Ave.
Alton Rd.
Lenox Ave.

16th St.

15th St.

Espanola Way

14th St.
Miami Beach Post Office
13th St.

12th St.

Michigan Ave.
Meridian Ave.

Flamingo Park

11th St.

Washington Ave.
Ocean Dr.
Collins Ave.

Beach Patrol Station

Art Deco Welcome Center

10th St.

9th St.

Lummus Park

8th St.

Alton Rd.
Lenox Ave.
Michigan Ave.
Jefferson Ave.

7th St.

6th St.

Pennsylvania Ave.

Atlantic Ocean

5th St.
4th St.
3rd St.
2nd St.
1st St.

Washington Ave.
Collins Ave.
Ocean Dr.

Government Cut

South Pointe Park

0   .124 km
0   .2 mi

N

Bagel Factory **32**
Bice Restaurant **26**
Blue Door **8**
China Grill **24**
Chrysanthemum **13**
Grillfish **10**
Jeffrey's **3**
Joe's Stone Crab Restaurant **29**
L'Entrecote de Paris **25**
La Sandwicherie **12**
Larios on the Beach **18**
Les Deux Fontaines **16**
Lyon Freres **6**
Mercury **17**
Monty's Stone Crab/ Seafood House **27**
Mrs. Mendoza's Tacos al Carbon **31**
The Nemo Restaurant **28**
News Cafe **19**
Norma's **5**
Osteria del Teatro **9**
Pacific Time **1**
Puerto Sagua **20**
South Pointe Seafood House **30**
Sport Cafe **22**
Stephan's Gourmet Market & Cafe **11**
The Strand **21**
Tap Tap **23**
Thai House South Beach **15**
Toni's **14**
Van Dyke Cafe **2**
World Resources **4**
Yuca **7**

2095

83

The Blue Door's setting—with plump circular booths, billowy white curtains, and polished oak accents—could be a backdrop for a 1930s movie. Celebrity sightings are almost guaranteed; with Madonna as a part owner, you would expect no less. The problem is that everyone, including your waiter, thinks he is the next big star. In the dining room, a steady stream of beautiful people parade through a center corridor on their way to the Alice-in-Wonderlandesque pool deck, where more people are posing on the luxurious furnishings. You'll want to sit on the patio if the weather is nice.

Finally, if your waiter deigns to take your order, try the delicate crabcakes, two to an order, served on a peppery fennel and tomato salad. On a recent visit the stone crab claws were badly cracked, making the experience frustrating. The fish options, on the other hand, were fresh and prepared in a simple but elegant style. The choices include sea bass with a mashed combination of acorn squash and fennel, grilled lobster, salmon, and sautéed mahi mahi in a sweet vinegar sauce.

The chef, George Fistrovich, combines his background in Mediterranean, Asian, and European cooking to create a truly unique menu with offerings that change with the seasons. Sometimes he misses the mark, but generally seems to put out some fine dishes. The prices are as high as the noses. But who cares? You're at the Delano.

China Grill. 404 Washington Ave. (at the corner of Fifth St.), South Beach. ☎ **305/534-2211.** Reservations recommended. Main courses $19–$30. AE, DC, MC, V. Daily noon–midnight, Fri–Sat noon–1am. NEW WORLD CUISINE/MULTICULTURAL.

Imported from New York, like so many other Miami institutions, China Grill took Miami Beach by storm when it opened in late 1995. Unfortunately, the attitude and prices are so up there that it has only managed to attract the country-club crowd.

The menu and management explain that the prices are so high because the dishes are meant to be shared; however, when we tried that we were left hungry. Others have complained that the service is slow and the food inconsistent. I know that I could get addicted to the Confucius Chicken Salad, which has crispy fried noodles and a perfect blend of sesame and soy in the vinaigrette. Still, the duck salad was greasy and had a sour, dusty taste. The crispy spinach was surprisingly sweet and alluring, but the wasabi mashed potatoes, which sounded intriguing, were dry and uninspired.

It is worth going to the bar for a drink to soak up some atmosphere and to people-watch. But be warned, the food sounds better than it is in this nightclub pretending to be a restaurant.

EXPENSIVE

Bicé Ristorante. 455 Ocean Dr., South Beach. ☎ **305/673-1886.** Reservations recommended. Main courses $15–$22; pastas $10–$15.50. AE, DC, MC, V. Daily noon–midnight. NORTHERN ITALIAN.

The newest of nearly a dozen Bices (pronounced Bee-che) around the world, this elegant trattoria is straight out of a Milanese piazza, which is where the original Bice first opened in 1926. The rapidly growing sensation has branches in Beverly Hills, Palm Beach, and Chicago where it is a popular lunch spot for business executives and fashion industry–types. In Miami Beach, of course, the setting is oceanside in the newly hip area below 5th Street.

The menu changes weekly and consists of nearly a hundred traditional northern Italian dishes. Usually offered is a crude cut carpaccio of tuna, served over a pleasant mix of greens. The waiter will drizzle some virgin olive oil over the mound; don't be afraid to let him pour. Another good start is the crab cakes served with an arrabiata-style tomato sauce. More than a dozen fresh pastas include a rich, slightly orange bolognese, served over wide gently curled noodles. You'll finish the plate.

The crowd is pure Euro. You'll be surrounded by well-tanned, Versace-wearing smokers. The place is a little loud late nights on Thursdays when the adjacent disco and cozy bar are the in place to be.

Joe's Stone Crab Restaurant. 227 Biscayne St. (at the corner of Washington Ave.), South Beach. ☎ **305/673-0365.** Reservations not accepted. No shorts allowed. Market price varies but average $36.95 for jumbo crab claws; $26.95 for large claws. AE, CB, DC, MC, V. Tues–Sat 11:30am–2pm; Sun–Thurs 5–10pm, Fri–Sat 5–11pm (always until 11pm on Miami Heat home-game nights). Open year-round. SEAFOOD.

Open since 1913 and steeped in tradition, this restaurant is famous in Florida and beyond, as evidenced by the ubiquitous long lines waiting to get in. A full menu is available, but to order anything but stone crabs is unthinkable, and the snobby waiters will let you know it. Service is brusque and pushy.

Even after a $5-million renovation, which more than doubled the size of the place, the lines are still ridiculously long. Too many locals claim they "know someone" at the door, which usually means they were introduced through their mutual friend, Ben Franklin. Even after heavy tipping, the wait can exceed three hours. If you have to say you were there, brave it and enjoy drinks in the newly renovated oak bar. Otherwise, try the take-out bar next door for the same price and less hassle. The claws here are pricier than at other local restaurants, but you are paying for history. Stone crabs are not on the menu from May to October.

Monty's Stone Crab/Seafood House. 300 Alton Rd., South Beach. ☎ **305/673-3444.** Reservations recommended. Main courses $20–$37. AE, DC, MC, V. Sun–Thurs 5–11pm; Fri–Sat 5pm–midnight. SEAFOOD.

Many seafood fans have long been enamored of Monty's various menus in the Grove and in Boca. Finally they have opened a branch on the southern tip of South Beach, in what was a failed nightclub and restaurant. Fortunately, the former owners spent millions of dollars renovating the rambling bayfront Mediterranean-style restaurant.

Now, Monty's has moved in, burnished the rustic oak floor, set up a raw bar outside around a large swimming pool, and opened the doors for business. The best deal in town is still the all-you-can-eat stone crabs—$36.95 for jumbos—about the same price that Joe's, located two blocks away, charges for four claws. (But don't order stone crabs in summer.) Enjoy the incredible views and off-season fish specialties, including the Maryland she-crab soup that is rich and creamy without too much thickener in evidence. Year-round, you can enjoy the saffron and tomato-base bouillabaisse; it's always worth a trip. The Key lime pie is authentic—which means it's made with real yellow key limes, graham cracker crust, and topped with real whipped cream. If you are feeling really decadent, the cappuccino flan or Monty's Mortal Sin are both sinful.

The Nemo Restaurant. 100 Collins Ave., South Beach. ☎ **305/532-4550.** Reservations recommended. Main courses $17–$20; lunch $8–$12; sandwiches and platters $4–$12; Sun brunch $19. AE, MC, V. Mon–Fri noon–3pm and 7pm–midnight; Sat 6pm–midnight; Sun noon–3pm and 6–11pm. NEW WORLD CUISINE/MULTICULTURAL.

This super-stylish and dark hotspot is an oasis in a newly hip area of South Beach below 5th Street. Here models and celebrities rub elbows, literally, since the tables are so close together, brightened by only a pinpoint of light that dangles over each terra-cotta table top. Ask to be seated in the back room, which for some reason is considered less desirable, but I think it's the only place you'll hear your dining companions or your waiter. In the main dining room, the din is unbearable. In the back, you look out onto a pleasant garden and, with only six tables, feel as if you have a private dining room.

Somehow, Nemo has managed to find the only really professional and flawless serving staff on the beach. Here, the wait staff is personable, intelligent, and efficient. Amazing! They are full of helpful suggestions regarding the daily specials or the regular menu.

The menu tends to offer many fish dishes. One of the most popular is the charred salmon with a crisp sprout salad, toasted pumpkin seeds, and a soy vinaigrette. The flash cooking in a wok renders a unique flavor with a slightly blackened taste outside and a tender sweet flavor inside. If you are in the mood for something light, try the grilled portobello mushroom appetizer, served with creamy garlic polenta. This is a good old-fashioned comfort dish—the mushroom is as hearty as a sirloin and the polenta is warm and rich. The spicy Vietnamese Beef Salad is indeed very spicy. It's served with a crisp assortment of vegetables including red onions, but it's too small a portion. Daily specials are always superb. Try the pork loin if they've got it, and the side dish of roasted beets with a super-chunky Maytag blue dressing. The dessert choices are pretty standard, though well executed. A more exotic and delicious choice is the California figs soaked in port syrup and surrounded with balls of tamarind (said to be an aphrodisiac) ice cream.

Norma's. 646 Lincoln Rd., South Beach. ☎ **305/532-2809.** Reservations recommended. Main courses $12–$24; lunch $7–$15. AE, DC, MC, V. Tues–Thurs noon–11pm; Fri–Sat noon–midnight; Sun noon–10:30pm. FRENCH/JAMAICAN.

This tiny jewel on Lincoln Road sparkles with its eclectic mix of classical and Caribbean cooking. The multilingual staff is polite if sometimes slightly flustered. An extensive list of daily specials are always good, but you may want to call in advance to reserve whatever sounds best, because these dishes do sell out quickly.

For starters, if you want to have smoked fish that tastes like no other you've had, try the smoked marlin platter with cucumbers, capers, and onion, plus a spicy pepper salsa and a creamy dipping sauce. Cindy, the cook, has the tender fillets flown in weekly from Montego Bay, where the original Norma enjoys the reputation of Julia Child of the Caribbean. At lunch, a surprisingly tasty jerk tofu salad is served on callaloo (a slightly sweeter version of spinach) with tomatoes and onions. The seared jerk tuna has got a kick (like all the jerk-seasoned dishes) and is one of the Beach's best. If you prefer something milder, the rasta chicken is a casserole of chicken breast, roasted red and yellow peppers, cream cheese, and callaloo, layered to evoke the rastafarian red, green, and gold flag. A delicate white wine sauce melds the distinct flavors into a rich and satisfying main course. A different homemade soup is offered daily; carrot is one of the best. If you like it hot, ask for a splash of pepper sherry. To cool off, try the refreshing mango or guava mousse served with fresh tropical berries, melons, or tropical fruits. And don't drive after you've had the Appleton Rum cake and rum whipped cream. Share a piece and then wander along the road to reflect on this most exciting restaurant.

✪ **Osteria del Teatro.** 1443 Washington Ave. (at Española Way), South Beach. ☎ **305/538-7850.** Reservations recommended. Main courses $21–$25. AE, CB, DC, MC, V. Wed–Mon 6pm–midnight; Fri–Sat 6pm–1am. NORTHERN ITALIAN.

On the corner of Española Way, the curved entryway of this well-established enclave of reliable, if slightly overpriced, Italian is abuzz nightly. Reams of locals and tourists wait for a seat at one of the small tables. Move the fresh orchid aside to make room for a big basket of lightly toasted chunks of real Italian bread and then wait for your very knowledgeable waiter to recommend a daily special.

A good start is any of the grilled vegetables, particularly the portobello mushrooms with fontina or the garlic-infused peppers. All the pastas are handmade and are done to perfection. The risotto al'aragosta is a creamy rice dish with a decadent lobster and shrimp sauce full of tasty morsels of seafood. Of the five or so entrees offered nightly, usually at least three are seafood. The tuna loin is served with a rich mushroom sauce with just a hint of rosemary. The duck breast, doused in a sweet balsamic honey sauce and fanned over a bed of wilted radicchio leaves, is rightfully a very popular dish. Each slice of duck is perfectly seared on the outside and tender throughout without a hint of gamey flavor.

Pacific Time. 915 Lincoln Rd. (between Jefferson and Michigan avenues), South Beach. ☎ **305/534-5979.** Reservations recommended. Main courses $19.50–$32. AE, DC, MC, V. Sun–Thurs 6–11pm; Fri–Sat 6pm–midnight. ASIAN/NOUVELLE.

This exciting Lincoln Road eatery has received accolades from *The Miami Herald*, *Esquire* magazine, and *Bon Appetit.* Chef and co-owner Jonathon Eismann puts out some of the funkiest dishes ever spotted this side of the equator. One of the best for meat-eaters is the Mongolian lamb salad, which has a lightly sweet, earthy taste with a crunchy kick of onion. For a main course, the ever-changing menu offers many locally caught fish specialties, including grouper served on a bed of shredded shallots and ginger with a sweet sake-infused sauce and tempura-dunked sweet potato slivers on the side. Under the midnight-blue sky ceiling and against the pale yellow distressed walls, you'll probably see stars. I'm told Arnold Schwarzenegger recently ordered the famous chocolate bomb for his wife. It is every bit as decadent as they've said, with hot bittersweet chocolate bursting from the cupcake-like center. Some are put off by the exotic dishes, but more adventurous eaters return over and over again to wait in line at this stunning Pacific-inspired meteor.

✪ **South Pointe Seafood House.** 1 Washington Ave., South Beach. ☎ **305/673-1708.** Reservations recommended. Main courses $18–$34; lunch $9–$19. AE, DC, MC, V. Mon–Sat 11:30am–3pm; Mon–Thurs 5–11pm, Fri–Sat 5pm–midnight, Sun 5–10:30pm; Sun brunch 11am–3pm. SEAFOOD.

Seafood houses in South Florida abound. Good ones, however, are hard to come by. Many are priced out of bounds, some rely on questionably fresh seafood, others insist on battering and frying everything in sight. A notable exception on South Beach is the difficult-to-get-to but especially popular South Pointe Seafood House. Besides its spectacular view, casual atmosphere, and selection of home-brewed beers, South Pointe Seafood House has some of the most exquisitely prepared seafood on the beach. It's located in South Pointe Park, at the southernmost tip of South Beach; while you dine, you can watch the cruise and cargo ships slowly ease their way in and out of the Port of Miami.

I like the special Bahamian seafood chowder, a tomato-base soup chock-full of more fish than shellfish. Don't miss one of Miami's best crab cakes, a rich mixture of local stone crab and Canadian Snow crab meat delicately sautéed to a golden brown and artfully displayed on top of a bed of cole slaw and tomato aioli. At the crowded bar, you can order some eye-opening experiments in home brews, like a raspberry draft with a sparkly taste that even confirmed non-beer drinkers can't help but like.

✪ **Yuca.** 501 Lincoln Rd. (corner of Drexel), South Beach. ☎ **305/532-9822.** Reservations required. Main courses $18–$29. AE, CB, DC, MC, V. Daily 11:30am–5pm and 6pm–midnight. NOUVELLE CUBAN.

In 1996, its first year, the waitstaff was as green as the plantains the chef so expertly stuffs.

Yet as bad as the service was, the food was extraordinary. Each dish was packed with so many exciting flavors and so much substance, you could hardly hope to finish a whole meal. To enjoy your meal, however, you'll have to demand to be seated in the front of the restaurant, facing Lincoln Road; otherwise you'll be in the hectic path of the kitchen and too close to the very talented but loud salsa band that plays on weekends. The menu is badly translated, so don't be shy about asking for a waiter who is proficient in English if you don't *habla español*.

To start, we tried the lobster medallions with sautéed spinach and a portobello mushroom stuffed with vegetarian paella. The pieces of lobster tail were expertly grilled with a touch of oil over just-wilted greens. The mushroom was tasty, but the paella was a bit pasty. For a main course, the pork tenderloin stole the show. It must have marinated for days because it could be cut with a butter knife. The addition of a hearty *congri*, a mash of red beans and rice, and a green apple and mango salsa was a perfect balance. The veal loin, the menu's most expensive entree, had a rich meaty flavor but was a bit dry. The side dish of succulent lobster and purple potatoes made up for the disappointing veal. A full selection of traditional and exotic dessert choices are available as well as some of the best coffee in town.

MODERATE

Chrysanthemum. 1248 Washington Ave., South Beach. ☎ **305/531-5656.** Main courses $10–$15. AE, CB, DC, MC, V. Tues–Thurs and Sun 6–11pm, Fri–Sat 6pm–midnight. SZECHUAN/PEKINESE.

At first, the unpretentious atmosphere may be a surprise in glitzy South Beach, but once you have tried the simple and tasty dishes in what many consider to be the best Chinese restaurant in Miami, you'll want to come back. You can count on the service to be prompt but not solicitous.

Many vegetarian specialties include spicy eggplant strips in a rich balsamic vinegar sauce, and black mushrooms sautéed with tiny Shangai lettuce hearts. Start with the Chinese salad, which comes heaped with a fresh mix of greens, vermicelli, bean sprouts, and coriander. The steamed whole fish is best with the ginger and scallions. It comes with bones, but ask the waiter to remove them; he will gladly and expertly oblige. The duck in peppercorn sauce is a succulent and spicy dish that may take the place of crispy duck in my book.

Grillfish. 1444 Collins Ave. (corner of Española Way), South Beach. ☎ **305/538-9908.** Reservations recommended on weekends. Main courses $8–$13. AE, DC, MC, V. In season daily 6pm–midnight; off-season daily 6–11pm. SEAFOOD.

From the beautiful Byzantine-style mural and the gleaming oak bar that runs the length of the corner storefront of stylish Española Way, you'd think you were eating in a much more expensive restaurant. No doubt Grillfish manages to pay the exorbitant South Beach rent because the restaurant has a loyal following of locals, who come for the fresh and simple seafood in a relaxed but upscale atmosphere. As the name implies, fish, fish, and fish is what you'll get.

The waiters are friendly and know the limited menu well. The barroom seafood chowder is full of chunks of shellfish as well as some fresh white fish filets in a tomato broth. The small ear of corn, included with each entree, is about as close as you'll get to any type of vegetable offering besides the pedestrian salad. Still, at these prices, it's worth a visit to try some local fare including Mako shark, swordfish, tuna, marlin, and wahoo. They'll grill it or sauté it. Also, choose the spicy red sauce on the pasta as a great complement to this rustic, Italian-inspired seafood fare.

Jeffrey's. 1629 Michigan Ave. (half-block south of Lincoln Rd.), South Beach. ☎ **305/ 673-0690.** Main courses $11–$17. AE, DC, CB, MC, V. Tues–Sat 6–11pm, Sun 5–10pm. CONTINENTAL/BISTRO.

Jeffrey's is a real find on South Beach. Here you get a genuinely concerned and doting owner, Jeffrey, who treats everyone as a regular and calls grandmothers and children "kids." It's been called the most romantic restaurant on the beach, and that is certainly the case among South Beach's gay crowd. Old-fashioned lace curtains and candlelight are a welcome repast from the glitz and chrome of the rest of the island.

You can choose from a hearty chicken breast marinated in a balsamic sauce served with freshly mashed sweet potatoes over spinach or a basic burger. Some of the better seafood options include the conch fritters, which are not too oily, or the crab cakes. Jeffrey's is known for the perfectly dressed Caesar salad, which could use some more anchovies for my taste, but, nonetheless is delicious. Most desserts are tasty but the homemade tarte-tartin, a caramelly deep-dish apple tart, is superb. Go early before they sell out of it.

Larios on the Beach. 820 Ocean Dr., South Beach. ☎ **305/532-9577.** Reservations recommended. Main courses $8–$15; lunch $4–$7. AE, MC, V. Sun–Thurs 11:30am–midnight, Fri–Sat 11:30am–1:30am. CUBAN.

Gloria and Emilio Estefan brought their favorite Cuban chef from the mainland to create this ultra-stylish restaurant in the heart of South Beach hustle. Enjoy a few appetizers at the handsome chrome and wood bar while you wait for a seat amid the sea of Spanish-speaking regulars.

The menu runs the gamut, from diner-style *medianoches* (cuban sandwiches with pork and cheese) to a tangy and tender *serrucho en escabeche* (pickled kingfish) with just enough citrus to mellow the fishiness and still not cause a pucker. You could get away with ordering three or four *apertivos* and *ensaladas* (appetizers and salads) for a couple.

Portions are large and prices are reasonable, but Cuban food is not light and this is no exception. If you are still hungry, try the *camarones al ajillo* (shrimp in garlic sauce), *fabada asturiana* (hearty soup of black beans and sausage), or *Palomilla* (thinly sliced beef served with onions and parsley). Save room for the rich custard desserts, which include a few stunning variations on the standard *flan*. A spoonful of pumpkin or coffee-accented custard with a cup of *cortadito* (espresso-style coffee with milk and sugar) will get you prepped for a full night of dancing.

L'Entrecote de Paris. 413 Washington Ave., South Beach. ☎ **305/673-1002.** Reservations suggested on weekends. Prix-fixe $16 (includes potatoes and salad). MC, V. Daily 6pm–1am. FRENCH BRASSERIE.

Everything in this classy little bistro is simple. For example, for dinner you choose between salmon or steak. Yes, that's it. Meat or fish and maybe a few salads. But both are great, although the salmon, next to the savory filet mignon with its piquant sauce and pommes frittes to soak up the juices, looks like spa cuisine. The fish is served with a pile of bald steamed potatoes and a salad with pedestrian greens and an unmatchable vinaigrette.

The steak on the other hand, even for a non-meat enthusiast, is the stuff cravings are made of. Its salty and sharp sauce is rich but not thick and full of the beef's natural flavor. The slices are served on top of your own little habachi, which also keeps the skinny fries warm.

A half-dozen tables and booths are so cramped that you may be tempted to take a stab at your neighbor's plate while you wait for your own. Don't. Most diners are very Euro and pack a *petit* attitude. On the other hand, the waiters are super quick and professional, almost friendly, in a French kind of way. A short and very Franco-oriented wine list includes several well-priced bottles for under $20. Even if you are on a diet or have forsaken chocolate, try the *profiteroles au chocolat*, a perfect puff pastry filled with vanilla ice-cream and topped with a dark bittersweet chocolate sauce. The *crème brûlée* and *tarte aux pommes* are also excellent.

Les Deux Fontaines. 1230–38 Ocean Dr. (in the Ocean Front Hotel), South Beach. ☎ **305/ 672-2579.** Reservations recommended for weekend dinner. Main courses $11–$19; lunch sandwiches and salads $6–$11. AE, DC, MC, V. Daily 6:30am–1am. FRENCH.

This quaint bistro-style restaurant serves delicious Mediterranean French food on the beach. It's best for lunch when a niçoise salad or seared tuna over mixed greens is all you feel like eating in the heat. A number of celebrities have been known to stop in for a bite, including Cher and some local chefs; they enjoy the simple menu and elegant patio setting that overlooks, but is neatly tucked above, scenic Ocean Drive.

Mercury. 764 Washington Ave., South Beach. ☎ **305/532-0070.** Reservations recommended. Main courses $12–$21. AE, DC, MC, V. Daily 6pm–midnight, Fri–Sat 6pm–1am. AMERICAN/NOUVELLE.

Recently renamed by new owners, Mercury has kept on their innovative, pretty-boy chef, Kerry Simon, from the days of Max's South Beach. They have also retained many of the signature dishes, including the meatloaf and mashed potatoes, that is as comforting as it is delicious. On a bit more elegant note, the starters tend to be more elaborate and impressive in their execution. The tuna tartar with lemongrass and waffle potatoes is a tower of bright red fish accented with subtle eastern seasonings, crispy chips, and a healthy splash of green wasabi sauce.

While the decor, with a sweeping mahogany bar that rungs the length of the chrome and stone interior, conjures up images of an old speakeasy, this place is pure fun. It's noisy though; even on a slow night, the din can be deafening. If your waiter can hear you, try asking for a piece of Kerry's favorite banana cream pie; the pie is so chunky and full of bright yellow pudding that once you take a bite, you are sure you are eight years old again and the world is good. Some complain that this restaurant is overpriced, but the service, hearty food, and great people-watching make it a must in my book.

The Strand. 671 Washington Ave., South Beach. ☎ **305/532-2340.** Reservations recommended on weekends. Main courses $13–$24; pasta and vegetarian dishes $12–$16. AE, DC, MC, V. Sun–Thurs 6pm–midnight, Fri–Sat 6pm–1am. AMERICAN.

Still the place to be and be seen, this old standby has candlelit tables and a large, open-room layout, a setting conducive both to intimate dining and table hopping. The menu changes nightly, but the food and the service are extremely consistent. Lots of model types hang out at the bar where hundreds of people crunch into an expansive and elegant deco-style marble and glass area.

If it is in season, definitely consider the seafood and tropical salad, which combines stone crab, lobster, shrimp, and fish in a passion fruit vinaigrette. The crab cakes are very gently browned on the outside and super moist inside. Other Italian-inspired dishes, like the fusili con fungi or the penne all'arrabiata, are true to form with a slightly al dente noodle and a subtle hand with the sauce. The reasonably tasty lamb medallions are served with a fragrant herb sauce, sautéed vegetables, and plump spinach-and-mushroom-stuffed ravioli.

Nothing on the menu will disappoint you, which explains why after more than 10 years (an eternity for South Beach) The Strand is still going strong. It's kept up with the times and still offers an exceptional value with enough glitz to keep it popular.

Tap Tap. 819 Fifth St. (between Jefferson and Meridian aves., behind the Shell station), South Beach. ☎ **305/672-2898.** Reservations recommended in season and for special events. Main courses $8–$15. Sun, all-you-can-eat brunch buffet $12. AE, DC, MC, V. Daily 11:30am–11pm, Fri–Sat 11:30–midnight. HAITIAN.

The whole place looks like an overgrown *tap tap*, a brightly painted jitney common in Haiti. Every space of wall and floor and furniture is painted with a neon blue or pink or purple and every color in between. The atmosphere is always fun. It's where the Haiti-philes and Haitians hang out, from journalists to politicians. Even Manno Charlemagne, the mayor of Port-au-Prince, shows up when he can to play his old brand of protest music and drink lots of Rhum Barbancourt.

You don't really come here for the food, although meals aren't bad, when you can get served. On crowded nights, the service is impossible. The young and handsome waitstaff tends to disappear entirely or show up flustered with someone else's order. I recommend going for appetizers and drinks. The *Lanbi nan citron*, a tart marinated conch salad, is perfect with a tall tropical drink and maybe some goat tidbits. The lightly grilled pieces of goat are served in a savory brown sauce and are less stringy than a typical goat dish. A super-satisfying dish itself is the pumpkin soup, a rich brick-colored purée of subtly seasoned pumpkin with a dash of pepper. An excellent salad of avocado, mango, and watercress is a great finish. Even if you don't stay for a full meal, try the pumpkin flan with coconut caramel sauce, an ultra-Caribbean sweet-treat.

Thai House South Beach. 1137 Washington Ave., South Beach. ☎ **305/531-4841.** Reservations recommended on weekends. Main courses $7–$13 ($15–$18 for fish). AE, MC, V. Daily 11:30am–2am. THAI.

The third in a series of successful Thai Houses in Miami, this most recent addition has perhaps the most complete and inspired menu. A whole page of tofu options for vegetarians includes massaman tofu with sweet potato, snow peas, and pineapple in a curry-based sauce.

After years of searching and tasting I have finally found the pad Thai to label "the best." Here, the subtlety of the flavors distinguishes this warm noodle dish, with a hint of fish and just a tinge of sweetness. The shrimp are few and small, but the peanut flavor and the scallions provide the required bulk. As a side, try the Thai fries, strips of *boniato* (a sweet potatolike root) dunked in coconut meat and deep fried.

The service in this quaint little storefront is spotty at best, but pleasant nonetheless. For a taste of South Beach with your meal, sit in the sidewalk area, which overlooks the hectic Washington Avenue where club-hoppers and teeny-boppers perform nightly.

You'll find other Thai Houses at: 715 East 9th St., Hialeah; and 2250 NE 163rd St., North Miami Beach.

Toni's. 1208 Washington Ave., South Beach. ☎ **305/673-9368.** Reservations recommended. Main courses $11–$22; rolls $3.50–$8.50. AE, MC, V. Daily 6pm–midnight, Fri–Sat 6pm–1am. SUSHI/JAPANESE.

One of Washington Avenue's first tenants, Toni's has withstood the test of time on fickle South Beach. By serving local fish caught daily and some imports from the Pacific and beyond, Toni has created a vast menu with options from teriyaki to hand rolls. Plus the atmosphere is comfortable and even allows for quiet conversation—a rarity on the beach.

Consider the seaweed salad, a crunchy and salty green plant that is dressed with a light sesame sauce. The miso soup is hearty and a bit sweet. Some fun appetizers from the sushi bar include Miami Heat, which contains slabs of tuna with bits of scallion in a peppery sesame oil. The hundreds of appetizers and rolls you can order makes this a fun place to go with a group and share. I suggest skipping the entrees unless you are somehow still hungry after all the warm-ups. Many main dishes are good, like the lobster teriyaki in a dark sweet sauce over white rice.

INEXPENSIVE

Bagel Factory. 1427 Alton Rd., South Beach. ☎ **305/674-1577.** Sandwiches $1–$7. No credit cards. Mon–Sat 5:30am–7pm, Sun 5:30am–3pm. BAGELS/DELI.

There are bagel joints all over South Beach, but this narrow storefront on Alton Road is one of the best. The Rishty family makes the city's best hand-rolled bagels in every imaginable flavor, from sunflower to banana raisin to sundried tomato. The bagels are deliciously chewy, but not too doughy. Add to that the phenomenal salads, including a range of decent fat-free options, and you'll understand why every weekend hungry customers wait in a line that goes out the door. Stake out a spot at one of the three small inside tables to take the order to go, like most loyal patrons do.

La Sandwicherie. 229 14th St. (behind the Amoco station), South Beach. ☎ **305/532-8934.** Sandwiches and salads $4.50–$7. No credit cards. Daily 10am–4am; Fri–Sat 10am–5am. FRENCH SNACK BAR.

If you want the most incredible gourmet sandwich you've ever tasted, stop by the green-and-white awning that hides this fabulously French lunch and snack counter. Choose pâté, saucisson, salami, prosciutto, turkey, tuna, ham, roast beef, or any of the perfect cheeses (Swiss, mozzarella, cheddar, or provolone). You could make a meal of the optional sandwich toppings, which include black olives, cornichons, cucumbers, lettuce, onions, green or hot peppers, or tomatoes. Many people do and they call it a Vegetarian. The toppings are included in the sandwich price. The fresh French bread has a slightly golden crust and is just thick enough to hold all you'll want to have stuffed in it. You can choose to have your sandwich made on a croissant, though I find them pretty uninspired compared to some of the flakier ones elsewhere on the beach.

If the six or so wooden stools are all taken, don't despair; you can stand and watch the tattoo artist do his work through the glass wall next door. Or, douse your creation with the light and tangy vinaigrette and bring lunch to the beach. That is if you can make it two blocks without eating the whole thing. In addition to the cans and bottles of teas, sodas, juices, and waters, you can get a killer cappuccino here.

Lyon Freres. 600 Lincoln Rd., South Beach. ☎ **305/534-0600.** Main courses $4–$9; sandwiches and salads $4–$8. AE, MC, V. Daily 7:30am–7:30pm; Fri–Sat 7:30am–midnight. GOURMET/DELI.

Consider this surprisingly good food for a casual breakfast, lunch, or dinner, and enjoy the view of in-line skaters, strolling lovers, and dog-walkers along the road. This high-ceilinged glass-and-chrome gourmet deli and grocery store has a dozen or more marble tables at the wine bar and at least as many outside on the sidewalk.

You choose your food from glass cases where dozens of homemade salads like fresh lentil salad, roasted vegetables, herbed goat cheese, curried chicken salad, and dozens more are served cafeteria style for $5 for a half-pound. A loyal following of locals sit all morning reading the *New York Times* and sipping *café au laits*.

The wine bar offers perhaps the largest selection of by-the-glass reds and whites from all over. They are kept in a pressurized and temperature-controlled case which guarantees a good glass every time. It's also a great opportunity to taste an interesting looking wine before committing to buying a bottle from the store's well-stocked shelves.

Mrs. Mendoza's Tacos al Carbon. 1040 Alton Rd., South Beach. ☎ **305/535-0808.** Main courses $3–$5; side dishes 79¢–$3. No credit cards. Mon–Sat 11am–10pm; Sun noon–9pm. FAST FOOD/MEXICAN.

This hard-to-spot storefront is a godsend. It's the only fresh California-style Mexican place where the steak and chicken are grilled as you wait and then stuffed into homemade flour or corn wrappings. You order at the tile counter and pick up your dish on a plastic tray in minutes. This is a popular spot for locals and those who work in the area.

The vegetarian offerings are huge and hearty. One of my favorites is the veggie burrito, which includes rice, black beans, cheese, lettuce, and guacamole doused in tomato salsa. They offer three types of salsa, from mild to super hot. You can see the fresh-cut cilantro and taste the super-hot chilies. The chips are hand cut and flavorful but a bit too coarse. Skip them and enjoy an order of the rich and chunky guacamole with a fork.

There's another location at Doral Plaza, 9739 NW 41st St.

News Café. 800 Ocean Dr., South Beach. ☎ **305/538-6397.** Continental breakfast $2.75; salads $4–$8; sandwiches $5–$7. AE, MC, V. Daily 24 hours. AMERICAN.

Of all the chic spots around trendy South Beach, News Café has been around the longest. Inexpensive breakfasts and cafe fare are served at about 20 perpetually congested tables. Most of the seating is outdoors, and terrace tables are most coveted. This is the regular meeting place for Ocean Drive's multitude of fashion photography crews and their models and where they can get all the international newspapers and magazines.

The food isn't remarkable but the people-watching is. Delicious and often health-oriented dishes include yogurt with fruit salad, various green salads, imported cheese and meat sandwiches, and a choice of quiches.

Puerto Sagua. 700 Collins Ave., South Beach. ☎ **305/673-1115.** Main courses $7–$17; sandwiches and salads $3–$9. AE, DC, MC, V. Daily 7:30am–2am. SPANISH/CUBAN.

This bar and restaurant has a steady stream of regulars who range from *abuelitos*, little old grandfathers, to hipsters who stop in after clubbing. The dingy brown-walled diner is one of the only real old hold-outs on South Beach. It has endured because the food is good.

The faded plastic sign on the corner boasts: *Famoso por sus Mariscos*, translated as "famous for its seafood." It is, though the style of cooking tends to be greasy. Some of the less heavy dishes are a super-chunky fish soup with pieces of whole flaky grouper, the chicken and seafood paella, or the marinated kingfish. Also good are most of the shrimp dishes, especially the shrimp in garlic sauce served with white rice and salad.

This is one of the most reasonably priced places left on the beach for simple and hearty fare. Don't be intimidated by the hunched older waiters in their white button shirts and black pants. Even if you don't speak Spanish, they're usually willing to do charades. Anyway, the extensive menu, which includes BLTs to grilled lobsters to yummy fried plantains, is translated into English. Hurry, before another boutique goes up in its place.

✪ **Sport Cafe.** 538 Washington Ave., South Beach. ☎ **305/674-9700.** Reservations accepted for four or more. Main courses $6.95–$9.95; sandwiches and pizzas $4.50–$7. MC, V. Daily noon–1am; sometimes earlier for coffee. ITALIAN.

Inside the decor is dark and smoky, with a beautiful wooden bar and a large-screen TV that dominate the small dining room. But don't expect to see the latest football or baseball games here; instead it's more likely that a soccer match or bicycle race will be on the screen. This is a European crowd.

The Sport Cafe's owners, brothers Tonino and Paolo Doino, hail from Rome. They've put together an authentic Italian menu, listing only three entrees and a few pizzas. Ask for the day's specials and order one of them. Always good is the penne with salmon served with a pink sauce. The noodles are perfectly *al dente,* and the chunks of fish add a slightly salty and warm flavor. Even though the portions are large, the sauce is so delicious and light you can finish a whole bowl. Rosa, the Doino boys' mother, also makes the very best eggplant parmigiano in the county. It's not on the menu, but it's available almost every day. There is no heavy breading, oily residue, or excessive cheese that mar so many versions of this dish elsewhere.

It can be a challenge placing your order with one of the Italian waiters, but do try to ask for a plate of fresh crushed garlic when they bring your bread and oil. The crusty dense loaf benefits from the dose of oil, pepper, and pungent bulb. Also try the great tiramisu, which, unlike the more common cake or pudding style, is served *semi-freddo,* or partially frozen, like an ice cream.

The atmosphere is rustic and young and the prices so cheap that on some nights you may have to wait for a seat, especially for the sidewalk tables. Thanks to their great success on Washington Avenue, the brothers have opened a second and similar restaurant called Al Vicolo Caffe on Lincoln Road.

⑨ **Stephan's Gourmet Market & Cafe.** 1430 Washington Ave. (at Española Way), South Beach. ☎ **305/674-1760.** Main courses $6–$12; dinner special for two with salad and a bottle of wine $24.95. AE, MC, V. Daily 10am–midnight; Fri–Sat 10am–2am; dinner special served daily 5:30–11pm. DELI/ITALIAN.

This deli, which could be in New York's Little Italy, sells a huge assortment of fresh pastas, breads, and salads as well as cold cuts, cheeses, and grocery items. But upstairs in a tiny loft used to store wine bottles is a cozy dining room with space for about 10 couples. Dinner is also served out on the sidewalk or delivered to your hotel.

A chalkboard displays the chef's special, usually a pasta dish with some kind of chicken or fish. One of my favorites is the linguini Alfredo with tender pieces of chicken breast mixed into the light and cheesy sauce. While you wait, you'll want to eat baskets and baskets full of the garlicky garlic bread and get started on the bottle of wine that comes with the daily special. The red is an excellent full-bodied Italian Merlot. However, I find the pinot grigio undrinkable. If the special doesn't strike you, consider any of the other moderately priced dishes like rotisserie chicken with potatoes and vegetables, ziti, sausage and peppers, or eggplant parmigiano. You can choose whatever looks good to you from the glass case downstairs or see what else the chef is dishing out.

Van Dyke Cafe. 846 Lincoln Rd., South Beach. ☎ **305/534-3600.** Reservations recommended for evenings. Main courses $6–$11. AE, DC, MC, V. Daily 8am–midnight; Fri–Sat 8am–2am. AMERICAN.

Owned by the same group who owns the successful News Café, the Van Dyke has utilized the same formula to guarantee its longevity on Lincoln Road. The smart, upscale decor inside and European sidewalk cafe outside are always crowded due to the diner-like prices and fast, friendly service.

There is nothing too ambitious on the menu, which offers basic sandwiches and salads, and best of all, breakfast all day long. The pastas are decent, though not too exciting. House specialties include an excellent smoked salmon on a rustic and thick black bread and a smooth and lemony hummus with pita chips. Also, since you are in Miami Beach, you may want to consider a nice hot bowl of cure-all chicken soup with matzoh balls. In the evenings the sounds of a talented jazz band waft down from the dark and elegant club upstairs.

World Resources. 719 Lincoln Rd., South Beach. ☎ **305/534-9095.** Main courses $6–$8; sushi hand rolls $3–$4. AE, DC, MC, V. Daily noon–midnight. SUSHI/THAI.

World Resources is an excellent little cafe and sushi bar masquerading as an Indonesian furniture and bric-a-brac store. Local hippy types and hipsters frequent this downright cheap hangout instead of cooking at home. Offerings include some of the freshest and most-innovative sushi in Miami, plus many Thai specialties. The portions are generous and the cooking simple. The basil chicken, for example, is a tasty combination of white meat sautéed in a coconut sauce with subtle hints of basil and garlic. The Thai salad is heaped with fresh vegetables including cauliflower, sprouts, and cucumbers. Although you can get better pad Thai at a number of spots on the beach, you can't beat the atmosphere here, which includes dozens of outside tables surrounding a tiny pond and stage where World Beat musicians perform nightly. From African drumming to Indian sitar playing, there is always some action at this standout on the Road. They also offer a vast selection of coffees, teas, wines, beers, and cigarettes from around the world.

4 Miami Beach: Surfside, Bal Harbour & Sunny Isles

The area north of the Art Deco District—from 21st Street to 163rd Street—had its heyday in the 1950s with the huge hotels and gambling halls blocking the view of the ocean. Now many of those hotels have been converted into condos and the bayfront mansions renovated by and for wealthy entrepreneurs, families, and speculators, leaving the area with many more residents, albeit seasonal, than visitors. On the culinary front, the result is a handful of super-expensive restaurants and a number of value-oriented spots.

VERY EXPENSIVE

✪ **Dominique's.** 5225 Collins Ave., (in The Alexander All-Suite Luxury Hotel), Miami Beach. ☎ **305/861-5252.** Reservations recommended, especially at dinner. Jackets requested. Main courses $20–$30 at dinner, $10–$15 at lunch. AE, CB, DC, MC, V. Daily 7am–11pm. MODERN FRENCH/CONTINENTAL.

Worth mentioning as one of the most elegant restaurants in Miami, Dominique's consistently draws rave reviews from locals and visitors who don't mind paying for superior service and food.

Although the decor is heavy, with huge drapes framing a dazzling view of the Atlantic, the food is not. The chef, Jean-Claude Philon, creates a masterfully balanced menu that combines classical French favorites, like marinated rack of lamb chops and prime steak, with more updated and healthful offerings, such as buffalo sausage, tender alligator scaloppini, and fresh diamondback rattlesnake salad.

EXPENSIVE

The Forge Restaurant. 432 Arthur Godfrey Rd. (41st St.), Miami Beach. ☎ **305/538-8533.** Reservations required. Main courses $18–$25. AE, DC, MC, V. Sun–Thurs 4pm–midnight, Fri–Sat 5pm–3am. AMERICAN.

English oak paneling and Tiffany glass suggest high prices and haute cuisine, and those are exactly what you can expect from the Forge. Each elegant dining room possesses its own character and features high ceilings, ornate chandeliers, and high-quality European artwork. The Forge attracts a mix of young, well-dressed Euros, Saudi royalty, and moneyed Miami families. The atmosphere is elegant but not too stuffy.

The Forge's huge American menu has a northern Italian bias, evidenced by a long list of creamy pasta appetizers. Equal attention is given to fish, veal, poultry, and beef dishes, many prepared on the kitchen's oak grill. Look for appetizers like oak-grilled tomatoes with mozzarella or shrimp cocktails the size of a child's fist. Finally, it is important to note that the Forge has one of Miami's best wine lists, selected from the on-premises wine cellar. Ask the very knowledgeable and affable head wine steward, Gino Santangelo, for a tour.

The Palm. 9650 E. Bay Harbor Dr., Bay Harbor Island. ☎ **305/868-7256.** Reservations highly recommended. Main courses $17–$29. AE, CB, DC, MC, V. Daily 5–11pm. CONTINENTAL.

You feel like you're in New York in this dark and clubby steakhouse. Known for their enormous sirloins and jumbo Maine lobsters, the prices are as big as the portions. The same celebrity caricatures and photos adorn the walls as in the other Palms in Los Angeles and New York. There are currently more than a dozen branches throughout the country all known for pleasing a demanding corporate and tourist crowd. The waiters are professional but brusque.

You can't go wrong with this limited and simple menu filled with old standbys, like Caesar salad, shrimp cocktail, clams oreganata, salmon, broiled chicken, and veal. A selection of steak ranges from filet mignon to chopped steak. You'll find more martini drinkers than health-conscious types here.

To get to The Palm, turn west onto 96th Street, at Bal Harbor Shops, go over a small bridge, and turn right onto East Bay Harbor Drive. The restaurant is on the left.

MODERATE

⑤ Cafe Prima Pasta. 414 71st St. (half a block east of the Byron movie theater), Miami Beach. ☎ **305/867-0106.** Main courses $12–$14; pastas $7–$9. No credit cards. Mon–Thurs and Sun 6–11pm; Fri–Sat 6pm–midnight. ITALIAN.

Here's another tiny pasta joint that serves phenomenal homemade noodles with good old Italian sauces like carbonara, dioliva, putanesca, and pomodoro. There are only 30 seats, so you might feel a bit cramped, but the crowd, a young laid-back set, is generally easy to sit close to. The stuffed agnolotti with either pesto, spinach, and ricotta or tomato are so delicate and flavorful that you'll think you're eating dessert. Speaking of which, you'll want to try their apple tart with a pale golden caramel sauce. Ask for it à la mode and plan to come back again for more.

Its location, closer to Collins Avenue, makes it more popular than Oggi just a few miles west. In fact, I found this place after an unsuccessful search for Oggi. It was sort of like Columbus's navigational mistake, but it worked out all right.

Cafe Ragazzi. 9500 Harding Ave. (on corner of 95th St.), Surfside. ☎ **305/866-4495.** Reservations not accepted. Main courses $11–$15; lunch specials $7, including soup, salad, and daily pasta. MC, V. Mon–Thurs 11:30am–3pm and 5:30–10:30pm; Fri 11:30am–3pm and 5:30–11pm; Sat 5:30–11pm; Sun 5–10pm. ITALIAN.

A relative newcomer in an area of long-standing delis and diners, this little Italian cafe with its rustic decor and handsome waitstaff enjoys great success for its tasty and simple pastas. The spicy putanesca sauce with a subtle hint of fish is perfectly

Miami Beach Dining

DINING:

Cafe Prima Pasta 6
Cafe Ragazzi 3
Chef Allen's 14
Crystal Cafe 10
Curry's 5
Dominique's 8
The Forge Restaurant 9
The Gourmet Diner 14
Here Comes the Sun 13
Mark's Place 13
Miami Beach Place 7
New Delhi Restaurant 12
Oggi Caffe 11
The Palm 2
Sheldon's Drugs 4
Wolfie Cohen's Rascal House 1

97

prepared with just enough bits of tomato to give it some weight. Also recommended is the salmon with raddicchio. You can choose from many decent salads and carpacci, too. The mostly Italian/Argentinian staff are limited in their ability to communicate sometimes, yet the service tends to be pretty efficient. Expect a wait on weekend nights.

✪ **Crystal Cafe.** 726 41st St., Miami Beach. ☎ **305/673-8266.** Reservations recommended on weekends. Main courses $13–$22. AE, MC, V. Tues–Sun 5–11pm. CONTINENTAL/ NOUVELLE.

The setting is sparse, decorated in black and white, with Lucite salt and pepper grinders and a bottle of wine as the only centerpiece on each of the 15 or so tables. I promise you won't need the seasoning. Chef Klime (pronounced Klee-me) has done it all with the help of a superb waitstaff and his affable wife. Enjoy his unique sparkle at this little-known hideaway.

They have created a neighborhood bistro that attracts stars like Julio Iglesias and other musical talents and makes even the little old man from over the bridge feel like a celebrity. The attentive staff never seems obtrusive yet is always there to refill a water glass, inquire about your needs, or tempt you with yet more of the most delicious foods on the planet.

With something like 30 entrees listed on the ever-changing menu, it is incomprehensible how each comes out perfectly prepared with some unexpected addition. Here you get no listing of each and every spice and ingredient used in a dish. The shrimp-cake appetizer, for example, is the size of a bread plate and rests on top of a small mound of lightly sautéed watercress and mushrooms. Surrounding the delicately breaded disc are concentric circles of beautiful sauces—tomato and a basil mayonnaise. The veal marsala is served in a luscious brown sauce that is thickened not with heavy cream or flours but with delicate vegetable broth and a hearty mix of mushrooms.

The osso buco is renowned among Miami foodies with good reason. It is a masterpiece. The tender, almost buttery meat is steeped in chicken broth and piled high with an assortment of vegetables. Desserts are tempting but hard to manage after such generous portions. But if you have room, consider the crêpe stuffed with warm berry compote with a nutty topping.

Oggi Caffe. 1740 79th St. Causeway (in the White Star shopping center next to the Bagel Cafe), North Bay Village. ☎ **305/866-1238.** Reservations accepted. Main courses $12–$20; pastas $8–$10. Mon–Thurs 11:30am–2:30pm and 6–10:30pm; Fri 11:30am–2:30pm and 6–11:30pm; Sat 6–11:30pm; Sun 5:30–10:30pm. ITALIAN.

Tucked away in a tiny strip mall on the 79th Street Causeway, this neighborhood favorite makes fresh pastas daily. Every one, from the agnolotti stuffed with fresh spinach and ricotta to the wire-thin spaghettini, is tender and tasty. Also notable are the daily soups. A hearty *pasta e fagiola* is filled with beans and vegetables and could almost be a meal. The creamy spinach soup, when on the menu, is also delicious and not laden with starch or other thickeners. Though you could fill up on the starters, the entrees, especially the grilled dishes, are superb. The salmon is served on a bed of spinach with a light lemon-butter sauce. The place is tiny and a bit rushed, but it's well worth the slight discomfort for this authentic and inexpensive food.

INEXPENSIVE

Curry's. 7433 Collins Ave., Miami Beach. ☎ **305/866-1571.** Reservations not accepted. $8–$11, including appetizer, main course, dessert, and coffee. AE, MC, V. Mon–Sat 4:30–9:30pm, Sun 4–9:30pm. AMERICAN.

Established in 1937, this large dining room on the ocean side of Collins Avenue is one of Miami Beach's oldest restaurants. Neither the restaurant's name nor the Polynesian wall decorations are indicative of the menu's offerings, which are straightforwardly American and reminiscent of the area's heyday. Broiled and fried fish dishes are available, but the best selections, including steak, chicken, and ribs, come off the open charcoal grill perched by the front window. Prices are incredibly reasonable here, and all include an appetizer, soup, or salad, as well as a potato or vegetable, dessert, and coffee or tea.

Miami Beach Place. 6954 Collins Ave., Miami Beach. ☎ **305/866-8661.** Main courses (served with spaghetti, vegetables, or rice and garlic rolls) $10–$13; pizzas and pastas $7–$16. MC, V. ITALIAN/PIZZA.

This Brazilian-owned pizza parlor is packed most weekends, not only because of their good inexpensive pastas and pizzas, but also because of the fun Brazilian bands that play most weekends after 9pm. By midnight the place is packed with Portuguese-speaking dancers who enjoy a late-night buffet and lots of wine and beer. I think the light and garlicky garlic rolls wrapped in golden twists are addictive. While the pizza tends to be too cheesy for my taste, it is topped with fresh toppings instead of the canned variety offered at other places. If you've never tasted the ubiquitous Brazilian soda, *Guaraná*, I suggest trying a sip; it's like a rich ginger ale with not as much zing.

Sheldon's Drugs. 9501 Harding Ave., Surfside. ☎ **305/866-6251.** Main courses $4.50–$5; soups and sandwiches $2–$5. AE, DISC, MC, V. Daily 7am–8pm. AMERICAN/DRUGSTORE.

This typical old-fashioned drugstore counter serves eggs and oatmeal and a good tuna melt. A blue-plate special might be a generic spaghetti and meatballs or grilled frankfurters. The food is not bad, and you can't beat the prices.

More importantly, this was a favorite breakfast spot of Isaac Bashevis Singer. In 1978, he was sitting at Sheldon's, eating a bagel and eggs, when his wife got the call that he had won the Nobel prize for Literature. The menu hasn't changed much since then. Consider stopping into this historic site for a good piece of pie and a side of history.

Wolfie Cohen's Rascal House. 17190 Collins Ave., Sunny Isles. ☎ **305/947-4581.** Omelets and sandwiches $4–$6; other dishes $5–$14. MC, V. Daily 7am–12:45am. JEWISH/DELICATESSEN.

Opened in 1954 and still going strong, this historical, nostalgic culinary extravaganza is one of Miami Beach's greatest traditions. Simple tables and booths as well as plenty of patrons fill the airy 425-seat dining room. The menu is as huge as the portions; try the corned beef, schmaltz herring, brisket, kreplach, chicken soup, or other authentic Jewish staples. Take-out service is available.

5 Key Biscayne

Key Biscayne has some of the world's nicest beaches, hotels, and parks, yet it is not known for its great food. Most visitors eat at the largest hotel on the island where the food is always reliable if not outstanding. Local, or "Key rats" as they are known, tend to go off-island for meals or take-out from some good local grocery and produce stores. But here are some good on-the-island choices.

EXPENSIVE

Rusty Pelican. 3201 Rickenbacker Causeway, Key Biscayne. ☎ **305/361-3818.** Reservations recommended. Main courses $16–$20; lunch about half-price. AE, CB, DC, MC, V. Daily 11:30am–4pm; Sun–Thurs 5–11pm, Fri–Sat 5pm–midnight. CONTINENTAL.

The Pelican's private tropical walkway leads over a lush waterfall into one of the most romantic dining rooms in the city, located right on beautiful blue-green Biscayne Bay. The restaurant's windows look out over the water onto the sparkling stalagmites of Miami's magnificent Downtown. Inside, quiet wicker paddle fans whirl overhead and saltwater fish swim in pretty tableside aquariums.

The restaurant's surf-and-turf menu features conservatively prepared prime steaks, veal, shrimp, and lobster. The food is good, but the atmosphere is even better, especially at sunset, when the view over the city is magical.

Stefano's. 24 Crandon Blvd., Key Biscayne. ☎ **305/361-7007.** Reservations recommended on weekends. Main courses $15–$23; pastas $11–$15. AE, DC, MC, V. Daily 6–11:30pm; Fri–Sat 6pm–12:30am. Disco open later. NORTHERN ITALIAN.

For retro-elegance, Stefano's has no match. The restaurant and disco share the same strobe-lit atmosphere. Food is traditional and reliable. You'll find an older country club crowd here in the evenings enjoying steaks and pastas and seafood. One of the best entrees is the *Delfino Livornese*, a dolphin sautéed with a spicy sauce of tomato, olives, capers, and onions. Stefano's also serves some rare game, such as guinea hen in wine sauce and quails wrapped in pancetta. I recommend sticking with the pastas and fish. Overall, the food is fine if a little pricey.

After 7:30pm the band starts playing pop American and Latin favorites. Some nights you feel as if you accidentally happened upon your long lost cousin's wedding as you watch the parade of taffeta dresses and tipsy uncles. Stefano's has continued to do well over time because of its dependable service and kitchen.

Sundays on the Bay. 5420 Crandon Blvd., Key Biscayne. ☎ **305/361-6777.** Reservations accepted; recommended for Sunday brunch. Main courses $15–$24; Sunday brunch $18.95. AE, CB, DC, MC, V. Mon–Sat 11:30am–5pm; Mon–Wed and Sun 5pm–2am, Thurs–Sat 5pm–2:30am; brunch Sun 10:30am–3:30pm. AMERICAN.

Although the food is fine, Sundays is really a fun tropical bar that features an unbeatable view of Downtown, Coconut Grove, and the Sunday's marina.

The menu features local favorites—grouper, tuna, snapper, and good shellfish when in season. Competent renditions of such classic shellfish dishes as oysters Rockefeller, shrimp scampi, and lobster fra diablo are also recommendable. Sunday brunches are particularly popular, when a buffet the size of Bimini attracts the city's late-rising in-crowd.

The lively bar stays open all week until 2:30am, with a DJ spinning Thursday through Sunday from 9pm. Some legal trouble put the owners in hot water in 1995, leaving the future of this old crazy reggae scene up in the air.

INEXPENSIVE

Ⓢ Bayside Seafood Restaurant and Hidden Cove Bar. 3501 Rickenbacker Causeway, Key Biscayne. ☎ **305/361-0808.** Reservations accepted only for groups of more than 15. Raw clams or oysters $7 per dozen; appetizers, salads, and sandwiches $4.50–$6; platters $7–$13. AE, MC, V. Daily noon–10:30pm, Fri–Sat noon–midnight. SEAFOOD.

Known by locals as "the Hut," this ramshackle restaurant and bar is a laid-back outdoor tiki hut and terrace that serves pretty good sandwiches and fish platters on paper plates. A blackboard lists the latest catches, which can be prepared blackened, fried, broiled, or in a garlic sauce. I prefer the blackened, which is super crusty, spicy, and dark. The fish dip is wonderfully smoky and moist if a little heavy on mayonnaise. Lately the Hut has been offering great happy hours on weekday evenings with open bar and snacks for $25 per person. It's a good deal if you drink a lot. On weekends, the house band plays live reggae and calypso.

But if you come here, do bring bug spray or ask the waiters for some (they usually keep packets behind the bar). For some reason this place is plagued by mosquitoes even when the rest of town is not. Local fishermen and yacht owners share this rustic outpost with equal enthusiasm and loyalty.

✪ **La Boulangerie.** 328 Crandon Blvd. (in Eckerd's shopping mall), Key Biscayne. ☎ **305/ 361-0281.** Sandwiches and salads $5–$7. MC, V. Mon–Sat 7:30am–8pm; Sun 7:30am–6pm. FRENCH BAKERY.

Beware. You'll stop into this inconspicuous French bakery for a loaf of bread and find yourself walking out with your arms full of the freshest sandwiches, salads, groceries, and pastries anywhere. You can also sit and enjoy a great breakfast, lunch, or early dinner with the jet-set in their designer sweatsuits. The little breadshop now has about 15 tables inside where diners enjoy vegetarian omelets, gourmet sandwiches, and dangerous desserts. The prosciutto and goat cheese sandwich on crusty French bread is unbeatable. There must be something in the mustard.

The friendly proprietors behind the counter will no doubt talk you into a heavenly fruit tart, like the pointy-tipped apricot tart with plump fruit halves painted with a thin layer of sweet glaze. Try any of the cakes or rustic breads, too.

Another Boulangerie is located at 3425 Main Highway, Coconut Grove.

The Oasis. 19 Harbor Dr. (on corner of Crandon), Key Biscayne. ☎ **305/361-5709.** Main courses $4–$12; sandwiches $3–$4. No credit cards. Daily 6am–9pm. CUBAN.

Even Hurricane Andrew couldn't blow down this rugged little shack where everyone, from the city's mayor to the local handymen, meet for delicious paella or a good Cuban sandwich. In fact, after the storm, the place expanded and now provides seating for those who used to gather around the little window for super-powerful *cafesitos* and rich *croquetas*. It's a little dingy, but the food is good and cheap.

6 Downtown

Downtown Miami is a large sprawling area divided by the Brickell bridge into two distinct areas: Brickell Avenue and the bayfront area near Biscayne Boulevard. Although these areas are not far from each other, you wouldn't walk from one to the other because it's too far a distance, plus it's unsafe at night. Convenient metro-mover stops do adjoin the areas, so for a quarter, it's better to hop on the scenic sky-tram.

Some shopkeepers in the area have tried to revitalize the nighttime scene, but in general, if your hotel is not Downtown and you aren't going to a show at the Gusman, The Knight Center, or Bayside, put your visit off until the afternoon when you'll join Latin American shoppers, college students, and lots of professionals in suits. Downtown Miami shuts down after dark though a few of the better restaurants, especially in the hotels, stay open late.

VERY EXPENSIVE

Le Pavillon. 100 Chopin Plaza (in the Hotel Inter-Continental), Downtown. ☎ **305/ 577-1000.** Reservations recommended. Main courses $18–$24. AE, CB, DC, MC, V. Mon–Sat 6:30–10:30pm. NEW WORLD CUISINE.

Private club by day, deluxe restaurant by night, Le Pavillon maintains its air of exclusivity with leather sofas and an expensive salon setting. Dark-green marble columns divide the spacious dining room, while well-spaced booths and tables provide comfortable seating and a sense of privacy. The menu features both heavy club-room fare and lighter dishes prepared with a masterful Miami Regional hand. Prices here are rounded off to the highest dollar and spelled out in lieu of numerals—a practice that might seem a touch pretentious, until your food arrives.

Standouts include the chilled trout appetizer, stuffed with seafood and basil, and an unusual grilled shrimp cocktail with pineapple relish and citrus-flavored lobster mayonnaise. Skillfully prepared dishes include boneless quail Louisiana, stuffed with oysters and andouille sausage. Meat, fish, and chicken dishes are abundant, as are a host of creative pastas, including ravioli stuffed with artichokes, garlic, truffles, and cheese. The Hotel Inter-Continental is located adjacent to the Bayside Marketplace.

EXPENSIVE

The Fish Market. 1601 Biscayne Blvd. (The Crown Plaza, corner of 16th St.), Downtown. ☎ **305/374-4399.** Reservations recommended. Main courses $17–$22. AE, CB, DC, MC, V. Mon–Fri 11:30am–2:30pm; Mon–Sat 6–11pm. SEAFOOD.

One of Miami's most celebrated seafood restaurants is this understated, elegant dining room right in the heart of the city. Located in an unassuming corner, just off the fourth-floor lobby of the Crown Plaza, the restaurant is both spacious and comfortable, featuring high ceilings, marble floors, reasonable prices, and a sumptuous dessert table centerpiece.

Don't overlook the appetizers, which include meaty Mediterranean-style seafood soup and delicate yellowfin tuna carpaccio. Local fish prepared and presented simply, either sautéed or grilled, is always the menu's main feature.

MODERATE

East Coast Fisheries. 360 W. Flagler St., Downtown (south). ☎ **305/372-1300.** Reservations recommended. Main courses $9–$15, most under $14; lunch from $7. AE, DC, MC, V. Daily 11am–10pm. SEAFOOD.

East Coast Fisheries is a no-nonsense retail market and restaurant offering a terrific variety of the freshest fish available. The dozen or so plain wood tables are surrounded by refrigerated glass cases filled with snapper, salmon, mahi mahi, trout, tuna, crabs, oysters, lobsters, and the like. The absolutely huge menu features every fish imaginable, cooked the way you want it—grilled, fried, stuffed, Cajun-style, Florentine, hollandaise, or blackened. However, the smell of frying grease detracts from the otherwise quaint old-Miami feel.

Service is fast, but good prices and good food still mean long lines on weekends. The restaurant is located on the Miami River, at the edge of West Flagler Street. From I-95 South, exit at NW 8th Street. Drive straight to NW 3rd Street and turn right. The next block is River Drive. Turn left, and you'll see the restaurant three blocks down on the right-hand side.

🛇 **Fishbone Grille.** 650 S. Miami Ave. (SW 7th Ave., next to Tobacco Rd.), Downtown. ☎ **305/530-1915.** Reservations recommended on weekends. Entrees $6–$16; pizzas and pastas $7–$12. AE, DC, MC, V. Mon–Thurs 11:30am–10pm; Fri 11:30am–11pm; Sat 5:30–11pm. SEAFOOD.

Located in a small strip center it shares with Tobacco Road, this sensational fish shop prepares dozens of outstanding specials daily. This is by far Miami's best and most reasonably priced seafood restaurant. The atmosphere is nothing to speak of, although at one cool table you can stare into a fish tank.

Try the excellent ceviche, which has just enough spice to give it a zing, yet doesn't overwhelm the super-fresh fish flavor. The stews, crab cakes, and all the starters are superb. If you like a nice Caribbean flavor, try the jerk Covina (the Biblical fish), or one of the excellent dolphin specialties.

Greenwich Village. 1001 S. Miami Ave. (one block west of Brickell), Downtown. ☎ **305/ 372-1716.** Reservations recommended. Main courses $17–$25; pastas $13–$15; lunch entrees $6–$12. AE, DC, DISC, MC, V. Mon–Fri 11:30am–3pm; daily 5:30–11pm. NORTHERN ITALIAN.

This pretty wicker and green Downtown spot is the place for high-powered bankers and brokers to meet and eat. At lunch-time, professionals appreciate the usually quick service and the well-priced, varied menu.

Dinner, too, gets hectic when a variety of locals show up for pricey but terrific pastas that range from the mundane angel hair in tomato sauce to the decadent squid-scented fettuccine with a creamy marinara sauce and sautéed shrimp. A huge array of soups and salads, plus a dessert table to tempt the most disciplined dieters, are reason enough to visit this well-run and time-tested hotspot. Don't miss the pudding-style tiramisu.

Las Tapas. 401 Biscayne Blvd. (in the Bayside Marketplace), Downtown. ☎ **305/372-2737.** Reservations accepted. Tapas $4–$7; main courses $12–$19; lunch about half-price. AE, CB, DC, DISC, MC, V. Sun–Thurs 11am–midnight, Fri–Sat 11am–1am. SPANISH.

Occupying a large corner of Downtown's Bayside Marketplace, glass-wrapped Las Tapas is a fun place to dine in a laid-back, easy atmosphere. *Tapas,* small dishes of Spanish delicacies, are the featured fare here. Good chicken, veal, and seafood main dishes are on the menu, but it's more fun to taste a variety of the restaurant's tapas. The best include shrimp in garlic, smoked port shank with Spanish sausage, baby eel in garlic and oil, and chicken sauté with garlic and mushrooms.

The open kitchen in front of the entrance greets diners with succulent smells. The long dining room is outlined in red Spanish stone and decorated with hundreds of hanging hams. Bayside Marketplace is on Biscayne Bay in the middle of Downtown.

INEXPENSIVE

Caribbean Delite. 236 NE First Avenue (across the street from Miami Dade Community College), Downtown. ☎ **305/381-9254.** Menu items $5.50–$9; lunch platters $4–$7. AE, MC, V. Mon–Sat 8:30am–7pm. JAMAICAN.

You would never spot this tiny storefront diner on a one-way street, although you might smell it from the sidewalk. The aroma of succulent jerk chicken or pork beckon regulars back over and over again.

Try Jamaican specialties like the oxtail stew or the curried goat, tender and tasty pieces of meat on the bone in a spicy yellow sauce. The kitchen can be stingy with its spectacular sauces, leaving the dishes a bit dry, so ask for an extra helping on the side. They are happy to oblige. Also, if you come early in the day, you can get a taste of Jamaica's national dish, salt fish and ackee (usually served for breakfast), outlawed in the United States. Ask chef and owner Carol Whyte to tell you the story of this interesting dish made with "brain fruit" or quiz one of the many Jamaicans who stop in while they are in port off the cruise ships a few blocks away.

The Crepe Maker. 200 S. Biscayne Blvd. (in front of First Union Bank), and Southeast Third Avenue and First Street (in front of Republic National Bank), Downtown. ☎ **305/274-2265** (for catering questions only). Crêpes $2–$6. No credit cards. CREPES.

Inspired by the wooden crêpe carts in Paris, Christopher Hoffman and his wife Maria decided Miamians would appreciate the cheap, healthful ease of fresh meats and vegetables quickly sautéed at sidewalk carts. They were right. The couple operates two carts where lawyers and students and tourists wait in line to watch the little pancakes turn golden brown on the edges in time for a cheerful chef in a flouncy white hat to throw a dash of olive oil and a handful of spinach leaves in the center.

Specials change daily but include classics like Cordon Bleu with ham and chicken and cheese and innovations like Havana chicken with sweet red peppers, black beans, and sweet pesto. You can also design whatever you like. Of course for dessert, there are fruit-and-jam-filled specialties. If you don't mind standing, The Crepe Maker carts prepare some of the freshest and most delicious fare available Downtown.

🅢 **Raja's.** 243 E. Flagler St. (in the Galeria International mall), Downtown. ☎ **305/539-9551.** Menu items $3–$6; specials, including salad, rice, and vegetable side dishes $5–$7. No credit cards. Thurs–Tues 9am–6:30pm, Sun 9am–4:30pm. SOUTH INDIAN/FAST FOOD.

Nearly impossible to find, this tiny counter in the hustling Downtown food court serves some of the feistiest chicken stews and vegetarian dishes in Miami. It's surrounded by mostly Brazilian fast-food places that are packed with tour groups on shopping sprees.

If you like it spicy, try the rich Masala Spicy Chili Chicken. For vegetarians, the heaping platters of dahl, cauliflower, eggplant, broccoli, and chickpeas are a valuable find in otherwise meat-laden Downtown. For those who know to request them, there are half a dozen tasty condiments, including lemon chutney with fresh orange rinds, bright green cilantro sauce, and glistening gold mango chutney that will compliment the rough stews and tasty soups. The Masala Dosa (rice crêpes stuffed with vegetable mash) is made fresh when ordered and is a filling lunch or dinner. Also, the side salad with fresh onions, cucumbers, and lettuce is free with the specials, but only if you ask for it. Try a mango lassi to finish it off and to cool your tongue if you sampled one of their signature hot dishes.

S & S Restaurant. 1757 NE Second Ave., Downtown. ☎ **305/373-4291.** Main courses $5–$11. No credit cards. Mon–Fri 6am–7pm, Sat 6am–2:30pm (later on Heat game nights). DINER.

This tiny chrome-and-linoleum-counter restaurant looks like a truck stop in some other town. But here in the middle of Downtown since 1938, only locals keep coming back. Expect a wait at lunch time while the mostly male clientele, from lawyers to linemen, wait patiently for old-fashioned fast food in large quantities.

A slice of pie and a slice of Miami history at the same time is what you'll find at S & S. Although the neighborhood around S & S has changed to a pretty undesirable one, its food—basic diner fare with some excellent stews and soups—hasn't changed in years. It's one of the only places in town I know that serves creamed chicken on toast. Also good when it's on the specials board is the stuffed cabbage roll in a pale brown sauce. In addition to super cheap breakfasts, the diner serves up some of the most comfortable comfort food in Miami.

7 Little Havana

The main artery of Little Havana is a busy commercial strip called Southwest 8th Street, or *Calle Ocho.* Auto body shops, cigar factories, and furniture stores line this street, and on every corner there seems to be a pass-through window serving super-strong Cuban coffee and snacks. In addition, many of the Cuban, Dominican, Nicaraguan, Peruvian, and Latin American immigrants have opened full-scale restaurants ranging from intimate candlelit establishments to bustling stand-up lunch counters.

EXPENSIVE

Victor's Cafe. 2340 SW 32nd Ave. (one block south of Coral Way), Little Havana. ☎ **305/445-1313.** Reservations recommended. Main courses $19–$29. AE, DC, DISC, MC, V. Mon–Thurs and Sun noon–midnight; Fri–Sat 3pm–1am. CUBAN.

From *Ceviche* to *Picadillo*: Spanish Cuisine at a Glance

In Little Havana and wondering what to eat? Many restaurants list menu items in English for the benefit of *norteamericano* diners. But in case you're wondering what to eat, here are translations and suggestions for filling and delicious meals.

Arroz con pollo   Roast chicken served with saffron-seasoned yellow rice and diced vegetables.

Café cubano   Very strong black coffee, served in thimble-size cups with lots of sugar. It's a real eye-opener.

Camarones   Shrimp.

Ceviche   Raw fish marinated in vinegar and citrus to "cook" it, seasoned with spice and vegetables.

Croquettas   Golden-fried sticks of ham, chicken, or fish.

Paella   A Spanish dish of chicken, sausage, seafood, and pork mixed with saffron rice and peas.

Palomilla   Thinly sliced beef, similar to American minute steak, usually served with onions, parsley, and a mountain of french fries.

Pan cubano   Long, white crusty Cuban bread. Ask for it *tostada*, toasted and flattened on a grill with lots of butter.

Picadillo   A rich stew of ground meat, brown gravy, peas, pimientos, raisins, and olives.

Platano   A deep-fried, soft, mildly sweet banana.

Pollo Asado   Roasted chicken with onions and a crispy skin.

Ropa vieja   A delicious shredded beef stew, whose name literally means "old clothes."

Sopa de Pollo   Chicken soup, usually with noodles or rice.

Tapas   A general name for Spanish-style hors d'oeuvres, served in grazing-size portions.

At Victor's, you'll get average food in an upscale setting—it's a place for tourists and celebrations. Strolling guitarists add an air of romance to this kitschy old Havana–style restaurant. In adjacent rooms the lively salsa music wafts through the regal dining room where attentive waiters look after most details. Stick around for the wild cabaret most nights after 11pm. Ask to sit on El Patio where oversized umbrellas shade you from the sun and create a private little cocoon overlooking the lush courtyard.

The cooking takes liberties with Cuban classics with generally good results. Some of the best dishes are the fish and shrimp plates, all of which are served with rice and beans. My favorite appetizer is the snapper ceviche marinated in Cachucha pepper and lime juice. The beef dishes also win favor among meat fans. The *bistec alo Victor con tamal en balsa* is a tender oak-grilled top sirloin served with Cuban-style polenta.

MODERATE

✪ **Casa Juancho.** 2436 SW 8th St., Little Havana. ☎ **305/642-2452.** Reservations recommended, but not accepted Fri–Sat after 8pm. Tapas $6–$8; main courses $11–$20; lunches $6–$12. AE, CB, DC, MC, V. Sun–Thurs noon–midnight, Fri–Sat noon–1am. SPANISH/CUBAN.

Perhaps one of Miami's finest Hispanic restaurants, Casa Juancho offers an ambitious menu of excellently prepared main dishes and tapas. The several dining rooms are decorated with traditional Spanish furnishings and enlivened nightly by strolling Spanish musicians. Try not to be frustrated with the older staff who don't speak English or respond quickly to your subtle glance. They are used to an aggressive clientele.

I suggest ordering lots of tapas, small dishes of Spanish "finger food." Some of the best include mixed seafood vinaigrette, fresh shrimp in hot garlic sauce, and fried calamari rings. A few entrees stand out, like roast suckling pig, baby eels in garlic and olive oil, and Iberian-style snapper.

Centro Vasco. 2235 SW 8th St., Little Havana. ☎ **305/634-9606.** Reservations recommended. Main courses $11–$22; lunch platters $6–$9. AE, DC, DISC, MC, V. Tues–Sun noon–midnight. CUBAN/SPANISH.

This ranch-style restaurant serves up traditional food to the suit-clad movers and shakers at lunch time and to a more festive evening crowd who come to enjoy the nightly entertainment. The rising star of Cuban music, Albita Rodriguez, got her start here.

One of the best lunch specials is the broiled dolphin with red pepper and potatoes. Or consider *Pollo Andaluza*, a quarter chicken baked with olives, tomatoes, and raisins over rice. For dinner, an even larger selection of meats and fishes are offered along with some hearty paellas with vegetables or fish.

The ease of dinner contrasts dramatically with the crazy atmosphere afterwards. If you are coming for dinner, definitely insist on a good table for the show. Considering the relatively high dinner prices, you deserve it. And if you wait to be escorted to the front by a helpful maître d', you'll find yourself halfway out the door of the packed music room. Push like you're a local, and you'll get respect and only a few harsh glances.

INEXPENSIVE

Hy-Vong. 3458 SW 8th St. (between 34th and 35th Aves.), Little Havana. ☎ **305/446-3674.** Reservations not accepted. Main courses $8–$12. No credit cards. Tues–Sun 6–11pm. Closed two weeks in Aug. VIETNAMESE.

Expect to wait for hours for a table, and don't even think of mumbling a complaint. The owner/chef/waitress will be sure to forget to stop by your small wooden table to refill your glasses or take an order if you do. So enjoy the wait with a traditional Vietnamese beer and lots of company. Outside this tiny storefront restaurant, you'll meet interesting students, musicians, and foodies who come for the large and delicious portions, not for the plain wood-paneled room or painfully slow service.

It's worth it. Vietnamese cuisine combines the best of Asian and French cooking with spectacular results. Food at Hy-Vong is elegantly simple and super spicy. Appetizers include small, tightly packed Vietnamese spring rolls, and *kimchee*, a spicy, fermented cabbage. Star entrees include pastry-enclosed chicken with watercress cream-cheese sauce and fish in tangy mango sauce.

La Carreta. 3632 SW 8th St., Little Havana. ☎ **305/446-4915.** Main courses $3–$9. DC, MC, V. Daily 24 hours. CUBAN.

This cavernous family-style restaurant is filled with relics of an old farm and college kids eating *media noches* (midnight sandwiches with ham, cheese, and pickles) after partying all night. Waitresses are brusque but efficient and will help anglos along who may not know all the lingo.

The menu is vast and very authentic. Try the *sopa de pollo*, a rich golden stock loaded with chunks of chicken and fresh vegetables or the *ropa vieja*, a shredded beef stew in a thick brown sauce.

Due to its immense popularity and low price, La Carreta has opened several branches throughout Miami. Check the white pages for locations.

⑤ Versailles. 3555 SW 8th St., Little Havana. ☎ **305/444-0240.** Soup and salad $2–$5; main courses $5–$8. DC, MC, V. Mon–Thurs 8am–2am, Fri 8am–3:30am, Sat 8am–4:30am, Sun 9am–2am. CUBAN.

Versailles is the meeting place of Miami's Cuban power brokers, who meet daily over café con leche to discuss the future of the exiles' fate. A glorified diner, the place sparkles with glass, chandeliers, murals, and mirrors meant to evoke the French palace. There's nothing fancy here—nothing French either—just straightforward food from the home country. The menu is a veritable survey of Cuban cooking and includes specialties like Moors and Christians (flavorful black beans with white rice), ropa vieja, and fried whole fish.

8 West Dade

As all of South Florida expands westward, good restaurants will follow as well. So far, however, only a few have distinguished themselves, and they are reviewed here.

EXPENSIVE

Shula's Steak House. 7601 NW 154th St. (Miami Lakes Golf Resort off the Palmetto Expy.), Miami Lakes. ☎ **305/820-8102.** Reservations recommended. Main courses $18–$58. AE, CB, DC, MC, V. In season Mon–Fri 7am–2:30pm and 6–11pm; Sat–Sun 7–11am and 6–11pm; call for hours off-season. STEAKHOUSE.

This is the place to get huge slabs of red meat cooked however you like. A limited à la carte menu lists their entrees by the weight.

You could start with the petite 12-ounce filet mignon that is so tender and juicy you could almost cut it with the back of a fork. Or if you are a linebacker or have that size appetite, consider the 48-ounce porterhouse. I haven't tried it myself, but am told it's one of the best. Potatoes and a few vegetables are available, but don't bring your vegetarian friends here. They'd go hungry.

Retired Miami Dolphin coach Don Shula is said to be spending more time around this shrine to his old Dolphins as he puts the final touches on his new location in downtown Miami's Hyatt Hotel, due to open in 1997. Another Shula's is in Tampa.

MODERATE

Tony Roma's. 6728 Main St. (at Ludlum Rd.), Miami Lakes. ☎ **305/558-7427.** Main courses $9–$14; sandwiches $6. AE, DC, DISC, V. Mon–Thurs 11am–11pm, Fri–Sat 11am–1am. BARBECUE.

Rib lovers rave over this Miami-based chain that now has more than a dozen locations in South Florida. In Miami Lakes the place is packed with regulars who order full slabs of slick and meaty pork with the usual side dishes like cole slaw and a crispy onion loaf. You can't beat the prices and the dark woody atmosphere makes you feel like you're in a much pricier place.

Other locations include: 15700 Biscayne Blvd., North Miami (☎ 305/949-2214); 18050 Collins Ave., Miami Beach (☎ 305/932-7907); and 2665 SW 37th Ave., Coral Gables (☎ 305/443-6626).

9 North Dade

Although there aren't many hotels in North Dade, the population in the winter months explodes due to the large number of seasonal residents who come down from the Northeast to enjoy the fair weather and calm of this suburban area on the mainland. A number of exclusive condominiums and country clubs, including William's Island, Turnberry, and The Jockey Club, breed a demanding clientele, many of whom dine out nightly. That's good news for visitors who can find superior service and cuisine at value prices.

VERY EXPENSIVE

❸ **Chef Allen's.** 19088 NE 29th Ave., North Miami Beach. ☎ **305/935-2900.** Reservations accepted. Main courses $20–$27. AE, MC, V. Sun–Thurs 6–10:30pm, Fri–Sat 6pm–midnight. NEW WORLD CUISINE.

For one of South Florida's finest dining experiences, Chef Allen's is a must. Owner/chef Allen Susser, of New York's Le Cirque fame, has built a classy yet relaxed restaurant with art deco furnishings, a glass-enclosed kitchen, and a hot-pink swirl of neon surrounding the dining room's ceiling.

The delicious homemade breadsticks are enough to hold you, but don't let them tempt you away from an appetizer that may include lobster-and-crab cakes served with strawberry-ginger chutneys or baked Brie with spinach, sun-dried tomatoes, and pine nuts. Served by an energetic young staff, favorite main dishes include crisp roast duck with cranberry sauce and mesquite-grilled Norwegian salmon with champagne grapes, green onions, and basil spaetzle. Local fish dishes, in various delectable guises, and homemade pastas are always on the menu.

The extensive wine list is well chosen and features several good buys. Handmade desserts are works of art and sinfully delicious. The restaurant is on the mainland at 190th Street, near the Dade County line.

EXPENSIVE

Mark's Place. 2286 NE 123rd St., North Miami. ☎ **305/893-6888.** Reservations recommended. Main courses $10–$15 for pasta and pizza, $16–$20 for meat and fish; lunch about half-price. AE, MC, V. Mon–Fri noon–2:30pm; Mon–Thurs 6–10:30pm, Fri–Sat 6–11pm, Sun 6–10pm. NEW WORLD CUISINE.

This restaurant attracts an upscale but leisurely crowd. Its claim to fame is owner/chef Mark Militello, an extraordinarily gifted artist who works primarily with fresh, natural, local ingredients. A smart, modern bistro, Mark's Place shines with off-white walls, an aquamarine ceiling, contemporary glass sculptures, and a friendly open kitchen.

Mark's food is extremely inspired, often unusual, and it rarely misses the mark. Appetizers include oak-grilled mozzarella and prosciutto, curry-breaded fried oysters, and a petite pizza topped with smoked chicken and Monterey jack cheese. The best main dishes are braised black grouper, Florida conch stew, and flank steak in sesame marinade. Try one of Mark's suggestions, plus the fresh home-baked bread. Desserts like Icky Sticky Coconut Pudding are equally unusual and baked with the same originality as the rest of the menu.

MODERATE

The Gourmet Diner. 13951 Biscayne Blvd. (between NE 139th and 140th Sts.), North Miami Beach. ☎ **305/947-2255.** Reservations not accepted. Main courses $10–$17. No credit cards. Mon–Fri 11am–11pm; Sat 8am–11:30pm; Sun 8am–10:30pm. BELGIAN/FRENCH.

👪 Family-Friendly Restaurants

Beverly Hills Cafe *(see p. 110)*   This restaurant offers a varied selection for children under 10 years old. Choices include the regular offerings of hamburgers, hot dogs, and grilled cheese sandwiches, as well as healthier options such as pasta marinara and a turkey sandwich. For just $3.50, the entrees include french fries, soda, apple juice, or milk.

Señor Frogs *(see p. 118)*   This Coconut Grove restaurant, with its lively atmosphere and universally appealing Mexican dishes, plus margaritas for the adults, is a good choice for the entire family. The service is generally efficient, and the food is reasonably priced. If you ask for half portions of some of the more popular dishes, like the quesadilla, the kitchen will happily oblige. High chairs and booster chairs are available.

Versailles Restaurant *(see page 106)*   This quirky, bustling Cuban diner is great for kids. Although there is no specific children's menu, the place is used to catering to patrons of all ages. You'll find *abuelitos* and *ninos*, little old grandparents and children, as well as high-powered politicians and teenage revelers. The prices are cheap, and there are plenty of choices for even the most finicky eater. Try *croquettas*, fried sticks of ham or chicken or fish, or Cuban sandwiches.

This retro 1950s-style diner serves plain old French fare without pretensions. The atmosphere is a bit brash and the lines are often out the door. You'll want to get there early anyway to taste some of the house specialties like beef Burgundy, the trout amandine, and frog legs Provençale—these dishes tend to sell out quickly.

Check the blackboard, which depending on where you are seated can be hard to see. The salads and soups are all prepared to order. Even a simple hearts of palm becomes a gourmet treat under the simple and tangy vinaigrette. A well-rounded wine list with reasonable prices makes this place a standout and a great deal. The homemade daily pastries are also delicious.

The Lagoon. 488 Sunny Isles Blvd. (163rd St.), North Miami Beach. ☎ **305/947-6661.** Reservations accepted. Main courses $12–$22; lobster special $19.95. AE, CB, MC, V. Daily 4:30–11pm; early-bird dinner 4:30–6pm. SEAFOOD/CONTINENTAL.

This old bayfront fish house has been around since 1936. Major road construction that makes The Lagoon nearly impossible to get to should have guaranteed its doom years ago, but the excellent view and incredible specials make it a worthwhile stop.

Yes it's true! Lobster lovers can get two 1¼ pounders for $19.95. Broiled is best with a light buttery seasoned coating. This dish is not only inexpensive but incredibly succulent, too. Side dishes include fresh vegetables like broccoli or asparagus as well as a huge baked potato, stuffed or plain. The salads are good but come with too much commercial-tasting dressing. I've tried a few and all are disappointing. To be safe, ask for oil and vinegar on the side. Actually, I recommend skipping all the accoutrements to save room for the lobster.

The bathrooms could use a good cleaning, as could the whole cavernous restaurant. Disregard that and the nonchalant service and you'll find the best-priced juicy Maine lobsters around.

The Melting Pot. 3143 NE 163rd St. (in Sunny Isles Plaza shopping center), North Miami Beach. ☎ **305/947-2228.** Reservations recommended on weekends. Main courses $9–$10 for cheese fondue, $11–$16 for meat and fish fondues. AE, MC, V. Sun–Thurs 5:30–11pm, Fri–Sat 5:30pm–midnight. FONDUE.

Dipping your own chunks of bread into pots of sizzling cheese is certainly a different dining experience. Traditional fondue is supplemented by combination meat-and-fish dinners, which are served with one of almost a dozen different sauces. Dates seem to love it here. The place, with its lace curtains and cozy booths, was voted most romantic restaurant in the local alternative paper several years ago.

As more diners become health conscious, the owners have introduced a more healthful version of fondue in which you cook vegetables and meats in a low-fat broth. It tastes good, though this version is less fun than watching drippy cheese flow from the hot pot. But best, perhaps, is dessert: chunks of pineapple, bananas, apples, and cherries you dip into a creamy chocolate fondue. No liquor is served here, but the wine list is extensive, and beer is available.

The restaurant is located on the north side of 163rd Street, between U.S. 1 and Collins Avenue. A second Melting Pot is located at 9835 SW 72nd St. (Sunset Drive) in Kendall (☎ 305/279-8816).

New Delhi Restaurant. 11730 Biscayne Blvd., North Dade. ☎ **305/899-0557.** Reservations accepted. Main courses $8–$16. AE, DC, MC, V. Daily 11:30am–2:30pm and 5:30–11pm. INDIAN.

The owner came from Washington, D.C. in 1995 to take over the former Akash of London. Though there are a handful of loyal followers who enjoy this fine Indian cuisine, the place just never seems to get full. Truth is Miami is not a town that attracts many Indians, and locals, especially those who live north of the more cosmopolitan Downtown and South Beach areas, seem to hanker only for pasta or corned beef.

The service is attentive with the owner himself waiting tables some evenings. If you like it hot, you'll have to beg them to spice up their dishes since the chef has adapted somewhat to American palettes by toning it down. Still, I can't figure why it's usually only got a table or two of nationals eating with relish (and a superb mango and cilantro chutney, too). With these prices and the tasty Southern and Northern Indian food here, like the spicy chicken masala or the snapper patia in a creamy mustard sauce, the place would be packed if it were in New York.

INEXPENSIVE

Beverly Hills Cafe. 17850 West Dixie Hwy, North Miami Beach. ☎ **305/935-3660.** Salads and sandwiches $5–$7; main courses $8–$13. AE, DISC, MC, V. Mon–Thurs 11:30am–9:30pm; Fri–Sat 11:30am–10pm. AMERICAN.

It isn't pink, and it isn't in Los Angeles, but this pleasant little spot in a cobble-pathed mini-mall is a perfect choice for an affordable business lunch or family dinner. The menu is varied with choices of Mexican dishes like quesadillas and fajitas or good old classics like Caesar salads or Philly cheese steak sandwiches. Some more healthful options include a fragrant stir-fried chicken on saffron-flavored rice, or a blackened dolphin sandwich. While none of the dishes are overly ambitious, the presentation and large portions make this a popular place for the predominantly budget-conscious diners in the neighborhood. The pastas, including a particularly good Southwestern chicken penne dish with grilled pepper and onions, is a spicy and recommendable choice for those who enjoy a little heat. Be warned that you can fill up on the toasty warm bread before one of the well-meaning but overworked waitresses arrives to take your order. You'll have to hold off to save room for the renowned tollhouse pie, a hot-fudge-sundae slab of ice cream atop a chocolate chip cookie dough crust. A limited but affordable selection of wines and beers is available.

A special children's menu is available for kids younger than 10 years old. For $3.50, kids can order a hamburger, hot dog, grilled cheese sandwich, pasta marinara, or a turkey sandwich, and get french fries and their choice of soda, apple juice, or milk.

Another Beverly Hills Cafe is located at 1559 Sunset Dr., Coral Gables (☎ 305/666-6618.

Here Comes the Sun. 2188 NE 123rd St. (west of the Broad Causeway), North Miami. ☎ **305/893-5711.** Reservations recommended in season. Main courses $10–$14; early-bird special $7.95; sandwiches and salads $5–$7.50. AE, DC, DISC, MC, V. Mon–Sat 11am–8:30pm. AMERICAN/HEALTH FOOD.

One of Miami's early health-food spots, this bustling grocery-store-turned-diner serves hundreds of plates a night, mostly to blue-haired locals. It's noisy and hectic but worth it. In season, all types pack the place for a $7.95 special, served between 4 and 6:30pm, which includes one of more than 20 choices of entrees, soup or salad, coffee or tea, and a small frozen yogurt. Fresh grilled fish and chicken entrees are reliable and served with a nice array of vegetables. The miso burgers with "sun sauce" are a vegetarian's dream.

Irie Isle. 168 NE 167th St. (between 1st and N. Miami Aves.), North Miami Beach. ☎ **305/354-7678.** Main courses $6–$8; lunch $3–$6. No credit cards. Mon–Thurs 10am–9pm; Fri–Sat 10am–10pm; Sun noon–8pm. JAMAICAN/FAST FOOD.

The area just off Route 826 in North Miami Beach has become something of a little Kingston, with dozens of Jamaican grocery stores, record shops, and restaurants sprouting up along the main drag, 167th Street. One of the best is a pleasant little counter called Irie Isle, where the curry is rich and spicy and the jerk is just like you get it at a beachside cookshack in Jamaica.

Unfortunately they don't make roti, though you'll find plenty here to satisfy any Caribbean cravings you might have. Every Sunday, the place serves up my favorite dish, ackee and salt fish; it's the national dish of Jamaica and is worth a taste. The ackee is a butter yellow fruit about the size of a tangerine. It grows almost exclusively in the island but is starting to be harvested here, against the wishes of the FDA who outlawed the fruit some years ago because of its toxicity when improperly prepared. When sautéed with onions, tomatoes, and salt cod, it is a heavenly and comforting food for breakfast, lunch, or whenever you can get it.

The Juice Bar. 18315 W. Dixie Hwy. (one block west of Biscayne Blvd.), North Miami Beach. ☎ **305/935-9544.** Sandwiches and salads $4–$6. No credit cards. Daily 8:30am–6pm. HEALTH FOOD.

This brightly painted stand in the middle of a busy road attracts a varied crowd from young pony-tailed Europeans to bikers who stop in for a fresh smoothie or vegetable juice made on the spot. If you don't mind a bit of car exhaust with your snapper sandwich, consider this landmark in North Dade.

The food is made on the premises and includes one of the most unusual tuna salads I've ever run across. There is no trace of fishiness and the smooth paste is served in a pita with tons of crisp vegetables, including alfalfa sprouts, tomato, and lettuce. The hummus is superb, though garlic lovers might want a hint more spark.

Laurenzo's Cafe. 16385 West Dixie Hwy. (at corner of 163rd St.), North Miami Beach. ☎ **305/945-6381.** Main courses $4–$5; salads $2–$5. AE, MC, V. Mon–Sat 8am–7pm, Sun 8am–4pm. SOUTHERN ITALIAN CAFETERIA.

This little lunch counter in the middle of a chaotic grocery store has been serving delicious buffet lunches to the *paesanos* for years. A meeting place for the minuscule Italian population in Miami, the store has been open for more than 40 years. Daily specials usually include a lasagna or eggplant parmigiana and two or three salad options.

Choose a wine from the vast selection and take your meal to go or sit in the trellis-covered seating area amidst busy shoppers buying their evening's groceries. You'll get to eavesdrop on some great conversations over your plastic tray of real southern-style Italian cooking.

Laurenzo's cotillion offers a good Italian fixed-price dinner with slightly more atmosphere and service. It's just down the street at 2255 NE 164th St. (☎ 305/948-8008).

10   Coral Gables & Environs

VERY EXPENSIVE

Christy's. 3101 Ponce de Leon Blvd., Coral Gables. ☎ **305/446-1400.** Reservations required. Main courses $17–$30; lunch $12–$20. AE, CB, DC, MC, V. Mon–Fri 11:30am–4pm; Mon–Thurs 4–11pm, Fri 4–11:45pm, Sat 5–11:45pm, Sun 5–11pm. AMERICAN.

Arrive famished. It's easy to be fooled into thinking you're going to be served peacock-size portions by Christy's demure Victorian style. One of the Gables' most expensive and elegant establishments, this New American eatery is known primarily for its generous cuts of thick, juicy steaks and ribs. Some say it's one of the most romantic spots in Miami. I say it's just okay.

The prime rib is so thick even a small cut weighs about a pound. New York strip, filet mignon, and chateaubriand are all on the menu here, and all steaks are fully aged without chemicals or freezing. Each entree is served with a jumbo Caesar salad and a baked potato. Seafood, veal, and chicken dishes also are available. Yet ordering anything but a steak at this pricey little candlelit spot would be a disappointment.

Norman's. 21 Almera Ave. (between Douglas and Ponce de Leon), Coral Gables. ☎ **305/446-7909.** Reservations highly recommended. Main courses $25–$32. Mon–Thurs noon–2pm and 6–10:30pm; Fri noon–2pm and 6–11pm; Sat 6–11pm. AE, DC, MC, V. NEW WORLD CUISINE.

Master chef and one of the originators of what has become known as New World Cuisine, Norman Van Aken re-emerged after a two-year break from restauranting to open what he has called his "culmination." The result is an open kitchen where a handful of silent and industrious chefs prepare Asian- and Caribbean-inspired dishes surrounded by well-dressed diners. The atmosphere is comfortable and subdued with hand-painted walls and an upstairs gallery looking down on the marble first floor.

Eating here is an experience where the food is the main focus of attention. It's difficult to not let the exotic-sounding list of ingredients on the menu be the topic of conversation. Some think it's pretentious or overwrought. I think there's plenty to enjoy like pizzas and pastas with a good glass of wine and a hunk of bread. Despite the run-on descriptions, the fish, too, is out of this world. "The Rhum and pepper painted grouper on mango-Habanero Mojo . . . " is an exotic-tasting dark-fleshed fish with an explosion of sauces to complement its heavy flavor.

The staff is adoring and professional and the atmosphere tasteful without being too formal. The portions are realistic, but still be careful not to overdo it. You'll want to try some of the wacky desserts like mango ice cream served with Asian pears and crushed red pepper (the pepper really just adds color to the plate). Like the restaurant, it's hot but very approachable.

Dining in Coral Gables, Coconut Grove & Downtown

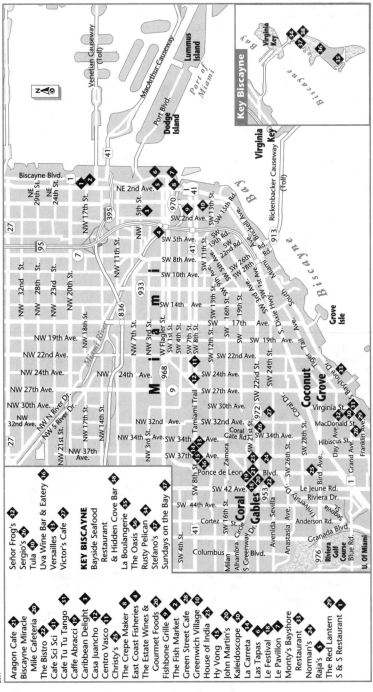

EXPENSIVE

Aragon Café. 180 Aragon Ave., (in the Omni-Colonnade Hotel), Coral Gables. ☎ **305/ 448-2600.** Reservations recommended. Jackets required. Main courses $15–$22. AE, DC, MC, V. Tues–Sat 6–11pm. NEW WORLD CUISINE.

Like the hotel in which it's located, the hand-crafted mahogany-and-marble Aragon Café exudes a quiet elegance with an international flair. The 85-seat restaurant features period furniture and a formal atmosphere.

Appetizers include blue-crab cakes with fried shredded leeks and radicchio-wrapped lobster. Seafood is the house specialty, and salmon is the fish of choice; several preparations each claim individual flavors. Other main choices include Muscovy duck with duck sausage and various veal selections. For dessert, the lemon torte with raspberry sauce takes the cake.

The Bistro. 2611 Ponce de Leon Blvd., Coral Gables. ☎ **305/442-9671.** Reservations recommended. Main courses $16–$26; lunch $4–$14. AE, CB, DC, MC, V. Mon–Fri 11:30am– 2pm; Mon–Thurs 6–10:30pm, Fri–Sat 6–11pm. FRENCH.

The Bistro's intimate atmosphere is heightened by soft lighting, 19th-century European antiques and prints, and an abundance of flowers atop crisp white tablecloths.

Co-owners Ulrich Sigrist and André Barnier keep a watchful eye over their experienced kitchen staff, which regularly dishes out artful French dishes with an international accent. Look for the *terrine maison*, a country-style veal-and-pork appetizer that is the house specialty. Common French-bistro fare like *escargots au Pernod* and *coquilles St-Jacques* are prepared with uncommon spices and accoutrements, livening a rather typical continental menu. Especially recommended are the roasted duck with honey-mustard sauce and the chicken breasts in mild curry sauce, each served with fried bananas and pineapple.

✪ **Caffe Abracci.** 318 Aragon Ave. (between LeJeune Rd. and Miracle Mile), Coral Gables. ☎ **305/441-0700.** Reservations recommended for dinner. Main courses $16–$24; pasta $14–$20; lunch $10–$16. AE, DC, MC, V. Mon–Fri 11:30am–2:30pm; Sun–Thurs 6–11pm, Fri–Sat 6pm–midnight. ITALIAN.

You'll be greeted with a hug by the owner and maître d' Nino, who oversees this remarkable spot as only an Italian could. The food is remarkable, yet the spot is not known to many outside of the Gables. Still, it's packed on weekends by those in the know. You are guaranteed perfect service in a pretty wood and marble setting, with the only drawback being the unfortunately loud dining room.

It's hard to get beyond the appetizers here, which are all so good that you could order a few and be satisfied. My favorite is the shrimp with a bright pesto sauce that has just enough garlic to give it a kick, but not so much you won't get a kiss later. The risottos are excellent and served in half portions so that you'll have room for the indescribable fish dishes. A snapper entree comes in a light olive oil and wine sauce dotted with fresh marjoram and tomatoes. The grilled tuna and the swordfish are also flawless.

Le Festival. 2120 Salzedo St., Coral Gables. ☎ **305/442-8545.** Reservations required for dinner. Main courses $16–$20; lunch about half-price. AE, CB, DC, MC, V. Mon–Fri 11:45am– 2:30pm; Mon–Thurs 6–10:30pm, Fri–Sat 6–11pm. FRENCH.

Le Festival's contemporary, sharp pink awning hangs over one of Miami's most traditional Spanish-style buildings, hinting at the unusual combination of cuisine and decor that awaits inside. In fact, the modern dining rooms, enlivened with New French features and furnishings, belie the traditional highlights of a well-planned menu.

Shrimp and crab cocktails, fresh pâtés, and an unusual cheese soufflé are star start-ers. Both meat and fish are either simply seared with herbs and spices or doused in wine and cream sauces. Dessert can be a delight if you plan ahead: Grand Marnier and chocolate soufflés are individually prepared and must be ordered at the same time as the entrees. There's also a wide selection of other homemade sweets.

Le Festival is located five blocks north of Miracle Mile, in an area slightly removed from other Coral Gables restaurants.

MODERATE

John Martin's. 253 Miracle Mile, Coral Gables. ☎ **305/445-3777.** Reservations recom-mended on weekends. Main courses $12–$20; sandwiches and salads $4–$8. Lunch $7–$10. AE, DC, DISC, MC, V. Mon–Thurs 11:30am–midnight; Fri–Sat 11:30am–1am. IRISH PUB.

This Irish pub serves food that's a step above your average pub fare. The basic menu is loaded with fried bar snacks as well as some big Irish specialties like bangers and mash and shepherd's pie. Some decent salads include a blackened chicken Caesar salad with nice pieces of white meat doused in a spicy seasoning.

Of course to wash it down, you'll want to try one of the ales on tap or one of the more than 20 single-malt scotches. The crowd is upscale and chatty as is the young waitstaff. Check out happy hour on weeknights, plus the Sunday brunch with loads of hand-carved meats and seafood.

Uva Wine Bar & Eatery. 3850 SW 8th St., Coral Gables. ☎ **305/529-2264.** Reservations recommended for weekend dinners. Main courses $11–$19; lunch $7–$12. AE, DC, MC, V. Mon–Fri 11am–3pm and 5–11pm; Sat–Sun 5–11pm. CUBAN/ITALIAN.

The pairing of Cuban and Italian flavors result in outrageously delicious specialties at this dark and cozy restaurant way down Calle Ocho. Although the salads are uninspired, other starters like the ceviche modo nostrum and the crostini with mush-rooms and mozzarella are quite good.

The truth is I come here only for the incredibly buttery seafood risotto that is so good, I've been known to get an order to go and eat it in the car. Beyond that, I know they've got a decent selection of wines and a pleasant staff who speak some English. It doesn't matter much since the place is mostly populated with well-dressed Latinos who come for the live music and woodsy bar scene. By the way, there's also a rather elegant little cigar room upstairs.

INEXPENSIVE

Biscayne Miracle Mile Cafeteria. 147 Miracle Mile, Coral Gables. ☎ **305/444-9005.** Main courses $3–$4. Cash only. Mon–Sat 11am–2:15pm and 4–8pm; Sun 11am–8pm. SOUTHERN AMERICAN.

Here you'll find no bar, no music, and no flowers on the tables—just great southern-style cooking at unbelievably low prices. The menu changes, but roast beef, baked fish, and barbecue ribs are typical entrees, few of which exceed $4.

Food is picked up cafeteria-style and brought to one of the many unadorned Formica tables. The restaurant is always busy. The kitschy 1950s decor is an asset in this last of the old-fashioned cafeterias, where the gold-clad waiters are proud and attentive. Enjoy it while it lasts.

The Estate Wines & Gourmet Foods. 92 Miracle Mile, Coral Gables. ☎ **305/442-9915.** Main courses $6–$8. Cash only. Mon–Fri 10am–8pm, Sat 10am–6pm. EUROPEAN/AMERICAN.

This storefront, in the heart of Coral Gables' main shopping strip, is primarily a wine shop. But one of the friendliest storekeepers in Miami also serves gourmet meals to a handful of lucky diners. Deliciously thick soups are served with pâtés, salads, and sandwiches around an overturned barrel that can accommodate only about a dozen diners. They have no food license though the city winks their eyes at the technicality. The only advertisement is word of mouth, and knowledgeable locals are dedicated regulars.

House of India. 22 Merrick Way, Coral Gables (near Douglas and Coral Way). ☎ **305/ 444-2348.** Reservations accepted. Main courses $7–$10; lunch buffet, served weekdays 11:30am–3pm and Sat noon–3pm, $6.95. AE, MC, V. Mon–Thurs 11:30am–10pm, Fri–Sat 11:30am–11pm, Sun 5–10pm. INDIAN.

House of India's curries, kormas, and kebabs are very good, but the restaurant's well-priced all-you-can-eat lunch buffet is unsurpassed. All the favorites are on display, including tandoori chicken, naan bread, various meat and vegetarian curries, as well as rice and dal (lentils).

The restaurant is not fancy (in fact, I've heard it described as a greasy spoon), but it is nicely decorated, with hanging batik prints. The place could use a good scrub down. It's located one block north of Miracle Mile.

Sergio's. 3252 Coral Way, Coral Gables. ☎ **305/529-0047.** Reservations not accepted. Main courses $5–$7; lunch $2–$5. AE, DC, MC, V. Sun–Thurs 6am–midnight, Fri–Sat 24 hours. CUBAN/AMERICAN.

Located across from Coral Gables' Miracle Center Mall, Sergio's stands out like a Latin-inspired International House of Pancakes, with red-clothed tables, neon signs in the windows, and video games along the back wall.

Serving everything from ham-and-eggs breakfasts to grilled steak–sandwich lunches and dinners, the family-style restaurant specializes in native Cuban-style dishes, as well as grilled chicken, fajitas, and a variety of sandwiches. Low prices and late-night dining keep it popular with locals.

11 Coconut Grove

Coconut Grove was long known as the artists' haven of Miami. But the rush of developers trying to cash in on the laid-back charm of this old settlement has turned it into something of an overgrown mall. A few old haunts that retain the flavor of the hippy days still remain, and a few good newcomers are worth a visit. Saturday nights are a scene with young and wealthy Latin kids cruising down Main Highway in convertibles with the loud music. The area's popular streets are shrinking as muggings and car break-ins cause more and more people to stay within the relatively safe confines of the Cocowalk and Mayfair areas.

EXPENSIVE

Cafe Sci Sci. 3043 Grand Ave., Coconut Grove. ☎ **305/446-5104.** Reservations accepted. Main courses $12–$17 for pasta, $16–$23 for meat and fish; lunch about half-price. AE, MC, V. Tues–Sun noon–3pm; Sun–Thurs 3pm–12:30am, Fri–Sat 3pm–1am. ITALIAN.

The original Sci Sci cafe (pronounced "shi shi") was a turn-of-the-century Naples eatery and a meeting place for international artists and intellectuals. That restaurant also claims it was the site where gelato—the silky-smooth Italian ice cream—was perfected. Like its namesake, Cafe Sci Sci in the Grove is also an inviting place to linger, one of Miami's European-style cafes. It's a pleasing combination of old and new, both visually and gastronomically.

The large menu offers both hot and cold antipasti, including carpaccio, sautéed mussels, ham and melon, and fried mozzarella with marinara sauce. Pasta entrees feature homemade black fettuccine with vodka, tomato, cream, and black pepper; tortellini filled with smoked cheese in Gorgonzola sauce; and Papardella

Rustiche—wide noodles with shrimp, saffron, peas, and cream. Meat, fish, and chicken dishes also combine traditional and contemporary styles.

The pace here is relaxed, as every order is freshly prepared. The restaurant is at the Groves' primary intersection, at the top of Main Highway.

S Kaleidoscope. 3112 Commodore Plaza, Coconut Grove. ☎ **305/446-5010.** Reservations recommended. Main courses $12–$15 for pasta, $14–$20 for meat and fish; lunch about half-price. AE, CB, DC, DISC, MC, V. Mon–Fri 11:30am–3pm; Mon–Sat 6–11pm, Sun 5:30–10:30pm. NOUVELLE AMERICAN.

I'd recommend Kaleidoscope, in the heart of Coconut Grove, even if it was located somewhere less exciting. The atmosphere is relaxed, with low-key, attentive service, comfortable seating, and a terrace overlooking the busy sidewalks below. Dishes are well prepared, and pastas, topped with sauces like seafood and fresh basil or pesto with grilled yellowfin tuna, are especially tasty. The linguini with salmon and fresh dill is prepared to perfection.

Although there is no special pre-theater dinner, many locals stop into this reliable and reasonable second-floor spot for an elegant dinner before a show down the street at The Coconut Grove Playhouse.

MODERATE

Green Street Cafe. 3110 Commodore Plaza, Coconut Grove. ☎ **305/567-0662.** Reservations not accepted. Main courses $6–$12; breakfast $3–$6. AE, MC, V. Sun–Thurs 6:45am–11:30pm, Fri–Sat 6:45am–1am. CONTINENTAL.

Green Street is located at the "100% corner," the Coconut Grove intersection of Main Highway and Commodore Plaza that 100% of all tourists visit. This enviable location—loaded with outdoor seating that's great for people-watching—relieves the pressure on Green Street to turn out great meals, but the food is well above average. Continental-style breakfasts include fresh croissants and rolls, cinnamon toast, and cereal. Heartier American-style offerings include eggs and omelets, pancakes, waffles, and French toast. Soup, salad, and sandwich lunches mean overstuffed chicken, turkey, and tuna-based meals. Dinners are more elaborate, with several decent pasta entrees as well as fresh fish, chicken, and burgers, including one made of lamb.

Monty's Bayshore Restaurant. 2560 S. Bayshore Dr., Coconut Grove. ☎ **305/858-1431.** Reservations recommended upstairs on weekends. Main courses $19–$35; sandwiches $6–$8; platters $7–$12. AE, CB, DC, MC, V. Daily 11am–3am. SEAFOOD.

This place comes in three parts: a lounge, a raw bar, and a restaurant. Among them, Monty's serves everything from steak and seafood to munchies like nachos, potato skins, and Buffalo chicken wings. This is a fun kind of place, usually with more revelers and drinkers than diners. At the outdoor, dockside bar, there is live music nightly, as well as all day on weekends. Upstairs, an upscale dining room serves one of the city's best Caesar salads and respectable stone-crab claws in season. Be sure, however, not to order the claws from May until October since they will serve you some imported version that simply doesn't compare. In season, however, splurge on the all-you can-eat jumbo claws for $36.95—about the same price as a plateful at Joe's Stone Crab Restaurant in South Beach.

The Red Lantern. 3176 Commodore Plaza (Grand Ave.), Coconut Grove. ☎ **305/529-9998.** Main courses $9–$20. AE, MC, V. Mon–Thurs 11:30am–11pm; Fri 11:30am–midnight; Sat 2:30pm–midnight; Sun 2:30–11pm. CANTONESE.

Finally, here's a pleasant Chinese place that breaks the mold of cheap and uninteresting ones around town. Specialties include shark's fin with chicken and steamed whole snapper with black-bean sauce. Plus an assortment of vegetarian dishes and some excellent soups keep lots of locals happy. My favorite is the clay-pot stew of chicken in a ginger broth. Although the atmosphere is nothing to speak of, the varied menu and interesting preparation make a meal here worthwhile.

Señor Frogs. 3008 Grand Ave., Coconut Grove. ☎ **305/448-0999.** Reservations recommended on weekends. Main courses $9–$12. AE, CB, DC, MC, V. Mon–Sat 11:30am–2am, Sun 11:30am–1am. MEXICAN.

You know you're getting close to Señor Frog's when you hear laughing and singing spilling out of the restaurant's courtyard. Filled with a college-student crowd, this restaurant is known for a raucous good time, its mariachi band, and its powerful margaritas. The food at this rocking cantina is as good as its atmosphere, featuring excellent renditions of traditional Mexican/American favorites. The mole enchiladas, with 14 different kinds of mild chilies mixed with chocolate, is as flavorful as any I've tasted. Almost everything is served with rice and beans in quantities so large that few diners are able to finish.

Tula. 2957 Florida Ave. (across the street from the Mayfair Hotel), Coconut Grove. ☎ **305/441-1818.** Main courses $13–$19. AE, DC, MC, V. Daily 6pm–midnight. ITALIAN.

From thick-crust pizzas baked in a brick oven to perfect rosemary lamb chops, Tula is a great find in the Grove. It caters to a more sophisticated crowd than you'll find elsewhere in town with an attentive wait staff and homemade pastas and soups that are as close to perfect as you'll find. There's nothing glitzy here—just good food that's a bit pricey but worth it. Ask for wine specials; they're not advertised but often available in small quantities. For months they had a superb Italian Barollo for less than $20 that was perfect with the mushroom risotto.

INEXPENSIVE

Cafe Tu Tu Tango. 3015 Grand Ave., (on the second floor of Cocowalk), Coconut Grove. ☎ **305/529-2222.** Reservations not accepted. Main courses $4–$8. AE, MC, V. Sun–Wed 11:30am–midnight, Thurs 11:30am–1am, Fri–Sat 11:30am–2am. SPANISH/INTERNATIONAL.

In the bustling microcosm of CocoWalk, this second-floor restaurant is designed to look something like a disheveled artist's loft. Dozens of original paintings—some only half-finished—hang on the walls and studio easels. Seating at sturdy wooden tables and chairs is either inside, on wooden floors among the clutter, or outdoors, overlooking the Grove's main drag.

Flamenco and other Latin-inspired tunes complement a menu with a decidedly Spanish flare. Hummus spread on rosemary flat bread and baked goat cheese in marinara sauce are two recommendable starters. Entrees include roast duck with dried cranberries, toasted pinenuts, and goat cheese, plus Cajun chicken eggrolls filled with corn, Cheddar cheese, and tomato salsa. Pastas, ribs, fish, and pizzas round out the eclectic offerings, and several visits have proved each consistently good. Try the sweet and potent sangria and enjoy the warm and lively atmosphere from a seat with a view. Especially when the rest of the Grove has shut down, Tu Tu Tango is an oasis.

12 South Miami

This mostly residential area has some very good dining spots scattered mostly along U.S. 1. Since Hurricane Andrew, most have rebuilt and are better than ever.

MODERATE

Anacapri. 12669 S. Dixie Hwy. (in the South Park Center at 128th St. and U.S. 1), South Miami. ☎ **305/232-8001.** Main courses $8–$16. AE, DC, DISC, MC, V. Sun–Mon and Wed–Thurs 5–10:30pm, Fri–Sat 5–11:30pm. ITALIAN.

Neighborhood fans wait in line happily with a glass of wine and pleasant company for this somewhat heavy but flavorful Italian cuisine. Prices are reasonable and everyone is treated like a member of the family. If you are in the area, check it out.

An antipasto with thinly cut meats and cheeses and some good green peppers is a great start to a hearty meal. Stick with the basics here, like pastas with red sauce, which are flavorful although a bit heavy on the garlic and oil.

Cafe Hammock. 500 SW 177th Ave. (in the Miccosukee Indian Gaming site on Krome Ave. and Tamiami Trail). ☎ **305/222-4600.** Reservations accepted. Main courses $10–$22; dinner specials $5–$6. MC, V. Daily 11am–1am. CONTINENTAL.

In the clanging environs of the Native American gaming village way down south, you can dine on stone-crab claws and decent steak for a few bucks while overlooking hundreds of fanatical bingo players. If you can keep away from the dealers and slots and don't mind a bit of smoke, you'll be amazed at the excellent service and phenomenal specials they run to entice gamblers to this bizarre outpost. But don't expect Native Americans in native dress; you'll find servers from New Jersey and California before you see a Miccosukee serving burgers here.

Call in advance to see if there are any worthwhile specials. Otherwise, the regular menu with intriguing sounding offerings like Cajun-style cod nuggets and Bahamian conch fritters are disappointing. Some entrees like frog legs and grilled portobello mushrooms are delicious, but no bargain. The alligator, too, is tasty, though a bit dry. (See the Everglades National Park map in Chapter 11.)

INEXPENSIVE

$ **Shorty's.** 9200 S. Dixie Hwy. (between U.S. 1 and Dadeland Blvd.), South Miami. ☎ **305/670-7732.** Main courses $5–$9. MC, V. Daily 11am–11pm. BARBECUE.

A Miami tradition since 1951, this hokey log cabin is still serving some of the best ribs and chicken in South Florida. People line up for the smoke-flavored slow-cooked meat that is so tender it seems to jump off the bone into your mouth.

The secret, however, is to ask for your order with sweet sauce. The regular stuff tastes bland and bottled. All the side dishes, including cole slaw, corn on the cob, and baked beans look commercial but are necessary to complete the experience. This is B-B-Q, with a neon B.

A second Shorty's is located in Davie at 5989 S. University Dr. (☎ 305/944-0348).

The Tea Room. 12310 SW 224th St. (at Cauley Square), South Miami. ☎ **305/258-0044.** Sandwiches and salads $6–$7; soups $3–$4. AE, MC, V. Mon–Sat 11am–4pm. ENGLISH TEA.

Do stop in for a spot of tea at this recently rebuilt tea room in historic Cauley Square off of U.S. 1. The little lace-curtained room is an unusual site in this heavily industrial area better known for its warehouses than its doilies.

Sample some simple sandwiches like the turkey club with potato salad and a small lettuce garnish or an onion soup that is full of rich brown broth and stringy cheese. Daily specials, like spinach-and-mushroom quiche, and delectable desserts are a must before beginning your explorations of the old antique and art shops in this little enclave of civility down south.

Pollo Tropical. 18710 S. Dixie Hwy. (at 186th St.), South Miami. ☎ **305/225-7858.** Main courses $3–$6. No credit cards. Sun–Thurs 11am–10pm, Fri–Sat 11am–11pm. CUBAN/FAST FOOD.

This Miami-based chain is putting up new terra cotta–arched fast-food places so fast you can hardly finish an order of garlic-drenched yucca before another one has taken root.

This is lucky for Miamians and the Southeast, where dozens of these restaurants provide hot and tender chicken with a variety of healthful side dishes, like fresh chunks of carrots, onions, zucchini, and squash on wooden skewers and a variety of salads.

The chicken is marinated in a seriously secret sauce and served with well-seasoned black beans and rice. The menu, though Latin inspired, is clearly spelled out in English. Pollo Tropical is a good place to get an education in Latin *sabor* or taste.

Other locations include 1454 Alton Rd., Miami Beach (☎ 305/672-8888); and 11806 Biscayne Blvd., North Miami (☎ 305/895-0274). Check the phone book for others.

What to See & Do 7

Unlike the theme-park landscape of central Florida, Miami is a real working city that just happens to call tourism its number-one industry. Many pale-faced locals who work daily jobs in fields not related to tourism find the idea of visitors flocking here somewhat aggravating. A popular bumper sticker reads: "Some of us are *not* on vacation."

It's not that visitors are treated with disdain, but rather that Miami is so geared toward its normal operation that many folks just don't notice quite how bustling tourism can be around the city. Since so many tourist attractions double as local entertainment, you'll find yourself among residents taking their children to parks and the many fun places to go around town.

The truth is the best things to do in Miami are not the man-made attractions, but the treasures that nature put here, like the Everglades National Park or the sea and sand, and the places that locals built for their own enjoyment, like Villa Vizcaya or Coral Castle. Of course much of the city was, and is still, built to court dollar-generating visitors from around the world, and many of these efforts make for fantastic entertainment. Some of the city's older attractions, such as Monkey Jungle, Parrot Jungle, and the Seaquarium, attract visitors as well as a steady stream of locals.

Add to all the resources here a new wave of world-class exhibitions, like the Wolfsonian and the plethora of sports- and water-related activities. You'll find yourself frustrated with not enough vacation to do it all. But, figuring on your limited schedule, check out the suggested itineraries for a good guide on how to spend your time.

SUGGESTED ITINERARIES

If You Have 1 Day

If you arrive early, take the morning to explore Key Biscayne and Virginia Key, where you'll find a beautiful beach-necklaced island with a fantastic state park at its tip. Take a swim off the sandy tip of Bill Baggs State Park or tour the area on foot, looking at the lush native landscape, birds, and wildlife. Have a bite at the snack shop, El Farito, as you gear up to make the short trip—really just an exaggerated U-turn—to South Beach. Make your way to the Art

Deco District, and tour the area's whimsical architecture along Ocean Drive. Park at Lincoln Road to walk the strip, and choose any of the excellent restaurants to have a late-afternoon snack or dinner.

If You Have 2 Days

You can spend a little more time on Key Biscayne on your first day (as just described above). You can also include a trip to the Miami Seaquarium, especially if you have children along; kids love the killer whales and performing dolphins. Tour South Beach in the evening when the lively cafe scene and nightlife will keep you up late. On your second day, drive down to Greater Miami South to visit one or more of the attractions described in this chapter, such as Parrot Jungle, Monkey Jungle, or Miami Metrozoo. On your way, consider a quick tour of Coral Gables and see the spectacular Biltmore Hotel. Or, if shopping is your thing, head Downtown where you can browse galleries in the Design District and stroll in Bayside Marketplace, where, if you are feeling ambitious, you can enjoy an evening boat cruise.

If You Have 3 Days

Spend the first two days as described above and plan to really delve into South Beach on your third day when you can visit the Wolfsonian, The Bass Museum, the Ho-locaust Memorial, and the Jewish Museum. Punctuate the afternoon with some in-line skating or biking on the boardwalk, and stops into one or more of the many cafes lining Ocean Drive. In the evening drive down Calle Ocho for dinner and a show, or head to Coconut Grove for your meal. Afterwards, enjoy a Latin nightclub or a bar in CocoWalk, or some live music.

If You Have 5 or More Days

You've only just begun to get a flavor of this multifaceted region. With a few extra days, take advantage of all you can do outdoors. Spend a day at the beach, collect-ing shells, working on your tan, or being a little more active. You can rent a charter boat to catch your own dinner, sail from the Coconut Grove Marina, jet ski, or kayak through the mangroves. You can take a tour of Villa Vizcaya, a historic tour of the city, or a funky Art Deco District walking tour. With an extra day, you can drive across the the Everglades (see Chapter 11) or down to the Keys (see Chapter 12). You could even hop on a one-day cruise to Freeport or Nassau in the Bahamas (see Chapter 11).

1 Miami's Beaches

There are more than 35 miles of pristine beaches in Dade County. The character of each of Miami's many beaches are as varied as the city's population. Some are shaded by towering palm tress, while others are darkened by huge condominiums. Some attract families or old-timers, others a chichi singles scene. In short, there are two distinct beach alternatives: Miami Beach and Key Biscayne.

MIAMI BEACH'S BEACHES   Collins Avenue fronts more than a dozen miles of white-sand beach and blue-green waters from 1st to 192nd streets. Although most of this stretch is lined with a solid wall of hotels, beach access is plentiful, and you are free to frolic along the entire strip. There are lots of public beaches here, com-plete with lifeguards, toilet facilities, concession stands, and metered parking (bring lots of quarters). Miami Beach's beaches are both wide and well maintained. Except for a thin strip close to the water, most of the sand here is hard-packed—the result of a $10-million Army Corps of Engineers Beach Rebuilding Project meant to pro-tect buildings from the effects of eroding sand.

In general, the beaches on this barrier island become less crowded the farther north you go. A wooden boardwalk runs along the hotel side of the beach from 21st to 46th streets—about 1¹/₂ miles—offering a terrific sun-and-surf experience without getting sand in your shoes. Aside from the "Best Beaches" listed below, Miami Beach's lifeguard-protected public beaches include **21st Street,** at the beginning of the boardwalk; **35th Street,** popular with an older crowd; **46th Street,** next to the Fontainebleau Hilton; **53rd Street,** a narrower, more sedate beach; **64th Street,** one of the quietest strips around; and **72nd Street,** a local old-timers spot.

KEY BISCAYNE'S BEACHES   If Miami Beach is not private enough for you, Key Biscayne might be more of what you have in mind. Crossing Rickenbacker Causeway ($1 toll) is almost like crossing into the Bahamas. The 5 miles of public beach here are blessed with softer sand and are less developed and more laid-back than the hotel-laden strips to the north.

THE BEST BEACHES

Here are my picks:

- **Best Picnic Beach:** I happened upon this incredible gem only because a local invited me to his apartment, which happened to overlook this gorgeous little island. When I asked what it was, he couldn't tell me, even though he had lived in the apartment for years. Well, after a bit of digging, I discovered that this beach was **Pelican Island,** a 10-acre picnickers' paradise that's owned by the county. It's accessible by a 35-seat pontoon boat that departs on weekends from the marina on the 79th Street Causeway. You can use any of the 18 barbecue grills, 200 picnic tables, horseshoe pits, and volleyball courts. And, while it isn't technically a beach, it is Miami's best spot anywhere for a picnic. For more information, call **305/754-9330.** You'll also find great picnic facilities at **Crandon Park** on Key Biscayne (see below).

- **Best Surfing Beach: Haulover Beach/Harbor House,** just north of Miami Beach, seems to get Miami's biggest swells. Go early and avoid the rush of young locals who wish they were in Maui.

- **Best Party Beach:** In Key Biscayne, **Crandon Park Beach,** on Crandon Boulevard, has 3 miles of oceanfront beach, 493 acres of park, 75 grills, 3 parking lots, several soccer and softball fields, and a public 18-hole championship golf course. The beach is particularly wide and the water is usually so clear you can see the bottom. Admission is $2 per vehicle. It's open daily from 8am to sunset.

- **Best Beach for People-Watching:** The ultra-chic **Lummus Park Beach,** which runs along Ocean Drive from about 6th to 14th streets in South Beach, is the best place to go if you're seeking entertainment as well as a great tan. On any day of the week you might spy models primping for a photo shoot, nearly naked sunworshipers avoiding tan lines, and the best abs anywhere.

- **Best Swimming Beach:** The **85th Street Beach,** along Collins Avenue, is the best place to swim away from the maddening crowds. It's one of Miami's only stretches of sand with no condos or hotels looming over sunbathers. Plus lifeguards patrol the area throughout the day.

- **Best Windsurfing Beach: Hobie Beach,** on the right side of the causeway leading to Key Biscayne, is not really a beach but a secluded inlet with the most predictable winds and a number of places where you can rent Windsurfers.

- **Best Shell-Hunting Beach:** You'll find plenty of colorful shells at **Bal Harbour Beach,** Collins Avenue at 96th Street, just a few yards north of Surfside Beach. There's also an exercise course and good shade—but no lifeguards.

Miami Area Attractions & Beaches

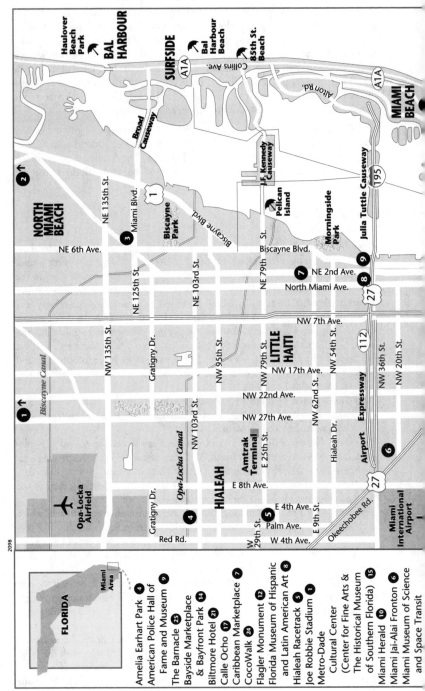

Amelia Earhart Park ❹
American Police Hall of
Fame and Museum ❾
The Barnacle ㉕
Bayside Marketplace
& Bayfront Park ⑭
Biltmore Hotel ㉑
Calle Ocho ⑰
Caribbean Marketplace ❼
CocoWalk ㉔
Flagler Monument ⑫
Florida Museum of Hispanic
and Latin American Art ❽
Hialeah Racetrack ❺
Joe Robbie Stadium ❶
Metro-Dade
Cultural Center
(Center for Fine Arts &
The Historical Museum
of Southern Florida) ⑮
Miami Herald ⑩
Miami Jai-Alai Fronton ❻
Miami Museum of Science
and Space Transit

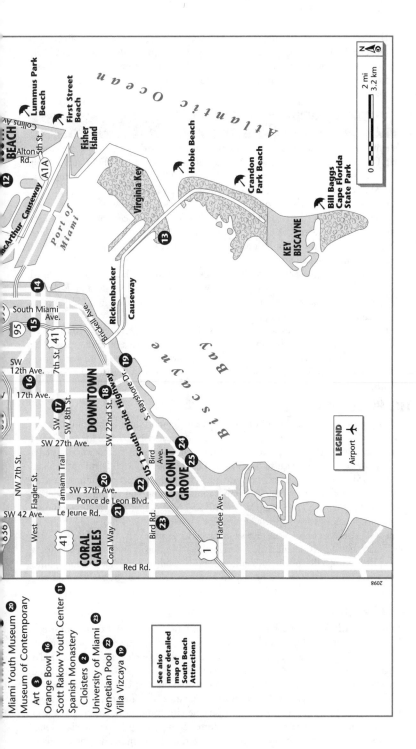

- **Best All-Around Tannning Beach:** Although the state has been trying to pass ordinances to outlaw nudity, several nude beaches are thriving in the region. In Dade County, **Haulover Beach,** just north of the Bal Harbour border, attracts nudists from around the world and has created something of a boom for area businesses that cater to them.

2 The Art Deco District

Miami's best sight is not a museum or an amusement park but a part of the city itself. Located at the southern end of Miami Beach, the ✪ Art Deco District is a whole community made up of outrageous and fanciful 1920s and 1930s architecture that shouldn't be missed. In Chapter 8, you'll find a map of this neigborhood (page 159) as well as a detailed walking tour.

The Art Deco District is roughly bounded by the Atlantic Ocean on the east, Alton Road on the west, Sixth Street on the south, and Dade Boulevard (along the Collins Canal) on the north. Plans are underway to extend the Deco District designation south to South Pointe Park.

Eating, drinking, and sunning are the primary activities of the international crowd who visit here. Fashion types, stylish Europeans, bikini-clad locals, and T-shirted tourists sit at sidewalk cafes and stroll along Ocean Drive. On any day, you'll no doubt find a fashion shoot in progress.

For maps and brochures, stop by the **Art Deco Welcome Center,** at 1001 Ocean Dr., the corner of 10th Street and Ocean Drive on the beach side of the street. The center also stocks Deco memorabilia, postcards, and souvenir items. It's open Monday to Saturday from 11am to 6pm, often later on Thursday, Friday, and Saturday nights.

THE BUILDINGS

After years of neglect and calls for the wholesale demolition of its buildings, South Beach got a new lease on life in 1979. Under the leadership of the Miami Design Preservation League, an approximate square mile of South Beach was granted a listing on the National Register of Historic Places. The Art Deco District was born.

Leonard Horowitz, a gifted young designer, began to cover the buildings' peeling beige paint with his now-famous flamboyant colors. Long-lost architectural details were highlighted with soft sherbets, and the colors of peach, periwinkle, turquoise, and purple received worldwide attention. Developers soon moved in, and the full-scale refurbishment of the area's hotels was underway.

Today, new hotels, restaurants, and nightclubs continue to open, and South Beach is on the cutting edge of Miami's cultural and nightlife scene. New condominiums are being built right on the beach, and hotels continue to be refurbished and reopened.

THE BEACH

Lummus Park Beach, which runs along Ocean Drive from about 6th to 14th streets in South Beach, is quite hip and hot. If you put your towel down here or lounge on a beach chair, you'll get a great tan plus a great spot to people-watch. It's a popular place for photo shoots and models. Volleyball nets are set up along the beach, and there are swings for children. And have you noticed the lifeguard stations?

When Hurricane Andrew knocked down the flimsy old lifeguard stands, Miami Beach didn't just build new ones. Instead, the city commissioned local architect William Lane to indulge his fancy. Now dotted along a 9-block commercial stretch of Ocean Drive are the whimsical structures that resemble anything but the mundane lifeguard stands that they are. You can't miss the Jetson's Tower on 10th Street, which was designed with the help of pop artist Kenny Scharf. This multicolored spaceship looks like it came right off the pages of a cartoon strip. Other innovative designs include a boomerang putting green at 14th Street, and a Mayan/Japanese/Shinto-inspired cyclinder that looks like an airport observation tower at 6th Street.

WALKING, BIKING & BLADING AROUND

I've outlined a walking tour in Chapter 8, but if you're not up for a self-guided tour, here are some suggestions.

On Thursday evenings and Saturday mornings, **The Miami Design Preservation League** (☎ 305/672-2014) sponsors walking tours that offer a fascinating inside look at the city's historic Art Deco District. Tourgoers meet at the Art Deco Welcome Center, 1001 Ocean Dr., for a 1¹/₂-hour walk through some of America's most exuberantly "architectured" buildings. The Design Preservation League led the fight to designate this area a National Historic District and is proud to share the splendid results with visitors. Walking tours cost $6 per person and depart on Saturdays at 10:30am and Thursdays at 6:30pm; call for schedules.

If you'd rather bike or in-line skate around the area, catch the Sunday morning **Art Deco Cycling Tour.** Since the bicycle seems to be the most efficient mode of transportation through the streets of South Beach, what better way to view the historic Art Deco District than perched on the seat of a bike. Tours depart Sundays at 10:30am and 12:30pm from the Miami Beach Bicycle Center, 601 5th St. (☎ 305/672-2014 or 305/674-0430). The tour costs $5 per person, plus another $5 if you rent a bike. Call the Welcome Center to reserve a spot.

"See Miami like a native" is the motto of **Deco Tours Miami Beach,** 420 Lincoln Rd., Suite 412, Miami Beach (☎ 305/531-4465). Not only will you get the history on Miami Beach's deco buildings, you'll also learn which big stars are in town shooting a flick, which new restaurants and clubs are hot, and where to get your hair done. Who said learning wasn't fun? Tours cost $10, and leave Monday to Friday at 10:30am and 4pm (none offered in July and August). Meet at the Miami Beach Chamber of Commerce on Meridian Avenue and Dade Boulevard.

3 Animal Parks

Kids of all ages will enjoy Miami's animal parks, which feature everything from dolphins to lions to parrots. See the "Attractions in Greater Miami South" map (page 135) for locations.

Miami Metrozoo. SW 152nd St. and SW 124th Ave., south of Coral Gables. ☎ **305/251-0403.** Admission $6 adults, $3 children 3–12. Daily 9:30am–5:30pm. Ticket booth closes 4pm. From U.S. 1, take SW 152nd St. exit west 3 blocks to the Metrozoo entrance.

Rarely does a zoo warrant mention as a city's top attraction, but Miami Metrozoo is different. This huge 290-acre complex is completely cageless; animals are kept at bay by cleverly designed moats. The original Mufasa and Simba of Disney fame were modeled on Metrozoo's lions who are still here. Star attractions include two rare white Bengal tigers, a Komodo dragon, rare koala bears, and a monorail "safari." Especially appealing for both adults and children is PAWS, a unique petting zoo. You can even ride an elephant.

Miami Seaquarium. 4400 Rickenbacker Causeway (south side), Key Biscayne. ☎ **305/361-5705.** Admission $18.45 adults, $14.45 seniors over 65, $13.95 children 3–9. Daily 9:30am–6pm. Ticket booth closes 4:30pm. From downtown Miami, take I-95 South to the Rickenbacker Causeway.

It takes about four hours of your time to tour the 35-acre oceanarium, if you want to see all four daily shows starring the world's most impressive ocean mammals. Trained dolphins, killer whales, and frolicking sea lions take your breath away. If you're inclined, you can even volunteer for one of their big wet fishy kisses! For those who remember Flipper's show (he wasn't really called Flipper but Bebe), come see one of the original dolphins who played the title role. She just celebrated her 30th birthday.

Monkey Jungle. 14805 SW 216th St., Greater Miami South. ☎ **305/235-1611.** Admission $10.50 adults, $9.50 seniors and active-duty military, $5.35 children 4–12. Daily 9:30am–5pm. Tickets sold until 4pm. Take U.S. 1 South to 216th St.; it's about 20 minutes from Downtown.

See rare Brazilian golden lion tamarins. Watch the "skin diving" Asian macaques. Yes, folks, it's primate paradise! Visitors are protected, but there are no cages to restrain the antics of the monkeys as they swing, chatter, and play their way into your heart. Where else but in Florida would an attraction like this still be popular after 60 years? Screened-in trails wind through acres of "jungle," and daily shows feature the talents of the park's most progressive pupils. You've got to love primates to get over the heavy smell of the jungle.

Parrot Jungle and Gardens. 11000 SW 57th Ave., Greater Miami South. ☎ **305/666-7834.** Admission $10.95 adults, $7.95 children 3–12. Daily 9:30am–6pm. Take U.S. 1 South, turn left at SW 57th Ave., and continue straight for 2¹/₂ miles.

Not just parrots, but hundreds of magnificent macaws, prancing peacocks, cute cockatoos, and fabulous flamingos occupy this over-50-year-old park. Alligators, tortoises, and iguanas are also on exhibit. But it's the parrots you came for, and it's parrots you get. With brilliant splashes of color, these birds appear in every shape and size. Continuous shows in the Parrot Bowl Theater star roller-skating cockatoos, card-playing macaws, and more stunt-happy parrots than you ever thought possible. Other attractions include a wildlife show focusing on indigenous Florida animals, an area called "Primate Experience," a children's playground, and a petting zoo.

Parrot Jungle is planning to move to its own island closer to downtown Miami; the move is scheduled to be completed by 1998.

4 Miami's Museum & Art Scene

Miami's museum scene has always been quirky, interesting, and inconsistent at best. Though several exhibition spaces have made forays into collecting nationally acclaimed work, limited support and political infighting has made it a difficult proposition. Recently, with the opening of the Wolfsonian in 1995 and MOCA in 1996, the scene has improved dramatically. It is now safe to say that world-class exhibitions start here. Listed below is an excellent cross-section of the valuable treasures that have become a part of the city's cultural heritage, and as such, are as diverse as the city itself.

IN SOUTH BEACH

The Bass Museum of Art. 2121 Park Ave. (at the corner of 21st St.), South Beach. ☎ **305/673-7530.** Admission $5 adults, $3 students with I.D. and senior citizens, children under 6 free; Wed by donation. Tues–Sat 10am–5pm, Sun 1–5pm (every second and fourth Wed open 1–9pm). Closed holidays.

The Bass is the most important visual-arts museum in Miami Beach. European paintings, sculptures, and tapestries from the Renaissance, baroque, rococo, and modern periods make up the bulk of the small permanent collection. Temporary exhibitions

South Beach Attractions

To Central Miami Beach

The Bass Museum of Art

Collins Park

Dade Boulevard

Miami Beach Convention Center

20th St.
19th St.
18th St.
17th St.

Lincoln Road Mall and Arts District

Lincoln Rd.

16th St.
15th St.

Espanola Way

14th St.
13th St.
12th St.
11th St.
10th St.
9th St.
8th St.
7th St.
6th St.
5th St.
4th St.
3rd St.
2nd St.
1st St.

Miami Beach Post Office

Beach Patrol Station

Art Deco Welcome Center

Lummus Park

West Ave.
Alton Rd.
Lenox Ave.
Michigan Ave.
Meridian Ave.
Euclid Ave.
Jefferson Ave.
Pennsylvania Ave.
Washington Ave.
Collins Ave.
Ocean Dr.
James Ave.

Flamingo Park

Atlantic Ocean

South Pointe Park

Government Cut

0   .124 km
     .2 mi

N

SOUTH BEACH ATTRACTIONS
Bass Museum of Art ❷
Bayshore Golf Course ❶
Holocaust Memorial ❸
Sanford L. Ziff Jewish Museum of Florida ⓱
The Wolfsonian ⓮
BIKE & BLADE RENTALS
Fritz's Skate Shop ❽
Gary's Megacycles ⓬
Miami Beach Bicycle Center ⓰
Skate 2000 ⓭
GYMS
Club Body Tech ⓫
South Beach Gym ⓯
ART SPACES
Colony Theater ❿
Jackie Gleason Theater of Performing Arts ❻
Lincoln Theatre ❼
Miami City Ballet Studio ❾
Performing Art Network Building ❺
INFORMATION
Miami Beach Chamber of Commerce ❹

2092

alternate between traveling shows and rotations of the Bass's stock, with themes ranging from 17th-century Dutch art to contemporary architecture.

Built from coral rock in 1930, the Bass sits in the middle of six tree-topped, landscaped acres. Wander the grounds to enjoy the changing outdoor sculpture exhibits. The museum is directly behind the public library on the right.

Holocaust Memorial. 1933 Meridian Ave., Miami Beach. ☎ **305/538-1663.** Free admission. Daily 9am–9pm. From Alton Rd., turn left on Dade Blvd., and turn right on Meridian Ave. The memorial is half a block on the left.

This heart-wrenching memorial of the genocide that took place in 1940s Europe is hard to miss and would be a shame to overlook. The powerful centerpiece is a bronze statue by Kenneth Treister that depicts millions of men, women, and children crawling into an open hand to freedom. You can walk through an open hallway lined with photographs and the names of concentration camps and their victims; it's a moving reminder of one man's unfathomable cruelty. From the street, you'll see the outstretched arm, but do stop and tour the sculpture at ground level. What's hidden behind the beautiful stone facade is quite moving and powerful.

Sanford L. Ziff Jewish Museum of Florida. 301 Washington Ave. (corner of 3rd St.), Miami Beach. ☎ **305/672-5044.** Admission $4 adults, $3 senior citizens and students, $9 family ($2.50 adult in groups of 20 or more with reservations), free on Sat and for children under 6. Tues–Sun 10am–5pm. Closed New Years, Thanksgiving, and Jewish high holidays.

Built on the site of a decaying synagogue, this spectacular museum is a time capsule of old Miami Beach. You'll find unbelievable old photos and documents as well as a number of traveling exhibitions from around the world detailing Jewish life. Please call to find out the schedule, since the museum is closed on many Jewish holidays and in between shows.

✪ The Wolfsonian. 1001 Washington Ave., South Beach. ☎ **305/531-1001.** Admission $7 adults, $5 senior citizens, students, and children 6 to 12, free for children under 6, members, and Thurs 6–9pm. Tues–Wed, Fri–Sat 10am–6pm, Thurs 10am–9pm, Sun 12–5pm.

Micky Wolfson, Jr., an eccentric collector of late 19th- and 20th-century art and other paraphernalia, was spending so much money storing his booty that he decided to buy the warehouse. Now his incredibly diverse and controversial collection is housed in the former storage company. And the warehouse has been retrofitted with such painstaking detail that it's the envy of curators around the world.

They won't call it a museum or a gallery, but whatever it is, what's on display is definitely worth a look. The collection of more than 70,000 pieces is being shown on a constantly rotating schedule. For 1997, in addition to an eclectic display of items commemorating Miami's centenntial, curators are planning an exhibition on culinary arts, transportation, and advertising and propaganda.

IN & NEAR DOWNTOWN

The Florida Museum of Hispanic and Latin American Art. 1 NE 40th St. (corner of NE 40th St. and North Miami Ave.), Miami. ☎ **305/576-5171.** Admission $2 adults, $1 children 6–12. Tues–Fri 11am–5pm; Sat 11am–4pm. Closed major holidays and in August.

In addition to their permananent collection of contemporary artists from Spain and Latin America, this museum hosts monthly exhibitions of works from Latin America and the Caribbean Basin. Usually the group shows focus on a theme, such as International Women or Surrealism. There is more than 3,500 square feet of exhibition space. Lectures and classes are offered throughout the year.

A group of young art enthusiasts run this museum on a shoestring budget; they work around the clock to obtain funding and sponsors for upcoming shows.

The dedicated staff relies on many volunteers who are passionate about the works of otherwise unknown artists from throughout the Caribbean and Latin America.

Metro-Dade Cultural Center. 101 W. Flagler St., Miami. ☎ **305/375-1700.**

The Metro-Dade Cultural Center is an oasis for those seeking cultural enrichment during their trip to Miami. The center houses the main branch of the Metro-Dade Public Library and sometimes features art and cultural exhibits. In addition to the library, the Metro-Dade Cultural Center houses the Historical Museum of Southern Florida and the Center for Fine Arts (see listings below).

From I-95 North, take NW 2nd St. exit and turn right, continue east to NW 2nd Ave., turn right and park at the Metro-Dade Garage. From I-95 South, exit at Orange Bowl–NW 8th St. and continue south to NW 2nd St. Turn left at NW 2nd St. and go 1¹/₂ blocks to NW 2nd Ave., turn right and park at the Metro-Dade Garage (50 NW 2nd Ave.). Bring ticket to lobby for validation.

Center for Fine Arts. 101 W. Flagler St. (in the Metro-Dade Cultural Center), Miami. ☎ **305/375-3000.** Admission $5 adults, $2.50 for senior citizens and students with I.D., free for children under 12; free Thurs 5–9pm. Tues–Fri 10am–5pm (Thurs until 9pm), Sat–Sun 12–5pm. Closed major holidays.

The Center for Fine Arts features an eclectic mix of modern and contemporary works by such artists as Eric Fischl, Max Beckman, Jim Dine, and Stuart Davis. Rotating exhibitions span the ages and styles. Call for updated schedules.

The Historical Museum of Southern Florida. 101 W. Flagler St. (in the Metro-Dade Cultural Center), Miami. ☎ **305/375-1492.** Admission $4 adults, $2 children 6–12, children under 6 free. Group discounts for groups of 20 or more with advanced reservations. Mon–Sat 10am–5pm, Thurs 10am–9pm, Sun 12–5pm. Closed major holidays.

The Historical Museum's primary exhibit is "Tropical Dreams," a state-of-the-art chronological history of the last 10,000 years in South Florida. The hands-on displays, audiovisual presentations, and hundreds of artifacts are intriguing. The museum also hosts hundreds of lectures and tours throughout the year, highlighting the fascinating history of Florida, and in particular, the state's southern region.

The American Police Hall of Fame and Museum. 3801 Biscayne Blvd., Miami. ☎ **305/573-0070.** Admission $6 adults, $3 children under 12, $4 seniors over 61. Daily 10am–5:30pm.

Unless you come from a family of police or you are particularly fascinated with law enforcement, America's Police Museum is a bust. Inside the building, which has a real police car affixed to its side, is a combination of reality and fantasy that's part thoughtful tribute, part Hollywood-style drama. Just past the police car featured in the motion picture *Blade Runner* is a mock prison cell, in which visitors can take pictures of themselves pretending they're doing five to ten. Also displayed are execution devices, including a guillotine and an electric chair. In the entry is a touching memorial, à la the Vietnam Memorial, to the more than 3,000 police officers who have lost their lives in the line of duty.

IN NORTH MIAMI BEACH

✪ **Museum of Contemporary Art.** Joan Lehman Building, 770 NE 125th St., North Miami. ☎ **305/893-6211.** Admission $4 adults, $2 seniors and students with I.D., children under 12 free. Tues–Sat 10am–5pm, Thurs 10am–9pm, Sun 12–5pm. Closed major holidays.

The recently expanded Museum of Contemporary Art, or MOCA as it is known locally, recently acquired a new 23,000-square-foot space in which to display its impressive collection of internationally acclaimed art with a local flavor. You can see works by Jasper Johns, Roy Lichtenstein, Larry Rivers, Duane Michaels, and Claes

Oldenberg. Guided tours are offered in English, Spanish, French, Creole, Portuguese, German, and Italian.

In addition, a new screening facility allows for film presentations that will compliment the exhibitions. Although the $3.75-million project was built in an area that otherwise is an unchartered tourist destination, MOCA is worth a drive to view important modern art in South Florida.

IN CORAL GABLES & COCONUT GROVE

Miami Museum of Science and Space Transit Planetarium. 3280 S. Miami Ave., Coconut Grove. ☎ **305/854-4247,** general info; 305/854-2222, for planetarium show times. Science museum admission $6 adults, $4 children 3–12 and seniors, under 3 free. Planetarium admission $5 adults, $2.50 children and seniors. Combined admission $9 adults, $5.50 children and seniors. Science museum, daily 10am–6pm. Call for planetarium show times. Closed Thanksgiving and Christmas. Take I-95 South to Exit 1 and follow signs. Alternatively, ride the Metrorail to Vizcaya Station.

The Museum of Science features over 140 hands-on exhibits that explore the mysteries of the universe. Live demonstrations and collections of rare natural history specimens make a visit here fun and informative. Two or three major traveling exhibits are usually on display as well.

The adjacent Space Transit Planetarium projects astronomy and laser shows as well as interactive demonstrations of upcoming computer tecnology and cyberspace features.

Miami Youth Museum. 3301 Coral Way, level U of the Miracle Center Mall, Coral Gables. ☎ **305/446-4FUN.** Admission $3.50 anyone over 1 year old. Mon–Fri 10am–5pm, Sat–Sun 11am–6pm. Closed most major holidays.

This interactive "museum" is more like a theater than a museum, since it's a place where kids can explore hands-on their interests in the "grown-up world." If you are in the Gables and want to placate (and educate) the kids, check this museum out. It's located inside the Miracle Mile Shopping Center, so Mom and Dad can treat the kids to a fun time after shopping. The museum has a mini grocery store complete with cashier and stock-boy assignments for role playing. Maybe the kids want to pretend to be Dr. Smiles, the dentist, or publish their own newspaper from the "Hot off the Press" exhibit.

5 More Attractions

✪ **Villa Vizcaya.** 3251 S. Miami Ave., just south of Rickenbacker Causeway, north Coconut Grove. ☎ **305/250-9133.** Admission $10 adults, $5 children 6–12, under 6 free. Daily 9:30am–5pm; gardens open until 5:30pm. Ticket booth closes 4:30pm. Closed Christmas. Take I-95 South to Exit 1 and follow signs to Vizcaya.

Sometimes referred to as the "Hearst Castle of the East," this magnificent villa was built in 1916 as a winter retreat for James Deering, co-founder and former vice president of International Harvester. The industrialist was fascinated by 16th-century art and architecture, and his ornate mansion—which took 1,000 artisans five years to build—became a celebration of these designs. Most of the original furnishings, including dishes and paintings, are still intact.

Pink marble columns, topped with intricately designed capitals, reach up toward hand-carved European-style ceilings. Antiques decorate 34 of the 70 rooms, which are filled with baroque furniture and Renaissance paintings and tapestries. The spectacularly opulent villa wraps itself around a central courtyard. Outside, lush formal gardens, accented with statuary, balustrades, and decorative urns, front an enormous swath of Biscayne Bay, neighboring on present-day homes of Sylvester Stallone and Madonna.

The Barnacle. 3485 Main Hwy., Coconut Grove. ☎ **305/448-9445.** Admission $1. Open for group tours Mon–Thurs (with advance reservations) 10am, 11:30am, 1pm, and 2:30pm on the main house porch. From downtown Miami, take U.S. 1 South to S. Bayshore Dr. Continue to the end, turn right onto McFarlane Ave. and left at the traffic light on to Main Hwy. The museum is 5 blocks on the left.

The former home of naval architect and early settler Ralph Middleton Munroe is now a museum in the heart of Coconut Grove, one block south of Commodore Plaza. The house's quiet surroundings, wide porches, and period furnishings illustrate how Miami's privileged class lived in the days before skyscrapers and luxury hotels. Enthusiastic and knowledgeable state park employees offer a wealth of historical information.

Coral Castle. 28655 S. Dixie Hwy., Homestead. ☎ **305/248-6344.** Admission $7.75 adults, $6.50 seniors, $5 children 7–12. Daily 9am–6pm, except Thanksgiving and Christmas Eve, when it closes at 3pm. Closed Christmas. Take U.S. 1 South to SW 286th St. in Homestead.

There's plenty of competition, but Coral Castle is probably the zaniest attraction in Florida. In 1923, the story goes, a crazed Latvian, suffering from unrequited love, immigrated to South Florida and spent the next 25 years of his life carving massive amounts of stone into a prehistoric-looking, roofless "castle." It seems impossible that one rather short Latvian could have done all this but there are scores of affidavits from neighbors swearing it happened. Apparently experts have used this South Florida phenomenon to help figure out how the Great Pyramids and Stonehenge were built.

Listen to the audio tour to learn about the bizarre spot, now on the National Register of Historical Places. The commentary lasts about 25 minutes and is available in four languages. Although the Coral Castle is a bit overpriced and under maintained, if you're in the area, especially with kids in tow, visit this monument to one man's madness.

Spanish Monastery Cloisters. 16711 W. Dixie Hwy. at the corner of 167th St., North Miami Beach. ☎ **305/945-1462.** Admission $4.50 adults, $1 children under 12, $2.50 seniors. Mon–Sat 10am–4pm, Sun noon–4pm. From Downtown, take U.S. 1 North and turn left onto 163rd St. Make the first right onto W. Dixie Hwy. The Cloisters are 3 blocks ahead on the right.

Did you know the oldest building in the Western Hemisphere dates from A.D. 1141 and is located in Miami? Well, it is. The Spanish Monastery Cloisters were first erected in Segovia, Spain. Centuries later, newspaper magnate William Randolph Hearst purchased and brought the Cloisters to America in pieces. The carefully numbered stones were quarantined for years until they were finally reassembled on the present site in 1954.

Venetian Pool. 2701 DeSoto Blvd., at Toledo St., Coral Gables. ☎ **305/460-5356.** Admission $4 adults, $3.50 children 13–17, $1.60 children under 13. Children under 36 months not allowed in the water. June–Aug, weekdays 11am–7:30pm; Sept–Oct and Apr–May, Tues–Fri 11am–5:30pm; Nov–Mar, Tues–Fri 11am–4:30pm; year-round Sat and Sun 10am–4:30pm.

Miami's most unusual swimming pool, dating from 1924, is hidden behind pastel stucco walls and is honored with a listing in the National Register of Historic Places. Underground artesian wells feed the free-form lagoon, which is shaded by three-story Spanish porticos and features both fountains and waterfalls. During summer, the pool's 800,000 gallons of water are drained and refilled nightly, ensuring a cool, clean swim. Visitors are free to swim and sunbathe here year-round, just as Esther

Williams and Johnny Weissmuller did decades ago. For a modest fee, you or your children can learn to swim during special summer programs.

6 Nature Preserves, Parks & Gardens

The Miami area is a great place for outdoors-minded visitors, with beachs, parks, and gardens galore. Plus, South Florida is the country's only area with two national parks; see Chapter 11 for coverage of the Everglades and Biscayne National Park.

BOTANICAL GARDENS & A SPICE PARK

In Miami, **Fairchild Tropical Gardens,** 10901 Old Cutler Rd. (☎ 305/667-1651), feature a veritable rainforest of both rare and exotic plants on 83 acres. Palmettos, vine pergola, palm glades, and other unique species create a scenic, lush environment. It is well worth taking the free hourly tram to learn what you always wanted to know about the various flowers and trees on a 30-minute narrated tour.

Although there are picnic facilities sprinkled throughout the park, the new Chachi House is a must for that feeling of breaking bread in an authentic rainforest. Built by the Chachi Indians of Northers Ecuador, this large hut has a thatched roof and no walls for an open-air lunch. It is situated near one of Fairchild's many lakes.

Admission is $8 for adults, free for children under 13 accompanied by an adult. Open daily 9:30am to 4:30pm. Take I-95 South to U.S. 1, turn left on LeJeune Rd. Follow straight to the traffic circle and take Old Cutler Rd. 2 miles to the park.

A testament to the unusual climate of Miami, here at the ⑤ **Preston B. Bird and Mary Heinlein Fruit and Spice Park,** 24801 SW 187th Ave., Homestead (☎ 305/247-5727), you'll find rare fruit trees that cannot survive elsewhere in the country. You'll see Jamaicans getting weepy at the abundance of the plants from their native country, including ackee, mango, ugly fruits, carambola, and breadfruit.

Definitely ask for a guide. If a volunteer is available, they'll tell you some fascinating things about this 20-acre living plant museum where the most exotic varieties of fruits and spices grow on strange-looking trees with unpronounceable names. One daily tour is offered at 10am by group reservation.

The best part is you are free to sample anything that falls to the ground. You'll also find dishes of interesting fruits, muffins, and jellies made from the parks bounty in the gift store. Cooks who like to experiment must visit the park store, which carries hard-to-find ingredients like callaloo, burnt orange maramalades, Indian and Caribbean spices, plus cookbooks, posters, and explanatory pamphlets on hundreds of topics.

Admission to the spice park is $1.50 for adults, 50¢ children. Open daily from 10am to 5pm (closed Thanksgiving, Christmas, and New Year's). Take U.S. 1 South, turn right on SW 248th St., and go straight for 5 miles to SW 187th Ave.

MORE PARKS IN MIAMI

Luckily, Miami also has hundreds of incredibly well-maintained park facilites that run the gamut from grassy strips to lake-filled playgrounds with picnic facilities and park rangers. Here are a few of the city's best.

The **Amelia Earhart Park,** at 401 E. 65th St., Hialeah (☎ 305/685-8389), is a veritable treasure trove for outdoor lovers. You'll find five lakes stocked with bass, brim, and mullet for fishing; a private island for kids to swing to and tunnel around; playgrounds; picnic facilities; and a big red barn that houses cows, geese, and goats for petting and ponies for riding. There is also a country store and dozens of old-time farm activities like horseshoeing, sugar-cane processing, and more. Parking admission

Attractions in Greater Miami, South

Coral Castle **6**
Fairchild Tropical Gardens **2**
Miami Metrozoo **3**
Monkey Jungle **4**
Parrot Jungle **1**
Preston B. Bird and Mary Heinlein
Fruit and Spice Park **5**

costs $3.50 per car, $6 bus. Beach admission is $4 for adults, $1.50 youth, $1.25 senior citizen. Open daily from 9am to sunset. To drive here, take I-95 North to the NW 103rd St. exit, and then go west to East 4th Ave. Turn right. Parking is 1 1/2 miles down the street.

In Key Biscayne, the historic **Bill Baggs Cape Florida State Park,** 1200 Crandon Blvd. (☎ 305/361-5811), features a recently re-opened lighthouse. You can explore the unfettered wilds and enjoy some of the most secluded beaches in Miami. A rental shack rents bikes, hydro-bikes, sailboats, kayaks, jet skis, and many more water toys. It's also a great place to picnic, plus a newly constructed restaurant serves homemade Cuban food, including great fish soups and sandwiches. Just be careful the raccoons don't get your lunch, because the furry black-eyed beasts are everywhere. Admission is $3.25 per car with up to eight people. Open daily from 8am to sunset.

In Miami, the **Larry and Penny Thompson Park,** at 11451 SW 184th St. (☎ 305/232-1049), with four lakes for fishing and swimming, is popular among campers, fishers, and day-trippers. Many fishing contests are held at the freshwater lake, which is filled with bass, blue gill, and catfish. You can stroll through the park's more than 270 acres of South Florida woodlands, hiking paths, and bridle trails. For camping enthusiasts, this place is a paradise; there are laundry facilities and hot showers. Open daily from sunrise to sunset.

Popular with the locals, **Tropical Park,** at 7900 SW 40th St. (☎ 305/226-0796), has it all. Enjoy a game of tennis and raquetball for a minimal fee or swim and sun yourself on their secluded little lake. If fishing is more your style, you can use their fishing pond for free, and they'll even supply you with the rods and bait. If you catch anything however, you're on your own. Open daily from sunrise to sunset.

7　Especially for Kids

Florida's vacationland has always been family-oriented, so there's many programs and activities exclusively for children. Several beachfront resort hotels provide excellent supervised activities for kids, including the Sonesta Beach Hotel on Key Biscayne and the Fontainebleau and Doral hotels in Miami Beach (see Chapter 5, "Accommodations"). The Greater Miami Convention and Visitors Bureau (☎ 305/539-3063 or 800/283-2707) can supply you with information on these and other family packages. Here's a round-up of what kids will especially enjoy.

AMELIA EARHART PARK *(see page 134)*　This is the best park in Miami for kids. They'll like the petting zoos, pony rides, and a private island with hidden tunnels.

THE MIAMI METROZOO *(see page 127)*　This completely cageless zoo offers such star attractions as a monorail "safari" and a petting zoo. Especially fun for kids are the elephant rides.

MIAMI MUSEUM OF SCIENCE AND SPACE TRANSIT PLANETARIUM *(see page 132)*　At the Planetarium, kids can learn about space and science by watching entertaining films and cosmic shows. The space museum also offers child-friendly explanations for natural occurences.

MIAMI SEAQUARIUM *(see page 127)*　Kids can volunteer to be kissed by a dolphin and watch performances by a dolphin who originally played Flipper on the 1960s television show.

MIAMI YOUTH MUSEUM *(see page 132)*　Here children can dabble in fantasy land, playing at what they're interested in. It's one huge game of "what do you want to be when you grow up."

SCOTT RAKOW YOUTH CENTER　Located at 2700 Sheridan Ave. (☎ 305/673-7767), this youth center is a hidden treasure on Miami Beach. This three-story facility boasts an ice-skating rink, bowling alleys, a basketball court, gymnasium equipment, and full-time supervision for kids. Call for a complete schedule of organized events. The only drag is that it's not open to adults (except on Sundays). Admission is $6 per day for children ages 9 to 17, $3 for residents. Open daily from 2:30 to 9pm.

8　Organized Tours

Similar to the tourist attractions, many of Miami's organized tours are interesting and offbeat. They are also fun and generally well-priced. Always call ahead to check prices and times. Reservations are usually suggested.

FLYING ABOVE MIAMI: AIR TOURS

Action Helicopter. 1901 Brickell Ave. B602, Miami. ☎ **305/358-4723.** Tickets $59 for 15 miles, $99 for 25 miles, $129 for 45 miles. $550 hourly rate for air taxi. Daily 9am–6pm. Helipad located on 950 McCarthur Causeway.

If you want to experience Miami from a bird's-eye view, try it from a helicopter. A short, exhilarating ride around the city and the beach will show you the Seaquarium, Bayside, and stars' homes from a decidedly different perspective.

Fun Flight Miami Inc. Rickenbacker Causeway at marina, Key Biscayne. ☎ **305/754-4222,** or pager 305/478-9055. Tickets $55 for a half hour, $100 per hour. Weekends 9:30am–4:30pm weather-permitting.

For the brave soul, there's an air tour over Miami and Key Biscayne on an ultra light. For those who've never seen it, an ultra light is a small open plane of sorts with a small motor. There's no better way to see ALL of Miami. Fun flight does live up to its name however, and can even certify you to fly one of their planes and join their ranks.

Pan Am Air Bridge. 1000 McCarthur Causeway, Miami. ☎ **305/371-8628.** Tickets $39.50 adults, $29.50 children ages 2 to 11. Departs every Sat at 2pm. Reservations requested three days in advance, and reconfirm the day before. Flights depart from the Watson Island Seaplane Base.

Pan Am airlines is back! They have teamed up with one of Florida's oldest airlines, Chalk's International, to offer air tours of all of Miami. Their weekly half hour tour on a 17-passenger seaplane offers views of the city's greatest sights from a height of 500 to 1,500 feet. The pilots have even been known to be coaxed into skimming the water upon landing. A narrator describes the riches below, including the luxurious island of Key Biscayne (a former coconut plantation), Miami Beach, Fisher Island, Star Island, all the way up to Palm Beach.

To get to the Watson Island Seaplane base from Miami Beach, take 395 East (The MacArthur Causeway). You'll see signs on your left to the base, across from the cruise ships in the Port of Miami.

BOAT & CRUISE-SHIP TOURS

Gondola Adventures. Bayside Marketplace Marina, 401 Biscayne Blvd., Downtown. ☎ **305/ 573-1818.** Rates $5–$499 daily.

A real gondola in Miami? Well, it may not be the canals of Venice, but with a little imagination, the Bayside Marina will do. You can go on a simple ride around Bayside for $5, or have lunch or champagne and even go on your own private and cozy sunrise cruise to an island.

Heritage *Miami II* Topsail Schooner. Bayside Marketplace Marina, 401 Biscayne Blvd., Downtown. ☎ **305/442-9697.** Tickets $12 adults, $7 children under 12.

More adventure than tour, this relaxing ride aboard Miami's only tall ship is a fun way to see the city. Two-hour cruises pass by Villa Vizcaya, Coconut Grove, and Key Biscayne and put you in sight of Miami's spectacular skyline. Cruises are offered September through May only. The two-hour tours leave daily at 1:30pm, 4pm, and 6pm, and on weekends also at 9pm, 10pm, and 11pm. Call to make sure the ship is running on schedule.

Lady Lucille. 4441 Collins Ave. (docked across from the Fontainebleau Hotel), Miami Beach. ☎ **305/534-7000.** Tickets $12.50 adults, $6 children under 12.

If you've seen enough of Miami's natural beauty on other sightseeing cruises, set your sights and sails on Miami's man-made beauty—Millionaire's Row. You can cruise along Biscayne Bay and check out Cher's or Fitipaldi's mansions all in the comfort of an air-conditioned 150-passenger boat, complete with snacks and two full bars. The three-hour cruise leaves daily at 11am, 1:30pm, and 4pm.

Sea Kruz. 1280 5th St., Miami Beach. ☎ **305/538-8300** or 800/688-PLAY. Tickets $19.95 weekdays, $24.95 weekends.

If you don't have time to hit the Caribbean on this trip and you like to gamble, consider one of the many mini-cruises to nowhere. The *Sea Kruz* takes you three miles off the coast into international waters so you can indulge in a little hedonistic pleasure on your visit to Miami.

For $5 more on the lunch cruise, there's an all-you-can-eat soup-and-salad bar, and for an additional $9 on the dinner cruise, there's an all-you-can-eat dinner with a carving station. Throw in a little dancing to a live band, and the evening's complete. Ask for free chips or coupons, usually offered for the asking. Cruises run Sunday to Thursday at 1:30pm, 5:30pm, 7:30pm, and 12:30am; Friday and Saturday at 1:30pm, 5:30pm, 7:30pm, and 1am.

Water Taxi. 651 Seabreeze Blvd., Ft. Lauderdale. ☎ **305/467-6677.** Tickets $15 all-day pass, $7.50 trip Downtown only. Daily 10am–1am.

Here's a novel way to get around Miami—on a boat. You can work on your tan while the old port boats or canal boats ferry you all over downtown Miami, Bayside, and Miami Beach. The water taxis run every 25 minutes, but if you buy an all-day pass, you'll be picked up when you call. Visit the Seaquarium, Viscaya, The Hard Rock Cafe, and even exclusive Fisher Island. While it is not the most effective mode of transportation, the Water Taxi can guarantee you'll never get stuck in traffic.

BUS SIGHTSEEING TOURS

Deco Tours Miami Beach. 420 Lincoln Rd., Suite 412, Miami Beach. ☎ **305/531-4465.** Admission $39–$49 adults, $25 children. Mon–Fri 8am–5pm. Group of 15 necessary for departure. Hotel pickup available.

If you have an entire day to devote to a complete tour of the area, give Deco Tours a call and embark on a seven-hour bus trip through Miami's remotest and often-neglected corners. Deco offers narrated tours through not only South Beach and Miami, but also Little Havana and Little Haiti, one of Miami's best-kept secrets. Deco Tours bills themselves as a customized tour planner; they'll take you on any Miami tour you could wish for with enough notice.

Miami Nice Excursion Inc. Travel and Service. 19250 Collins Ave., Miami Beach. ☎ **305/949-9180.** Admission $27–$39 adults, $25 children. Daily 7am–10pm. Call ahead for directions to various pick-up areas.

Pick your destination. The Miami Nice tours will take you by bus to the Everglades, Fort Lauderdale, the Seaquarium, or even the Bahamas. Included in most Miami trips is a fairly comprehensive city tour narrated by knowledgeable guides who can share what they know in Spanish or German too. The company is one of the oldest in town and has grown to accomodate the increased interest in destinations throughout South Florida.

WALKING TOURS

I recommend taking ✪ **Dr. Paul George's Tours;** Dr. Paul George is Mr. Miami, who happens to be a history teacher at Miami-Dade Community College and a historian at the Historical Museum of Southern Florida. Although there's a set calendar, any of his tours would be fascinating to South Florida buffs. Tours focus on themes or neighborhoods, from a tour of Little Havana, Brickell Avenue, or Key Biscayne, to the City of Miami Cemetery Tour. Call ahead for the agenda (☎ 305/375-1492). Tours cost $15 to $25; reservations are needed. Tours leave from the Historical Museum of Southern Florida at the Metro-Dade Cultural Center, 101 W. Flagler St.

If you've never been to the **Biltmore Hotel Coral Gables,** take advantage of the free walking tours offered Sundays at 1:30pm, 2:30pm, and 3:30pm to enjoy the hotel's beautiful grounds and building. The Biltmore is chock-full of history and mystery, so go out there and uncover it. It's located at 1200 Anastasia Ave., Coral Gables; call 305/445-1926 for more information.

If you're in Coral Gables the first Friday of the month from 7 to 10pm, you can join the **Coral Gables Art and Gallery Tour.** Vans shuttle art lovers to more than 20 galleries in Coral Gables. Viewers can sip wine as they view American folk art, African, Native American, and Latin art, as well as photography. Most galleries are on Ponce De Leon Boulevard between SW 40th Street and SW 24th Street. The vans run every 15 minutes from 7 to 10pm. For more information, call Richard Arregui at 305/447-3973.

9 Water Sports

BOATING & SAILING

You can rent sailboats and catamarans through the beachfront concessions desk of several top resorts, such as the Doral Ocean Beach Resort, Sheraton Bal Harbour Beach Resort, or the Dezerland Surfside Beach Hotel (see listings in Chapter 5).

Private rental outfits include **Beach Boat Rentals,** 2380 Collins Ave., Miami Beach (☎ 305/534-4307), where 50-horsepower 18-foot powerboats rent for some of the best prices on the beach. Rates are $50 for an hour, $125 for four hours, and $255 for eight hours. Cruising is exclusively in and around Biscayne Bay, as ocean access is prohibited. Renters must be over 21 and must present a current passport or driver's license. The rental office is at 23rd Street, on the inland waterway in Miami Beach, and it is open daily from 9am to 5pm (weather permitting).

Boat Rental Express, at the Sunny Isles Marina, 4000 Sunny Isles Blvd., Miami Beach (☎ 305/944-4500), rents 18- to 20-foot powerboats and 22-foot sportdecks if you want to run with the big boys. You must be at least 21 and have prior boating experience. Rentals are available from 8:30am to 5:50pm Friday to Wednesday. Rates are $54 per hour for powerboats, $44 per hours for sportdecks, with a two-hour minumum.

Club Nautico of Coconut Grove, 2560 S. Bayshore Dr., Coconut Grove (☎ 305/858-6258), rents high-quality powerboats for fishing, waterskiing, diving, and cruising in the bay or ocean. All boats are Coast Guard–equipped with VHF radios and safety gear. Rates begin at $199 for four hours and $299 for eight hours and go up to as much as $419 on the weekends. Club Nautico is open daily from 9am to 5pm (weather permitting). Other locations include Crandon Park Marina, 400 Crandon Blvd., Key Biscayne (☎ 305/361-9217) with the same rates as the Coconut Grove location; and Miami Beach Marina, Pier E, 300 Alton Rd., South Beach (☎ 305/673-2502). Rates are $229 for four hours and $299 for eight hours to rent a 20-foot boat. A 24-footer will run you $259 for half a day and $359 for a full day. Nautico on Miami Beach is open daily from 9am to 5pm.

Key Biscayne Boat Rental, 3301 Rickenbacker Causeway, Key Biscayne (☎ 305/361-RENT), is next to the Rusty Pelican. If you want to cruise Key Biscayne's lovely waters, a 21-footer costs $175 for a half day to $250 for a full day. If you're looking for just a few hours of thrills, a two-hour minimum for $100 is available. Key Biscayne Boat Rental is open Monday to Friday from 9am to 5pm, and will open earlier for special fishing requests.

If speedboats are not your style, **Sailboats of Key Biscayne Rentals and Sailing School,** Crandon Marina next to Sundays on the Bay, 4000 Crandon Blvd., Key Biscayne (☎ 305/361-0328 days, 305/279-7424 evenings), offers a slightly more subdued ride. A 22-foot sailboat can be rented for $27 an hour, or $81 for a half day. A 23-foot Hunter or Catalina is availalable for $35 an hour, or $110 for a half day. If you've always had a dream to win the America's Cup but can't sail, Sailboats will get you started. They offer a 10-hour course over five days for $250 for one person and $100 for each additional person. Open 9am to sunset daily, weather permitting.

Shake a Leg, 2600 Bayshore Dr., Coconut Grove (☎ 305/858-5550), is a unique sailing program for disabled and able-bodied people alike interested in sailing. The program pairs up sailors for day and evening cruises and offers sailing lessons as well. Consider a moonlit cruise (offered monthly) or a race clinic. The group is a lot of fun and can teach you a lot. Shake-a-Leg members welcome able-bodied volunteers for activities on and off the water. It costs $50 for non-members to rent a boat for three hours; free for volunteers. Open Saturday from 9am to 1pm.

JETSKIS

At **Fun Watersports Waterski & Jet-Ski Rentals,** 5101 Blue Laggon Dr., West Miami (☎ 305/261-7687), the lake you ride on is small and in an odd location (right next to Miami International Airport), but if you've never jetskied, it's somewhat safer than braving the sometimes-heavy chop of the ocean. For $25 a half hour and $45 an hour, you can rent a jetski and learn how to operate it. For $35 a half hour and $60 an hour, a waverunner is available if you prefer to sit rather than balance on a moving jetski. Fun Watersports is open daily from 10am to 6pm.

Tony's Jet Ski Rentals, 3601 Rickenbacker Causeway, Key Biscayne (☎ 305/361-8280), rents jetskis, Yamaha Wave Runners, and Kawasaki two-seaters. This is the city's largest rental shop, located on a private beach in the Miami Marine Stadium lagoon. Jetskis rent for $38 per half hour and $60 an hour. Waverunners rent for $45 per half hour and $70 per hour. Tony's is open daily from 10:30am to 6:30pm.

KAYAKS & CANOES

If you've taken the Biscayne National Park boat tour, no doubt all that cruising has inspired you to do it yourself. I think that renting a canoe and paddling your way through clear blue water and mangroves is something almost every visitor should do while in Miami. This national treasure has a host of natural beauty to explore. You can rent canoes from **Biscayne National Park Boat Tours,** east end of SW 328th St., Homestead (☎ 305/230-1100), for $7 an hour, or $20 for a half day. Open daily from 10am to 4pm.

Though his company, **Mangrove Coast Seakayaks,** 5794 Commerce LN., South Miami (☎ 305/663-3364; internet: http://www.webcom.com/~mangrove/), is based in Miami, David Berman launches most of his trips from Key Largo (about 1 1/2-hour drive from Miami). It is there that you can see some of the most unadulterated terrain in the state. On the scheduled trips, usually on Sunday mornings at 7:30am, you'll tour wild mangrove islands and stop along the way for snacks, including native tropical juice and fruit. If you want to kayak in the area you are staying, David and his very helpful staff will be happy to arrange an individual trip. Manatees and dolphins have been known to cozy up to kayakers, thinking the human-powered low-draft boats are a friendly species. They usually are.

Trips, offered year-round, are scheduled according to the tides; call for departure times. A guided tour costs $85 per person, a private custom tour $250. These rates are higher than other kayaking companies because they use only high-quality fiberglass sea kayaks with rudders that are contolled with your feet. These very stable boats are easy to control, though the paddling does take time to master. Although it's fun, it's also hard work. Bring waterproof clothing and a change of clothes, because you'll get soaked.

The laid-back **Urban Trails Kayak Company** rents boats from two nearby locations in North Dade: 10800 Collins Ave., Miami Beach (☎ 305/947-1302); or 17530 W. Dixie Hwy. (☎ 305/919-7689). Both offer scenic routes through rivers with mangroves and islands as your destination. Most of the kayaks are sit-on-tops, which is what it sounds like. Most boats are plastic, though there are some fiberglass ones available too. Rates are $8 an hour, $20 for up to four hours, $25 for more than four people. Tandems are $15 an hour, $35 for up to four hours, $40 for the day. Open daily from 9am to 5pm.

The outfitters give interested explorers a map to take with them and quick instructions on how to work the paddles and boats. If you want a guided tour, you'll need at least four people and will pay $35 per person for a half day. This is a fun, great way to experience some of Miami's unspoiled wildlife. But be sure to pump up at the gym before tackling the paddle. It's a lot harder than it looks!

SCUBA DIVING

In 1981, the government began a wide-scale project designed to increase the number of habitats available to marine organisms. One of the program's major accomplishments has been the creation of nearby artificial reefs, which have attracted all kinds of tropical plants, fish, and animals. In addition, Biscayne National Park (see Chapter 11) offers a protected marine environment just south of Downtown.

Several dive shops around the city offer organized weekend outings, either to the reefs or to one of over a dozen old shipwrecks around Miami's shores. Check "Divers" in the yellow pages for rental equipment and for a full list of undersea tour operators.

Divers Paradise of Key Biscayne, 4000 Crandon Blvd. (☎ 305/361-3483), offers two dive expeditions daily to the more than 30 wrecks and artificial reefs off the coast of Miami Beach and Key Biscayne. A two-week certification course costs $159, and a dive trip costs about $90 for those with no equipment and only $35 if you show up prepared. It's open Monday to Friday from 10am to 6pm, Saturday and Sunday from 9am to 6pm. Call ahead for times and locations of dive trips.

Team Divers on South Beach, at 300 Alton Rd. (☎ 305/673-3483), can certify those who have always wanted to explore the ocean floor. A two-week course costs $150; those in a hurry can take an abbreviated three-day course for $425. They offer dive trips off Key Biscayne and Miami Beach, including some breathtaking reef and wreck dives for more-experienced divers. The dives cost $57, including the equipment, or $45 if you bring your own mask, snorkel, and fins. Call ahead for dive and course information.

SWIMMING

Obviously, with all of the beachfront areas in Miami, you can swim all of the time. In addition, most hotels have pools.

If you need swimming lessons, try the **Dick Cutrera School of Swimming,** 462 Hampton Lane, Key Biscayne (☎ 305/361-5441 or 305/361-5502). Dick Cutrera is a swimmimg legend in Miami and Key Biscayne. In business for 35 years, he has taught grandmothers and their grandchildren to swim from his own home. He charges $30 for a half hour of swimming lessons to children, and $60 an hour to teach adults. He claims he can teach someone to swim in as little as three hours. He charges extra to drive to a hotel or condo pool to meet clients. Dick Cutrara is available seven days a week by appointment.

Summer swimming lessons for adults and children are also offered at the **Venetian Pool,** 2701 DeSoto Blvd. at Toledo St., Coral Gables (☎ **305/460-5356**). A two-week course for children costs $25, and adults pay $4 per lesson.

WINDSURFING

Many upscale Miami hotels rent windsurfers to their guests. However, if the hotel hosting your stay does not have a water-sports concession stand, head for Key Biscayne to solve the problem yourself.

Sailboards Miami, Rickenbacker Causeway, Key Biscayne (☎ 305/361-SAIL), operates out of big yellow trucks on Hobie Beach (see "Miami's Beaches," above), the most popular windsurfing spot in the city. For those who've never wind-surfed but want to try their hand at it, for $39, Sailboards Miami offers a two-hour lesson that's guaranteed to turn you into a wave warrior or you get your money back. After that, you can rent a windsurf board for $20 an hour, or $37 for two hours. If you want to make a day of it, a 10-hour card costs $130. Open daily from 10am to 6pm.

10 More Places to Play, Both Indoors & Out

BIKING & SCOOTERS

The hard-packed sand that runs the length of Miami Beach is one of the best places in the world to ride a bike. An excellent alternative to the slow pace of walking, biking up the beach is great for surf, sun, sand, exercise, and people-watching. You may not want to subject your bicycle to the salt and sand, but there are plenty of oceanfront rental places here. Most of the big beach hotels rent bicycles, as does **Miami Beach Bicycle Center,** 601 5th St. (☎ 305/674-0150). Located in South Beach, the shop rents bicycles for $3 per hour or $14 a day. It's open Monday to Saturday from 10am to 7pm, Sundays from 10am to 5pm.

Bikers can also enjoy more than 130 miles of paved paths throughout Miami. The beautiful and quiet streets of Coral Gables and Coconut Grove beg for the attention of bicyclists. Old trees form canopies over wide, flat roads lined with grand homes and quaint street markers. Several bicycle trails are spread throughout these neighborhoods, including one that begins at the doorstep of **Dade Cycle,** 3216 Grand Ave., Coconut Grove (☎ 305/444-5997); it's open Monday to Saturday from 9:30am to 5:30pm, Sunday from 10:30am to 5:30pm. MasterCard, Visa, and Discover are accepted.

Although the shopkeeper and his employees tend to be a little disorganized, **Gary's Megacycles,** 1260 Washington Ave., South Beach (☎ 305/534-3306), rents the best bikes on the beach. Aluminum-frame bikes, helmets, and locks rent for $5 an hour or $15 for the day. Consider junking the rental car and cruising South Beach on one of these hot wide-rimmed combination bikes. There are a lot of styles to choose from. Just be sure to lock up. It's open Monday to Saturday from 10am to 7pm, Sundays from 10am to 4pm.

If the park isn't flooded from excess rain, **Shark Valley** in the Everglades National Park is South Florida's most scenic bicycle trail. Many locals haul their bikes out to the Glades for a relaxing day of wilderness trail-riding. You can ride the 17-mile loop with no other traffic on the paved flat road except other bikers and a menagerie of wildlife. Don't be surprised to see a gator lounging in the sun, a deer munching on some grass, or a picnicker eating a sandwich along the mangrove shore. **The Shark**

Seasonal Pleasures: Pick Your Own Produce

There is a singular pleasure in getting your fingers stained red by berry juice while friends up North shovel snow. But as South Florida's farm region gets gobbled up by tract homes and shopping malls, the area's self-pick farms are disappearing, too. Some of the remaining berry fields offer ambitious pickers a chance to find their own treasures beneath the trailing vines of strawberry rows for about $2.25 a pound.

If you don't feel like waking up early to pick the juicy red jewels, at least stop by to buy a few boxes of South Florida's winter's bounty. Nothing tastes like just-picked berries. They bloom between January and April, but be sure to call to see if there are any in the fields. Also, at other times you may find vegetable and herbs, including carrano; cayenne, jalapeño, and orange peppers; eggplant; zuchini; lettuce; cabbage; and broccoli.

The four strawberry farms mentioned here are scattered throughout South Dade and can be reached by driving south on U.S. 1. **Burr's Berry Farms,** 12741 SW 216th St., in Goulds (☎ 305/235-0513), makes outrageous fruit milk shakes and ice creams. Open daily from 9am to 5:30pm. To get to Burr's, drive south on U.S. 1 and turn right on SW 216th Street. The fruit stand is about one mile west of U.S. 1 on the same road as the Monkey Jungle.

Go early to snatch up some of the fast-selling pastries, tarts, and jams at **Knaus Berry Farm,** 15980 SW 248th St., in Redland (☎ 305/247-0668). At all hours a line of anxious ice-cream lovers waits for fresh fruit treats from a little white window. You'll also find flowers, herbs, and other seasonal vegetables. Open Monday to Saturday from 8am to 5:30pm. Knaus is slightly further south on U.S. 1. Turn right on 248th Street, and the stand is about 2 1/2 miles down on the left-hand side.

You should bring your sunglasses and a big appetite to **Strawberries of Kendall,** with locations at SW 137th Avenue at 94th Street; SW 117th Avenue, at 160th Street; and SW 144th Street west of the turnpike. It's best to drive around the area west of U.S. 1 and see who is open and who has berries in the field.

Straight-up strawberry picking is available at **Rainbow Farms,** located at 18001, 20800, and 22601 Krome Ave. (☎ 305/342-9340). Get there before the sun does.

Valley Tram Tour Company (☎ 305/221-8455) rents old-fashioned coaster-brake bikes on the premises for $3.25 an hour and accepts MasterCard or Visa.

Or, if you'd like an audio-guided tour, call Follow the Yellow Brick Road, a bike tour company run by **Gary's Megacycles,** at 1260 Washington Ave., South Beach (☎ 305/534-3306). For $25, a representative will pick you up from anywhere from Miami Beach to Hollywood. Along with a high-tech Coloi bike, you'll get an audio-taped guide in any of four languages, a map, a helmet, and all the accoutrements. They're open from 10am to 7pm and accept reservations 24 hours a day. Pay with MasterCard or Visa.

Intra Mark, 350 Ocean Dr., Key Biscayne (☎ 305/365-9762), rents scooters for $15 an hour or $45 for a half day, and bicycles for $5 an hour or $10 for four hours. The eco-minded staff directs bikers to the best paths for nature-watching. You'll find them off the Rickenbacker bridge across from the Rusty Pelican every day between 10am and 5pm.

Key Cycling, 61 Harbor Dr., Key Biscayne (☎ 305/361-0061), rents mountain bikes and beach cruisers for $3 per hour. They are open daily from 10am to 5pm.

BINGO

Well, why not? This is Miami after all. You can play bingo at **Miccosukee Indian Gaming,** 500 SW 177th Ave., west of Miami (☎ 305/222-4600 or 800/741-9600). This huge glitzy casino isn't Las Vegas, but you can play slot machines, all kinds of bingo, and even poker (with a $10 maximim pot). The crowd is your standard crazed-eyed bunch of grandmas and young couples looking for a big win, but you can have fun and get some great deals on meals. (See the Cafe Hammock listing in Chapter 6; it's also plotted on the Everglades National Park map in Chapter 11).

North Collins Bingo, 18288 Collins Ave., Sunny Isles (☎ 305/932-7185), features games every day from noon to midnight (with a break from 4 to 7pm). It costs $5 to $20 a night. There are no-smoking areas, door prizes nightly, and "the largest cash prizes allowed by law."

FISHING

Bridge fishing is popular in Miami; you'll see people with poles over most every waterway.

Some of the best **surf casting** in the city can be had at Haulover Beach Park, at Collins Avenue and 105th Street, where there is a bait-and-tackle shop right on the pier. South Pointe Park, at the southern tip of Miami Beach, is another popular fishing spot and features a long pier, comfortable benches, and a great view of the ships passing through Government Cut.

You can also choose to do some **deep-sea fishing,** although the cost is pretty steep. **Kelley Fishing Fleet** at the Haulover Marina, 10800 Collins Ave., at 108th St., Miami Beach (☎ 305/945-3801), has half-day, full-day, and night fishing aboard diesel-powered "party boats." The fleet's emphasis on drifting is geared toward trolling and bottom fishing for snapper, sailfish, and mackerel; but it also schedules two-, three-, and four-day trips to the Bahamas. Half-day and night fishing trips are $19.75 for adults and $12.75 for children; full-day trips are $29.75 for adults and $18.75 for children; rod-and-reel rental is $4.25. Daily departures are scheduled at 9am, 1:45pm, and 8pm; reservations are recommended.

Also at the Haulover Marina is **Charter Boat *Helen C,*** 10800 Collins Ave., Haulover (☎ 305/947-4081). Although there is no shortage of private charter boats here, Capt. Dawn Mergelsberg is a good pick, since she puts individuals together to get a full boat. Her *Helen C* is a twin-engine 55-footer, equipped for big-game "monster" fish like marlin, tuna, dolphin, and bluefish. The cost is $70 for up to 6 people, and sailings are scheduled for 8am to noon and 1 to 5pm daily; call for reservations.

Key Biscayne also offers some deep-sea fishing to those willing to get their hands dirty. The competition among the boats is fierce, but the prices are basically the same no matter which boat you choose. The going rate is about $400 to $450 for a half day, and $600 to $700 for a full day of fishing. These rates include a party of six, and the boats supply you with rods and bait as well as instruction for first timers. Some will take you out to Key Biscayne and even out to the Upper Keys if the fish aren't biting in Miami.

You might consider the following boats, which all sail out of the Key Biscayne marina; call for reservations: *Sunny Boy III* (☎ 305/361-2217); *Abracadabra* (☎ 305/361-5625); *Queen B* (☎ 305/361-2528); and *L & H* (☎ 305/361-9318).

GOLF

There are more than 50 private and public golf courses in the Greater Miami area. Contact the Greater Miami Convention and Visitors Bureau (☎ 305/539-3063 or 800/283-2707) for a complete list of courses and costs.

✪ **The Links at Key Biscayne,** 6700 Crandon Blvd., Key Biscayne (☎ 305/ 361-9129), is the number-one-ranked municipal course in the state and one of the top five in the country. The park is situated on 200 bayfront acres and offers a pro shop, rentals, lessons, carts, and a lighted driving range. The course is open daily from dawn to dusk; greens fees (including cart) are $68 per person during the winter and $37.50 per person during the summer. Special twilight rates are available.

Another recommended public course is **Bayshore Par Three Golf Course,** 2795 Prairie Ave., Miami Beach (☎ 305/674-0305). You'll have fun trying to avoid all the water traps at this inexpensive and gorgeous course just north of the Miami Beach Convention Center. The course is open daily from 6:30am to sunset; greens fees are $7 to $10 per person during the winter and $5 to $7 during the summer. Special twilight rates are available.

One of the most popular courses among real enthusiasts is the **Doral Park Golf and Country Club,** 5001 NW 104th Ave., West Miami (☎ 305/591-8800); it's not related to the Doral Hotel or spa. Call to book in advance since this challenging 18-holer is so popular with locals. The course is open from 6:30am to 6pm during the winter and until 7pm during the summer. Cart and greens fees vary so call 305/ 594-0954 for information.

Known as the best in Miami, ✪ **Golf Club of Miami,** 6801 Miami Gardens Dr., at NW 68th Ave. (☎ 305/829-8456), has three 18-hole courses of varying degrees of difficulty. You'll encounter lush fairways, rolling greens, and some history. Designed in 1961 by Robert Trent Jones and updated in the 1990s by the PGA, this was where Jack Nicklaus played his first professional tournament and Lee Trevino won his first professional championship. The course is open daily from 6:30am to sunset. Cart and greens fees are $45 to $75 per person during the winter, $20 to $34 per person during the summer. Special twilight rates are available.

Good for beginners and pros, the par-36 course at **Greynolds Park,** 17530 West Dixie Hwy., North Miami Beach (☎ 305/949-1741), is one of the county's most popular nine-hole courses. Mark Mahanna designed the 3,100-yard course in 1964. The snack shop and pro shop are good. The course is open daily from 7am to 5pm during the winter, and until 7pm during the summer. Greens fees are $10 per person during the winter and $8 per person during the summer. Cart fees are $10 for two people. Special twilight rates are available.

Amateurs practicing their game or golfers on a budget looking for some cheap practice time will appreciate **Haulover Park,** 10800 Collins Ave., Miami Beach (☎ 305/ 940-6719). The longest hole on this par-27 course is 125 yards in a pretty bayside location. The course is open daily from 7:30am to 5:30pm during the winter, until 7:30pm during the summer. Greens fees are $5 per person during the winter, $4 per person during the summer. Hand carts cost $1.38.

HEALTH CLUBS

Although many of Miami's full-service hotels have fitness centers (see Chapter 5, "Accommodations," for details), don't count on them in less upscale establishments or in the small Art Deco District hotels. Several health clubs around the city will take nonmembers in on a daily basis.

In Coral Gables, try **Body and Soul Fitness Club,** 355 Greco Ave. (☎ 305/ 443-8688). This club has top-of-the-line Body Master machines, aerobic machines, and free weights. You'll be charged $9.50 per aerobics class and per workout. Special packages are available at a reduced cost: 4 visits for $36, and 10 visits for $85, including aerobics and weights. Hours are Monday to Friday from 5:30am to 9:30pm, Saturday from 8am to 6pm, and Sunday from 8am to 4pm.

If you're already a member at the mega health club chain **Bally's Total Fitness,** you're in luck—just dial 800/777-1117 for a complete listing of their South Florida clubs.

At **Club Body Tech,** 1253 Washington Ave. (☎ 305/674-8222), in South Beach, you'll work out with Cindy Crawford, Madonna, and a host of super models when they're in town. Trendy Club Body Tech offers star appeal and top-of-the-line equipment for a post-aerobic toning session. Workouts are $14 daily, $52.19 weekly, and $94.79 monthly. Hours are Monday to Friday from 6am to 7pm, Saturday from 8am to 9pm, and Sunday from 9am to 7pm.

Also in South Beach is **The Gridiron Club,** 1676 Alton Rd. (☎ 305/531-4743), a muscle gym for sure. Come on in and sweat with the BIG boys on South Beach. Aerobics classes are offered for those watching their girlish figure. A daily workout will run you $9; talk to the manager about extended rates. Hours are Monday to Friday from 5:30am to 11pm, Saturday from 8am to 8pm, and Sunday from 8am to 6pm.

Olympia Gym, 20335 Biscayne Blvd., in North Miami Beach (☎ 305/ 932-3500), is a huge, top-of-the-line gym where the elite of North Miami Beach meet. If you don't mind working out to the music of beepers and cellular phones, Olympia Gym has much to offer, including a juice bar on the premises and an extra-large aerobics room. Daily workouts cost $10, weekly $30, and monthly $75. Hours are Monday to Friday from 5am to 10pm, Saturday from 8am to 7pm, and Sunday from 8am to 5pm.

On the second floor of the Clevelander Hotel is the **South Beach Gym,** 1020 Ocean Dr., South Beach (☎ 305/672-7499). Although there are no aerobics classes offered, this gym offers a workout with an ocean view. Model-watch on the stairclimbers with Ocean Drive at your feet. It costs $15 daily, $35 weekly, and $60 monthly. Hours are Monday to Friday from 7am to 11pm, Saturday from 9am to 9pm, and Sunday from 10am to 6pm.

IN-LINE SKATING

In-line skates are popular in South Florida where the consistently flat terrain makes in-line skating an easy endeavor. Do remember to keep a pair of sandals or sneakers with you since many area shops won't allow you inside with skates on. The following rental outfits can help chart an interesting course for you and provide you with all the necessary gear.

In South Beach, **Fritz's Skate Shop,** 726 Lincoln Rd. Mall (☎ 305/532-1954), rents their skates for $8 an hour and $24 a day. If you're an in-line skate virgin, an instructor will hold your hand for $25 an hour.

Also in South Beach, **Skate 2000,** 1200 Ocean Dr. (☎ 305/538-8282), will help you keep up with the beach crowd by renting in-line skates and the associated safety accessories. Rates are $8 per hour or $24 per day. Skate 2000 also offers free lessons by a certified instructor on South Beach's boardwalk every Sunday at 10am. You can either rent or bring your own skates.

In Coral Gables, **Extreme Skate & Sport,** 7876 SW 40th St. (☎ 305/261-6699), is one of South Florida's largest in-line skate dealers. Even if you know nothing about this trendy new sport, a knowledgable sales staff and a large selection to choose from ensures that you can't go wrong.

JOGGING

Throughout Dade County you'll find a number of safe and well-planned jogging courses. The following are only a sampling of some of the best. For more good routes in your area or for running buddies, call the Miami Runners Club at 305/227-1500.

In Key Biscayne, **Crandon Park,** at 4000 Crandon Blvd., has a 15-station fitness course as well as great secluded trails that run along the island's east side, past the old zoo and over the Causeway. In **Coconut Grove,** jog along the South Bayshore Drive on a clearly marked path along the bay.

In North Miami Beach, **Greynolds Park,** 17530 W. Dixie Hwy., has many trails winding past lakes and hills as well as a 15-station Vita-Course. At **Haulover Beach Park,** 10801 Collins Ave., in Miami Beach, you can run along the sandy paths with the ocean at your side through a rigorous 20-station fitness course. The **Miami Beach Boardwalk,** a wood-decked course, runs along the ocean from 21st to 46th streets. Though you share the well-lighted path with strollers and walkers, it is a beatiful route in a safe area.

The **Larry and Penny Thompson Park,** 12451 SW 184th St., in Homestead, has more than 250 acres of park land with trails running through varied terrain. They also have a 20-station fitness course if you're feeling ambitious.

TENNIS

Hundreds of tennis courts in South Florida are open to the public for a minimal fee. Most courts operate on a first-come first-serve basis, and most are open from sunrise to sunset. For information and directions to the one nearest where you're staying, call one of these government offices: City of Miami Beach Recreation, Culture, and Parks Department (☎ 305/673-7730); City of Miami Parks and Recreation Department (☎ 305/461-1313); or the Metro-Dade Park and Recreation Department (☎ 305/533-2000).

The three hard courts and seven clay courts at the **Key Biscayne Tennis Association** at the Links, located at 6702 Crandon Blvd. (tel 305/361-5263), get crowded on weekends since they are some of Miami's nicest courts. There's a pleasant, if limited, pro shop, plus many good pros. Only four courts are lit at night, but if you reserve at least 48 hours in advance you can usually take your pick. The lush foliage surrounding the courts makes you feel as though you are on an exclusive island somewhere, which you are, in Key Biscayne. It costs $4 to $5 per person per hour. The courts are open daily from 8am to 9pm.

In Coral Gables, **Salvadore Park,** 1120 Andalusia Ave. (☎ 305/460-5333), is a favorite local spot with eight clay courts (the most popular) and five hard courts. All courts are lighted at night. Though plans are in the works to get a real pro shop, the current facilities can string racquets, sell balls, and offer snack-vending machines. It costs $4 to $5 per person per hour. The courts are open Monday to Friday from 8am to 10pm, weekends 8am to 7pm. To get here, take I-95 until it turns into U.S. 1 South. After about 5 miles, look for Grenada Boulevard and turn right. Turn left on Andalusia Avenue, and the park is one block down on the left.

11 Spectator Sports

Miami's spectacular sports scene includes several major professional franchises, including football, basketball, and baseball, plus an eclectic variety of international games, including cricket, soccer, and jai alai. Check the *Miami Herald*'s sports section for a daily listing of local events and the paper's Friday "Weekend" section for comprehensive coverage and in-depth reports.

For last-minute tickets, call the stadium directly since many season ticket holders sell singles and return used tickets. Expensive tickets are available from brokers or individuals, listed in the classified sections of the local papers. It's usually possible to get tickets for Dolphins or Heat games.

BASEBALL

The National League **Florida Marlins,** one of baseball's newest expansion teams, played their first (and quite successful) season in 1993. Home games are at the Joe Robbie Stadium, 2269 NW 199th St., Greater Miami North (☎ 305/626-7417). The team currently holds spring training in Melbourne, Florida. Tickets are $4 to $30. Box office hours are Monday to Friday 8:30am to 6pm, Saturday and Sunday 8:30am to 4pm, and prior to games; tickets are also available through Ticketmaster, (☎ 305/358-5885).

The **University of Miami Hurricanes** play about 45 home games in the 5,000-seat Mark Light Stadium, on the U of M's Coral Gables Campus. The season lasts from February to May, with both day and evening games scheduled. For information, call 305/284-2263 or 800/GO-CANES in Florida. Tickets are $3 to $6. Box office hours are Monday to Friday 9am to 5pm, Saturday 9am to noon.

Although no major-league teams are currently planning to hold spring training in the Miami area, "Grapefruit League" enthusiasts should contact the offices of Major League Baseball (350 Park Ave., New York, NY 10022; ☎ 212/339-7800) to get an update or to find out about teams within day-trip distance of Miami, in Fort Lauderdale and north.

BASKETBALL

The **Miami Heat**, now coached by celebrity coach Pat Riley, made its NBA debut in November 1988. Predictably, it is also one of Miami's hottest tickets. The season of approximately 41 home games lasts from November to April, with most games beginning at 7:30pm at Miami Arena, 1 SE 3rd Ave. For information, call 305/577-HEAT. Tickets are $14 to $41. Box office hours are Monday to Friday 10am to 4pm (until 8pm on game nights); tickets are also available through Ticketmaster (☎ 305/358-5885).

DOG RACING

Greyhound racing is Miami's most popular spectator sport. The dogs circle the oval at speeds averaging 40 miles per hour. Betting is simple, and track workers are willing to give you a hand. Note that racing is held from April 27th to the end of November.

The fun, high-stakes **Flagler Greyhound Track,** 401 NW 38th Court (☎ 305/649-3000), features some of America's top dogs, with racing seven days a week. The track hosts the $110,000 International Classic, one of the richest races on the circuit. Admission is $1 general, $3 clubhouse. Parking costs 50¢. Post times are Monday to Sunday at 7:30pm, with matinees Tuesday, Thursday, and Saturday at 12:30pm.

An average crowd of 10,000 fans wager a collective $1 million nightly at the **Hollywood Greyhound Track,** considered by experts to be one of the best in the country. It's located at 831 N. Federal Hwy., at Pembroke Rd., Hallandale (☎ 800/959-9404). If you've never been to the dog track before, arrive half an hour early for a quick introduction to greyhound racing, shown on the track's TV monitors. Admission is $1 general, $2 clubhouse. Parking is free. Post times are Monday through Sunday at 7:30pm in late December through late April, with matinees Tuesday, Thursday, and Saturday at 12:30pm.

FOOTBALL

Football is as big in Miami as it is around the rest of the country. Miami's golden boys are the **Miami Dolphins,** the city's most recognizable team, followed by thousands of "dolfans." With Don Shula's retirement, it will be interesting to see what the new coach, Jimmy Johnson, can do with this once-unstoppable team. The team plays at least eight home games during the season, between September and December, at 7500 SW 30th St., Davie (☎ 305/452-7000). Tickets cost about $30. The box office is open Monday to Friday from 10am to 6pm; tickets are also available through Ticketmaster (☎ 305/358-5885). Call for schedules.

The **University of Miami football Hurricanes** play at the famous Orange Bowl from September through November. The stadium, at 1501 NW 3rd St., is seldom full, and games here are really exciting. If you sit high up, you will have an excellent view over Miami. Call for the schedule (☎ 305/284-CANE or 800/GO-CANES in Florida). Tickets start at $13. Box office hours are Monday to Friday 8am to 6pm and prior to all games.

HORSE RACING

Wrapped around an artificial lake, **Gulfstream Park** is both pretty and popular. Large purses and important races are commonplace at this suburban course, and the track is often crowded. It's located at U.S. 1 and Hallandale Beach Boulevard, Hallandale. Call for schedules (☎ 305/931-7223). Admission is $2 grandstand, $4.50 clubhouse. Parking costs from $1. Post times from January 4th to March 16th are Tuesday to Sunday at 1pm.

You've seen the **Hialeah Park's** pink flamingos on "Miami Vice," and indeed, this famous colony is the largest of its kind. This track, listed on the National Register of Historic Places, is one of the most beautiful in the world, featuring old-fashioned stands and acres of immaculately manicured grounds. It's located at 2200 E. 4th Ave., Hialeah. Admission is $2 grandstand, $4 clubhouse; children under 18 are free with an adult. Parking costs from $1.50. Races are held mid-November to mid-May, but the course is open year-round for sightseeing Monday to Saturday from 10am to 4pm. Call for post times (☎ 305/885-8000).

JAI ALAI

Jai alai, a sort of Spanish-style indoor lacrosse, was introduced to Miami in 1924 and is regularly played in two frontons in South Florida. Although the sport has roots stemming from ancient Egypt, the game as it is now played was invented by Basque peasants in the Pyrenees Mountains during the 17th century.

Players use woven baskets, called *cestas,* to hurl balls, *pelotas,* at speeds that sometimes exceed 170 miles per hour. Spectators, who are protected behind a wall of glass, place bets on the evening's players.

Miami Jai Alai Fronton, 3500 NW 37th Ave., at NW 35th St. (☎ **305/ 633-6400**), is America's oldest jai alai fronton, dating from 1926. It schedules 13 games per night. Admission is $1 grandstand, $5 clubhouse. Open year-round, except for a four-week recess in the fall. The first game starts Monday and Wednesday to Saturday at 7pm, with matinees on Monday, Wednesday, and Saturday at noon.

8 Driving & Strolling Around Miami

Miami is made up of many small neighborhoods, some of which are more car-centric than others. If you're Downtown or in Coral Gables without a car, then you may as well plan on sitting by the pool for your whole vacation. In these neighborhoods, attractions, restaurants, and shopping are spread out over many miles, and sidewalks are virtually non-existent. To explore the greater Miami area and the beaches, you'll want a car. But if you're staying in South Beach, you'll find a car superfluous, and, when it comes to paying valets, even annoying (unless, of course, you're driving a convertible Rolls-Royce or a Lamborghini—then expect scantily-clad guys or girls to jump in the front seat when it's unoccupied).

The two driving tours below highlight the different sides of Miami, the city's architectural, cultural, and ethnic diversity. And when you're set to stroll South Beach, the walking tour will show you the way.

DRIVING TOUR 1
Miami Panorama

Start and Finish: Bayside Marketplace, 401 Biscayne Blvd. (Downtown).

Time: Approximately one hour, excluding stops and allowing for light traffic.

Best Times: Weekday working hours, when the roads tend to be less busy.

Worst Times: Weekday rush hours, from 8 to 10am and 4 to 6pm.

This driving tour follows a circular route, which will give you a good feel for the city in general. You'll drive through Miami's varied neighborhoods, from the Art Deco District to Downtown skyscrapers, from the beach to Little Haiti.

Start at the:

1. **Bayside Marketplace** (401 Biscayne Blvd.). Perched on the edge of Miami's expansive bay just across from the busy port, this curvaceous retail marketplace boasts dozens of colorful carts selling souvenirs and ethnic wares, as well as some fun restaurants and retail shops.

Driving Tour: Miami Panorama

1. Bayside Marketplace
2. Port of Miami Expansion
3. Port of Miami
4. Palm, Hibiscus, and Star Islands
5. Ocean Drive
6. The Loews Miami Beach Hotel
7. Deco hotels
8. Burger King
9. Fontainebleau Mural
10. Doral and Eden Roc Hotels
11. Normandy Isle
12. North Bay Village
13. Little Haiti
14. Caribbean Marketplace
15. Omni International Mall

Just past Bayside and the port bridge on the right, you'll see:

2. **Miami's Port Expansion.** In the works is a multimillion-dollar expansion of the portside area to include new slips for the mega-liners, a retail shopping area, a maritime museum, underground parking, plus a lushly landscaped park.

Drive north along U.S. 1 (Biscayne Blvd.) about 10 blocks and turn east onto the MacArthur Causeway (Rte. 41). When crossing the bridge, look back toward Downtown to see one of the world's prettiest cityscapes. To your right you can see the:

3. **Port of Miami,** just across a thin strip of water. If they are not out at sea, several large cruise ships will be docked here; they'll look so close it will seem like you can almost touch them.

To your left, as you cross the bridge, you'll see some of the most luxurious waterfront homes in Miami Beach. You'll pass three private islands:

4. **Palm Island, Hibiscus Island, and Star Island.** Many of Miami's elite live here, including Gloria Estefan and her husband Emilio.

Once the causeway reaches Miami Beach, stay in the right lane and continue straight onto Fifth Street, the southern boundary of South Beach's Art Deco District. Fifth Street terminates at:

5. **Ocean Drive,** the Art Deco District's most celebrated strip. Turn left and drive slowly. Lined with pretty hotels, tall palm trees, and a long stretch of beach, this unusual road offers some of the best people-watching in Miami. For a more in-depth look at this historic area, see "A Walking Tour," later in this chapter.

TAKE A BREAK   The **News Café,** 800 Ocean Dr. (☎ 305/538-NEWS), is a great place to relax. This cheap and trendy sidewalk cafe is just across from the beach. It serves excellent breakfasts, terrific soups, salads, sandwiches, and the like, plus good coffee and herbal teas. (See listing in Chapter 6, "Dining.")

At 15th Street you will be forced to turn left. Make the turn, and look right to see:

6. **The Loews Miami Beach Hotel,** currently under construction. This is the only convention hotel to be built on South Beach in more than 30 years. The Loews company is investing in excess of $135 million to build an 800-room mega-structure to handle the demand of conventioneers.

Drive one block on 15th Street, and then turn right onto Collins Avenue. You are now heading north along Miami Beach's most celebrated street, which will give you a good perspective on the diversity of the beach. Look to your right and take time to admire the:

7. **Deco hotels,** like the **Delano** (no. 1685), **National** (no. 1687), and **Shelborne** (no. 1801). These hotels are some of the region's prettiest skyscrapers. On the northwest corner of Collins Avenue and Lincoln Road is:

8. **Burger King,** Miami's only true art deco fast-food outlet, complete with a blue-and-yellow tropical exterior, neon lights, and trademark art deco curves.

Continue north, past the huge hotels and condominiums, and you will soon see a lush tropical garden behind huge Roman-style columns. This fancy greenery is just an illusion; it's really the:

9. **Fontainebleau Mural** at Collins Avenue and 44th Street. The lagoon and water-falls pictured actually exist behind the wall in the rear of the famous Fontainebleau Hilton (4441 Collins Ave.). Stop by and take a look.

Farther along Collins Avenue, you will pass the:

10. **Eden Roc** (4525 Collins Ave.), **Doral** (4833 Collins Ave.), and many more of Miami Beach's monolithic hotels. Continue north and turn left onto 71st Street. You now are heading toward the 79th Street Causeway, named for its terminus on the mainland. You will see:

11. **Normandy Isle,** as the route to the causeway winds its way through. This exclusive and pretty Biscayne Bay enclave is riddled with French-sounding street names. In the middle of the bay, the causeway crosses:

12. **North Bay Village,** a couple of residential islands built from the soil dredged from Biscayne Bay.

Once back on the mainland, continue straight, about six blocks past Biscayne Boulevard, and turn left onto NE 2nd Avenue. You now are driving through the heart of:

13. **Little Haiti.** This region's main thoroughfare contains dozens of stores with signs announcing their goods in Creole, French, and sometimes English. Drive south until you reach the:

14. **Caribbean Marketplace,** located at the corner of 60th Street. The colorful building's architecture is based on the Iron Market in Port-au-Prince. The marketplace was forced to close due to financial failure; it used to contain shops selling traditional foods and merchandise.

Turn left on any street and make your way back to U.S. 1. Then turn right and head south on U.S. 1. This relatively tame-looking main thoroughfare is, by night, one of Miami's seediest strips. After dark, prostitutes walk the streets, and drug transactions are commonplace. Keep your eyes open during the day, too. There are a variety of fast-food joints and cheap motels, plus annoying traffic lights.

15. **The Omni International Mall** (1601 Biscayne Blvd.) will soon appear on your left, after which you will drive under the bridge leading to the MacArthur Causeway and end up back at the Bayside Marketplace.

DRIVING TOUR 2
Downtown, Coconut Grove & Coral Gables

Start and Finish: Bayside Marketplace, 401 Biscayne Blvd. (Downtown).

Time: Approximately 1¹/₂ hours, excluding stops.

Best Times: Two hours before sunset, when the city will be breathtakingly illuminated.

Worst Times: Weekday morning rush hour, from 8 to 10am.

After driving through Downtown, this tour takes you to two of Miami's oldest and best-known neighborhoods: Coconut Grove and Coral Gables.

Coconut Grove, annexed by the City of Miami in 1925, was established by northeastern artists and writers and has a reputation as being an "in" spot for bohemian-minded intellectuals. The first hotel in the area was built in 1880.

Coral Gables, one of Miami's first planned developments, was created by developer George Merrick in the early 1920s. Many houses were built in a Mediterranean style along lush tree-lined streets that open onto beautifully carved plazas. The best architectural examples of the era have Spanish-style tiled roofs and are built from Miami oolite, a native limestone, commonly called "coral rock."

Start at the:

1. **Bayside Marketplace** (401 Biscayne Blvd.) and drive south along Biscayne Boulevard. Take note of the:

2. **Southeast Financial Center** (200 S. Biscayne Blvd.). This 55-story steel-and-glass tower is the tallest building east of Dallas and south of Manhattan. At its bottom, Biscayne Boulevard doglegs and reveals:

3. **International Place** (100 SE First St.). Formerly owned by the ruined Centrust Bank, this spectacular wedge-shaped building, designed by celebrated architects I. M. Pei & Partners, is illuminated nightly at a cost of more than $100,000 a year. For Independence Day, the night lights are red, white, and blue; for Deco weekend, pastel colors.

   Stay in the left lane and cross the drawbridge over the Miami River, the mainland's most beautiful waterway and a sewer of illegal activities. Be patient—the bridge regularly opens to let tugboat-led barges through.

   You are now on Brickell Avenue, home to the largest concentration of international banks in the United States. Drive slowly. Each one of these architectural masterpieces deserves attention.

   South of SE 15th Street, Brickell Avenue becomes residential, and an equally extraordinary block of condominiums rises up along the avenue's east side. Lush foliage makes it hard to see these palaces, so you might want to stop your car for a better view. Three of these apartment buildings:

4. **The Palace** (1541 Brickell Ave.), **The Imperial** (1617 Brickell Ave.), and **The Atlantis** (2025 Brickell Ave.), were designed by Arquitectonica, Miami's world-famous architectural firm. The Atlantis sports a square hole in its center, sprouting a lone palm tree over the outdoor Jacuzzi. **Villa Regina** (1581 Brickell Ave.) would be almost plain-looking if it were not for its spectacular rainbow-colored exterior, painted by Israeli artist Yacov Agam.

   A few blocks past the turn-off toward Key Biscayne you will come to a second set of traffic lights. Bear left onto South Miami Avenue, which quickly becomes South Bayshore Drive. This two-lane road runs along Biscayne Bay, on the southern edge of Coconut Grove. Just before the sign to the Villa Vizcaya, turn left and drive around the large cul-de-sac. On the right you'll see:

5. **Sylvester Stallone's bayfront mansion** with a huge coral gate. Keep following the road and look right to find **Madonna's mansion.**

   After you've driven around the cul-de-sac, return to South Bayshore Drive and immediately look out on your left for the entrance to:

6. **Villa Vizcaya** (3251 S. Miami Ave.; ☎ 305/250-9133), the elegant and opulent estate of International Harvester pioneer James Deering. The magnificent house and grounds are worth wandering. The house is open daily from 9:30am to 5pm, the gardens until 5:30pm. (See "More Attractions" in Chapter 7.)

   Continuing along tree-covered South Bayshore Drive, you'll pass the:

7. **Grand Bay Hotel** (2669 S. Bayshore Dr.) on your right and **Miami City Hall,** at the end of Pan American Drive, on your left.

   At its end, South Bayshore Drive turns right, into McFarlane Road, a short street that terminates at Coconut Grove's most important intersection. Make a sharp left onto Main Highway and cruise slowly. This is the heart of the:

8. **Grove's business district** and home to dozens of boutiques and cafes.

   ☕ **TAKE A BREAK**   For a light snack or a long lunch, there are plenty of places to choose from. The **Green Street Café,** 3110 Commodore Plaza (☎ 305/567-0662), is located on one of the Grove's busiest corners, the intersection of Main Highway and Commodore Plaza. But the cafe is a relaxed place, serving breakfast, lunch, and dinner to loungers who linger at the sidewalk tables. (See the listing in Chapter 6, "Dining.")

Driving Tour: Downtown, Coconut Grove & Coral Gables

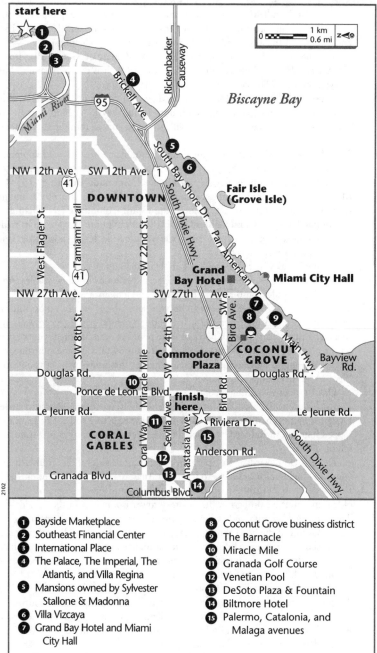

start here

Biscayne Bay

NW 12th Ave.   SW 12th Ave.

DOWNTOWN

Fair Isle
(Grove Isle)

West Flagler St.

Tamiami Trail

SW 22nd St.

Grand
Bay Hotel   **Miami City Hall**

NW 27th Ave.   SW 27th   Ave.

SW 8th St.

SW 24th St.

Commodore
Plaza

**COCONUT
GROVE**   Bayview
Rd.

Douglas Rd.   Douglas Rd.

Miracle Mile

Ponce de León   Blvd.

Le Jeune Rd.   finish
here   Le Jeune Rd.

Coral Way

Sevilla Ave.

Anastasia Ave.

**CORAL
GABLES**   Riviera Dr.

Bird Rd.

Granada Blvd.

Columbus Blvd.   Anderson Rd.

Rickenbacker Causeway

Brickell Ave.

Miami River

South Bay Shore Dr.

South Dixie Hwy.

Pan American Dr.

Main Hwy.

Bird Ave.

2102

1. Bayside Marketplace
2. Southeast Financial Center
3. International Place
4. The Palace, The Imperial, The Atlantis, and Villa Regina
5. Mansions owned by Sylvester Stallone & Madonna
6. Villa Vizcaya
7. Grand Bay Hotel and Miami City Hall

8. Coconut Grove business district
9. The Barnacle
10. Miracle Mile
11. Granada Golf Course
12. Venetian Pool
13. DeSoto Plaza & Fountain
14. Biltmore Hotel
15. Palermo, Catalonia, and Malaga avenues

155

Two blocks south of Commodore Plaza, you will see the entrance to:

9. The Barnacle, 3485 Main Hwy. This former home of naval architect and early settler Ralph Middleton Munroe is now a museum open to the public (☎ 305/448-9445). Tours are given Thursday through Monday at 9am, 10:30am, 1pm, and 2:30pm. Admission is $2. (See "More Attractions" in Chapter 7.)

On the next block, on your right, is the **Coconut Grove Playhouse** (3500 Main Hwy.). Built as a movie theater in 1926, it is one of Miami's oldest showplaces. (See "The Performing Arts" in Chapter 10.)

Main Highway ends at Douglas Road (SW 37th Avenue). Turn right, drive north about 10 miles, and make a left onto Coral Way (SW 22nd Street). You are now entering Coral Gables via the village's most famous thoroughfare, dubbed the:

10. Miracle Mile. This stretch of shops and eateries dates from the development's earliest days and is the heart of downtown Coral Gables. To your right, on the corner of Ponce de Leon Boulevard, stands the **Colonnade Building** (133–169 Miracle Mile), a structure that once housed George Merrick's sales offices and has recently been rebuilt into a top hotel, the Omni Colonnade (see Chapter 5, "Accommodations"). **Coral Gables City Hall** (405 Biltmore Way), with its trademark columned rotunda, is at the end of the Miracle Mile. It's open weekdays from 8am to 5pm; admission is free.

Follow Coral Way to the right of City Hall and past the:

11. Granada Golf Course, one of two public teeing grounds in Coral Gables. After four blocks, turn left onto DeSoto Boulevard and look for the:

12. Venetian Pool (2701 DeSoto Blvd.) on your left. This is Miami's most unusual swimming pool, dating from 1924. It is hidden behind pastel stucco walls and shaded by three-story Spanish porticos. The pool has been honored with a listing on the National Register of Historic Places. It costs $4 to swim and sunbathe, but if you just want to look around for a few minutes, the cashier may let you in free. (See "More Attractions" in Chapter 7.)

One block farther along DeSoto Boulevard is the:

13. DeSoto Plaza and Fountain, one of Coral Gables' most famous traffic circles. Designed by Denman Fink in the early 1920s, the structure consists of a column-topped fountain surrounded by a footed basin that catches water flowing from four sculpted faces.

DeSoto Boulevard picks up again on the other side of the fountain and continues for about four blocks to its end at Anastasia Avenue, in front of the:

14. Biltmore Hotel (1200 Anastasia Ave.). This grand hotel is one of Miami's oldest and prettiest properties. Its 26-story tower is a replica of the Giralda Bell Tower of the Cathedral of Seville in Spain. The enormous cost of operating this queen has forced the hotel through many hands in recent years. Bankruptcy shut the hotel in 1990, but the Biltmore is once again open and under the management of the Westin chain. Go inside and marvel at the ornate marble-and-tile interior, outfitted with mahogany furniture and a medieval fireplace.

Out back, the hotel's enormous swimming pool is the largest of its kind in America. Just beyond is the challenging and beautiful Biltmore Golf Course.

The fastest way back to downtown Miami is to continue east to the end of Anastasia Avenue, turn right on LeJeune Road, and then turn left onto U.S. 1. Take a detour on your way home to sightsee on:

15. Palermo, Catalonia, Malaga, and other interesting tree-lined avenues. If you drive along these streets, you'll see some of Miami's historic homes, built in the 1920s and 1930s in Spanish and Mediterranean styles.

A WALKING TOUR
South Beach: The Deco District

Start: Art Deco Welcome Center, 1001 Ocean Dr., South Beach.
Finish: Clevelander Hotel, 1020 Ocean Dr.
Time: Allow approximately 1 1/2 hours, not including browsing in galleries.
Best Times: Monday through Saturday between noon and 5pm.
Worst Times: Nights and Sundays, when galleries are closed.

The Art Deco District is roughly bounded by the Atlantic Ocean on the east, Alton Road on the west, Sixth Street on the south, and Dade Boulevard (along the Collins Canal) to the north. This approximately one-square-mile area is listed on the National Register of Historic Places. You'll certainly see plenty of people to watch while you're strolling around; there's amazing architecture to admire as well. This tour walks you past the Deco District's highlights.

Start at the:

1. **Art Deco Welcome Center** (1001 Ocean Dr.). This storefront has several informative giveaways, including maps and art deco architecture information. Art deco books, T-shirts, postcards, mugs, car sunshades, and other similarly styled items are sold. It's open Monday to Saturday from 11am to 6pm, usually later until 9pm on Thursday, Friday, and Saturday evenings.

   Turn right onto 10th Street. One block ahead, on the corner of Collins Avenue, you will see the:

2. **Essex House** (1001 Collins Ave.). Built in 1938, the Essex is an excellent example of Nautical Moderne, complete with octagonal porthole windows, curved design, and sleek "racing stripes" along its sides. Explore the lobby, which features etched glasswork and detailed crown moldings.

   Across the street is the pink-and-yellow:

3. **Fairmont Hotel** (1000 Collins Ave.), best known for its extremely stylish garden restaurant just beside it. Although the restaurant's angles and colors blend in with the surroundings, its decorations are contemporary.

   Continue down (left, as you face the Fairmont) Collins Avenue to the:

4. **Sherbrooke Cooperative** (901 Collins Ave.), which has a beautiful porch railing, porthole windows, and multilevel rounded eyebrows that give elegance to an otherwise simple design.

   On the corner of 8th Street is the:

5. **Tiffany Hotel** (801 Collins Ave.), an attractive building boasting an imposing metal spire. Now painted plain white, the hotel would benefit from a color scheme that highlighted its special design.

   Turn right onto 8th Street, walk one block, and make a left onto Washington Avenue. Most of the storefronts along this street are original commercial exteriors. Like many establishments on the block, the aqua-colored:

6. **Strand Restaurant** (671 Washington Ave.) features ornate moldings and a ziggurat roof line. Formerly the Famous, a popular Jewish restaurant, the Strand has maintained the original wide-open but warm interior.

   Walk south, turn left on Sixth Street, and continue two blocks to the beach. Make a left on Ocean Drive and stroll along one of South Beach's most beautiful strips. Most buildings on this stretch are hotels built in the late 1930s and early 1940s. The:

7. **Park Central** (640 Ocean Dr.) is one of the street's most successful designs, flaunting a fluted tin eave, etched-glass windows, and a geometric guardrail. The:

A Deco District Glossary

You don't have to be an architect to enjoy the fanciful styles that are so prevalent in these parts; the intrinsic beauty of these buildings is easy to see. Still, it always helps knowing what to look for. Here's what to call what you're looking at:

Eyebrows   Colorfully painted cantilevered window shades are a common ornament on Streamline Moderne buildings.

Etched Glass   Flamingos, fish, palm trees, and other tropical motifs are found in many area lobbies.

Finial, Spire, or Trylon   These futuristic-looking vertical ornaments are located atop a building's highest point.

Neon Light   This seems to be an area trademark.

Porthole Windows   Nautical imagery is one of South Beach's most important motifs.

Rounded Corners   These reflect most obviously the influence of airplanes, automobiles, trains, and ships on Streamline Moderne architecture. Fast, sleek, aerodynamic designs looked futuristic in the 1930s and 1940s.

Terrazzo   This mosaic flooring is frequently arranged in geometric patterns.

Ziggurat or Stepped Pediment   Seen on roofs and incorporated into other areas, this Egyptian style is common in art deco design.

8. Imperial and **Majestic hotels** (650 and 660 Ocean Dr.) are also excellent examples of the period. Like many hotels in the area, these buildings are cantilevered over their front terraces and are supported by columns.
   On the next block, the:
9. Colony Hotel (736 Ocean Dr.) stands out because of the huge neon sign affixed to its curved-entry overhang.

   ☕ **TAKE A BREAK**   Take a break from your tour to relax at the **News Café,** 800 Ocean Dr. (☎ 305/538-NEWS). (For details, see Driving Tour 1 earlier in this chapter or the listing in Chapter 6.)

   Having regained your energy, walk a little farther along Ocean Drive to the:
10. Waldorf Towers (860 Ocean Dr.), a corner building with a cylindrical turret capped by a rooftop tower. Glass bricks and eyebrows are also incorporated into the building's design. At night, a spectacular neon light sculpture shines in the uppermost windows.
    On the next block is the:
11. Locust Apartments (918 Ocean Dr.), the only Mediterranean Revival building on the street. It features attractive pointed-arch windows reminiscent of those found in medieval Venetian edifices.
    A block farther down is the:
12. Clevelander Hotel (1020 Ocean Dr.), one of the few in the area with an original swimming pool and deco-style sun deck area. The huge outdoor stage, located behind the pool, hosts live rock and reggae bands most every night, when the Clevelander becomes one of the liveliest locales on the beach.
    Turn west again and make your way to Washington Avenue, where you should turn right to head north. On the left side of the street, you'll see the magnificent:

Walking Tour: South Beach: The Deco District

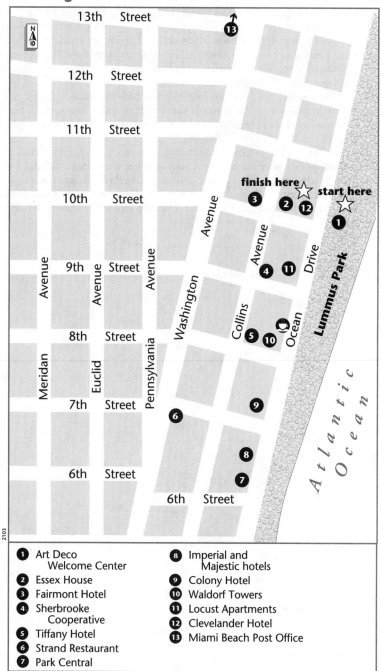

1 Art Deco
Welcome Center

2 Essex House

3 Fairmont Hotel

4 Sherbrooke
Cooperative

5 Tiffany Hotel

6 Strand Restaurant

7 Park Central

8 Imperial and
Majestic hotels

9 Colony Hotel

10 Waldorf Towers

11 Locust Apartments

12 Clevelander Hotel

13 Miami Beach Post Office

13. Miami Beach Post Office (1300 Washington Ave.), completed in 1938 and designed by Howard L. Cheney as part of the Works Progress Administration project. The building is in the Depression Moderne style. Step into the skylit-domed lobby where you'll see a turret with a lantern filial and gleaming gold post boxes beneath a classic, uplifting WPA mural depicting Ponce De Leon landing in Florida and fighting with the Native Americans.

Head east on 13th Street to make your way back to Ocean Drive. On your way, observe how many of the simple buildings have similar deco features. Many have been repainted in brighter colors than the originals to highlight the unusual features. Turn right and walk three blocks.

You'll find yourself back at the Art Deco Welcome Center, where you began this tour. Staff here are happy to answer any questions you might have. Other good places to stroll include the pedestrian mall along Lincoln Road, between 16th and 17th streets west of Washington, and Española Way, a pretty street with Mediterranean Revival architecture, between 14th and 15th streets, starting at Collins Avenue.

Shopping 9

A mecca for hard-core shoppers from Latin America, the Caribbean, and the rest of Florida, Miami has everything you could ever want and things you never dreamed of. Where else could you find a Neiman-Marcus just miles from an authentic Cuban cigar factory? A place selling exotic saltwater fish down the street from a warehouse full of opulent 15th-century French furniture? Only in Miami.

This shopping capital has strip malls, boutiques, and enclosed malls in every conceivable nook and cranny of the city, which makes for lots of competition among retailers and good bargains for those who like to hunt. In addition to the mega-malls, like Dadeland and Aventura, the city entices buyers with block after block of fancy boutiques and second-hand stores in areas like Lincoln Road and Miracle Mile. Driving along the side streets you'll spot dozens of interesting ethnic food and clothing shops to explore. In this chapter, I've listed some of my favorite places to shop.

1 The Shopping Scene

Almost every major street in Miami is lined with an infinite variety of small stores, restaurants, motels, and fast-food joints. This is, after all, primarily a tourist town. Below I've described some of the popular retail areas, where many stores are concentrated for easy browsing.

As a general rule, **shop hours** are Monday through Saturday from 10am to 6pm and Sunday from noon to 5pm. Many stores stay open late (usually until 9pm) one night of the week (usually Thursday). Shops in trendy Coconut Grove are open until 9pm on Sunday through Thursday and even later on Friday and Saturday nights. Department stores and shopping malls keep longer hours, staying open from 10am to 9 or 10pm Monday to Saturday and noon to 6pm on Sunday.

The 6.5% state and local **sales tax** is added to the price of all non-food purchases.

Most Miami stores can wrap your purchase and **ship** it anywhere in the world via the United Parcel Service (UPS). If they can't, you can send it yourself, either through UPS (☎ 800/742-5877) or through the U.S. Mail (see "Fast Facts: Miami" in Chapter 4).

Someday . . . Miami will become the great center of South American trade.

—Julia Tuttle, Miami's founder, 1896

SHOPPING AREAS

If you're looking for discounts on all types of goods—from watches and jewelry to luggage and leather—downtown Miami is the best district to visit. However, watch out for some unscrupulous businesses. You also should look around Flagler Street and Miami Avenue for all kinds of cluttered bargain stores. Most signs around there are printed in both English and Spanish, for the benefit of locals and tourists alike.

Coconut Grove   Downtown Coconut Grove is one of Miami's few pedestrian-friendly zones. Centered around Main Highway and Grand Avenue and branching onto the adjoining streets, the Grove's wide sidewalks, lined with cafes and boutiques, provide hours of browsing pleasure. You can't escape Miami's ubiquitous malls, however—there's one near this cozy village center (see "Mayfair Shops in the Grove" under "Malls"). Coconut Grove is best known for its dozens of avant-garde clothing stores, funky import shops, and excellent sidewalk cafes. See "City Layout" in Chapter 4 for more information about this area.

Coral Gables—Miracle Mile   Actually only a half-mile long, this central shopping street was an integral part of George Merrick's original city plan (see "Neighborhoods in Brief" in Chapter 4). Today, the strip still enjoys popularity for its old-fashioned ladies shops, haberdashers, bridal stores, and gift shops. Lined primarily with small 1970s storefronts, the Miracle Mile, which terminates at the Mediterranean-style City Hall rotunda, also features several good and unusual restaurants (see Chapter 6, "Dining"). It's worth a stop on your tour of Coral Gables.

South Beach—Lincoln Road   This luxurious pedestrian mall, originally designed in 1957 by Morris Lapidus, recently underwent a multimillion-dollar renovation that includes new lighting and more than 500 palm trees. Here shoppers can find an array of clothing, art, and a menagerie of South Beach's finest restaurants. Future plans include the construction of a movie theater and a major grocery store. Enjoy an afternoon of gallery hopping and be sure to look into the open studios of the Miami City Ballet. Monthly gallery tours, periodic jazz concerts, and a weekly farmer's market are just a few of the offerings on "The Road." See "City Layout" in Chapter 4 for more information about this area.

MALLS & DEPARTMENT STORES

There are so many malls in Miami that it would be impossible to mention them all, but what follows is a list of the biggest and the best shopping centers.

You can find any number of department stores such as Saks, Neiman-Marcus, and Lord & Taylor in the Miami malls listed below, but Miami's own is **Burdines,** at 22 E. Flagler St., Downtown (☎ 305/835-5151), and 1675 Meridian Ave. in Miami Beach (☎ 305/674-6311). One of the oldest and largest department stores in Florida, Burdines specializes in high-quality, middle-class home furnishings and fashions.

Aventura Mall. 19501 Biscayne Blvd., Aventura. ☎ **305/935-4222.**

Enter this large enclosed mall, and you'll find it easy to imagine you're on the outskirts of Omaha . . . or anywhere else in America for that matter. More than

---

Best Buys

Miami's best buys are fruit and fish, the region's specialties. Nowhere will you find fresher local seafood and citrus products. Here's where to shop.

CITRUS FRUIT   There was a time when it seemed as though almost every other store was shipping fruit home for tourists. Today such stores are a dying breed, although a few high-quality operations still send the freshest oranges and grapefruit. **Todd's Fruit Shippers,** 260 Minorca Ave. (☎ 305/448-5215), can take your order over the phone and charge it to American Express, MasterCard, or Visa. Boxes are sold by the bushel or fractions thereof and start from about $20.

SEAFOOD   **East Coast Fisheries,** 330 W. Flagler St., Downtown (☎ 305/577-3000), a retail market and restaurant (see the review in Chapter 6), has shipped millions of pounds of seafood worldwide from its own fishing fleet. It is equipped to wrap and send 5- or 10-pound packages of stone-crab claws, Florida lobsters, Florida Bay pompano, fresh Key West shrimp, and a variety of other local delicacies to your door via overnight mail.

Miami's most famous restaurant is **Joe's Stone Crab,** located at 227 Biscayne St., South Beach (☎ 305/673-0365 or 800/780-CRAB). Joe's makes overnight air shipments of stone crabs to anywhere in the country, but note that Joe's only sells stone crabs during the crab season, which runs from October through May.

---

200 generic shops are complemented by the megastores J.C. Penney, Lord & Taylor, Macy's, and Sears. It's located at Biscayne Boulevard and 197th Street near the Dade–Broward county line. Parking is free.

Bal Harbour Shops. 9700 Collins Ave., Bal Harbour. ☎ **305/866-0311.**

There's not much in the way of whimsy here, just the best-quality goods from the fanciest names. Ann Taylor, Fendi, Joan & David, Krizia, Rodier, Gucci, Brooks Brothers, Waterford, Cartier, H. Stern, Tourneau—the list goes on and on. The Bal Harbour Shops are the fanciest in Miami. With Neiman-Marcus at one end and Saks Fifth Avenue at the other, the mall itself is a pleasant open-air emporium, featuring covered walkways and lush greenery. The Bal Harbour Shops are located at 97th Street, just opposite the tall Sheraton Bal Harbour Hotel. Parking starts at $1 with an endorsed ticket.

Bayside Marketplace. 401 Biscayne Blvd., Downtown. ☎ **305/577-3344.**

The marketplace, filled with lively and exciting shops, has a stunning location—16 beautiful waterfront acres in the heart of downtown Miami. Downstairs, about 100 shops and carts sell everything from plastic fruit to high-tech electronics (some of the more unique specialty shops are listed separately). The upstairs eating arcade is stocked with dozens of fast-food choices, offering a wide variety of inexpensive international eats. Some restaurants stay open later than the stores, which close at 11pm Monday to Saturday and 8pm on Sunday. Parking is $1 per hour.

✪ **Dadeland Mall.** 7535 N. Kendall Dr., Kendall. ☎ **305/665-6226.**

The granddaddy of Miami's suburban mall scene, Dadeland features more than 175 specialty shops, anchored by 5 large department stores—Burdines, J.C. Penney, Jordan Marsh, Lord & Taylor, and Saks Fifth Avenue. Sixteen restaurants serve from the adjacent Treats Food Court. The mall is located at the intersection of U.S. 1 and SW 88th Street, 15 minutes south of Downtown. Parking is free.

The Falls. 8888 Howard Dr., Kendall area. ☎ **305/255-4570.**

Tropical waterfalls are the setting for this outdoor shopping center with dozens of moderately priced, slightly upscale shops. Miami's only Bloomingdales is here, as are Polo, Ralph Lauren, Caswell-Massey, and more than 60 other specialty shops. The Falls is located at the intersection of U.S. 1 and 136th Street, about 3 miles south of Dadeland Mall. Parking is free.

Mayfair Shops in the Grove. 2911 Grand Ave., Coconut Grove. ☎ **305/448-1700.**

The small and labyrinthine Mayfair Shops complex, just a few blocks east of Commodore Plaza, conceals several top-quality shops, restaurants, art galleries, and nightclubs. The emphasis is on chic, expensive elegance, and intimate European-style boutiques. Valet parking is available for $1 for the first two hours and $1 each additional hour; $6 after 6pm.

Sawgrass Mills. 12801 W. Sunrise Blvd., Sunrise. ☎ **305/846-2300.**

Although this mammoth mall is actually located in Broward County, west of Fort Lauderdale, it is a phenomenon worth mentioning. Since the most recent expansion, which added more than 30 new designer outlet stores, this behemoth now holds more than 300 shops and kiosks in nearly 2.5 million square feet covering 50 acres. Wear your Nikes to trek around the shops that include: Donna Karan, Saks Fifth Avenue, Levi's, Sunglass Hut, Ann Taylor, Barneys New York, Cache, Waterford crystal, and hundreds more selling at 30% to 80% below retail.

From Miami, buses run three times daily; the trip takes just under an hour. Call for exact pick-up points along Collins Avenue and Downtown. If you are driving, take I-95 North to 595 West until Flamingo Road. Exit and turn right, driving 2 miles until Sunrise Boulevard. You can't miss this monster on the left. Parking is free. But don't forget where you parked your car.

2 Shopping A to Z

ART & ANTIQUES

Miami's art and antiques shops are scattered in small pockets around Miami. Some are located in North Miami Beach, along West Dixie Highway or Miami Gardens Drive. You'll find the bulk of the antique district in Coral Gables, where many antique and art galleries are within walking distance of each other along Ponce De Leon Boulevard, extending from U.S. 1 to Bird Road. Listed below is a selection of galleries both in and out of these districts; of course there are many more stores to browse in.

If you happen to be in town on the first Friday of a month, you can take a free trolley tour of the Coral Gables art district. The tour runs from 7 to 10pm; meet at Ambrosino (listed below) or any of the other participating galleries in the area. Some shops stay open later hours and serve refreshments to art lovers who want to turn shopping into a night out.

Ambrosino Fine Arts Inc. 3155 Ponce de Leon Blvd., Coral Gables. ☎ **305/445-2211.**

This well-respected gallery shows works by contemporary Latin American artists. The knowledgeable staff is always willing to answer questions.

Dietel's Antiques. 6572 Bird Rd., Coral Gables. ☎ **305/666-0724.**

An active trade business here means lots of different styles are revolving constantly. You'll find baubles of every assortment. Stop into this little jewel as you make your way through this quaint antique district.

Elite Fine Art. 3140 Ponce De Leon Blvd., Coral Gables. ☎ **305/448-3800.**

Touted as one of the finest galleries in Miami, Elite features modern and contemporary Latin American painters and sculptors.

✪ **Evelyn S. Poole Ltd.** 3925 N. Miami Ave., Miami. ☎ **305/573-7463.**

Known as the most fine of the fine antique dealers, the Poole collection of European 17th-, 18th-, and 19th-century decorative furniture and accesories is housed in 5,000 sguare feet of space in the newly revived Decorator's Row. On her local client list are Paloma Picasso and Gianni Versace, who shop for that special "statement piece" in these vast museumlike galleries.

Gallery Antigua. 5103 Biscayne Blvd. (in the Boulevard Plaza Building). ☎ **305/759-5355.**

With Florida so close to the Carribean, it's no surprise that an entire gallery dedicated to Afro-American and Carribean artists would prosper. Gallery Antigua boasts a vast collection of prints and reproductions, as well as masks and sculptures. They do framing on the premises and will ship purchases for you.

Meza Fine Art. 275 Giralda Ave., Coral Gables. ☎ **305/461-2723.**

This gallery specializes in Latin American artists, including Carlos Betancourt, Javier Marin, and Gloria Lorenzo.

Miami Twice. 6562 SW 40th St., Coral Gables. ☎ **305/666-0127.**

Here you'll find the Old Florida furniture and decorations, such as lamps and ashtrays, that define South Florida's unique style. In addition to deco memorabilia there are some fun old clothes, shoes, and jewelry. Since the prices can be a bit steep, bargain like you would anywhere else.

BAKERIES

Andalusia Bake Shops. 248 Andalusia Ave., Coral Gables. ☎ **305/445-8689.** Other locations at 3015 Aventura Blvd., North Miami Beach (☎ 305/935-2253); and 901 Alton Rd., Miami Beach (☎ 305/531-2253).

This ever-expanding chain has won fame among locals who praise it for its outstanding cakes, pastries, and breads. Also, most of the locations have a to-die-for prepared food counter serving up everything from chicken curry salad to hummus and pot pies.

Biga Corporation. 1701 Alton Rd., Miami Beach. ☎ **305/538-3335.** Another location at 305 Alcazar, Coral Gables (☎ 305/446-2111).

Six dollars for a loaf of bread! Yes, and sometimes more. You'll be happy to pay it when you sink your teeth into these inimitable old-world style loaves. Flavors range from seven grain to marble pumpernickel/rye, which is my favorite. There's a great wine and cheese selection, too.

La Boulangerie. 3425 Main Highway, Coconut Grove. ☎ **305/443-0776.** Other locations at 328 Crandon Blvd., Key Biscayne (☎ 305/361-0281); or in Bal Harbor Shops, 9700 Collins Ave., Miami Beach (☎ 305/867-8307).

Stop here for delicious sandwiches and fruit tarts (see review in Chapter 6).

La Brioche Doree. 4017 Prairie Ave., Miami Beach. ☎ **305/538-4770.**

No one makes a better croissant anywhere. Period.

Vie de France. 19575 Biscayne Blvd. (in the Aventura Mall), North Miami. ☎ **305/935-3005.**

After a hard day of shopping, sit back and relax in Vie de France's cafe, sip a cup of "joe," and enjoy one of their delicious "mille feuilles" pastries. It's as close to authentic as you'll get.

BEACHWEAR

You'd expect a plethora of beachwear stores in Miami, and there are. However, if you want to get away from the cookie-cutter styles available at any local mall, try these stores listed below. You're likely to find a bathing suit that makes you stand out while you're basking on the beach or out giving the waves a workout.

Alice's Day Off. 5900 SW 72nd St., South Miami. ☎ **305/284-0301.**

Alice's may have a corner on the neon trend, but they also come out season after season with pretty and flattering floral patterns. If an itsy-bitsy bikini is not your style, Alice's has a range of more modest cuts that won't make you look like one of the local retirees.

Aqua. 650 Lincoln Rd., South Beach. ☎ **305/674-0942.**

If the thought of cavorting on the beaches practically "au naturel" doesn't make you blush, head straight to Aqua. They have a great selection of Brazilian-cut suits all in bold colors.

Bird's Surf Shop. 250 Sunny Isles Blvd., North Miami Beach. ☎ **305/940-0929.**

If you're a hard-core surfer or just want to hang out with them, head to Bird's Surf Shop. Although Miami doesn't regularly get huge swells, if you're here during the winter and one should happen to hit, you'll be ready. The shop carries more than 150 boards. Call their surf line (☎ 305/947-7170) before going out to find the best waves from South Beach to Cape Hatteras and even the Bahamas and Florida's West coast.

Island Trading. 1332 Ocean Dr., South Beach. ☎ **305/673-6300.**

One more part of music mogul Chris Blackwell's empire, Island sells everything you'll need to wear in the tropical resort town, like batik sarongs, sandals, sundresses, bathing suits, cropped tops, and more. Many of the unique styles are designed on the premises by a team of young and innovative designers.

Island Water Sports. 237 NE 167th St., North Miami Beach. ☎ **305/652-2573.**

You'll find everything from booties to gloves to baggies. Check-in here before you rent that Waverunner or Windsurfer.

X-Isle Surf Shop. 437 Washington Ave., South Beach. ☎ **305/534-7873.**

Prices are slightly higher at this beach location, but the young staff is knowledgeable and tubular.

BOOKS

If you enjoy curling up with a good book in front of a blasting air conditioner—we are in Miami after all—Miami's bookstores do the trick.

A Kid's Book Shoppe. 1985 Miami Gardens Dr., North Miami Beach. ☎ **305/937-2665.**

If the kids get bored during long car trips around Miami, stop in here and pick up a book or an educational game. This store specializes in books for children of all ages as well as teaching materials that can stimulate a young, restless mind.

Books & Books. 296 Aragon Ave., Coral Gables. ☎ **305/442-4408.** Another location at 933 Lincoln Rd., South Beach (☎ 305/532-3222).

Here the literati arrive in BMWs. Enjoy the antiquarian room, which specializes in art books and first-edition literature. If that's not enough intellectual stimulation for you, the shop hosts free lectures from noted authors and experts almost nightly as well as a poetry line where you can hear a new poem every day (☎ 305/444-POEM).

At the Lincoln Road location, you'll rub elbows with tanned and buffed South Beach bookworms sipping cappuccinos at the Russian Bear Cafe located inside the store. Check your in-line skates at the door please.

Coco Grove Antiquarian. 3318 Virginia St., Coconut Grove. ☎ **305/444-5362.**

One of very few out-of-print bookstores in Miami, Coco Grove Antiquarian specializes in books about Florida and the Carribean, but also boasts a large selection of out-of-print cookbooks, sci-fi, and first editions.

Cuba Art and Books. 2317 Le Jeune Rd., Coral Gables. ☎ **305/567-1640.**

This shop specializes in old Cuban books about the island nation, and also sells some prints and paintings by Cuban artists. Most titles are in Spanish and focus on art and politics.

CHOCOLATE

If you know and love chocolate, you'll appreciate all of the following stores: **Godiva Chocolatier,** at 19575 Biscayne Blvd., Miami (☎ 305/682-0537), and 7429 N. Kendall Dr., South Miami (☎ 305/662-2429); **Krone Chocolatier,** 9700 Collins Ave., Miami Beach, in the Bal Harbor Shops (☎ 305/868-6670); **Le Chocolatier,** 1834 NE 164th St., North Miami Beach (☎ 305/944-3020); and **Leonidas Chocolate,** 1231 Washington Ave., Miami Beach (☎ 305/673-8088).

CIGARS & CIGARETTES

Although it is illegal to bring Cuban cigars into this country, somehow *Cohibas* show up at every dinner party and nightclub in town. Not that I condone it, but if you hang around the cigar smokers in town, no doubt one will be able to tell you where you can get some of the highly prized contraband. Be careful, however, of counterfeits.

Some of the stores listed below sell excellent hand-rolled cigars made with domestic and foreign-grown tobacco. Many of the *viejos* (old men) got their training in Cuba working for the government-owned factories in the heyday of Cuban cigars.

Ba-balú. 432 Española Way, Miami Beach. ☎ **305/538-0679.**

Including an extensive collection of Cuban memorabilia from pre-1959 Cuba, Ba-balú offers a taste of Cuba, selling not only their hand-rolled cigars (they do about a thousand a week) but T-shirts, baseball caps, Cuban coins, bills, postcards, stamps, and coffee. Enjoy live bongo music nightly, and ask owner Herbie Sosa for a free shot of Cuban coffee.

La Gloria Cubana. 1106 SW 8th St., Little Havana. ☎ **305/858-4162.**

This tiny storefront shop employs about 45 veteran Cuban rollers who sit all day rolling the very popular torpedoes and other critically acclaimed blends. They've got back orders until next Christmas, but it's worth stopping in. They *will* sell you a box and show you around.

Miccosukee Tobacco Shop. 850 SW 177th Ave. (Krome Ave. and Tamiami Trail), Miami. ☎ **305/226-2701.**

At this remote outpost, you are spared the state taxes on cigarettes and can pick up national brands for $14 a carton, generics from $8 to $13.

Mike's Cigars. 1030 Kane Concourse (at 96th St.), Bay Harbor Island. ☎ **305/866-2277.**

Mike's recently moved to this location, but it's one of the oldest smoke shops in town. Since 1950, Mike's has been selling the best from Honduras, the Dominican Republic, and Jamaica, as well as the very hot local brand La Gloria Cubana. Most say they have the best prices, too.

South Beach News and Tobacco. 1701 Washington Ave., Miami Beach. ☎ **305/673-3002.**

A walk-in humidor stocks cigars from the Dominican Republic, Honduras, and Jamaica, plus a hand roller comes in as he pleases to roll for the tourists. You'll also find a large selection of wines, coffees, and cigar paraphernalia in this pleasant little shop.

ELECTRONICS

Electronics are a big market in Miami, and many people travel to Miami from South America and other areas of the world to buy playthings and gadgets. You'll find many electronics stores around, but most are concentrated in downtown Miami. And a trip to downtown Miami to shop for a good Walkman or television can be both amazing and scary. The streets are littered with bargain electronics stores, but shop with care. Make sure any equipment you buy comes with a warranty, and it's wise to charge your purchase instead of paying cash. I've listed a few reputable stores with several chain locations where you can safely shop.

A Sharper Image. 401 Biscayne Blvd. (in the Bayside Marketplace). ☎ **305/374-8539.** Another location in the Dadeland Mall, at 7507 N. Kendall Dr., South Miami. ☎ 305/667-9970.

This store is electronic shopping from A to Z, so if you're an electronics nut, you'll love this store. It tends to be high-end, both in merchandise and price. But it's free just to look and touch (yes, you're allowed), so even if you're not buying, visit the store to see what's new in the high-tech world.

Incredible Universe. 7800 NW 25th St., Miami. ☎ **305/716-5800.**

It's incredible! It's scary! This store is essentially an electronics department store. Once you get over the size and all the promotional gimmicks that masquerade as entertainment, you can find some really great deals. Check out the "Black Hole," a section of the store where items that have been bruised are sold at deeply disounted prices. And you can bring the kids. There's a supervised computer play room to keep kids occupied while Mom and Dad spend.

Sound Advice. 1220 SW 85th St., Kendall. ☎ **305/594-4434.** Other locations at 1595 NE 163rd St., North Miami Beach (☎ 305/944-4434); and 1222 S. Dixie Hwy., Coral Gables (☎ 305/665-4434).

An audio-junkie's candy store, Sound Advice features the latest in high-end stereo equipment, as well as TVs, VCRs, and telephone equipment. Techno-minded, but sometimes pushy salesmen, are on hand to help.

Spy Shops International Inc. 350 Biscayne Blvd., Downtown. ☎ **305/374-4779.** Another location at 2900 Biscayne Blvd. (☎ 305/573-4779).

This store is perfect for James Bond wanna-bes who want to buy electronic-surveillance equipment, day and night optical devices, stun guns, mini safes, door-knob alarms, and other anti-crime gadgets.

FASHIONS
WOMEN'S

A B S Clothing Collection. 226 8th St., South Beach. ☎ **305/672-8887.**

This California-based chain store fits right into South Beach. You'll find trendy and professional stuff here, from zebra-print minis to tailored pantsuits. It's perfect for something to wear strolling on Ocean Drive.

Betsey Johnson. 805 Washington Ave., South Beach. ☎ **305/673-0023.** Another store at 3117 Commodore Plaza., Coconut Grove. ☎ 305/446-5478.

Here you'll find slightly wild clothes for the young and young at heart, made of stretchy materials, velvet, knits, and more.

Loehmann's. 18703 Biscayne Blvd. (Fashion Island), North Miami Beach. ☎ **305/932-4207.**

Loehmann's is the Queen of discount women's clothing. If you don't mind fighting other zealous shoppers and communal dressing rooms, you'll find some great deals here on everything from bathing suits to evening wear.

North Beach Leather. 9700 Collins Ave. (in the Bal Harbor Shops), Miami Beach. ☎ **305/866-0951.**

Looking for a leather outfit in any imaginable color and style? Check out the great mark-down section.

Ungaro. 9700 Collins Ave.(in the Bal Harbor Shops), Miami Beach. ☎ **305/866-1401.**

Here you'll find elegant apparel—what everyone wears to shop at Bal Harbour.

MEN'S

Brooks Brothers. 9700 Collins Ave. (in the Bal Harbor Shops), Miami Beach. ☎ **305/865-8686.**

If you need a new navy blazer or some khaki trousers to roll up for an oceanfront stroll, shop here for the classics.

Giorgio's. 208 Miracle Mile, Coral Gables. ☎ **305/448-4302.**

One of the finest custom men's stores, Giorgio's features an extensive line of Italian suits and all the latest by Canelli.

Hugo Boss. 9700 Collins Ave., Miami Beach. ☎ **305/864-7753.**

Hipsters and business men alike love this place, where you'll find T-shirts and suits all priced over the top.

UNISEX

More than 100 retail outlets are clustered in Miami's mile-square **Fashion District**, just north of Downtown. Miami's fashion center, which surrounds Fashion Avenue—NW Fifth Avenue—is second in size only to New York's. The district features European- and Latin-influenced designs with tropical hues and subdued pastels, and is known for swimwear, sportswear, high-fashion children's clothing, and glittery women's dresses. Most stores offer medium-quality clothing at a 25% to 70% discount, as well as on-site alterations. Most are open weekdays from 9am to 5:30pm.

RESALE SHOPS

Anonymous Consignment Boutique. 3315 Rice St., Coconut Grove. ☎ **305/940-3212.**

On a good day, you can find unusually young and hip designer clothes in good condition. There are tons of hangers on dozens of racks. Patience can yield some great finds like a $15 Versace sundress or a $75 silk Armani blouse.

Douglas Gardens Jewish Home and Hospital Thrift Shops. 5713 NW 27th Ave., North Miami Beach. ☎ **305/638-1900.**

Lately they got smart and started to raise prices. Still, for housewares and books you can do all right. Call to see if they are offering any specials for seniors or students.

Rags to Riches. 654 NE 125th St., North Miami. ☎ **305/891-8981.**

This is an old-time consignment shop in the thrift-store row. You may find some decent rags, and maybe even some riches. Not as upscale as it used to be, this place is still a good spot for costume jewelry and shoes.

Second Hand Rose. 18509 W. Dixie Hwy., North Miami Beach. ☎ **305/932-9888.**

You've got to dig, but sometimes you can come up with a few good finds in women's designer clothes.

The Children's Exchange. 1415 Sunset Dr., Coral Gables. ☎ **305/666-6235.**

Selling everything from layettes to overalls, this pleasant little shop is chock-full of good Florida-style stuff for kids to wear to the beach and in the heat.

SHOES

Battaglia. 360 Miracle Mile, Coral Gables. ☎ **305/461-1190.** Also at Omni, Aventura, and Dadeland malls.

If you're looking for fantastic sandals and high heels at good prices, try this shoe store.

The Leathery. 3460 Main Hwy., Coconut Grove. ☎ **305/448-5711.**

This store sells men's and women's Timberland, Birkenstocks, Bass, Clogs, TEVAs, and more.

Little Feet and More. 7216 Red Rd., South Miami. ☎ **305/666-9655.**

You'll find Nike, Reebok, Cole Hahn, Keds, and Baby Jacks for the whole family.

FOOD MARKETS & STORES

Apple a Day Natural Food Market. 1534 Alton Rd., Miami Beach. ☎ **305/538-4569.**

This grocery store with a natural accent caters to South Beach's health-conscious crowd with your basic nuts and berries as well as some great prepared foods and hard-to-find misos and seaweeds.

Bombay Bazaar. 2008 NE 164th St., North Miami Beach. ☎ **305/948-7258.**

This redolent little storefront is filled with bags and boxes of exotic spices, rices, and beans. Also, a small section of saris, jewelry, scarves, magazines, and videos sell well to the little Indian community that has formed around North Miami Beach. Don't bother trying to call, because an incomprehensible machine picks up, and no one ever calls back.

Epicure. 1656 Alton Rd., Miami Beach. ☎ **305/672-1861.**

You've never seen tomatoes like they sell them here at Epicure. A cluster of plump fire engine–red beauties from Holland sell for more than $4! They are the best. You'll not only find fancy produce, like portobello mushrooms the size of a yarmulke, but pineapples, cherries, and salad greens like you can't imagine. Epicure stocks all the usual prepared foods as well, including great chicken soup and smoked fishes. It's the beach's Scotty's, and you've got to love them. But when you pull out your wallet, you'll be thinking about how much money you have to pull out.

Gardner's Market. 7301 Red Rd., South Miami. ☎ **305/667-9953.**

Anything a gourmet or novice cook could desire can be found here. This fancy grocery store in South Miami offers the freshest and best products, from fish to cheese.

Key Biscayne Farmer's Market. 95 Harbor Dr., Key Biscayne. ☎ **305/361-1300.**

At this farmer's market, you'll find a picturesque bounty of fresh and organic fruits, vegetables, and herbs at prices that are not too insane, considering you're in Key Biscayne.

Kingston Miami Trading Company. 280 NE 2nd St., Downtown. ☎ **305/372-9547.**

With a disorganized array of canned goods, spices, and bottles, this little grocery store in downtown Miami has some great Jamaican specialties, including salt cod fish, scotch bonnet sauces, hard-do bread, jerk seasoning, and lots of delicious drinks like Irish moss, Ting, and young coconut juice.

Ⓢ **Laurenzo's Italian Supermarket and Farmer's Market.** 16385 and 16445 W. Dixie Hwy. ☎ **305/945-6381** and 305/944-5052.

These landmarks in North Miami Beach, or NMB as old-timers say, are the meeting place for those in the know. Anything you want from homemade ravioli to hand-cut imported Romano cheese to smoked salmon to fresh fish and ground pork can be found here. The smells alone emanating from the bakery are enough to make you gain a few pounds. Be sure to see the neighboring store full of just-picked herbs, salad greens, and every type of vegetable from around the world. Incredible daily specials, like 10 Indian River pink grapefruits for 99¢, lure thrifty shoppers from all over the city.

Scotty's. 3117 Bird Ave., South Miami. ☎ **305/443-5255.**

Like Epicure listed above, Scotty's is a similarly stocked and priced market with the most exotic goods in town. You don't have to know how to cook to be a gourmet here, you just have to know how to shop.

A Taste of Old Florida

Old-fashioned smoke houses used to dot U.S. 1 and Biscayne Boulevard, but as Miami grew, the old smokers were driven out of business. As popular as they were, the old shacks couldn't generate enough money to compete with condominiums and shopping centers. Sadly, I've watched dozens disappear over the years.

One that remains is **Jimbo's** on Virginia Key. There's no address, since as Dan, an employee, likes to say: "We're out in the boonies."

Most days, depending on the seasons and the tides and who feels like shopping, Jimbo sells marlin and salmon. Really, their primary business is selling bait shrimp to fisherman. But there is always some odoriferous fish splayed out for the pungent smoke to do its magic on. Usually, it's just been brought in from one of Jimbo's fishermen friends.

If you can find them, you'll see the old crew of Italians playing baci, smoking, and drinking out on the bay, in a tiny sliver of backwater life tucked away from civilization. It's worth it. They work most days that the sun shines and stay until it sets.

To get to Jimbo's, drive over the Rickenbacker Causeway en route to Key Biscayne. Look out on your left side once you have passed the second light on Crandon Boulevard, just past the MAST Academy. Turn left. Drive about a mile until you see some old wooden fishing shacks that are used as movie props. You'll find Jimbo's Shrimps across the way. To find out what they're smoking, call 305/361-7026.

Sedano's. 13794 SW 152nd.St., South Miami. ☎ **305/255-3386.**

Sedano's caters to the large Hispanic community scattered throughout Little Havana and South Miami with an assortment of ethnic fare including fresh produce such as yuca, platanos, mamey, avocado, boniato, and guanabanas. You'll also find basic dry goods such as coffees, beans, rice, cornmeal, and spices.

Vinham Oriental Market. 372 NE 167th St., North Miami Beach. ☎ **305/948-8860.**

Blue crabs, rice cookers, and cookbooks, this store is a one-stop shop for anything you might need for Chinese cooking. A helpful owner will instruct you.

GOLF

Alf's Golf Shop. 524 Arthur Godfrey Rd., Miami Beach. ☎ **305/673-6568.** Another location at 15369 S. Dixie Hwy., Miami (☎ 305/378-6068).

The best pro shop on the beach, Alf's can sell you balls, clubs, gloves, and instructional videos. The knowledgeable staff has equipment for golfers of every level. Plus, the neighboring golf course offers discounts to Alf's clients.

Edwin Watts Golf Shops. 15100 N. Biscayne Blvd., North Miami Beach. ☎ **305/944-2925.**

They have more than 30 stores throughout the Southeast and are one of the most popular golf stores in Miami. This full-service golf retail shop has it all, including clothing, pro-line equipment, gloves, bags, balls, videos, and books. Plus you can ask the pros for advice on the best courses in town, as well as request coupons for discounted greens fees on various courses.

Nevada Bob's. 36th St. and NW 79th Ave. (near the airport), Miami. ☎ **305/593-2999.**

This chain store has everything for golfers at a discount: Greg Norman and Antigua clothing, pro-line equipment, and steel-shafted conventional clubs to the high-tech Yonex clubs. There's more than 6,000 square feet of store; you can practice your swing at an indoor driving range with a radar gun. You won't find commission salespeople here; the staff are a laid-back crew and very up on the latest soft and hard equipment.

HONEY

At **Bee Natural Honey Co.,** 1420 SW 256th St. (☎ 305/258-1110), you can watch them harvest your fresh take of glistening sweet honey on one of Miami's only remaining bee farms.

HOUSEWARES

Dish. 939 Lincoln Rd., Miami Beach. ☎ **305/532-7737.**

Offering an eclectic collection of dinnerware from the deco era to contemporary designs, this funky little boutique is a must-see for the curious or the collector.

Linge de Maison Veronique. 305 Alcazar Ave., Coral Gables. ☎ **305/461-3466.**

Fussy Coral Gables housewives flock here for beautiful wares, including custom and hand-embroidered linens, layettes, bed and bath accessories, and tableware to match your china pattern.

Mr. Pottery. 18721 Biscayne Blvd., North Miami Beach. ☎ **305/937-2638.** Other locations at 11301 S. Dixie Hwy. (☎ 305/238-8985), and in the Town & Country Center Mall (☎ 305/274-7268).

Good prices on a vast selection of everything for the home keep this store busy year-round.

Pratesi Linens Inc. 9700 Collins Ave. (in the Bal Harbour Shops), Miami Beach. ☎ **305/ 861-5677.**

The quality of this Italian linen is unmatchable. But you could buy a car with what you'll pay for a full set of king-size hand-embroidered sheets.

JEWELRY

The International Jeweler's Exchange. 18861 Biscayne Blvd. (in the Fashion Island), North Miami Beach. ☎ **305/931-7032.**

At least 50 jewelers hustle their wares from individual counters at one of the city's most active jewelry centers. Haggle your brains out for excellent prices on timeless antiques from Tiffany's, Cartier, or Bulagari to unique designs you can create yourself. Closed Sunday.

The Seybold Building. 3601 NE 1st St., Downtown. ☎ **305/377-0122.**

Jewelers of every assortment gather here daily to sell their diamonds and gold. The glare is blinding as you enter this multi-level retail marketplace. You'll see handsome and up-to-date designs, but note that there aren't too many bargains to be had here.

LINGERIE

Bare Essence Lingerie. 1245 Washington Ave., South Beach. ☎ **305/532-0304.**

Bare Essence displays a decent collection of underwear and bras, including Cosa Bella, plus a more racy section of negligees that border on the obscene. You'll also find some decent exercise gear.

Belinda's. 827 Washington Ave., South Beach. ☎ **305/532-0068.**

This German designer makes some of the most beautiful and intricate teddies, night-gowns, and wedding dresses. The styles are a little too Stevie Nicks for me to actually consider wearing in public, but the creations are absolutely worth admiring. The prices are appropriately up there.

Corset Corner. 300 Miracle Mile, Coral Gables. ☎ **305/444-6643.**

As the name suggests, this little old store on Miracle Mile sells the basic, good old-fashioned gear.

Flash Lingerie. 9700 Collins Ave. (in the Bal Harbor Shops), Bal Harbour. ☎ **305/868-7732.**

Extremely tasteful and elegant lingerie is what this shop specializes in. You'll find Cotton Club, La Perla, Lou, and other luxurious imports.

Victoria's Secret. 3015 Grand Ave., Coconut Grove. ☎ **305/443-2365.** Other locations at 401 Biscayne Blvd., Miami (☎ 305/374-8030); and Aventura Mall (☎ 305/932-0150).

You've seen the sexy catalogues, now see it up close. The many shops in town stock the basic undergarments in shimmery rayons and polys as well as a few Chinese silk robes and undies. You'll find one of the largest selections of thongs anywhere.

MUSIC

Blue Note Records. 16401 NE 15th Ave., North Miami Beach. ☎ **305/940-3394.**

This place has hard-to-find progressive and underground music and a good bunch of music aficionados who can tell you a thing or two. There are new and used and discounted CDs and old vinyl, too.

Casino Records Inc. 1208 SW 8th St., Little Havana. ☎ **305/856-6888.**

The young hip sales staff speaks English and tends to be music buffs themselves. Here you'll find the largest selection of Latin music in Miami, including pop icons like

Willy Chirino, Gloria Estefan, Albita, and local boy Nil Lara. Their slogan translates to "If we don't have it, forget it." Believe me, they've got it.

CD Solution. 13150 Biscayne Blvd., North Miami. ☎ **305/892-1048.**

Buy, sell, or trade your old CDs at this eclectic music hut.

Revolution Records and CDs. 1620 Alton Rd., Miami Beach. ☎ **305/673-6404.**

Here you'll find a quaint and fairly well-organized collection of CDs, from hard-to-find jazz to original recordings of Buddie Rich. They'll search for anything and let you hear whatever you like.

Specs Music. 2982 Grand Ave., Coconut Grove. ☎ **305/461-9109.** Other locations at 1655 Washington Ave., South Beach (☎ 305/534-6533); and 12451 Biscayne Blvd., North Miami Beach (☎ 305/899-0994).

Call to find out who is playing at this mega-music mall. In addition to a great collection of multicultural sounds, you'll find a lively scene most weekends. Plus the South Beach and Coconut Grove locations have coffee bars with donuts and pastries and sometimes play live music.

PETS & EXOTIC ANIMALS

The tropical climate plus the constant trade with remote lands makes Miami a perfect point for exotic-animal lovers to find any furry or scaly thing imaginable.

Birdland of Miami. 6615 SW 8th St., Coral Gables. ☎ **305/261-9861.**

You'll find anything feathered here, from blue or yellow finches or cockatoos to birds that are either quiet or loquacious. If you have a special request, give them a few days, and they'll find it. The store also offers a full range of supplies, including beautiful gilded cages and fun bird toys.

Exotic Aquariums. 7399 SW 40th St., South Miami. ☎ **305/266-0978.**

Many local divers make a living collecting exotics on their dive trips. Although the practice infuriates conservationists, aquarium owners love it. Here you'll find saltwater and freshwater fish from all over the world.

Natural Selections. 14316 SW 142nd Ave., South Miami. ☎ **305/255-3357.**

Every slimy thing that made your mother screech can be had here, including geckos, lizards, snakes, and iguanas. Call for the gory details of the day.

WINES & SPIRITS

Crown Liquors. 6751 Red Rd., Coral Gables. ☎ **305/669-0225.** Another location at 1296 NE 163rd St. (☎ 305/949-2871).

This liquor store offers one of the most diverse selections in Miami. Its ever-rotating stock comes from estate sales around the country and worldwide distributors. And since there are several stores in the chain, the owners get to buy in bulk, which results in lower prices for oenophiles. If you want one of the tastiest and most affordable champagnes ever, try their exclusive import, Billecarte Salmon.

The Estate Wines & Gourmet Foods. 92 Miracle Mile (at Douglas and Galiano), Coral Gables. ☎ **305/442-9915.**

This exceedingly friendly storefront in the middle of Coral Gables' main shopping street offers a small but well-chosen selection of vintages from around the world. They also sell a great array of gourmet cheeses, pâtés, salads, and sandwiches.

Laurenzo's. 16385 and 16445 W. Dixie Hwy., North Miami Beach ☎ **305/945-6381** and 305/944-5052.

In Laurenzo's, a few small aisles are dedicated to their superb wine collection. A full-time expert can help you choose a bottle. While discounts are available for purchases of a case or more, you'll also get an attitude if you're a novice.

Sunny Isles Liquor. 18180 Collins Ave., North Miami Beach. ☎ **305/932-5782.**

The well-located store has on-hand hundreds of brands of imported beer and hard-to-find liquor. They will search and find decanters and minis for your collection.

10 Miami After Dark

Miami nightlife is as varied as its population. On any night, you'll find world-class opera or dance as well as grinding rock and salsa. Restaurants and bars are open late and many clubs, especially on South Beach, stay open past dawn.

South Florida's late-night life is abuzz, too, with South Beach the center of the scene. The Art Deco District is the spawning ground for top international acts, such as Latin artist Julio Iglesias; controversial rappers 2 Live Crew; jazz man Nestor Torres; and rockers Expose, Nuclear Valdez, The Mavericks, Nil Lara, and, of course, Gloria Estefan. It's no secret that Cuban and Caribbean rhythms are extremely popular, and the sound of the conga, inextricably incorporated into Miami's club culture, makes dancing irresistible.

One of the most striking aspects of the city is the recent growth of world-class music, dance, and theater. Miami proudly boasts a top opera company and symphony orchestra, as well as respected ballet and modern dance troupes.

The one thing Miami seems to have trouble sustaining is consistently good live music. In the past few years Miami has watched more than a half dozen music clubs shut their doors. Some blame the lack of community support; others say it's Miami's remote geographic location, which is too far a drive for bands to include on their circuit; others claim promoters in town don't work hard enough to get the word out. The truth is that there are some excellent venues for live music, especially popular spots for jazz and Latin music. I hope these clubs will endure.

For up-to-date entertainment **listings,** check *The Miami Herald*'s "Weekend" section, which runs on Fridays, or the more comprehensive listings in *New Times,* Miami's free alternative weekly. Available each Wednesday, this award-winning paper prints articles, previews, and advertisements on upcoming local events. Several **telephone hotlines**—many operated by local radio stations—give free recorded information on current events in the city. These include Love 94 Concert hotline (☎ 800/237-0939) and the UM Concert Hotline (☎ 305/284-6477). Other information-oriented telephone numbers are listed under the appropriate headings below.

Tickets for many performances are handled by **TicketMaster;** call 305/358-5885 to charge tickets. For sold-out events, you might try **Ultimate Travel & Entertainment,** 3001 Salzedo, in Coral

Gables (☎ 305/444-8499). This well-known ticket broker is open Monday to Friday from 9am until 6pm, Saturday from 10am until 4pm.

1 The Performing Arts

THEATER

In Miami, an active and varied selection of dramas and musicals are presented throughout the year. Thanks to the support of many loyal theater aficionados, especially an older crowd of New York transplants, season subscriptions are common and allow the theaters to survive, even when every show is not a hit. Some traveling Broadway shows make it to town as well as some revivals by big-name playwrights like Tennessee Williams, David Mamet, Neil Simon, and Israel Horowitz. The best way to find out what is playing is to check the local paper or call the theaters directly. In the summer, most theaters are dark or show a limited schedule.

The Actors' Playhouse, at the newly restored Miracle Mile Theater in Coral Gables (☎ 305/444-9293), is a grand 1948 art deco movie palace with a 600-seat main theater as well as a smaller theater/rehearsal hall where a number of excellent musicals for children are put on throughout the year. Tickets run from $16 to $50.

The **Coconut Grove Playhouse,** on 35th and Main Highway in Coconut Grove (☎ 305/442-4000), was also a former movie house, built in 1927 in an ornate Spanish rococo style. Today, this respected venue is known for its original and innovative staging of both international and local dramas and musicals. The house's second, more intimate Encore Room is well suited to alternative and experimental productions. Tickets run from $15 to $35.

The **Florida Shakespeare Theatre,** on Anastasia Avenue in Coral Gables at the Biltmore Hotel (☎ 305/446-1116), stages at least one Shakespeare play, one classic, and one contemporary piece a year. In addition, this well-regarded theater usually tries to secure the rights to a national or local premiere as well. Tickets cost $20 and $22; $12 and $17 for students and seniors.

The recently renamed **Jerry Herman Ring Theatre** is on the main campus of the University of Miami in Coral Gables (☎ 305/284-3355). The University's Department of Theater Arts uses this stage for advanced-student productions of comedies, dramas, and musicals. Faculty and guest actors are regularly featured, as are contemporary works by local playwrights. Performances are usually scheduled Tuesday through Saturday during the academic year only. Tickets sell for $6 to $16.

The **New Theater,** 65 Almeira Ave., in Coral Gables (☎ 305/443-5909), recently celebrated its 10th birthday. This theater prides itself on showing world-renowned titles from America and Europe. As the name implies, you'll find mostly contemporary plays, with a few classics thrown in for variety. Performances are staged year-round, Thursday through Sunday. Tickets sell for $18 to $20, and are half-price for students. They don't widely advertise it, but on Thursdays you can get a second ticket for half-price.

ACTING COMPANIES

Miami's two well-known acting companies have suffered from poor financing and real-estate woes. At press time neither knew where they were going to be housed for the upcoming season. Luckily, both have use of the beautiful Colony Theater on Lincoln Road and the support of a loyal crew of theater aficionados. Call for schedules and locales.

The **Acme Acting Company** (☎ 305/576-7500) performs Wednesday to Saturday at 8pm, and Sunday at 7pm. They usually present off-beat contemporary plays to critical acclaim. Tickets are $15 to $25 depending on the venue, students and seniors pay $10 to $20.

The **Area Stage Company** (☎ 305/538-2187) lived on Lincoln Road for nearly seven years until rents drove them searching for a new space. This award-winning company has won respect from local and national audiences for their dramatic work in all manner of contemporary theater.

CLASSICAL MUSIC

In addition to a number of local orchestras and operas, which regularly offer high-quality music and world-renowned guests, each year brings with it a slew of special events and touring artists. One of the most important and longest-running series is produced by the **Concert Association of Florida (CAF),** 555 17th St., South Beach (☎ 305/532-3491). CAF regularly arranges the best "serious" music concerts for the city, plus performances by world-renowned dance companies. Since CAF does not have its own space, performances are usually scheduled in either the Dade County Auditorium or the Jackie Gleason Theater of the Performing Arts (see below). The performance season lasts from October through April, and ticket prices range from $20 to $60.

The New World Symphony. Lincoln Rd. in South Beach. ☎ **305/673-3331.** Tickets $10–$40. Student and senior discounts available.

Alternating performances between Downtown's Gusman Center for the Performing Arts and South Beach's Lincoln Theatre, this orchestral academy is a stepping stone for gifted young musicians seeking professional careers. Accepting artists on the basis of a three-year fellowship and led by artistic advisor Michael Tilson Thomas, the orchestra specializes in ambitious, innovative, energetic performances and often features guest soloists and renowned conductors. The symphony's season lasts from October through May.

Florida Philharmonic Orchestra. 169 East Flagler St., Suite 1534, Miami. ☎ **305/930-1812** or 800/226-1812. Tickets $15–$60.

South Florida's premier symphony orchestra, under the direction of James Judd, presents a full season of classical and pops programs interspersed with several children's and contemporary popular music dates. The Philharmonic performs Downtown in the Gusman Center for the Performing Arts, the Jackie Gleason Theater of the Performing Arts, and puts on childrens' concerts at the Dade County Auditorium.

Miami Chamber Symphony. 5690 N. Kendall Dr., Kendall. ☎ **305/858-3500.** Tickets $12–$30.

Renowned international soloists, such as Ida Haendel, Frank Cooper, Shura Scherkassky, Aldo Ciccolini, Richard Stoltzman, and Ivan Davis, regularly perform with this professional orchestra. The symphony performs October through May, and most concerts are held in the Gusman Concert Hall, on the University of Miami campus.

OPERA

✪ **Florida Grand Opera.** Coral Way in Coral Gables. ☎ **305/854-1643.** Tickets $18–$100. Student discounts available.

Nearing their 60th birthday, this company regularly features singers from America's and Europe's top houses. All productions are sung in their original language and staged with projected English supertitles. Tickets become scarce when Placido Domingo or Luciano Pavarotti (who made his American debut here in 1965) come to town.

The opera's season runs roughly from November through April, with performances five days per week. Most productions are staged in the Dade County Auditorium.

DANCE

Several local dance companies train and perform in the Greater Miami area. In addition, top traveling troupes regularly pass through the city, stopping at the venues listed above. Keep your eyes open for special events and guest artists.

✪ **Ballet Flamenco La Rosa at the Performing Arts Network.** 555 17th St., Miami Beach. ☎ **305/672-0552** or 305/757-8475 for tickets. Tickets $20 at door, $18 in advance, $15 for students and seniors.

For a taste of local latin flavor, see a lively troupe perform impressive Flamenco and other styles of dance. In addition to frequent performances on Miami stages, you'll find a host of classes offered by Miami's best Latin dancers. Call for schedules.

✪ **Miami City Ballet.** Lincoln Road Mall at 9th St., South Beach. ☎ **305/532-4880.** Tickets $17–$49.

Headquartered in a storefront in the middle of the Art Deco District's popular pedestrian mall, this Miami company has quickly emerged as a top troupe, performing both classical and contemporary works. The artistically acclaimed and innovative company, directed by Edward Villella, features a repertoire of more than 60 ballets, many by George Balanchine, and more than 20 world premieres. Stop by most afternoons to watch rehearsals through the large storefront window. The City Ballet season runs from September through April, with performances at the Dade County Auditorium.

Miami Ballet Company (MBC). Performing in the Gusman Theater on E. Flagler St. and downtown Miami. ☎ **305/667-5985.** Tickets $9–$50.

This nationally acclaimed company performs for a relatively limited season from December until March. If you are here for the Christmas season, don't miss the classic Nutcracker. Also, guest performers at the Spring gala draw crowds to the stunning Downtown auditorium.

MAJOR VENUES

After years of decay and a $1-million facelift, the **Colony Theater,** on Lincoln Road, South Beach (☎ 305/674-1026), has become an architectural showpiece of the Art Deco District. This multipurpose 465-seat theater stages performances by the Miami City Ballet and the Ballet Flamenco La Rosa, as well as various special events.

At the **Dade County Auditorium,** West Flagler Street at 29th Street, Miami (☎ 305/545-3395), performers gripe about the lack of space, but for patrons this 2,500-seat auditorium is comfortable and intimate. It is home to the city's Greater Miami Opera and stages productions by the Concert Association of Florida, many Spanish programs, and variety shows.

At the **Gusman Center for the Performing Arts,** East Flagler Street at 17th Street in downtown Miami (☎ 305/372-0925), seating is tight but the sound is superb at this elegant, 1,700-seat Downtown theater. In addition to producing a regular stage for the Philharmonic Orchestra of Florida, The Miami Film Festival, and the Ballet Theatre of Miami, the Gusman Center features pop concerts, plays, film-festival screenings, and special events. The auditorium was built as the Olympia Theater in

1926, and its ornate palace interior is typical of the era, complete with fancy columns, a huge pipe organ, and twinkling "stars" on the ceiling.

Not to be confused with the Gusman Center (above), the **Gusman Concert Hall**, 1314 Miller Dr., at 14th Street in Coral Gables (☎ 305/284-2438), is a roomy 600-seat hall that gives a stage to the Miami Chamber Symphony and a varied program of university recitals.

The **Jackie Gleason Theater of the Performing Arts** (TOPA), Washington Avenue at 17th Street in South Beach (☎ 305/673-7300), has been recently renovated in order to improve the acoustics and sightlines. It has become tradition for the American Ballet Theatre to open their touring season here during the last two weeks of January, after which TOPA, a 2,705-seat hall, is home to big-budget Broadway shows, classical music concerts, opera, and dance performances.

2 The Club & Music Scene

LIVE MUSIC & JAZZ

Despite the spotty success of local music, South Florida's jazz scene is very much alive with traditional and contemporary performers. Keep an eye out for guitarist Randy Bernsen, vibraphonist Tom Toyama, and flutist Nestor Torres, young performers who lead local ensembles. The University of Miami has a well-respected jazz studies program in its School of Music (☎ 305/284-6477) and often schedules low- and no-cost recitals. Frequent music shows also are scheduled at the Miami Metrozoo (see "Animal Parks" in Chapter 7). The lineup changes frequently, and it's not always jazz, but the quality is good, and concerts are included with zoo admission.

Additionally, many area hotels feature live music of every assortment. Schedules are listed in the newspaper entertainment sections. Try calling the **Blues Hotline** (☎ 305/666-MOJO) and the **Jazz Hotline** (☎ 305/382-3938) for the most up-to-date bookings in Miami. Cafe Nostalgia, listed in "The Latin Scene" section later in this chapter, also offers live music.

Churchill's Hideaway. 5501 NE Second Ave., Miami. ☎ **305/757-1807.** Cover $3, depends on band.

It's a dive, but if you want to sample Miami's local music scene, Churchill's is the place to go see a fledgling band before they make it big. The theme is a British pub (hence the name Churchill's) where you can snack on rustic shepherd's pie and good English brew. Call ahead for information on upcoming bands and open hours.

The Hungry Sailor. 3064 Grand Ave., Coconut Grove. ☎ **305/444-9359.** Cover Fri and Sat $5–$10.

This small English-style wood-paneled pub has Watney's, Bass, and Guinness on draught and reggae regularly on tap. The club attracts an extremely mixed crowd. A short British menu and high-quality live music are featured Wednesday through Saturday. Open Sunday to Thursday from 11am to midnight, Friday and Saturday from 11am to 2:30am.

MoJazz Cafe. 928 71st St., Miami Beach. ☎ **305/867-0950** or 24-hour information line 305/865-2636. Cover varies from none–$10.

This good smoky jazz club features great acts from all over. The owner Mo Morgen and his band play often. Ask for the big-spender option—if you spend $22 per person on food, drinks, or T-shirts, you skip the cover. From 5:30pm, Mexican food is served. Music plays Tuesday and Wednesday from 9pm to 1am, Thursday from 9pm to 1:30am, Friday and Saturday from 9pm to 2am, Sunday from 9pm to 1am.

Rose's Bar and Lounge. 754 Washington Ave., South Beach. ☎ **305/532-0228.** Cover $3–$25 on weekends, varies with show.

This hip South Beach bar features local music—live rock, jazz, or whatever else strikes your fancy or theirs—almost every night on their tiny stage. Get there early to beat the crowds and claim a spot among the sparse seating. Open every night from 5pm to 5am.

❂ **Tobacco Road.** 626 S. Miami Ave., Downtown. ☎ **305/374-1198.** Cover varies form none–$6.

This Miami institution is a must-see. It's been around since 1912 doing more in the back room than just dancing. These days you'll find a good bar menu along with the best live music anywhere—blues, zydeco, brass, jazz, and more. Some regulars include Dirty Dozen Brass band from New Orleans who play a mean mix of zydeco and blues with an actual dozen brass players; Bill Warton and the Ingredients who make a pot of gumbo while up on stage; Monkey Meet; Ico Ico; Chubby Carrier and his band; and many more. On Friday and Saturday nights, the music is played upstairs, and people dance like crazy, even though it's packed and there's no real dance floor. You can cool off in the backyard patio where air is a welcome commodity. The downright-cheap dinner specials, like a $9 lobster dinner, are quite good. Open Monday to Friday from 11:30am to 5am, Saturday and Sunday from 12:30pm to 5am.

❂ **Van Dyke Cafe.** 846 Lincoln Rd., Miami Beach. ☎ **305/534-3600.** No cover.

Live jazz seven nights and it's free! In an elegant little upstairs lounge, the likes of Eddie Higgins, Mike Renzi, and some locals, like Don Wilner, play strictly jazz for a well-dressed crowd of jazz enthusiasts. You can have a drink or two at the pristine oak bar or enjoy some snacks from the bustling restaurant downstairs (see the review in Chapter 6). Open Monday to Thursday and Sunday from 8pm to midnight, Friday and Saturday from 10pm to 2am.

DANCE CLUBS

In addition to quiet cafes and progressive poolside bars, Miami Beach pulsates with one of the liveliest night scenes in the city. Also check out "The Latin Scene" listings later in this chapter for more places to dance.

A new trend in Miami's club scene is the popularity of "one-off" nights—events organized by a promoter and held in established venues on irregular schedules. Word of mouth, local advertising, and listings in the free weekly *New Times* are the best way to find out about these hot events.

Amnesia. 136 Collins Ave., South Beach. ☎ **305/531-5535.** Cover $10.

This huge outdoor club spawned the wave of "foam parties" in South Beach, where the dance floor is flooded with bubbles and dancers grope for air and each other. Due to insurance concerns, the craze may not continue this season, but there is usually some good dance music and a fun crowd. Definitely call in advance to see if there is a special event. Open Thursday to Sunday from 11pm to 5am. The Safari private supper club is open Thursday to Sunday from 7pm to 5am.

Baja Beach Club. 3015 Grand Ave., Coconut Grove (CocoWalk). ☎ **305/445-0278** or 305/445-5499. Cover varies, none–$15.

How many bodies can fit in one club? Baja Beach Club has made it its mission to find out. If you're not blinded by the pulsating disco lights and gold chains, attending a "best legs" or "hunks in trunks" contests will do the trick. So if you love loud

---

Roots, Rhythms & Rituals: A Secret Beach Party

Honoring ancient healing ceremonies and the expansion of lights on the planet, this young group hosts a wild night of dancing and drumming and singing at varying secret beach locations. Roots, Rhythms, & Rituals encourages would-be musicians to bring their own shakers, rattles, or flutes—pots and pans will do, too. They meet at midnight at a designated beach spot and can get very funky with body painting and chanting as part of the celebration. Children are welcome as is a $10 donation per adult, which the group says helps "maintain the balance of energy." It's a Zen thing. Ceremonies start at 8pm under the gorgeous moon over Miami. Call 305/460-3365 or 305/460-3206 to find out when and where this beach party will be held.

---

dance music and scantily clad bodies, you'll enjoy this suburban bar scene. Wednesday is ladies night, and cover varies depending on the night and your age. Open Wednesday to Sunday from 9pm to 5am.

Bermuda Bar and Grill. 3509 NE 163rd St., North South Beach. ☎ **305/945-0196.** Cover $10 men Wed–Sun; $5 women Fri and Sun.

This huge North Miami Beach danceteria specializes in ladies' nights (Wednesday, Thursday, and Saturday no cover for women) as well as occasional contests awarding cash prizes to the woman with the skimpiest outfit. If you like to dance, however, they do have high-energy dance music that will get anyone but a dead person up on the floor. Thursday night is salsa night for those craving a Latin beat. Open Wednesday to Sunday from 5pm to 6am.

Cameo Theater. 1445 Washington Ave., South Beach. ☎ **305/532-0922.** Cover varies according to theme night.

The Cameo Theater is an institution on South Beach. The old converted theater enjoyed a renaissance of sorts when it became a regular concert spot and nightclub a few years ago. Theme nights do come and go, but the one that seems like it's there to stay is Sunday's Disco Inferno night, when the huge nightclub goes retro and Gloria Gaynor proves that she did survive. Open Friday to Sunday from 10pm to 5am.

Glam Slam. 1235 Washington Ave., South Beach. ☎ **305/672-4858.** Cover varies.

Opened by "the artist formerly known as Prince," this most happening club on South Beach has had its share of closings. With a large gay clientele it also has great dance music and fun, huge bar scene. In the back alley is a private club, The Fat Black Pussy Cat. If you can get the weekly password, usually obtainable by asking a hip-looking waiter at any South Beach restaurant, you'll get in. Open Wednesday to Sunday with various theme nights.

Groove Jet. 323 23rd St. (next to the Fina gas station), Miami Beach. ☎ **305/532-2002.** Cover usually $5 before midnight and $7 after.

This fantastic hidden spot north of the South Beach scene has been through many incarnations. Its most recent, Groove Jet, was closed down after a spate of crackdowns by Miami Beach police, but now it's back. It's happened before for one reason or another (usually something like selling drugs). Still, like a phoenix, it tends to resurface. So drive by this spot to see what's happening, whatever name it's going by.

Usually in the back it's acid-jazz and in the other two rooms inside you'll hear House and alternative or trance. Open Thursday to Sunday from 11pm to 5am.

La Voile Rouge Hotel & Beach Club. 455 Ocean Dr., South Beach. ☎ **305/535-0099.** No cover.

There's always something going on at this very Euro bar and disco where Bicé, the restaurant, resides. Thursday, however, is *the* night for an upscale disco with a cool DJ spinning. In addition, you'll find a cozy bar, piano bar, and main bar hopping till all hours. Call for hours, which vary depending on the season. The bar is generally open from noon to 2am, and weekend entertainment usually runs from 10pm to 2am.

Liquid. 1439 Washington Ave., South Beach. ☎ **305/532-9154.** Cover varies, $5–$10.

Liquid is reminiscent of the 80's New York club scene, so you can expect to wait at the ropes until a disdainful bouncer chooses you. Don't dare to wear the usual casual South Beach attire; they are looking for "casual chic." And if you are male, don't come unescorted. Women in slinky dresses are in big demand. Once inside, you'll find a cavernous space with up-to-the-minute dance music and two beautiful bars, plus lounge seating in a cozy back area. Open nightly from 11pm to 5am.

3 The Gay & Lesbian Scene

The gay and lesbian scene is super active in South Beach. Not only are there many clubs, but there's a thriving network of gay-owned businesses. Most hotels and restaurants are gay-friendly, and many clubs are hetero-friendly as well. An ultra-open lifestyle here allows for open display of affection among gay male or female visitors.

821. 821 Lincoln Rd., South Beach. ☎ **305/534-0887.** No cover.

821 is somthing between a neighborhood bar and a nightclub with a live DJ every night. Thursdays and Saturdays are for ladies, and women are welcome other nights as well. Offering good music and limited attitude in a basic black box, this hotspot is a staple on Lincoln Road. Open daily from 3 to 9pm for happy hour, then until 3 or 5am.

Kremlin. 727 Lincoln Rd., South Beach. ☎ **305/673-3150.** Cover $6 after 10:30pm.

Despite the rough sounding name, the Kremlin is a welcome, almost cozy addition to the gay scene on South Beach. Thursdays do bring out the boys in leather and chains. Call for schedules of special events. Open Thursday to Saturday from 9:30pm to 2am.

Twist. 1057 Washington Ave., South Beach. ☎ **305/53-TWIST.** No cover.

One of the beach's most popular cruise bars, Twist attracts mostly male clientele but has an open-door policy. Open daily from 1pm to 5am.

Warsaw Ballroom. 1450 Collins Ave., South Beach. ☎ **305/531-4555.** Cover $12.

One of Miami's oldest and funnest nightclubs, Warsaw hosts various theme nights and some of the best dance music in town. After all these years, regulars still line up down the sidewalk, waiting to get in. Open nightly from 8pm to 5am.

West End. 942 Lincoln Rd., South Beach. ☎ **305/538-9378.** No cover.

A mellow bar and pool hall, this Lincoln Road stand-by is a favorite hangout for women and men. Enjoy a relaxed atmosphere and a good place to meet people. Open daily from noon to 5am.

4 The Latin Scene

Considering that Hispanics make up the majority of Miami's population and there's a huge influx of Hispanic visitors, it's no surprise that there are some great Latin nightclubs in the city. What's interesting is that in recent years, many new clubs have opened and are attracting a mix of curious Anglos and Europeans as well. Plus, with the meteoric rise of the international music scene that's based in Miami, many international stars come through the offices of MTV Latino, SONY International, and a multitude of Latin TV studios based in Miami, and look for a good club scene on weekends.

Because of the increased competition, some of Miami's older Latin clubs have gone into decline. For example, Les Violins, a landmark in downtown Miami, recently put their property on the block. Thankfully, there are still many authentic clubs that are fun to check out. If you don't already know how to dance to Latin music, consider taking a salsa class and then head out to one of the following Anglo-friendly clubs.

Alcazaba. 50 Alhambra Plaza (in the Hyatt Regency Coral Gables), Coral Gables. ☎ **305/ 441-1234.**

The Hyatt's Top-40 lounge plays an eclectic mix of music but exudes a decidedly Mediterranean atmosphere that mixes fantasy with reality. Cool out with some tropical drinks and authentic tapas in between songs. Happy hour—Wednesday and Friday from 5 to 7pm and Saturday from 9 to 11pm—offers half-price beer, wine, and drinks, plus a free buffet.

Cafe Nostalgia. 2212 SW 8th St. (Calle Ocho), Miami. ☎ **305/541-2631.** Cover $10.

As the name implies, Cafe Nostalgia is dedicated to reminiscing about old Cuba. After watching a film with Celia Cruz, you can dance to the hot sounds of Afro-Cuban jazz. With pictures of old and young Cuban stars smiling down on you and a live band celebrating Cuban heritage, Cafe Nostalgia sounds like a bit much; it's more than that. Be prepared, it's packed after midnight and dance space is mostly between the tables. Open Wednesday to Sunday from 9pm to 4am. Films are shown from 10pm to midnight, followed by live music.

Casa Panza. 1620 SW 8th St. (Calle Ocho), Miami. ☎ **305/643-5343.**

Clap your hands or your castanets if you have them. Every Tuesday and Thursday night, Casa Panza in the heart of Little Havana becomes the House of Flamenco. Patrons of the restaurant can enjoy a flamenco show or don their own dancing shoes and participate in the celebration. Enjoy a fantastic dinner before the show or have a few drinks before you take a spin around the stage. Two free shows are held Tuesday and Thursday evenings at 8pm and 11pm.

Centro Vasco. 2235 SW 8th St. (Calle Ocho), Miami. ☎ **305/643-9606.** Cover $15 Fri and Sat, plus a two-drink minimum.

In the place that gave Sony's new Latin diva, Albita Rodriguez, her start you'll hear the best of son, guarija, salsa, flamenco, and more at the weekend show at 10pm. Make reservations early since the shows sell out, sometimes weeks in advance. (See the dining review in Chapter 6.) Shows at 10pm Friday to Sunday, but check for seasonal variations.

Mango's. 900 Ocean Dr., South Beach. ☎ **305/673-4422.** Cover $6–$15, varies by performer.

If you want to dance to a funky, loud Brazilian beat till you drop, check out Mango's on the beach. They feature nightly live Brazilian and some Latin music on a little

Where to Learn to Salsa

Are you feeling shy about hitting a Latin club because you fear your two left feet will step out? Then take a few lessons before tripping the light fantastic. Here are the names of several dance companies and dance teachers around the city that offer individual and group lessons to dancers of any origin who are willing to learn. These folks have made it their mission to teach merengue and flamenco to the wanna-be's.

Ballet Flamenco La Rosa, 555 17th St. (in the PAN building), Miami Beach (☎ 305/672-0552), wants to teach you how to flamenco with the best of them. They are the only professional flamenco company in the area, so their prices are steep. If you're feeling shy, $50 will buy you a private lesson, and $10 an hour will allow you to learn the art of the dance with a group of other Flamenco beginners.

Nobody salsas like **Luz Pinto** (☎ 305/673-9418), and she can help you master the basics with patience and humor. She charges between $45 and $50 for a private lesson for up to four people and $10 for a group lesson. A good introduction is her multi-level group class at 7pm Sunday evenings at the PAN building. Though she teaches everything from ballroom to merengue, her specialty is Casino-style salsa, popularized in the 1950s in Cuba, Luz's homeland. A mix between disco and country square dancing, Casino-style salsa is all the rage in Latin clubs in town. If you are a very good student, you may be able to talk Luz into chaperoning a trip to a nightclub to show off your moves. She'll work out a fee based on the number of participants and their ability.

Angel Arroya has been teaching salsa to the clueless out of his home for the past 10 years. $10 will buy you an hour's time in his "school," **The Salsa Workshop,** 16464 NE 27th Ave., North Miami Beach (☎ 305/949-7799). He traditionally teaches Monday and Wednesday nights, but call ahead to check for any schedule changes.

patio bar. When you need refreshment, you can choose from a schizophrenic menu of Caribbean, Mexican, vegetarian, and Cuban specialties. Open daily from 11am to 5:30pm.

Studio 23 (Studio Veinte Tres). 247 23rd St. (adjacent to Mama Vieja Restaurant), South Beach. ☎ **305/538-1196.** Cover $5 Sat only.

You've heard of the Macarena? Do it here—along with salsa, cumbia, merengue, vellenato, and house music. This neighborhood Latin disco and nightclub gets going after hours with wild strobe-lit atmosphere. If you don't know how to do it, just wait. You'll have plenty of willing teachers on hand. Open Wednesday to Sunday from 8pm to 4am.

Swiss Chateau Club. 2471 SW 32nd Ave., Miami. ☎ **305/445-3633.** Cover $5 for men on Sat night; couples and women are free.

If you're looking to sample some authentic Cuban nightlife, look no further than Swiss Chateau. Although the name sounds anything but Latin, the Chateau offers authentic salsa and merengue music every weekend for a mostly older crowd of *exilios*. When you've worked up an appetite, try a snack from the tapas menu, which includes steak, shrimp, and chicken *croquettas*. Open Friday to Sunday from 7pm to 4am.

5 Movies & More

CINEMAS

In addition to the annual Miami Film Festival and the Italian Film Festival, Miami is lucky to have three wonderful art cinemas showing a range of films from *Fresas y Chocolate* to *Crumb*.

The Alliance Cinema (☎ 305/531-8504) is tucked behind a tropical little walkway just next to Books & Books at 927 Lincoln Rd., Suite 119, in South Beach. It shows art films and many Latin American independent features. There's also the Anti-Film Festival in February, a showing of underground movies, and the Queen Flickering Light, a gay film festival in June. You may want to bring a pillow; the seats are old and rickety. Tickets cost $6.

Astor Art Cinema, at 4120 Laguna St. (☎ 305/443-6777), is an oasis in the midst of a sea of Cineplex Odeons and AMCs in Coral Gables. The quaint double theater hosts foreign, classic, independent, and art films and serves decent popcorn, too. Tickets are $5, $3 for seniors.

The Bill Cosford Cinema at the University of Miami, located on the second floor of the memorial building off Campo Sano Avenue (☎ 305/284-4861), is named after the deceased *Herald* film critic. This well-endowed little theater was recently revamped and boasts high-tech projectors, new air conditioning, and new decor. It sponsors independent films as well as lectures by visiting filmmakers and movie stars. Andy Garcia and Antonio Banderas are a few of the big names this little theater attracts. It also hosts the Italian Film Festival, The African American Film Festival, and a Student Film Festival, plus collaborations with the Fort Lauderdale Festival. Admission is $5.

THE LITERARY SCENE

Books & Books, in Coral Gables at 296 Aragon Ave., and in Miami Beach at 933 Lincoln Rd., hosts readings almost every night and is known for attracting top authors like Colleen McCullough, Jamaica Kincaid, and Paul Levine. For details on the free readings, call 305/444-9044.

To hear more about what's happening in Miami's literary scene, tune into the "Cover to Cover" show, broadcast at 8pm on Mondays on the public radio station, WLRN (91.3 FM).

6 Late-Night Bites

Although many dining spots in Miami stop serving at 10pm, South Beach eateries stay open very late, especially on weekends. So, if you want a quick bite after clubbing and it's 4am, don't fret. A vast number of pizza places lining Washington Avenue in Miami Beach are open past 6am.

In South Beach, **The Sandwicherie,** 229 14th St. (behind the Amoco station), serves up a great late-night sandwich until 4 and 5am. Another place of note in the up-all-night eateries is the **News Café,** 800 Ocean Dr. One of the first sidewalk cafes to open in the area, the trendy cafe serves up an eclectic selection of meals ranging from a middle-eastern platter to a fruit bowl or steak and potatoes.

If your night out was at one of the Latin clubs around town, stop in at **Versailles,** 3555 SW 8th St., in Little Havana. What else but a cuban *medianoche* (midnight sandwich) will do? Their hours extend well past midnight, catering to gangs of revelers, both young and old, who like to hang out, chatter, and laugh until dawn.

Side Trips from Miami 11

For as varied as Miami and its beaches are, many people like to use this centrally located spot as a jumping-off point for other destinations. Whether you'd like to explore Biscayne National Park or the Everglades, or skip over to one of the Bahamian islands, all are easily accessible from here.

1 Biscayne National Park

35 miles S of Miami

Many people who arrive at Biscayne National Park's main entrance at Convoy Point take one look around and exclaim "are we there?" You see, the park is very large—181,500 acres to be exact—but what some visitors don't realize is that 95% of it is underwater. In 1968, President Lyndon Johnson signed a bill to conserve the barrier islands off South Florida's east coast as a national monument, a protected status that's a rung below national park. After being twice enlarged, once in 1974 and again in 1980, the waters surrounding the northernmost coral reef in North America became a full-fledged national park.

There's not much for landlubbers here. The park's small mainland mangrove shoreline and 44 islands are best explored by boat. Its extensive reef system is extremely popular with divers and snorkelers. The concessionaire at Convoy Point rents canoes, runs dive trips, and offers popular glass-bottom boat tours.

Elliott Key, one of the park's 44 little mangrove-fringed islands, contains a visitors center, hiking trails, and a campground. Located about nine miles from Convoy Point, Elliott Key is only accessible by boat.

JUST THE FACTS

GETTING THERE   By Car   Convoy Point, the park's mainland entrance, is located 9 miles east of Homestead. To reach the park from Miami, take Florida's Turnpike to the Tallahassee Road (SW 137th Avenue) exit. Turn left, then left again at North Canal Drive (SW 328th Street) and follow signs to the park. If you're coming from U.S. 1, whether you're heading north or south, turn east at North Canal Drive (SW 328th Street). The entrance is approximately 9 miles away.

By Boat   Biscayne National Park is especially accessible to boaters. Mooring buoys abound, since it is illegal to anchor on coral. When no buoys are available, boaters must anchor on sand. Boaters should carry NOAA nautical chart no. 11451, which is available at Convoy Point. Even the most experienced yachtsman should be sure to carry a chart. Waters are often murky, making the abundant reefs and sandbars difficult to detect—and there are few less-interesting ways to spend a day than waiting for the tide to rise. There is a boat launch at adjacent Homestead Bayfront Park. There are 66 slips on Elliott Key, available free on a first-come, first-serve basis.

ACCESS POINTS   The park's mainland entrance is **Convoy Point,** located 9 miles east of Homestead.

VISITORS CENTERS & INFORMATION   General inquiries and specific questions should be directed to the **National Park Service,** P.O. Box 1369, Homestead, FL 33090 (☎ 305/230-7275).

For information on park activities and tours, contact **Biscayne National Park Underwater Tours,** P.O. Box 1270, Homestead, FL 33090 (☎ 305/230-1100).

The **Convoy Point Visitors Center,** at the park's main entrance (☎ 305/230-7275), is the natural starting point for any venture into the park. In addition to providing comprehensive information on the park, rangers will show you a 10-minute slide show and a short video about Hurricane Andrew, both on request. Open daily from 8:30am to 4pm and on Saturday and Sunday until 5pm.

ENTRANCE FEES & PERMITS   Entrance is free to **Biscayne National Park.** Back-country permits are also free, and available at the visitors center.

OPENING HOURS   Biscayne National Park is always open; the visitors centers are staffed daily from about 8:30am to 5pm.

SEEING THE HIGHLIGHTS

Since Biscayne National Park is primarily underwater, the only way to truly experience it is with snorkel or scuba gear. And you'll need a boat. Beneath the surface, the aquatic universe pulses with multicolored life: bright parrot and angelfish, gently rocking sea fans, and coral labyrinths abound. Before entering the water, be sure to apply waterproof sunblock or wear a T-shirt. Once you begin to explore, it's easy to lose track of time, and the Florida sun is brutal, even during the winter months.

Afterward, take a picnic out to Elliot Key, and taste the crisp salt air blowing off the Atlantic. Since the island is only accessible by boat, the beach is usually less crowded than those further north.

Biscayne National Park is more a preserve than a destination, a place that's meant to be experienced, not an event. I suggest using your time here to explore, but most of all, to relax.

SPORTS & OUTDOOR ACTIVITIES

CANOEING   Biscayne Park offers excellent canoeing, either along the coast or across open water to nearby mangrove islands. Since tides can be strong, only experienced canoeists should attempt to paddle far from shore. If you plan to go far, first obtain a tide table from the visitors center (see "Just the Facts," above) and paddle with the current. Free ranger-led canoe tours are scheduled for most weekend mornings. Phone for information. You can rent a canoe at the park; rates are $7 an hour or $20 for a half-day.

FISHING   Ocean fishing is excellent year-round; many people cast their lines right from the breakwater jetty at Convoy Point. A fishing license is required. Bait is not available in Biscayne, but is sold in adjacent Homestead Bayfront Park. Stone crabs and Florida lobsters can be found here, but are only allowed to be caught on the ocean side and when in season. There are strict limitations on size, season, number, and method of take (including spearfishing) for both fresh and saltwater fishing. The latest regulations are available at most marinas, bait and tackle shops, and at the park's visitors centers. Or you can contact the **Florida Game and Fresh Water Fish Commission,** Bryant Building, Tallahassee, FL 32301 (☎ 904/488-1960).

HIKING Since the majority of this park is underwater, hiking is not great, but there are some short trails. At Convoy Point you can walk along the 370-foot board-walk, and along the half-mile jetty that serves as a breakwater for the park's harbor. Even from here you can usually see brown pelicans, little blue herons, snowy egrets, and a few exotic fish.

Elliott Key is only accessible by boat, but once you're there, you have two good trail options. True to its name, the Loop Trail makes a 1.5-mile circle from the bayside visitors center, through a hardwood hammock and mangroves, to an elevated oceanside boardwalk. It's likely that you'll see purple and orange land crabs scurry-ing around the mangrove's roots.

The Old Road is a 7-mile tropical hammock trail that runs the length of Elliott Key. Because the visitors center is located about a third of the way along the trail, you can only walk (or bike) about 2¹/₂ miles north, or 4¹/₂ miles south before turn-ing around. This trail is one of the few places left in the world to see the highly endangered Schaus' swallowtail butterfly, recognizable by its black wings with diago-nal yellow bands. They're usually out from late April through July.

SNORKELING/SCUBA DIVING The clear, warm waters of Biscayne National Park are packed with colorful tropical fish that swim in the offshore reefs. Snorkel-ing and scuba gear are rented and sold at Convoy Point. Or bring your own.

Biscayne National Park Underwater Tours, P.O. Box 1270, Homestead, FL 33090 (☎ 305/230-1100), operates daily snorkel trips that last about four hours and cost $27.95 per person. They also run two-tank dives for certified divers, and instruc-tion for beginners. Prices are $34.50 per person. They are open daily from 8am until 5:30pm.

SWIMMING You can swim at the protected beaches of Elliott Key and adjacent Homestead Bayfront Park, but neither of these beaches match other South Florida beaches for width, softness, or surf.

ORGANIZED TOURS

Biscayne National Underwater Park Tours, located at the east end of SW 328th Street, Homestead FL 33090 (☎ 305/230-1100), offers regularly scheduled glass-bottom boat trips. For a fish-eye view of Biscayne National Park's aquatic wilderness, board the 52-foot *Bocachita* for a leisurely cruise. Biscayne National Park boasts almost 200,000 acres of mangrove shoreline, living coral reefs (the only one in the continental United States) and barrier islands. Unfortunately, it's fast disappearing due to pollution and divers' carelessness, so be sure to see it while it's still here. Boats depart year-round, daily from Convoy Point every half-hour from 10am to 1pm. Tours cost $16.50 for adults and $8.50 for children 12 and under. Reservations are required.

The company also offers guided scuba and snorkeling reef trips led by underwater naturalists. Snorkeling tours and one-tank scuba dives depart daily at 1:30pm, and cost $27.95 and $35 per person, respectively, including equipment rental. Two-tank dive trips are offered Wednesday, Saturday, and Sunday at 8:30am. Booking is essential.

Robert Is Here Selling Fruit

One of the best parts about the drive to the Everglades is a stop at one of Florida's best known fruit stands, called **Robert Is Here.** And he usually is. Homestead native Robert Moehling has been selling homegrown treats at this everexpanding roadside stand and adjacent farm for nearly 40 years. He's graduated from hawking cucumbers from a cardboard box to selling local and gourmet products from around the world. You'll find the freshest and biggest pineapples, bananas, papayas, mangos, and melons anywhere, as well as his famous shakes in unusual flavors like key lime, coconut, orange, and cantaloupe. In addition to what's usually found at greenmarkets, Robert also stocks exotic offerings like carambola, mamey, lychees, sugar apples, and sea grapes. The bottled jellies, hot sauces, and salad dressings make great souvenirs or gifts for foodie friends from home. To get there from Miami, take the Florida Turnpike or U.S. 1 to SW 344th Street or Palm Drive. Turn right. You'll see the stand about a mile down on the left at the corner of SW 192 Avenue. You can't miss it if you're headed to the Everglades National Park. To find out what's in season, call 305/246-1592.

CAMPING

There are no hotels in Biscayne National Park, but camping is plentiful—for those with water transportation. Campsites are on Elliott Key, and are only accessible by boat. They're equipped with showers, restrooms, and drinking fountains. With a backcountry permit, available from the ranger station, you can pitch your tent somewhere even more private. Camping is free.

2 Everglades National Park

35 miles SW of Miami

Encompassing more than 2,000 square miles and 1.5 million acres, Everglades National Park covers the entire southern tip of Florida and is one of America's most unusual regions. The Everglades' awesome beauty is more subtle than that of Yosemite and Grand Canyon national parks. In fact, it is not its geological grandeur that, in 1947, led lawmakers to preserve this remarkable place. Rather, the Everglades is a wildlife sanctuary, set aside for the protection of its delicate plant and animal life. Don't misunderstand, this park is gorgeous, though its beauty may not be immediately obvious. At first glance, the Glades appear to be only a river of sawgrass dotted with islands of trees. But stand still and look around: You'll notice deer, otters, and great white egrets. Follow a rustle, and a tiny tree frog appears. Hawks and herons flutter about, while baby—and bigger—alligators laze in the sun. You are in one of the world's most unusual jungles; the longer you stay, the more you'll perceive. However, beware of mosquitoes! Wear protective clothing and don't forget your repellent.

Hurricane Andrew, one of the costliest storms in American history, ripped straight through the South Florida Everglades in 1992. While human-built structures suffered damages amounting into the billions of dollars, scientists were fascinated by the resiliency of nature: Everglades National Park weathered the storm with what seems to be few ill effects. Trees were toppled and trails flooded, but nature has already buried its dead and grown anew. Although some of the people of South Florida may still feel shaken, the Everglades seems to have taken the storm in stride.

JUST THE FACTS

GETTING THERE   By Car   From Miami, there are two ways to approach the park—either from the east, through the Main Visitor Center, or from the north, via the Tamiami Trail (Hwy. 41).

The Main Visitor Center (☎ 305/242-7700) is located on the east side of the park, about 45 miles south of Downtown. From downtown Miami, take U.S. 1 South about 35 miles. Turn right (west) onto Route 9336 (follow the signs) and continue straight for about 10 miles to the park entrance. This is the park's official headquarters, which are open daily from 9am to 5pm.

The Tamiami Trail (Hwy. 41) runs east-west from downtown Miami to the Gulf of Mexico and follows the northern edge of the Everglades into Big Cypress National Preserve. Along the way you will pass a number of concerns offering airboat and other rides through the sawgrass of the Everglades.

By Boat   Several boat ramps are located throughout the park, but the Everglades' only marina—accommodating about 50 boats with electric and water hookups—is located in Flamingo. The well-marked channel to Flamingo is accessible to boats with a maximum four-foot draft, and is open year-round. Reservations can be made through park headquarters (see "Visitors Centers" below).

ACCESS POINTS & ORIENTATION   The Everglades National Park has three entrances. The aptly-named **Main Entrance,** located on the park's east side, is most popular and for good reason. From this entrance, a single 38-mile road wends its way southwest, allowing visitors greatest access to the park. The **Shark Valley Entrance,** located on the park's north side, is known for its 15-mile trail loop that's used for an excellent interpretive tram tour, bicycling, and walking. The trail leads to a tall observation tower (see "What to See & Do," below, for complete information). The **Everglades City Entrance,** on the northwest side of the park, is riddled with canoe trails and is the best approach for those wishing to explore the park by boat (see "Sports and Outdoor Activities," below, for information on boating and canoeing).

VISITORS CENTERS & INFORMATION   General inquiries and specific questions should be directed to **Everglades National Park Headquarters,** 40001 State Rd. 9336, Homestead, FL 33034 (☎ 305/242-7700). Ask for a copy of *Parks and Preserves,* a free newspaper that's filled with up-to-date information on goings-on in the Everglades.

Flamingo Lodge Marina & Outpost Resort, in Flamingo (☎ 305/253-2241, or 813/695-3101, or 800/600-3813), is the one-stop clearinghouse for in-park accommodations, equipment rentals, and tours.

The **Main Visitor Center,** located at the park's Main Entrance, has educational displays, free brochures outlining trails and activities, and information on tours and boat rentals. A small shop here sells postcards, film, insect repellent, unusual gift items, and the best selection of books about the Everglades.

The **Royal Palm Visitor Center,** a small nature museum located 3 miles past the park's Main Entrance, is a smaller information center located at the head of popular Anhinga and Gumbo-Limbo trails.

The **Shark Valley Information Center** at the park's northern entrance and the **Everglades City Gulf Coast Ranger Station** at the park's western entrance are also staffed by knowledgeable rangers who provide both brochures and personal insight into the goings-on in the park.

Everglades City Area Chamber of Commerce, P.O. Box 130, Everglades City, FL 33929 (☎ 941/695-3941), provides information on tours and outfitters operating near the park's northwestern entrance. The chamber staffs an office at the intersection of U.S. 41 and Fla. 29.

ENTRANCE FEES, PERMITS & REGULATIONS A seven-day permit for Everglades National Park costs $5 per vehicle at the Main Entrance and Everglades City, and $3 per vehicle at Shark Valley. Pedestrians and cyclists are charged $3 per person at the Main Entrance and Everglades City, and $2 per person at Shark Valley. An Everglades Park Pass, valid for a year's worth of unlimited entrances, is available for $15. U.S. citizens may purchase a 12-month Golden Eagle Passport for $25, which is valid for entrance into any U.S. national park. U.S. citizens aged 62 and older pay only $10 for a national park passport that's valid for life. A Golden Access Passport is available free to U.S. citizens with disabilities. Permits and passes are sold at each of the park's entrances or visitors centers.

Campers can pick up free permits, which are required, at either the Flamingo or Everglades City ranger station. Back-country campers must register at ranger stations either in Flamingo or Everglades City, and are only allowed to use designated camp sites, which are plentiful and well marked on visitor maps. Open fires are prohibited.

Those who want to fish must obtain a standard State of Florida fishing license. These are not available in the park, but can be obtained at any tackle shop or sporting goods store. A seven-day freshwater license costs $16. Those expecting to cast their lines in Florida Bay, the Gulf of Mexico, or other surrounding waters must purchase a separate saltwater license; three-day licenses cost $7, seven-day licenses, $17.

Firearms are not allowed anywhere in the park.

SEASONS There are two distinct seasons in the Everglades: high season and mosquito season. High season is also dry season, and lasts approximately from December through May. This is the best time to visit, as low water levels attract the largest variety of wading birds and their predators. As the dry season wanes, wildlife follows the receding water, and by the end of May, most of the big animals are clustered in the southernmost end of the Glades. During wet season, which lasts from June through November, migratory birds are absent, wildlife is harder to spot, and mosquitoes will deter even the most determined visitor. Even in the wet season, however, the river of grass rarely gets very deep, most trails remain accessible, and there's plenty to see for those who avail themselves to it.

Many establishments and operators in the area either close or curtail offerings in the summer, so always call ahead to check schedules.

OPENING HOURS Visitors may wander freely throughout Everglades National Park year-round. 24-hour access into and out of the park is available via each of the entrances. Shark Valley and Everglades City entrances are staffed daily from 8am to 5pm and the Main Entrance's Park Headquarters building is open 24 hours.

RANGER PROGRAMS More than 50 ranger programs, free with admission, are offered every month. On the **Glade Glimpses** walking tour, rangers point out flora and fauna and discuss issues affecting the Everglades' survival. These tours are scheduled at 10:15am, noon, and 3:30pm daily. The **Anhinga Ambles,** a similar program that takes place on the Anhinga Trail, starts at 10:30am, 1:30pm, and 4pm.

Occasionally a more interesting **Slough Slog** program is offered. On this journey, participants wade into the park and through the muck, stopping at an alligator hole, which is a particularly interesting and vital ecosystem unto itself. Lace-up shoes and long pants (preferably ones you don't care about) are required on this walking trip.

Times, programs, and locations of ranger programs vary from month to month. Schedules are available at any of the visitors centers (see above).

Everglades National Park

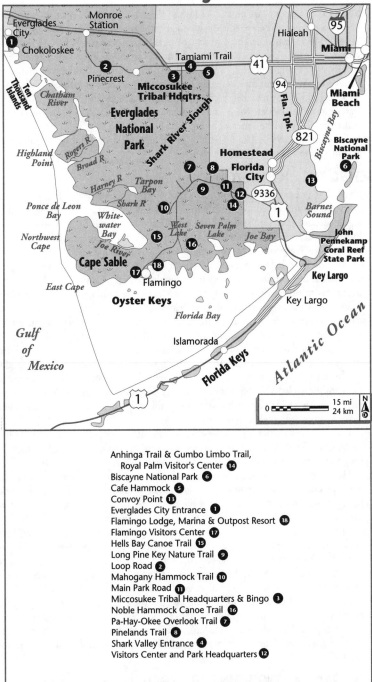

Anhinga Trail & Gumbo Limbo Trail,
  Royal Palm Visitor's Center ⑭
Biscayne National Park ⑥
Cafe Hammock ⑤
Convoy Point ⑬
Everglades City Entrance ①
Flamingo Lodge, Marina & Outpost Resort ⑱
Flamingo Visitors Center ⑰
Hells Bay Canoe Trail ⑮
Long Pine Key Nature Trail ⑨
Loop Road ②
Mahogany Hammock Trail ⑩
Main Park Road ⑪
Miccosukee Tribal Headquarters & Bingo ③
Noble Hammock Canoe Trail ⑯
Pa-Hay-Okee Overlook Trail ⑦
Pinelands Trail ⑧
Shark Valley Entrance ④
Visitors Center and Park Headquarters ⑫

SAFETY   Accidents are more common to the area than theft. Always let someone know your itinerary before you set out on an extended hike. It's mandatory that you file an itinerary when camping overnight in the back country. When on the water, watch for weather changes; severe thunderstorms and high winds often develop very rapidly. Swimming is not recommended due to the presence of alligators, sharks, and barracudas. Watch out for the region's four indigenous poisonous snakes: diamond-back and pygmy rattlesnakes; coral snakes (identifiable by their colorful rings); and water moccasins (which swim on the surface of the water). And bring insect repellent to ward off mosquitoes and biting flies.

First aid is available from park rangers. The nearest hospital is in Homestead, 10 miles from the park's Main Entrance.

SEEING THE HIGHLIGHTS

Shark Valley provides a fine introduction to the wonder of the Everglades, but visitors shouldn't expect to spend more than a few hours there. Bicycling or taking a guided tram tour can be the best way to immerse yourself in the area's rich ecological landscape. Boaters who choose to explore via the Everglades City entrance to the park are likely to see a lot of mangroves, and not much else.

For a more varied experience in the park that lets you see a greater array of plant and animal life, venture into the park through the Main Entrance, and dedicate at least a day to exploring from here. Stop first along the Anhinga and Gumbo Limbo trails, which start right next to one another, 3 miles from the park's Main Entrance. These trails provide a thorough introduction to the flora and fauna that inhabit the Everglades, and are highly recommended to first-time visitors. Arrive early to spot the widest selection of exotic birds, as many of them travel deeper into the park during daylight hours. And remember to take your time: At least an hour is recommended.

Those who love to mountain bike, and prefer solitude, should check out the infrequently traveled Old Ingraham Highway. This dirt road delves deeper into the Glades, and is avoided by most visitors. Since this pathway is sometimes closed, check at the visitors center when you arrive.

It's also worth climbing the observation tower at the end of the ¹/₄-mile-long Pa-hay-okee Trail. The panoramic view of undulating grass and seemingly endless vistas give the impression of a semiaquatic Serengeti.

However, if you're tired of merely watching and want to get closer to nature, a few hours in a canoe along any of the trails allows paddlers the chance to sense the park's fluid motion, and to become a part of the ecosphere. You'll feel more like an explorer than merely an observer (see "Sports & Outdoor Activities," below).

The Coastal Prairie Trail runs 15 miles beyond the end of the 38-mile-long Main Park Road. Hiking boots and a reasonable degree of fitness are required. The payoff? A land teeming with wildlife, one that hasn't been disturbed by ecological purges that afflicted other parts of the Everglades, and a sense that you're traveling back in time to discover unexplored and unsullied lands.

But no matter what options you choose (and there are many), I strongly recommend staying for the 7pm evening program at the Long Pine Key Amphitheatre. This talk by one of the park's rangers, along with the accompanying slide show, gives a detailed overview of the park's history, natural resources, wildlife, and threats to its survival.

THE TRAILS ALONG MAIN PARK ROAD

The majority of the Everglades' hiking trails are located along a single main road that winds its way for about 38 miles from the Main Visitor Center at the park's Main

Entrance to Flamingo, in the southwest corner of the state. They are listed geographically below.

ANHINGA TRAIL (3 miles from Main Entrance)   The ¹/₂-mile-long Anhinga Trail is named for a large black fishing bird that's a permanent resident in these parts. The birds are so habituated to humans that they often nest within plain view of the trail.

The first short stretch of Anhinga Trail is paved, as it was once part of the Ingraham Highway, the first Homestead-to-Flamingo road, built in 1922. The rest of the trail is an elevated wooden boardwalk that courses through sawgrass marsh and follows an artificial canal built along the edge of freshwater Taylor Slough (pronounced "slew"). Because the slough and adjacent canal are slightly deeper than the surrounding marshlands, there is more water and wildlife here than in most parts of the Everglades, especially during dry season. Alligators, turtles, river otters, herons, egrets, and other animals abound, making this one of the best trails for spotting wildlife. Many of the fish you see here are not native to Florida, but were introduced—usually accidentally—over the last century. The most common of these "exotic" species include oscar (from South America), poke killifish (from Central America), and blue tilapin (from Africa). The white flowers popping-up from the sawgrass are called swamp lilies. You can reach out and touch them, but beware: True to its name, the tall sawgrass blades can cut like a knife.

Because the trail is largely unprotected by tall trees, mosquitoes are less of a problem here than in many other parts of the Glades. The trailhead begins just behind the Royal Palm Visitor Center.

GUMBO-LIMBO TRAIL (3 miles from Main Entrance)   The Gumbo-Limbo Trail, which begins right next to the Anhinga Trail, is named for the gumbo-limbo tree, a subtropical hardwood that's sometimes called the "tourist tree" because it continuously sheds its bronze bark—much like a tourist peels after a few days in the hot Florida sun. Contrary to its monotonously flat appearance, the Everglades actually contains subtle topographic changes—elevations of just a few feet create entirely different environments. The Gumbo-Limbo Trail is on one of these elevated "hammocks," drier ground that provides firmer footing for an abundant variety of trees, including the gumbo limbo, poison wood, and the strangler fig. Sumac, red maple, and live oak—varieties that are more closely associated with temperate climates—can also be found here. Under the shade of the trees' dense canopy is a lushly vegetated protected environment that has a distinctive jungle feel. The cool Gumbo-Limbo Trail is dense with insects (including mosquitoes) and small animals like lizards, tree snails, frogs, and songbirds. Orchids, ferns, and bromeliads abound. Look up and you will see many species of "air plants" that use host trees for support. Most air plants are not parasitic, but obtain moisture and nourishment from the air. Their lofty positions are more favorable to growth than the shady forest floor.

LONG PINE KEY (5 miles from Main Entrance)   Twisting through a variety of habitats, Long Pine Key's 7-mile nature trail is one of the Everglades' longest. The wide, unpaved, hard-packed dirt road runs west, roughly parallel to the main park road. The majority of the route is characterized by a large stand of slash pines, a habitat of tall, skinny trees that's maintained by periodic burns managed by the National Park Service. The pines intermingle with satinleaf, smaller trees distinguishable by leaves that are dark green on top and satiny bronze underneath; when the wind blows, the trees appear to shimmer in the sun. A few times, the trees thin out to reveal open marshes. Pine Glades Lake, at the trail's end, is a popular fishing spot, despite posted warnings about mercury contamination.

PINELANDS TRAIL (6 miles from Main Entrance)   Pineland's ³/₄-mile loop through slash pine is recommended for hikers who want a quick look at this typical Everglades habitat without committing to a long trek. This trail also reveals plenty of oolitic limestone, the bedrock that underlies most of South Florida. Deposited over five million years ago, when Florida was covered by shallow sea, the rock is characterized by jagged outcroppings, as well as smooth hollows, called "solution holes." Varying in size from almost microscopic to several feet across, solution holes are created by rainwater mixed with acidic plant matter. During the dry season, some of the larger holes become important water reservoirs attracting quail, panther, deer, and other large animals.

The low, shrub-size palms growing under the pines are saw palmettos. These lush trees, along with wild tamarind, beauty berry, tetrazygia, and others, are marked along the trail with interpretive signs.

PA-HAY-OKEE TRAIL (11 miles from Main Entrance)   Short and sweet, this extremely accessible trail is perfect for day-trippers. Only a quarter of a mile long, the entire trail is actually a wooden boardwalk built over a sawgrass prairie that the Seminoles called *pa-ha-okee*, or grassy waters. The boardwalk ends at a two-story observation tower that affords visitors a panoramic view of low-lying marshlands and elevated hammocks. Along the boardwalk, stop to read the interpretive signs embedded in the railings, and look into the surrounding water for small white apple snails, the exclusive food of the endangered snail kite bird.

Pa-Hay-Okee Trail is located about a mile and a half past Rock Reef Pass, a three-foot high limestone ridge that forms the highest elevation in the park. More hospitable to vegetation than lower-lying areas, Rock Reef Pass is identifiable from the air by its thin line of large trees and shrubs.

MAHOGANY HAMMOCK TRAIL (18 miles from Main Entrance)   Another short, elevated boardwalk, the ¹/₂-mile Mahogany Hammock Trail winds its way through a subtropical hardwood forest that includes the largest living mahogany tree in the United States. Almost logged to extinction, mahogany trees were once common throughout the Everglades. The lanky, fan-shaped palms to your right, at the head of this trail, are threatened paurotis palms. Native to South Florida, these trees thrive in brackish marshes exclusively.

The entire trail is incredibly lush and junglelike, and the dense vegetation supports an enormous variety of wildlife. Take your time searching out frogs, insects, snails, and small birds. Patience might also reward you with a sighting (or hearing) of the barred owl, a normally nocturnal predator that makes this hammock its home. The pine trees across the park's Main Road from Mahogany Hammock are a roost for bald eagles. They are most likely to be spotted here during winter evenings.

WEST LAKE TRAIL (29 miles from Main Entrance)   West Lake's ¹/₄-mile-long elevated boardwalk cuts through a dense mangrove swamp before jutting out into large, brackish West Lake. The mangroves' complex, branchlike root system, often visible above the waterline, is the nursery ground for a majority of the Glades' marine animals. In late winter, hundreds of ducks can be seen here, along with alligators and several species of wading birds. There are plenty of interpretive signs along the route explaining important aspects of the mangrove ecosystem.

SPORTS & OUTDOOR ACTIVITIES

BICYCLING   The relatively flat 38-mile paved Main Park Road is excellent for bicycling, as are many park trails including Long Pine Key. Cyclers should expect to spend two to three hours along the path.

If the park isn't flooded from excess rain (which it has been for several months in recent years), Shark Valley in the Everglades National Park is South Florida's most scenic bicycle trail. Many locals haul their bikes out to the Glades for a relaxing day of wilderness trail-riding. You can ride the 17-mile loop with no other traffic in sight. Instead, you'll share the paved flat road only with other bikers and a menagerie of wildlife. Don't be surprised to see a gator lounging in the sun, a deer munching on some grass, or a picnicker eating a sandwich along the mangrove shore. Otters, turtles, alligators, and snakes are common companions in the Shark Valley area—although I don't think a single shark has been sighted lately.

You can rent bikes from **Flamingo Lodge Marina & Outpost Resort** (see "Where to Stay," below) for $12 per day, $7 per half-day (any five-hour period), and $3 per hour. Bicycles are also available from **Shark Valley Tram Tours,** at the park's Shark Valley Entrance (☎ 305/221-8455) for $3.25 per hour; rentals can be picked up from 8:30am and must be returned by 4pm. In Everglades City, **Ivey House Bed & Breakfast,** 107 Camellia St. (next to the Circle K store; ☎ 941/695-3299), rents bikes for $3 per hour or $15 for the day from November through May; they are open from 8:30am until 4:30pm daily.

If you'd like to try an audio-guided tour, call **Follow the Yellow Brick Road,** a bike tour company run by **Gary's Megacycles** at 1260 Washington Ave., Miami Beach (☎ 305/534-3306). For $25, a representative will transport you and a rental bike from anywhere from Miami Beach to Hollywood. Along with a high-tech Coloi bike, you'll get an audio-taped guide in any of four languages, a map, a helmet, and all the accoutrements. They are open from 10am to 7pm and accept reservations 24 hours a day; you can pay with MasterCard or Visa.

BIRDING More than 350 species of birds make their homes in the Everglades. Tropical birds from the Caribbean and temperate species from North America can be found here, along with exotics that have blown in from more distant regions. Eco and Mrazek ponds, located near Flamingo, are two of the best places for birding, especially in early morning or late afternoon in the dry winter months. Pick up a free birding checklist from a visitor center, and ask a park ranger what's been spotted in recent days.

BOATING Motorboating around the Everglades seems like a great way to see plants and animals in remote habitats. However, environmentalists are taking stock of the damage motorboats inflict on the delicate ecosystem. If you choose to motor, remember that most of the areas near land are "no wake" zones, and for the protection of nesting birds, landing is prohibited on most of the little mangrove islands. There is a long list of restrictions and restricted areas, so get a copy of the park's boating rules from National Park Headquarters before setting out (see "Just the Facts," above). Skiffs with 15-horsepower motors are available for rent at **Flamingo Lodge Marina & Outpost Resort** (see "Where to Stay," below). These low-power boats cost $65 per day, $47 per half-day (any five-hour period), and $15 per hour. A $50 deposit is required.

Motorboats are also available for rent on the west side of the Everglades, at **Chokoloskee Island Park,** on Chokoloskee Island, 3 miles south of Everglades City (☎ 941/695-2414). The cost is $40 for a half-day and $60 for a full day. Rentals are available Monday through Friday from 7am to 5pm, Saturday and Sunday from 6am to 5pm.

CANOEING The most intimate view of the Everglades comes from the humble perspective of a simple low-boat. From a canoe, you'll get a closer look into the park's shallow estuaries where water birds, sea turtles, and endangered manatees make their homes. Everglades National Park's longest "trails" are designed for boat and canoe travel and many are marked as clearly as walking trails. Noble Hammock Trail, a 2-mile loop, takes one to two hours, and is recommended for beginning canoers. Hell's Bay Trail, a 3- to 6-mile course for hardier paddlers, takes from two to six hours, depending on how far you choose to go. Park rangers can recommend other trails that best suit your abilities, time limitations, and interests.

Canoes can be rented at **Flamingo Lodge Marina & Outpost Resort** (see "Where to Stay," below), for $25 per day, $20 per half-day (any five-hour period), and $7 per hour. A $40 deposit is required. The concessionaire will shuttle your party to the trailhead of your choice, and pick you up afterward. Rental facilities are open daily from 6am to 5pm.

Canoes are also available at Everglades City, near the Park Ranger Station at the Everglades' western entrance, from **North American Canoe Tours,** P.O. Box 5038, Everglades City, FL (☎ 941/695-4666 or fax 941/695-4155 November to April, ☎ 203/739-0791 May to October). Seventeen-foot aluminum canoes can be rented with or without camping equipment, a personal guide, or fully outfitted tour. Canoes cost $20 per day. Canoes with camping supplies cost $50 per person per day.

FISHING   Open water comprises about one-third of Everglades National Park. Freshwater fishing is popular in brackish Nine-Mile Pond (25 miles from Main Entrance) and other spots along the Main Park Road, but due to high mercury levels found in the Everglades, freshwater fishers are warned not to eat their catches. Before casting, check in at a visitors center, as many of the park's lakes are preserved for observation only. Freshwater fishing licenses are required and cost $16 for seven days. They are not sold in the park, but you can purchase one from a tackle shop or sporting-goods store.

Separate saltwater licenses are sold at Flamingo Lodge Marina & Outpost Resort (see "Where to Stay" below), and are required for fishing in Florida Bay, the Gulf of Mexico, and the sounds that surround the park. Licenses for non-residents cost $7 for three days and $17 for seven days. Snapper and sea trout are plentiful and charter boats and guides are available for hire at Flamingo. Phone for information and reservations.

ORGANIZED TOURS

BY AIRBOAT   Although airboats are not allowed in the park proper, several operators on the western edge of the Everglades offer rides through the surrounding waterways. At the **Miccosukee Indian Village** (☎ 305/223-8380), you can take a half-hour, high-speed airboat tour through the rushes. Birds scatter as the boats approach, and when you slow down, alligators and other animals appear. This thrilling "safari" through the Everglades is one you will not soon forget—highly recommended. Rides are offered daily from 9am to 5pm and cost just $7. To get into the village, it costs $5 for adults, $3.50 for children.

To get to the village from Miami Beach, take 395 (the MacArthur Causeway) west to 836, which connects to the 826 (the Palmetto Expressway). Exit on SW 8th Street (Hwy. 41), and drive about 30 miles. You'll see the village on your left. Airboat rides are on the right side of the road.

BY MOTORBOAT   Both Florida Bay and backcountry tours are offered at **Flamingo Lodge Marina & Outpost Resort** (see "Where to Stay," below). Each are available in two or four-hour versions that cost $12 and $32 per person, respectively. Florida Bay tours cruise nearby estuaries and sandbars, while six-passenger back-country boats visit smaller sloughs. Tours depart throughout the day, and reservations are recommended.

Boat tours from Everglades City are offered by **Everglades National Park Boat Tours** (☎ 941/695-2591, or 800/445-7724 in Florida). The Mangrove Wilderness Tour explores the Glades' inland rivers and creeks at high tide. White ibis, cuckoos, egrets, herons, and other animals can often be seen through the thick mangroves. The Ten Thousand Islands Cruise navigates through the mangrove estuaries of the Gulf Coast. The endangered manatee can often be spotted, along with dozens of species of birds including the Southern bald eagle. Tours depart daily, every half hour from 9am to 5pm (less frequently during the off-season); last about 90 minutes; and cost $11 for adults, $5.50 for children. Reservations are not accepted. Tours depart from Park Docks, on Chokoloskee Causeway (Route 29), a half-mile south of the traffic circle by the ranger station.

Everyone raves about the narrated tours given by naturalists Frank and Georgia Garrett of ✪ **Majestic Everglades Excursions** (☎ 941/695-2777). They take up to six passengers on four-hour excursions through the islands on their covered deck boat and explain the bird, marine, animal, and plant life. The trips cost $65 for adults, $35 for children under 12. Reservations are required; pick-up is at Seas Store and Deli, across from the park entrance in Everglades City. Tours don't run in June or July.

BY CANOE   David Harraden and sons Jason and Jeremy of **North American Canoe Tours** (☎ 941/695-3299 or fax 941/695-4155 November to April; ☎ 203/739-0791 May to October) have been leading canoe expeditions into the Everglades every winter since 1978, offering trips ranging from one day to a week. The one-day trips cost $40 per person. They operate out of Everglades City, but also provide van shuttle service to and from Flamingo. The Harradens operate from November through April.

BY TRAM   At the park's Shark Valley Entrance open-air tram buses take visitors on two-hour naturalist-led tours that delve 7^1/$_2$ miles into the wilderness. At the trail's midsection, passengers can disembark and climb a 65-foot observation tower that offers good views of the Glades. The tour offers visitors considerable views that include plenty of wildlife and endless acres of sawgrass. Tours run from November through April only from 9am to 4pm, and are sometimes stalled by flooding or particularly heavy mosquito infestation. Reservations are recommended from December through March. The cost is $7.75 for adults, $4 for children, and $7 for seniors. For further information contact the Flamingo Lodge (see "Where to Stay," below).

WHERE TO STAY

Since the Everglades are so close to Miami, most visitors return to their city hotel rooms at night. If you want to stay in the park, however, Flamingo is not only the best but also the only place.

CAMPING IN THE PARK

You can camp overnight almost anywhere you want in the backcountry, but free permits are required, and you must file your itinerary with officials (see "Just the Facts," above). Many backcountry sites are chickees—covered wooden platforms on stilts. They are only accessible by canoe. Ground sites are located along interior bays and rivers, and beach camping is also popular. In summer especially, mosquito repellent is required gear.

Car camping can be done at Flamingo and Long Pine Key campgrounds, where there are more than 300 campsites designed for tents and RVs. They have level parking pads, tables, and charcoal grills. There are no electrical hook-ups and showers are cold. Permits cost $4 to $8 per site from September through May, and are free the rest of the year. Private ground fires are not permitted, but supervised campfire programs are conducted during winter months.

HOUSEBOATING

Houseboat rentals are one of the park's best-kept secrets. Available through the Flamingo Lodge, motorized houseboats make it possible to explore some of the park's more remote regions without having to worry about being back by nightfall. You can choose from two different types of houseboats. The first, a 40-foot pontoon boat, sleeps six to eight people in a single large room that is separated by a central head (bathroom) and shower. There's a small galley (kitchen) that contains a stove, oven, and charcoal grill. It rents for $254 per night (with a two-night minimum).

The newer, sleeker Gibson fiberglass boats sleep six, have a head and shower, air conditioning, and electric stove. There's also a full rooftop sundeck. These rent for $280 per night (with a two-night minimum).

Boating experience is helpful, but not mandatory, as the boats only cruise up to six miles per hour and are surprisingly easy to use. Reservations should be made very far in advance.

FLAMINGO & ENVIRONS

Flamingo Lodge Marina & Outpost Resort. 1 Flamingo Lodge Hwy., Flamingo, FL 33034. ☎ **941/695-3101** or 800/600-3813. Fax 813/695-3921. 103 rms, 24 cottages. A/C TV TEL. Nov–Dec 14 and Apr 1–30, $74 single or double; $87 cottage; $110 suite. Dec 15–Mar, $87 single or double; $102 cottage; $130 suite. May–Oct, $59 single or double; $72 cottage; $85 suite. Additional person $10 extra. Children under 12 stay free in parents' room. AE, DC, DISC, MC, V.

Flamingo Lodge is the only hotel located within the boundaries of Everglades National Park. An attractive and spacious motel, the air-conditioned lodge is situated right in the center of the action. Nothing's fancy, but there's a "fishing camp" feel and a very friendly atmosphere. Rooms are relatively simple and clean and overlook Florida Bay. Each has two double beds and a private bathroom. Cottages, which come with small kitchens, are larger, more private, and somewhat romantic. They are equipped with dishes and flatware.

Facilities include a restaurant and bar, freshwater swimming pool, gift shop, and coin-op laundry (available from 8am to 10pm). Binoculars can be rented at the front desk, which is open daily from 6am to 11pm. The hotel is open year-round and reservations are accepted daily from 8am to 5pm.

HOMESTEAD & FLORIDA CITY

Homestead and Florida City, two adjacent towns that were almost blown off the map by Hurricane Andrew, are located about 10 miles from the park's Main Entrance, along U.S. 1, 35 miles south of Miami.

Best Western Gateway to the Keys. 1 Strano Blvd. (U.S. 1), Florida City, FL 33034. ☎ **305/246-5100** or 800/528-1234. Fax 305/242-0056. 90 rms, 24 suites. A/C TV TEL. Dec–Apr, $79 single or double; from $99 suite. May–Nov, $65 single or double; from $85 suite. AE, DC, DISC, MC, V.

Opened in late 1994, this two-story, pink-and-white Best Western is contemporary in style and comfort. Each identical room has new beds with bright tropical spreads and matching window treatments that cover oversized picture windows. The business-oriented Best Western is well priced and well maintained, and is the most recommendable in the area. There's a swimming pool and a spa.

SHARK VALLEY

Everglades Tower Inn. SR Box E 4910, Ochopee, FL 33943. ☎ **305/559-7779.** Fax 305/220-5814. 20 rms. A/C TV. Dec 20–Jan 15, $55 single or double. Jan 16–Apr and Oct–Dec 19, $44 single or double. May–Sept, $34 single or double. MC, V.

Run by the indigenous Miccosukee tribe, this inn is a simple and basic motel located about 1 mile west of the Everglades' Shark Valley Entrance. All rooms have two double beds and private baths, but no telephones, no pool, no frills.

WHERE TO DINE
FLAMINGO

Flamingo Restaurant. In Flamingo Lodge, Flamingo. ☎ **941/695-3101.** Reservations recommended for dinner. Main courses $14–$17. AE, DC, DISC, MC, V. Oct–May, daily 7am–10am; year-round, daily 11:30am–3:30pm and 5:30–9pm. AMERICAN.

One can't mention Flamingo Restaurant without making immediate reference to its spectacular view of Florida Bay and numerous keys. The only restaurant that's actually within Everglades National Park, the Flamingo is so close to nesting habitats, it should provide birding checklists along with each menu. Food here is surprisingly good despite the restaurant's lack of competition. Meat and poultry dishes, including Caribbean steak marinated in jerk seasonings and citrus chicken marinated in fruit juices, are offered, but the kitchen is best noted for its fine fresh fish. Mahi mahi and native reef fish are prepared grilled, blackened, or deep fried and at dinner, all entrees come with salad or conch chowder, and steamed vegetables, black beans and rice, or baked potato. Lunches are lighter and include fish and chicken sandwiches, pastas, burgers, and salads.

HOMESTEAD & FLORIDA CITY

Capri Restaurant. 935 N. Krome Ave., Florida City. ☎ **305/247-1542.** Reservations accepted. Main courses $9–$13. AE, MC, V. Mon–Thurs 11am–10pm, Fri–Sat 11am–11pm. ITALIAN/AMERICAN.

Although Capri Restaurant was right in the path of Hurricane Andrew, it survived practically unscathed. It's no wonder. The restaurant occupies a squat one-story windowless stone building that looks something like a medieval fort. Inside the dark restaurant is a 1950s-style dining room and cocktail bar that's been an area landmark and meeting place since it opened in 1958. Richard Accursio, the restaurant's original owner, still oversees the daily preparations of Italian-American standards, be they appetizers or pastas or meat main courses.

Potlikker's. 591 Washington Ave., Homestead. ☎ **305/248-0835.** Reservations accepted. Main courses $6–$12; sandwiches $5–$6. AE, MC, V. Daily 7am–9pm. SOUTHERN AMERICAN.

This is one of the best restaurants in Homestead, but that's not much of a boast. Inside the restaurant's single A-frame dining room are wooden booths with paper placemats, loud lite-rock radio, and large windows that are always darkened with closed blinds. The menu, presented on a large erasable whiteboard, features hamburgers, hot dogs, and fried fish and shrimp baskets, along with barbecue chicken and ribs, roast pork, grilled fish, lots of local veggies, and more. It's a good southern feed at popular prices. The restaurant is located at the corner of NE 6th Street, between Krome Avenue and U.S. 1.

3 Quick Getaways to the Bahamas

CRUISES

Many people believe that taking a cruise means spending thousands of dollars and booking a ship far in advance. It's true that some big trips require serious advance planning, but most of the Caribbean-bound ships, sailing weekly out of the Port of Miami, are relatively inexpensive, can be booked without advance notice, and make for an excellent excursion.

Home to 22 cruise ships from all around the world, the Port of Miami is the world's busiest, with a passenger load of close to three million annually. The popularity of cruises shows no sign of tapering off, and the trend in ships is toward bigger, more luxurious liners. Usually all-inclusive, cruises offer value and simplicity compared to other vacation options.

All the shorter cruises are well equipped for gambling, and casinos open as soon as the ship clears U.S. waters—typically 45 minutes after leaving port. Usually, four full-size meals are served daily, with portions so huge they're impossible to finish. Games, movies, and other on-board activities ensure you are always busy. Passengers can board up to two hours prior to departure for meals, games, and cocktails.

There are dozens of cruises to choose from—from a one-day excursion to a trip around the world. A full list of options can be obtained from the **Metro-Dade Seaport Department,** 1015 North America Way, Miami, FL 33132 (☎ 305/371-7678). Open Monday through Friday from 8am to 5pm.

The cruise lines and ships listed below offer two- and three-day excursions to the Bahamas. Cruise ships usually depart Miami on Friday night and return Monday morning. If you want more information, contact the **Bahamas Tourist Office,** 19495 Biscayne Blvd., Suite 809, Aventura, FL 33180 (☎ 305/932-0051). All passengers must travel with a passport or proof of citizenship for re-entry into the United States.

Carnival Cruise Lines. 35201 Blue Lagoon Dr., Miami, FL 33126. ☎ **305/599-2200** or 800/327-9501. Ship: *Fantasy* and *Ecstasy*. Itinerary: 3–4 nights to Nassau. Depart/Return: Fri 4pm to Mon 7am. Cost from $360.

One of the largest cruise ships in the world, the *Fantasy* made its debut in March 1990 with lots of publicity. Several swimming pools, game rooms, and lounges surround a spectacular multistory foyer that has quickly made the *Fantasy* the centerpiece of Carnival's fast-growing fleet. The 70,000-ton ship can accommodate up to 3,000 passengers.

Norwegian Cruise Line. 95 Merrick Way, Coral Gables, FL 33134. ☎ **305/445-0866** or 800/327-7030. Ship: *Leeward*. Itinerary: 3 nights to Key West and Nassau. Depart/Return: Fri 6pm to Mon 7am. Cost from $430.

An intimate smaller ship, the 950-passenger *Leeward* spends a full day in Nassau or on Key West (they alternate weekly). As on other Caribbean-bound ships, you can choose to disembark at any destination or you can stay on board for food, drinks, and games.

Royal Caribbean Cruise Line. 1050 Caribbean Way, Miami, FL 33132. ☎ **305/539-6000** or 800/327-6700. Ship: *Nordic Empress*. Itinerary: 3 nights to Nassau and Coco Cay. Depart/Return: Fri 5pm to Mon 9am. Cost from $500.

In 1990 Royal Caribbean entered the three-night Caribbean market with the brand-new *Nordic Empress*. Beautifully streamlined and stylized, this special ship is fully outfitted and treats its 1,610 passengers to some of the world's swankiest seafaring. Coco Cay is the cruise line's private island, five hours from Nassau.

FLIGHTS & WEEKEND PACKAGES

For those who want a quick getaway to the Caribbean without the experience of cruising, many airlines and hotels team up to offer extremely affordable weekend packages.

For example, one of the Bahama's most elegant and newly renovated resorts, **The Atlantis,** hosts guests who like to play the slots, poker, or anything else in its active casinos. The Sun Club bought and totally revamped the 30-year-old club in 1994. Reasonably priced three-day packages start at about $390, depending on your departure date. It's generally cheaper to fly midweek. Flights on USAir prop-planes depart four or five times daily from Miami International. You can also choose to stay in the companies' other luxurious resorts, The Paradise Beach Resort or the Ocean Club.

Other groups that arrange competitively priced packages include **American Flyaway Vacations,** operated by American Airlines (☎ 800/321-2121); **Bahamas Air** (☎ 800/222-4262); **Pan Am Air Bridge** (☎ 305/371-8628); the slightly run-down **Princess Casino** in Freeport (☎ 305/359-9898); and **USAir** (☎ 800/842-5374). Call for rates, since they vary dramatically throughout the year and also depend upon what type of accommodations you choose.

12 The Keys

Juan Ponce de León, the 16th-century Spanish explorer who was searching for the Fountain of Youth, found the Florida Keys instead—islands he called *"Los Martieres"* (The Martyrs), because they looked to him like men in distress. *"Cayo"* is the Spanish word for "small island." To those of us with less-active imaginations, the Keys appear more like little tropical islands strung out in a chain that reaches from Miami halfway to Cuba. Although there are about 400 islands in the Florida Keys, the best known of these are the 34 that are connected to the mainland by the Overseas Highway (U.S. 1). The hundreds of small, undeveloped islands that surround these "mainland" keys are known locally as the "backcountry." Most backcountry islands are wildlife refuges protected by either the federal government or the Nature Conservancy, a private environmental organization.

The Keys are surrounded by the world's third-largest barrier-reef system, a variety of living corals that supports a complex and delicate ecosystem of plants and animals including sponges, anemones, jellyfish, crabs, rays, sharks, turtles, snails, lobsters, and thousands of types of fish.

The Keys are divided into three regions—Upper Keys, Lower Keys, and Key West—each with distinctive characteristics. The **Upper Keys** are commercial and overdeveloped—the result of their close proximity to Miami and merciless dredging and filling that occurred in the 1940s. Under a mandate by President Franklin Roosevelt, chemical-based mosquito-abatement programs were instituted, coral reefs were slashed, trees were chopped, and towns were built. There are few unspoiled spots left between the strip malls and condominium complexes, but several resort hotels and plenty of parks take advantage of the area's intrinsic beauty.

Like the Upper Keys, fishing and diving fuel the economic engine that drives the **Lower Keys,** but due to environmental activism and governmental protection, development here has been contained. As you head south, the discount stores give way to seashell shops and sandy beaches. A rich variety of indigenous plants and animals live here, including many endangered species. Eagles, egrets, and Key deer are some of the most visible, as are gumbo-limbo trees, mangroves, royal poincianas, banyans, and aloe.

Literally at the end of the road and famous for its relaxed atmosphere, **Key West** has reached legendary status for the way its residents jealously guard their island's independent identity. In 1982, when a federal Customs roadblock was thrown up across U.S. 1 to help reduce drug smuggling, locals responded with a mock secession from the United States and a declaration of an independent "Conch Nation."

ANNUAL EVENTS & ACTIVITIES IN THE KEYS

Anything goes in the Keys—just walk through downtown Key West and you'll be convinced. And in that spirit, the annual festivals that take place in Key West are wacky, to say the least. Plus fishing tournaments are so common in the Keys that there seems to be one every month. Here are some of the biggest and the best fishing and other festivals in Key West and the Keys.

In Key West, **Old Island Days** refers to a calendar full of special events scheduled every year from December through April. These activities usually occur on weekends and include garden tours, special readings, outdoor party events, and myriad other unusual activities. Contact the **Key West Chamber of Commerce,** 402 Wall St., Key West, FL 33040 (☎ 305/294-2587 or 800/527-8539), for a schedule of Old Island Days events.

The **Arts Expo Craft Show** (☎ 305/294-0431), usually held the last weekend of January, is a colorful explosion of local talent exhibiting and selling unique functional art. In early February, artists display their creation at the **Old Island Days Art Festival**. The **Annual House and Garden Tours** are an island tradition, showing off some of the Key's best homes during the last two weekends in February. Contact the Old Island Restoration Foundation (☎ 305/294-9501) for exact tour dates and ticket information.

In March is the **Annual Flagging of the Old Island Armada.** Dozens of private and commercial vessels parade in Key West's main channel, and flags are ceremoniously hoisted. Also in March is the **Key West Garden Club Flower Show** (☎ 305/294-3210), with its annual display of homegrown horticulture.

In April, the **Conch Republic Celebration** (☎ 305/296-8803) is one of the year's biggest parties. In an attempt to catch illegal aliens and drug smugglers, in April 1982, the U.S. Border Patrol blocked the highway connecting Key West to the mainland. Island leaders, furious about being treated like foreigners, mockingly declared Key West an independent "Conch Republic."

In early May, the **Texaco/Hemingway Key West Classic**, hailed as the top fishing tournament in Florida, is held. This-catch-and-release competition offers a $50,000 purse to the best angler for sailfish, marlin, and light tackle. For information, call 305/294-4440. In mid-May, the **Coconuts Dolphin Tournament** is the largest fishing tournament in the Keys, offering $5,000 and a Dodge Ram pickup truck to the person who breaks the record for the largest fish caught. The competition is fierce! For more information, call 305/451-4107. November brings **The Mercury Outboards Cheeca/Redbone Celebrity Tournament** to Islamorada. Curt Gowdy from American Sportsman hosts this tournament, whose proceeds go to finding a cure for cystic fibrosis. The likes of Wade Boggs and actor James B. Sikking compete almost yearly. For details, call 305/664-2002.

If you happen to be in the Keys during the summer, mark your calendar for late May and join the locals for the **Super Boat Racing Series** in downtown Key West. It's a day of food, fun, and powerboat racing sure to generate excitement. For information, call 305/296-8963.

In July, the **Looe Key Underwater Music Fest** comes to town. At this outrageous celebration, boaters go out to the underwater reef off Little Torch Key, drop speakers into the water, and pipe in music. It's entertainment for the fish and swimmers alike! The snorkeling Elvis' have been known to be the main act for this celebration. For details, call 305/872-2411. The **July Fourth Swim Around the Island** is one of the highlights of Key West's Independence Day celebrations. Look for beach parties and fireworks, along with the usual island shenanigans.

In late July, Key West puts on a massive shindig celebrating its most noteworthy resident, Ernest Hemingway, with the **Hemingway Days Festival.** For a week, the "conchs" and their visitors pay homage to the tortured novelist by putting on Ernest Hemingway look-alike contests attracting participants from all over the United States and sometimes other countries. You'd be surprised to find out how many men actually look like him! Writer's workshops and conferences are offered for more serious-minded visitors. For more details, call 305/294-4440.

In Key West for Halloween? It might feel like the rest of the world is joining you if you're around for the world-famous **Fantasy Fest** held in October. This insane gathering of thousands of people is Florida's version of Mardi Gras. Crazy costumes, wild parades, and even more colorful revelers gather for an opportunity to do things Mom said not to do. For information, call 305/296-1817. Check out the **Goombay Festival** that coincides with Fantasy Fest to sample Caribbean dishes and purchase art and ethnic clothing in this celebration with a Jamaican flair.

In November, the **Reef Relief's Cayo Festival** (☎ 305/294-3100), held in Key West, raises both money and consciousness for the protection of the Key's fragile coral reefs. Organized by a nonprofit organization, the festival features food, fun, and activities for all ages.

1 Exploring the Keys by Car

You'd think with just one main road running through the entire chain of the Keys there wouldn't be much to explore. But there is. You'll find plenty of hidden treasures off-the-beaten-path. And I've included in this chapter all you'll need to know about out-of-the-way spots and backwater adventures.

One of the best things about Key West is getting there, so unless you're really pressed for time don't even think of flying—driving is the way to go. Motoring across the Keys on U.S. 1 (the Overseas Highway), over 42 bridges and across 34 islands, is one of the greatest road trips anywhere. For much of the drive, expansive skies and sweeping water vistas surround you with innumerable shades of blue. The clear water appears to "blossom" with little mangrove islands that compete for your attention with families of ospreys nesting on the telephone lines that follow you all the way to Key West. At other points along the way, the road is clogged with shopping centers and billboards advertising restaurants, rest stops, and attractions.

Most of U.S. 1 is a narrow, two-lane highway, though in the Upper Keys it opens up to four lanes. The legal speed limit is 55 m.p.h. (45 m.p.h. on Big Pine Key and in commercial areas), and passing is restricted for most of the way. Still, on a good day you can make the trip to Key West from Miami in less than four hours. But don't rush. There are plenty of worthwhile places to stop along the way.

Please note that gasoline prices rise rapidly the farther south you go, but then descend slightly when you arrive on Key West. Fill up in Miami.

EN ROUTE: ALABAMA JACKS & HOLIDAY ISLE

Two stops are required on any trip to or from the Keys. The first, in Florida City, just south of Homestead, is known as **Alabama Jacks.** It's on Card Sound Road, also called the old road to the Keys. This landmark was built on a floating barge in 1953 and today is the meeting point for Harley owners, weekend cyclists, midwestern

The Keys

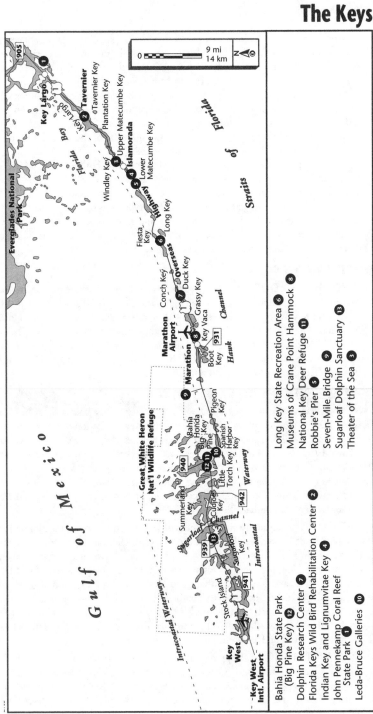

Bahia Honda State Park
(Big Pine Key) ⑫

Dolphin Research Center ⑦

Florida Keys Wild Bird Rehabilitation Center ②

Indian Key and Lignumvitae Key ④

John Pennekamp Coral Reef
State Park ①

Leda-Bruce Galleries ⑩

Long Key State Recreation Area ⑥

Museums of Crane Point Hammock ⑧

National Key Deer Refuge ⑪

Robbie's Pier ⑤

Seven-Mile Bridge ⑨

Sugarloaf Dolphin Sanctuary ⑬

Theater of the Sea ③

tourists, and hip couples from Miami. All these folks get together to drink beer and listen to a hokey cowboy band that plays on weekends from 2pm until closing (which is 7pm). Other days, enjoy the decent bar food, including some spicy crab cakes, and great waterfront atmosphere from 11am to 7pm. It's a great introduction to the Keys.

To get to Alabama Jacks, when you get off the Turnpike at its end in Florida City, turn right at the stoplight onto U.S. 1. You'll see the Mutineer restaurant on your left and signs for the toll plaza. Make a left onto Card Sound and drive about 11 miles. You can't miss the trucks parked on both sides of the road. The bar is at about Mile Marker 125 on the right before the toll.

The other place where you should stop is the renowned **Holiday Isle** and its **Tiki Bar,** 84001 Overseas Hwy., Mile Marker 84, Islamorada (☎ 800/327-7070). After a bright red rum-runner or two you may want to enter the limbo contest and be cheered on by an assortment of yuppie business types and kids in Hawaiian shirts. The most fun is to be had in the afternoons and early evenings when everyone is either sunburned, drunk, or just happy to be alive and dancing to reggae. For more details, see "The Upper Keys After Dark" below.

ROAD TRIP TIPS

FINDING AN ADDRESS   Most addresses in the Keys are delineated by Mile Marker (MM), small green signs on the right side of the road that announce the distance from Key West. The markers end with number 126, just south of the Florida mainland. The zero marker is in Key West, at the corner of Whitehead and Fleming streets. All addresses in this chapter are accompanied by a MM designation to help you determine its location on (or near) U.S. 1. Listings in this chapter are organized first by price, then by location, from north to south.

2 The Great Outdoors

BEACHES   Most people do not realize that the Keys really don't have any beaches to speak of. You'll find a few small man-made beaches at the hotels in Key West and a few others. Instead, most of the ocean activity takes place on boats or in grassy parks. But if you want to go to the beach, here are your options: Smathers Beach off South Roosevelt Boulevard west of the airport, Higgs Beach along Atlantic Boulevard between White Street and Reynolds Road, or Fort Zachary Beach located off the western end of Southard Boulevard.

BICYCLING   The almost flat 126 miles of U.S. 1 that run down the Florida Keys are tailor-made for cyclists, if it weren't for the cars. There are bike paths paralleling the road from Mile Markers 106 to 86, but the rest of the route is on narrow shoulders, making bicycling the Keys for serious cyclists only. Larger islands, like Marathon, Big Pine, and Key West, offer good family cycling on dedicated paths and smaller side streets. In Marathon, try Sombrero Beach Road, from the Overseas Highway to the public beach (at Mile Marker 50). On Big Pine, cruise along Key Deer Boulevard (at Mile Marker 30)—those with fat tires can ride into the National Key Deer Refuge. And on Key West, just about any street will do.

BIRD-WATCHING   A stopping point for migratory birds on the "Eastern Flyway," the Keys are populated with a large proportion of West Indian bird species, especially during spring and fall. The small vegetated islands of the Keys are the only nesting sites in the United States for the great white heron and white-crowned pigeons. It's also one of a very few breeding places for the reddish egret, the roseate spoonbill, the mangrove cuckoo, and the black-whiskered vireo. Many factors are threatening the health of these bird populations; paramount among them is loss of habitat. Forty percent of the shallow water mangrove pools on the Upper Keys were lost to human development between 1955 and 1985 and transitional wetlands, shallow water mangrove sites, freshwater ponds, and hardwood hammocks continue to be filled and developed. The Dry Tortugas, a chain of seven coral islands 70 miles west of Key West, is one of the best birding spots in the world. Accessible only by boat or plane, the islands are a mecca for the most serious birders. See "The Dry Tortugas," below, for complete information.

DIVING & SNORKELING   According to 22,000 votes cast by readers of *Scuba Diving* magazine, the Florida Keys are the best place to dive in America, topping even California and Hawaii. The Keys are surrounded by one of the world's largest barrier-reef systems in relatively shallow water, which attracts a plethora of sealife. John Pennekamp Coral Reef State Park (at Mile Marker 102.3) is an especially popular place to dive and snorkel (see "The Upper Keys," below), offering regular excursions to its protected reefs. If you aren't a certified diver, you can take a quick course that will allow you to go out with an instructor or you might want to try snuba-diving, a relatively new version of diving offered in Key Largo, where the swimmers go down attached to a communal air breathing unit without cumbersome tanks. Dive shops abound and are listed geographically below.

FISHING   South Florida and the Florida Keys might just have more boats, rods, and reels than any place else on earth. Almost two dozen local fish species—including amberjack, barracuda, snapper, king mackerel, sailfish, tarpon, swordfish, and white marlin—attain a weight of 50 pounds or more, the respectable minimum for seasoned trophy hunters. There are three different kinds of fishing in the Keys: deepsea fishing for big-game fish like marlin, sailfish, and tuna; reef fishing for "eating fish" like snapper and grouper; and backcountry fishing for bonefish, tarpon, and other "stalking" fish.

Unless you're fishing from land, a pier, or a sanctioned bridge, a saltwater-fishing permit is mandatory, and costs $7 for three days and $17 for seven days. Permits can be purchased from almost any bait or boat shop; many are listed geographically below.

If your catch will not be eaten or mounted, release your fish to preserve the area's severely depleted fish population. Always pay close attention to your baited hooks; they will tempt hungry birds. Over 80% of bird injuries are caused by fishing hooks and monofilament. Never discard fishing line in the water, and if you accidentally hook a bird, never allow it to fly off without first removing any attached fish line.

HIKING   You can hike throughout the Keys, on both marked trails and meandering coastlines. The best places to trek through nature are the Bahia Honda State Park (at Mile Marker 29.5), National Key Deer Refuge (at Mile Marker 30), Crane Point Hammock (at Mile Marker 50.5), Long Key State Recreation Area (at Mile Marker 68), and John Pennekamp Coral Reef State Park (at Mile Marker 102.3). See "What to See and Do," below, for complete information.

KAYAKING & CANOEING   The Overseas Highway (U.S. 1) only touches on a few dozen of the many hundreds of islands that make up the Florida Keys. I can think of no better way to explore the uninhabited shallow backcountry than by kayak or canoe. You can go places big boats just can't get to because of their large draft. Sometimes the lumbering ancient manatees will cuddle up to the boats thinking they are another friendly species. Most are. For a more enjoyable time, ask for a sit-inside-type boat—you'll stay drier. Also, a fiberglass boat with a rudder (as opposed to plastic) is generally more stable and easier to maneuver. Many area hotels rent kayaks and canoes to guests, as do a multitude of outfitters, listed geographically below.

3 The Upper Keys: Key Largo to Marathon

48 to 105 miles SW of Miami

Although it hardly looks like it from the busy main road, the Upper Keys are all about water and wilderness. This is the fishing and diving capital of America, and a profusion of outfitters and billboards never let you forget it. In Islamorada, the unofficial capital of the Upper Keys, both commercial and private fishing fleets are docked at most every inlet. Marathon, the Upper Keys' other main population center, is a curious mixture of modern tract-home community, tourist resort, and old fishing village. This island's highly developed infrastructure includes resort hotels, a commercial airport, and a highway that expands to four lanes. In between Islamorada and Marathon are about 35 miles of highway, alternating between wetlands, strip malls, nesting grounds, resort hotels, and blue waters.

ESSENTIALS

VISITOR INFORMATION   The **Key Largo Chamber of Commerce,** 105950 Overseas Hwy., Key Largo, FL 33037 (☎ 305/451-1414), is open daily from 9am to 6pm. The **Islamorada Chamber of Commerce,** in the Little Red Caboose, Mile Marker 82.5 (P.O. Box 915), Islamorada, FL 33036 (☎ 305/664-4503 or 800/322-5397), also offers maps and literature on the Upper Keys. The **Greater Marathon Chamber of Commerce,** 12222 Overseas Hwy., Mile Marker 48.7, Marathon, FL 33050 (☎ 800/842-9580), is located in a squat pink building on the right-hand side of the road (facing Key West).

GETTING THERE   **American Eagle** (☎ 800/433-7300), flies nonstop from Miami to Marathon, and charges from $128 to $234, round-trip.

If you're driving from Miami, take the Florida Turnpike south along the east coast to Exit 4, Homestead/Key West. This is the Turnpike Extension that meets U.S. 1 in Florida City. Islamorada is about an hour south. If you're coming from Florida's west coast, take Alligator Alley to the Miami exit, then turn south onto the Turnpike Extension.

Greyhound (☎ 800/231-2222) operates three buses daily, in each direction, between Miami and Key West. It stops in both Key Largo and Marathon, and costs $11 each way.

OUTDOOR SIGHTS & ATTRACTIONS

✪ **Indian Key and Lignumvitae Key.** Off Indian Key Fill, Overseas Hwy., Mile Marker 79 (P.O. Box 1052). ☎ **305/664-4815.**

Most of the Florida Keys that are not connected by the Overseas Highway are protected as wildlife preserves and off-limits to casual visitors. Two unusual exceptions are Indian Key and Lignumvitae Key, backcountry islands that offer visitors a glimpse of the "real" keys, before modern development. These two small islands, preserved and managed by the Florida Department of Natural Resources, are each located about 1 mile from U.S. 1 in Islamorada, and are only accessible by boat. Tours to each island depart regularly throughout the year.

Named for the lignum vitae ("wood of life") trees found there, 280-acre Lignumvitae Key supports a virgin tropical forest that is characteristic of the kind of vegetation that once thrived on most of the Upper Keys. Over the years, human settlers, importing "exotic" plants and animals to the Keys, have changed the botanical makeup of many backcountry islands. Sometimes the damage is incredibly devastating. When the Department of Natural Resources adopted Lignumvitae Key in 1971, they embarked on an aggressive campaign to remove all exotic vegetation and restore the key to its original state.

Indian Key, located on the Atlantic side of Islamorada, is a 10-acre historic site that was occupied by Native Americans for thousands of years. It was also the original seat of Dade County before the Civil War. An 1840 rebellion by Native Americans almost wiped out the island's once-growing population, leaving the ruins to posterity.

Boat tours to both islands depart Indian Key Fill (Mile Marker 79) Thursday through Monday at 8:30am for Indian Key, and at 1:30pm for Lignumvitae Key. In summer, tours operate Friday through Sunday only. The tour fee for each island is $20 per person. Reservations are required 48 hours in advance during the high season.

Museum of Crane Point Hammock. 5550 Overseas Hwy., Marathon. ☎ **305/743-9100.** Admission $7.50 adults, $6 seniors 65 and older, $4 students, free for children 6 and under. Mon–Sat 9am–5pm, Sun noon–5pm.

Most of the land surrounding Crane Point Hammock is highly developed; there's even a shopping mall across the street. This 64-acre nature area didn't escape the builders accidentally. It was purchased in 1949 by the Crane family, ardent conservationists who recognized the significance of this special parcel. Now managed by the Florida Keys Land and Sea Trust, Crane Point Hammock contains what is probably the last virgin thatch palm hammock in North America.

The Hammock's small nature museum teaches visitors about the Key's flora and fauna, both on land and underwater. A walk-through replica of a coral reef cave unravels the complexities of the tropical reef ecosystem, while life-sized wildlife dioramas teach about birds and Key deer. Other exhibits contain finds that illustrate over 5,000 years of human history in the Keys. A walkway leads to a single-room children's museum with interactive displays that include a miniature railway station and small saltwater touch tank.

Outside, visitors are encouraged to wander through the museum's quarter-mile nature trail, a self-guided loop that circles the palm hammock.

✪ **Seven Mile Bridge.** Overseas Hwy., Mile Markers 40–47.

Oil magnate Henry Flagler first visited Florida in 1878. Realizing the state's potential for growth, he built the Florida East Coast Railroad to shuttle northeasterners from Jacksonville to the warmth of Miami. After years of planning, the decision was made to extend the line to Key West, a project that pundits labeled "Flagler's Folly." Construction began in 1904, and thousands of workers battled against insects, hurricanes, intense heat, and water shortages, but on January 21, 1912, the Overseas Extension was completed. The railroad operated until 1935, when a Labor Day hurricane damaged the rails beyond repair. A large portion of the Overseas Highway (U.S. 1) was built on Flagler's abandoned rail bed. Many remnants of the rail line can still be seen along the highway; most notable is a large portion of the original Seven Mile Bridge that runs alongside the newer roadway. The islands' most celebrated span rests on 546 concrete piers, and rises to a 72-foot crest, the highest point in the Keys.

Heading south on the Overseas Highway, slow down just before the bridge and turn right, off the road, onto the unpaved parking lot at the foot of the bridge. From here you can walk or bicycle along the old bridge that goes for almost 4 miles before abruptly dropping off into the sea. The first half-mile of this "ghost bridge" is popular with area fishermen who use shrimp as bait to catch barracuda, yellowtail, and a host of other fish. At the far end of the bridge is the University of Miami's Institute of Marine Science, a research facility that's not open to the public.

ANIMALS OF THE KEYS

✪ **Florida Keys Wild Bird Rehabilitation Center.** 93600 Overseas Hwy., Mile Marker 94, Tavernier. ☎ **305/852-4486.** Free admission. Daily 8:30am–5pm.

Almost anytime you visit the Rehabilitation Center, you are likely to see naturalist Laura Quinn in her "operating room," removing a fish hook from a bird's throat or untangling fishing line from a broken wing. The ultimate goal of this center is to return wildlife to the wild, but when a bird arrives with a permanent injury, these protective wetlands become the animal's home. As a result, this is the best place in the Keys to get close to a large variety of native birds including broad-wing hawks, great white heron, brown pelicans, and even osprey. This is not a zoo built for gawkers; birds are exhibited reluctantly, as Laura Quinn's greatest wish is that the zoo could be closed for a lack of exhibits.

The Wild Bird Rehabilitation Center is a little hard to find. Look for wooden bird sculptures on the westbound lane of the highway.

Theater of the Sea. Overseas Hwy., Mile Marker 84.5 (P.O. Box 407), Islamorada. ☎ **305/664-2431.** Admission $14.25 adults, $7.95 children; Swim with the Dolphins, $80 per person. Daily 9:30am–4pm.

Established in 1946, Theater of the Sea is one of the world's oldest marine zoos. Although the facilities seem a bit tired, and sea mammal acts have fallen from political correctness, the theater's dolphin and sea lion shows can be both entertaining and informative, especially for children. Sharks, sea turtles, and other local creatures are also on display. Under the pretense of "education," the park offers visitors the opportunity to swim with the dolphins in their supervised ocean-water lagoon. Reservations for this pricey "Dolphin Adventure" must be made in advance.

Robbie's Pier. Overseas Hwy., Mile Marker 77.5, Lower Matecumbe Key. No phone. Admission $1. Daily 8am–5pm.

The steely tarpon is a fierce fighting fish and a prized catch for backcountry anglers who stalk them on the Florida Bay side of the Keys. You'll probably see these prehistoric-looking giants—which grow up to 200 pounds—stuffed and mounted on many local restaurant walls. To see them live, you either have to have a rod and reel and lots of patience, or head to Robbie's Pier, where tens, and sometimes hundreds, of these behemoths mill about waiting for free food. For $1, the proprietor will let you walk out onto Robbie's rickety wooden wharf and create a tumultuous feeding frenzy with a bag of food pellets. The pier is located beside U.S. 1, just southwest of Lignum Vitae Channel. Look for the "Hungry Tarpon" sign on the right.

✪ **Dolphin Research Center.** U.S. 1 and Mile Marker 59, on the bayside (see a 30-foot statue of a dolphin). ☎ **305/289-1121.** Swim with the Dolphins, $90 per person. Call on the first day of the month to book for the following month. Educational walking tours five times per day starting at 10am. Admission $9.50 adults, $6 children, $7.50 seniors. MC, V. Daily 9:30am–4pm.

If you have always wanted to touch, swim, or play with dolphins, this is the place. One of the only three such centers in the continental U.S. (all in the Keys), the Dolphin Research Center received positive reviews from a federal inspection of the program. The group's main goal is to protect the mammals and educate the public about these unusually smart beasts.

Although some people argue that training dolphins is cruel and selfish, the knowledgeable trainers at the Dolphin Research Center will tell you the dolphins need stimulation and enjoy human contact. They certainly seem to. They nuzzle and smile and kiss the lucky few who get to swim with them in the daily program. They have even been known to get a little amorous with female swimmers. The "family" of 15 dolphins swims in a 90,000 square feet coral natural saltwater pool carved out of the shoreline.

The procedure for making reservations is quite rigid. On the first of every month starting at 9am, the phone lines open for dolphin lovers to call and make reservations or be put on a lottery and hope to be chosen to swim. Kids should be at least 12 years old.

If you can't book your choice of dates, don't despair. You can still take a walking tour or a half-day class in how to do hand signals and feed the dolphins from docks. Yes, you can pet them.

EXPLORING THE NATURAL WONDERS OF THE KEYS

Although the Keys don't have all that much in the way of beaches, the ones that they do have are by and large located in the state parks. These are among the nicest and cleanest.

One of the best-known parks is the **John Pennekamp Coral Reef State Park,** located at Overseas Highway, Mile Marker 102.5 (P.O. Box 487), in Key Largo (☎ 305/451-1202). Named for a former *Miami Herald* editor and conservationist, the 188-square-mile park is the nation's first undersea preserve. It's a sanctuary for part of the only living coral reef in the continental United States. The original plans for Everglades National Park included this part of the reef within its boundaries, but opposition from local homeowners made its inclusion politically impossible.

Because the water is extremely shallow in many places, the 40 species of corals and more than 650 species of fish are particularly accessible to divers, snorkelers, and glass-bottom-boat passengers. Unfortunately the reef is a little *too* accessible, and the ecosystem is showing signs of stress from careless divers and boaters.

You can't see the reef from shore. To experience this park, visitors must take to the water. Your first stop should be the excellent visitor center, which is full of demonstrative fish tanks and a mammoth 30,000-gallon saltwater aquarium that re-creates a reef ecosystem. At the adjacent dive shop, visitors can rent snorkeling and diving equipment and join one of the boat trips that depart for the reef throughout the day. They also rent motorboats, sailboats, windsurfers, and canoes. Two-hour glass-bottom-boat tours take riders over coral reefs.

Canoeing around the park's narrow mangrove channels and tidal creeks is also popular. Canoes can be rented here, and during winter, naturalists lead canoe tours. Hikers have two short trails to choose from: a boardwalk through the mangroves, and a dirt trail through a tropical hardwood hammock. Ranger-led walks are usually scheduled daily from the end of November through April. Phone for schedule information and reservations (☎ 305/451-1202).

Park admission is $3.75 per vehicle, plus 50¢ per passenger; $1.50 per pedestrian or bicyclist. Glass-bottom-boat tours cost $13 for adults, $8.50 for children under 12. Sailing and snorkeling tours are $32 for adults, $25 for children under 18, including equipment. Scuba dives cost $37.50 per person, not including equipment. Reef boat rentals are $25 to $45 per hour, while canoes rent for $8 per hour, or $24 for four hours. Open daily from 8am to 5pm; phone for tour and dive times.

Another state park in the Upper Keys is the **Long Key State Recreation Area,** with the second nicest beach (the best is Bahia Honda in the Lower Keys). Situated atop the remains of ancient coral reef, the 965-acre park is one of the best places in the Upper Keys for hiking and canoeing. It's located on the Overseas Highway at Mile Marker 68 (P.O. Box 776), Long Key (☎ 305/664-4815).

Railroad builder Henry Flagler created the Long Key Fishing Club here in 1906, and the waters surrounding the park are still popular with game fish hunters. Sand beaches are rare in the Keys, and the ones here are accessible only by boat. In summer, giant sea turtles lumber onto the protected beaches to lay their eggs.

You can hike along two nature trails. Golden Orb Trail is a 1-mile loop around a lagoon that attracts a large variety of birds. Rich in West Indian vegetation, the trail leads to an observation tower that offers good views of the pond and beach. Layton Trail, the only part of the park that doesn't require an admission fee, is a $1/4$-mile shaded loop that goes through tropical hammock before opening up onto Florida Bay. The trail is well marked with interpretive signs; you can easily walk it in about 20 minutes.

The park's excellent $1^1/2$-mile Canoe Trail is also short and sweet, allowing visitors to loop around the mangroves in about an hour. It couldn't be easier. Canoes are rented at the trailhead, and cost $4 per hour. Long Key is also a wonderful picnic spot if you get hungry on your way to Key West.

Admission is $3.25 per car plus 50¢ each person (except for Layton Trail, which is free). Open daily from 8am to sunset.

SPORTS & OUTDOOR ACTIVITIES

AIRPLANING   **The Flight Department,** 9850 Overseas Hwy., Marathon Airport (☎ 305/743-4222), has half-hour tours over the reef that give you a bird's-eye view of the islands and the coral that surrounds them. Passengers can choose their itinerary from several different flight plans. Tours cost $75 per flight, for up to three passengers.

BOATING   **Captain Pip's,** Overseas Hwy., Mile Marker 47.5, Marathon (☎ 305/743-4403), rents 20-foot motorboats with 88-, 120-, and 150-horsepower engines for $110 to $130 per day.

Robbie's Rent-A-Boat, Overseas Hwy., Mile Marker 77.5, Islamorada (☎ 305/664-9814), rents 14- to 27-foot motorboats with engines ranging from 15 to 200 horsepower. Boats cost $60 to $205 for a half day and $80 to $295 for a whole day.

CANOEING & KAYAKING   **Florida Bay Outfitters,** Overseas Hwy., Mile Marker 104 (P.O. Box 2513), Key Largo (☎ 305/451-3018), one of the most respected outfitters in the area, rents canoes and sea kayaks for use in and around John Pennekamp Coral Reef State Park. Kayaks cost $25 for a half day and $40 for a whole day. Canoes cost $20 for a half day and $30 for a whole day. **Coral Reef Park Co.,** Mile Marker 102.5 (P.O. Box 1560), Key Largo (☎ 305/451-1621), is another rental outlet at John Pennekamp Coral Reef State Park. Canoes can be rented for $8 per hour, $24 for a half day.

At **Mangrove Bay Kayak Tours**, 5794 Commerce Lane, S. Miami (☎ 305/663-3364), David Berman and his partner sell and rent kayaks 365 days a year for use in Key Largo—where the bugs stay at bay even in the summer months. Their instructional eco-tours highlight not only the most pristine sealife in Florida, but also teach beginning kayakers how to handle a top-of-the-line fiberglass hull with rudder. The scheduled day trips that coincide with high tide are tailored to the desires of the participants but generally run about four to five hours. The cost is $85 per person, which includes native fruit and juice refreshments and very mangrove-savvy guides; there are never more than eight participants on a trip. We had three super-helpful guides and a lot of regulars on the last trip I took. It's hard work and a lot of fun. Private groups can be put together starting at $250 for one person and $350 for two; it's worth it for the individual attention and the superior quality of the fiberglass boats.

Mike Wedeking's Kayak Nature Tours, P.O. Box 861, Big Pine Key (☎ 305/872-2896), takes adventure travelers on expertly guided kayak journeys throughout the Florida Keys. A former U.S. Forest Service guide, Mike provides insightful narrative on observed fish, sponges, coral, osprey, hawks, eagles, alligators, raccoons, and deer. Three-hour tours cost $45 per person and include spring water and binoculars.

FISHING   Robbie's Partyboats & Charters, Overseas Hwy., Mile Marker 84.5, Islamorada (☎ 305/664-8070 or 305/664-4196), located at the south end of the Holiday Isle Docks (see "Where to Stay," below), offers day and night deep-sea and reef-fishing trips on 47- and 65-foot party boats. Big-game-fishing charters are also available, and "splits" are arranged for solo fishers. Party-boat fishing costs $25 for a half day, $40 for a full day, and $30 at night. Charters run $375 for a half day, $550 for a full day; splits begin at $65 per person. Phone for information and reservations.

Bud 'n' Mary's Fishing Marina, Overseas Hwy., Mile Marker 79.8, Islamorada (☎ 305/664-2461 or 800/742-7945), one of the largest marinas between Miami and Key West, is packed with sailors offering guided backcountry fishing charters. This is the place to go if you want to stalk tarpon, bonefish, and snapper. Deep-sea and coral-fishing trips are also arranged. Charters cost $375 to $450 for a half day, $575 to $700 for a full day, and splits begin at $125 per person.

The Bounty Hunter, 9500 Overseas Hwy., Mile Marker 48, Marathon (☎ 305/743-2446), offers full- and half-day outings. For years Capt. Brock Hook's huge sign has boasted NO FISH, NO PAY. You're guaranteed to catch something. Shark, barracuda, sailfish, and other trips are arranged. Prices are $300 per person half day; $450 per person full day.

SCUBA, SNUBA & SNORKELING   The **Florida Keys Dive Center,** Overseas Hwy., Mile Marker 90.5, Tavernier (☎ 305/852-4599), takes snorkelers and divers to the reefs of John Pennekamp Coral Reef State Park and environs every day. PADI-training courses are also available. Tours leave at 8:30am and 1pm and cost $25 per person to snorkel and $40 per person to dive.

At **Hall's Dive Center & Career Institute,** 1994 Overseas Hwy., Mile Marker 48.5, Marathon (☎ 305/743-5929), snorkelers and divers are shuttled to dive sites at Looe Key, Sombrero Reef, Delta Shoal, Content Key, and Coffins Patch. Tours are scheduled daily at 9am and 1pm and cost $41 per person to snorkel/$63 to dive.

With **Snuba Tours of Key Largo**, you can dive down to 20 feet with an attached breathing apparatus that really gives you the feeling of scuba diving without having to haul all that heavy equipment. You have a choice of two dive packages, both to beautiful shallow coral reefs where you will see hundreds of colorful fish and plant life. Reservations are required; call 305/451-6391 to find out where and when to meet. The cost for a 2½-hour tour is $25 including all equipment. The second trip makes two dives in John Pennekamp State Park and costs $70. If you choose option two you may require a one-hour lesson, which costs an additional $30. If it's your first experience breathing underwater, I would choose the shorter dive.

WHERE TO STAY

The Upper Keys have an eclectic selection of accommodations to choose from. Since the Keys are a must-see for visitors to Florida, a number of exclusive and pricey resorts have sprung up from the marshy wetlands that are the Keys. Those of you who are budget conscious, don't fret . . . there are a number of excellent, less-expensive hotels to balance out the big resorts. Some of the bigger hotel chains that operate in the Upper Keys are **Best Western** (☎ 800/462-6079) and **Holiday Inn** (☎ 800/843-5379).

VERY EXPENSIVE

✪ **Cheeca Lodge.** Overseas Hwy., Mile Marker 82 (P.O. Box 527), Islamorada, FL 33036.
☎ **305/664-4651** or 800/327-2888. Fax 305/664-2893. 203 rms, 64 suites. A/C MINIBAR
TV TEL. Winter $230–$575 double, $305 suite. Off-season $155–$425 double, $255 suite.
AE, CB, DC, DISC, MC, V.

Cheeca Lodge is the top-rated resort in the Upper Keys, known for its first-rate fishing and diving programs. Located on 27 beachfront acres, Cheeca's blue-and-white
plantation-style buildings surround Islamorada's most lushly landscaped gardens. The
main house is flanked by several two-story guest buildings sheltered by swaying palm.
Guest rooms at this low-key luxury resort are not particularly plush, but they are
roomy and furnished to a reasonably high standard. The bathrooms are contemporary but modest. Every room has a balcony, many of which overlook the water.

Dining/Entertainment: The Atlantic's Edge restaurant is one of the best in the
Upper Keys (see "Where to Dine," below). The more casual Ocean Terrace Grill has
indoor and outdoor seating overlooking the pool and ocean. The Light Tackle
Lounge is open daily and offers a light menu in the evenings.

Services: Room service, concierge, children's nature programs, free snorkeling
lessons, water aerobics, massages.

Facilities: VCR, six lighted tennis courts, nine-hole golf course, water-sports rentals, two swimming pools, saltwater lagoon, boutique, four hot tubs, nature trail,
bicycle rentals.

Hawk's Cay Resort. Overseas Hwy., Mile Marker 61, Duck Key, FL 33050. ☎ **305/743-7000**
or 800/432-2242. Fax 305/743-5215. 160 rms, 16 suites. A/C TV TEL. Winter $195–$346
double, $380–$850 suite. Off-season $130–$265 double, $245–$700 suite. Additional person
$25 extra. Children under 15 stay free. AE, DC, DISC, MC, V.

Located on its own 60-acre island, 10 miles north of Marathon, Hawk's Cay is a
major resort encompassing a marina and a saltwater lagoon that's home to a half-
dozen dolphins. Built in 1959, the expansive manicured grass grounds contain
several spread-out two- and three-story flamingo-colored buildings. Standard rooms
are all very similar to one another; views account for the differences in price. Rooms
are uniformly large, with walk-in closets, small refrigerators, and good-quality window treatments that can keep rooms dark throughout the morning. Every room has
a sliding-glass door that opens onto a private balcony, and some have good water
views. L-shaped junior suites have a separate seating area containing a pull-out sofa
and top-floor suites have large wraparound terraces.

Dining/Entertainment: Porto Cayo, the resort's top restaurant, serves Italian/
American cuisine, and is known for its seafood salad bar. The informal Cantina
Restaurant is located poolside for lunches, snacks, and dinners. The Pub serves
seafood and turf dinners dockside.

Services: Room service, concierge, overnight laundry, airport transportation.

Facilities: Eight lighted tennis courts, pool, fitness trail, two whirlpools, and
playground.

Jules' Undersea Lodge. 51 Shorelane Dr. (P.O. Box 3330), Mile Marker 103.2, Key Largo, FL
33037. ☎ **305/451-2353.** Fax 305/451-4789. 2 rms. A/C TV TEL. $195–$295 per person,
double occupancy year-round. Rates include breakfast and dinner. AE, DISC, MC, V.

Originally built as a research lab in the 1970s, this small underwater compartment
now operates as a single-room hotel. As expensive as it is unusual, Jules' is most popular with diving honeymooners and other active and romantic couples. The lodge rests
on pillars on the ocean floor. To get inside, guests swim under the structure and pop
up into the unit through a four-by-six-foot "moon pool" that gurgles soothingly all

night long. The 30-foot-deep underwater suite consists of a bedroom and galley, and sleeps up to six. Contrary to what you might expect, there's not a single starfish lamp or conch-shell ashtray in sight. You don't need to be a scuba specialist to stay here; tethered breathing lines are used in lieu of air tanks. The staff will deliver anything to your room, including pizza, but it's not necessary, as dinner (which is included) is delivered to your door in a waterproof container. Needless to say, this novelty is not for everyone. To reach the lodge from U.S. 1 south, turn left onto Transylvania Avenue, across from Central Plaza shopping mall.

Sheraton Key Largo Resort. 97000 S. Overseas Hwy., Mile Marker 97, Key Largo, FL 33037. ☎ **305/852-5553**, 800/826-1006, or 800/325-3535. Fax 305/852-8669. 200 rms, 10 suites. A/C MINIBAR TV TEL. Winter $215–$275 double, $390 suite. Off-season $165–$215 double, $290 suite. Additional person $15 extra. Children under 17 stay free in parents' room. AE, CB, DC, DISC, MC, V.

Well hidden behind a thick jungle that makes it invisible from U.S. 1, the Sheraton Key Largo is sheltered by 12 private acres of gumbo-limbo and hardwood trees and more than 1,200 feet of waterfront. Despite its hideaway location, the sprawling pink-and-blue four-story complex, built in 1985, is surprisingly large. A three-story atrium lobby is flanked by two sizable wings that face Florida Bay. Large guest rooms have floral window treatments and pull-out couches. The compact bathroom is augmented by a separate vanity area containing double sinks, and all rooms have a private balcony. Suites are twice the size of standard rooms and have better-quality natural wicker furnishings and double-sized balconies. Many also have private spa tubs and particularly good bathrooms with adjustable shower heads, bidets, and lots of room for toiletries.

Dining/Entertainment: Treetops, the hotel's top restaurant, offers terrific views of Florida Bay and surf-and-turf dinners nightly. Casual Cafe Key Largo serves breakfast, lunch, and dinner both inside and outdoors. Splashes Bar & Grill, located poolside, serves sandwiches, salads, and refreshments. The top-floor Fishtales lounge has a dance floor, pool table, and rattan furnishings.

Services: Room service, concierge.

Facilities: Two swimming pools, two lighted tennis courts, Jacuzzi, nature trails, small fitness room with Universal equipment, water-sports equipment rental, hair salon, gift shop.

MODERATE

Banana Bay Resort & Marina. 4590 Overseas Hwy., Mile Marker 49.5, Marathon, FL 33050. ☎ **305/743-3500** or 800/BANANA-1 (☎ 800/226-2621). Fax 305/743-2670. 60 rms. A/C TV TEL. Winter $95–$175 double. Off-season $75–$125 double. Rates include breakfast. Additional person $15. Children under 5 stay free. Weekend and other packages available. AE, DC, DISC, MC, V.

It doesn't look like much more than a motel from the sign-cluttered Overseas Highway. But turn into the arched entranceway and you're suddenly in one of the most bucolic and best-run properties in the Upper Keys. Built in the early 1950s as a fishing camp, the resort is a puzzle of pink and white two-story buildings hidden amongst banyans and palms. Banana Bay's 10 acres accommodate just 60 rooms—a very low population density that's evidenced by peace and quiet and little competition for use of the resort's facilities.

The accommodations and grounds of Banana Bay are particularly well maintained, certainly a function of hands-on management by the owners who live on-site. The guest rooms are all very similar to one another; the primary difference between them is views and price. Many of the moderately sized rooms have private balconies.

The Cabana Restaurant serves lunch and dinner both poolside and inside its 1950s-style dining room. A waterfront tiki bar offers great sunset views. Charter fishing, sailing, and diving are offered from the resort's 50-slip marina.

🅢 **Conch Key Cottages.** Near the Overseas Hwy., Mile Marker 62.3 (RR 1, Box 424), Marathon, FL 33050. ☎ **305/289-1377** or 800/330-1577. 10 units. A/C TV. Winter $96 efficiency, $605 weekly; $114 one-bedroom apartment, $720 weekly; $134 one-bedroom cottage, $845 weekly; $183 two bedroom cottage, $1,147 weekly. Off-season $70 efficiency, $441 weekly; $87 one-bedroom apartment, $550 weekly; $96 one-bedroom cottage, $605 weekly; $150 two-bedroom cottage, $945 weekly. Festivals $70–$96 efficiency, $441–$605 weekly; $87–$114 one-bedroom apartment, $550–$720 weekly; $96–$134 one-bedroom cottage, $605–$845 weekly; $150–$183 two-bedroom cottage, $945–$1,147 weekly. DISC, MC, V.

Occupying its own private micro-island just off the Overseas Highway, Conch Key Cottages is a unique midscale hideaway run by live-in owners Ron Wilson and Wayne Byrnes. You could walk around the entire island in about four minutes, if it weren't so full of mangroves. The best accommodations here are the one- and two-bedroom waterside cottages. The all-wood cabins overlook their own private stretch of natural, beach and have screened-in porches and cozy bedrooms and baths. Each has a hammock and barbecue grill. On the other side of the pool are a handful of efficiency apartments that are outfitted similar to the cottages, but enjoy no beach frontage. Both the efficiencies and cottages have fully equipped kitchens. There's also a small heated freshwater pool. Tailor-made for couples or families, Conch Key Cottages is the perfect place to get away from it all.

Faro Blanco Marine Resort. 1996 Overseas Hwy., Mile Marker 48.5, Marathon, FL 33050. ☎ **305/743-9018** or 800/759-3276. 100 rms, 23 condos. A/C TV TEL. Winter $65–$119 double cottage; $99–$198 double houseboat; $185 double lighthouse; $233 condominium. Off-season $55–$99 double cottage; $79–$145 double houseboat; $145 single or double lighthouse; $206 condominium. Additional person $10 extra. AE, DISC, MC, V.

Spanning both sides of the Overseas Highway and all on waterfront property, this huge, two-shore marina and hotel complex offers something for every taste. Freestanding, camp-style cottages with a small bedroom are the resort's least expensive accommodations. Built on concrete slabs, the very basic cottages mostly have two single beds and slightly faded interiors. They surround a small wooded park with a children's slide and swing. On the other end of the spectrum are extremely large, first class condominium apartments contained in a cluster of modern circular four-story "towers." Each has three bedrooms, two baths, a living room, and a kitchen.

Houseboats are the happiest of mediums. Permanently tethered in a relatively tranquil marina, these white rectangle boats look like buoyant mobile homes and are uniformly clean, fresh, and recommendable. They have colonial American-style furnishings, fully equipped kitchenettes, front and back porches, and water, water everywhere. The boats rock ever so slightly.

Finally, there are two unusual rental units located in a lighthouse on the pier; circular staircases, unusually shaped rooms and showers, and nautical decor make this quite a unique place to stay, but some guests might find it literally cramps their style.

Several restaurants on the property serve a variety of seafood, beef, veal, and poultry dishes.

Holiday Isle Resort. 84001 Overseas Hwy., Mile Marker 84, Islamorada, FL 33036. ☎ **305/664-2321** or 800/327-7070. Fax 305/664-2703. 180 rms, 19 suites. Winter $80–$190 double, $200–$395 suite. Off-season $50–$150 double, $135–$350 suite. AE, DC, DISC, MC, V.

A huge resort complex encompassing five restaurants, lounges, and shops, and four distinct (if not distinctive) hotels, Holiday Isle is one of the biggest resorts in the Keys. The company's marketing strategy is decidedly downscale, attracting a spring break–style crowd year-round. Their Tiki Bar claims the invention of the Rum Runner drink (151-proof rum, blackberry brandy, banana liquor, grenadine, and lime juice), and there's no reason to doubt it. Hordes of partiers are attracted to the resort's almost nonstop merrymaking, live music, and beachfront bars. As a result, some of the accommodations here can be noisy.

El Captain and Harbor Lights, two of the least-expensive hotels on the property, are both austere and basic. Like the other hotels here, frills are few, and "deferred" maintenance is in abundance, including broken hangers and door locks. Howard Johnson's, Holiday Isle's fourth hotel, is a little farther from the action and a shred more civilized.

INEXPENSIVE

③ Bay Harbor Lodge. 97702 Overseas Hwy., Mile Marker 97.7, Key Largo, FL 33037. ☎ 305/852-5695. 16 units. A/C TV TEL. $55 double, $70 efficiency, $80 cottage year-round. Additional person $8. MC, V.

A small simple retreat that's big on charm, Bay Harbor Lodge is an extraordinarily welcoming place made especially friendly by owners Laszlo and Sandra Simoga. The lodge is far from fancy, and the wide range of accommodations are not all created equal. Motel rooms are small in size and ordinary in decor, but even the least expensive is recommendable. Efficiencies are larger motel rooms with fully stocked kitchenettes. The underpriced oceanfront cottages are larger still, have full kitchens, and represent one of the best values in the Keys. None of the accommodations' vinyl-covered furnishings and old-fashioned wallpaper will win design awards, but elegance isn't what the "real" keys are about. The 1 1/2 lush acres of grounds are planted with lots of banana trees and several little barbecue grills. There's a new pool and outdoor hot tub, and rowboats, paddleboats, canoes, and kayaks are available for guests' use. Bring your own beach towels. The entrance to the lodge is from the southbound lane of U.S. 1.

Breezy Palms Resort. Overseas Hwy. (P.O. Box 767), Mile Marker 80, Islamorada, FL 33036. ☎ **305/664-2361.** Fax 305/664-2572. 39 rms, 23 efficiencies. A/C TV TEL. Winter $75–$90 double, $105–$180 efficiency. Off-season $65–$80 double, $100–$165 efficiency. AE, DISC, MC, V.

The appellation "resort" is used euphemistically at Breezy Palms, a simple, palm-studded pink-and-blue hotel in two parts. One side of this very well-maintained mom-and-pop property is a two-story motel with spacious bedrooms, big closets, and bathrooms with separate vanity areas. They have refrigerators, VCRs, and screened-in porches overlooking a large swimming pool. Rooms on the second floor enjoy ocean views. One-bedroom apartments, located across a large U-shaped driveway, have separate living areas with rattan furnishings, tropical prints, and VCRs. Each also has a separate small kitchen stocked with enough cookware to prepare and eat a simple meal. Good-size bathrooms have low-pressure, water-saving showerheads and plenty of counter space.

Breezy Palms is located oceanfront and has a sheltered harbor with plenty of dock space. There are volleyball and shuffleboard courts and barbecue pits on the beach. Complimentary coffee is served each morning. All in all, this hotel is a very good value.

Sea Cove Motel. 12685 Overseas Hwy., Mile Marker 54, Marathon, FL 33050. ☎ **305/ 289-0800** or 800/653-0800. 27 rms. A/C TV TEL. Winter $34–$49 double with shared bath, $49–$69 double with private bath, $79–$99 efficiency. Off-season $24–$39 double with shared bath, $39–$69 double with private bath, $59–$89 efficiency. Houseboats $69–$125. Additional person or pet $5. Children under 16 stay free. AE, DISC, MC, V.

It's surprisingly hard to find good budget accommodations in the Keys. Sea Cove's large, economical motel rooms are not the Ritz, but they are the very best available for the money. They have Oriental rug–covered concrete floors, plastic tables and chairs, small tiled bathrooms, overhead fans, and little porches in front of each. Some have kitchens.

Before committing, check out the motel's unusual "Floating Castle," a large, multi-unit houseboat that's anchored in the back of the property. Thin walls could make for hard sleeping if your neighbor snores, but otherwise this unusual floating home just might be one of the best deals in the Keys. Wood-paneled rooms are somewhat small and somewhat charming. Some rooms share a common bathroom. Snorkeling and dive trips leave from the harbor next door.

CAMPING

John Pennekamp Coral Reef State Park. Overseas Hwy., Mile Marker 102.3 (P.O. Box 487), Key Largo, FL 33037. ☎ **305/451-1202.** 47 campsites. $24–$26 per site. MC, V.

One of Florida's most celebrated parks (see above), Pennekamp offers 47 well-separated campsites, half available by advance reservation, the rest distributed on a first-come, first-served basis. The car-camping sites are small, but well facilitated with bathrooms and showers. A little lagoon, nearby, attracts many large wading birds. Reservations are held until 5pm and the park must be notified of late arrival by phone on the check-in date. Pennekamp opens at 8am and closes around sundown. Pets are not allowed.

Long Key State Recreation Area. Overseas Hwy., Mile Marker 67.5 (P.O. Box 776), Long Key, FL 33001. ☎ **305/664-4815.** 60 campsites. $24–26 per site for one to four people. Additional person (over four) $2. MC, V.

The Upper Key's other main state park is more secluded than its northern neighbor and somewhat more popular. All sites are located oceanside, and are as nice as paid legal camping can be. If possible, make reservations 60 days in advance.

WHERE TO DINE

The better restaurants in the Upper Keys are housed within the big resorts. Most eateries are small seafood, casual dining–style places to accommodate those seeking a quick bite on their way to Key West. I've listed those that are good places to stop.

VERY EXPENSIVE

✪ **Atlantic's Edge.** In the Cheeca Lodge, Overseas Hwy., Mile Marker 82 (P.O. Box 527), Islamorada. ☎ **305/664-4651.** Reservations recommended. Main courses $17–$32; fixed-price meals $25 and $29. AE, CB, DC, DISC, MC, V. Daily 5:30–10pm. AMERICAN/SEAFOOD.

One of the nicest restaurants in the Upper Keys, Atlantic's Edge is well known in these parts for its laid-back elegance and expertly prepared seafood. The white, window-wrapped beachfront dining room has an airy informality that's pleasantly countered by starched service. Sit by the window or in a corner booth for a roman-tic and cozy dinner experience. Said to be a favorite of former President George Bush, this elegant stand-by is worth the price.

Caribbean-influenced meals might start with a salad of lobster, avocado, roasted red pepper, and mango, or a cup of corn and crab soup. If you caught it, they'll cook it. If yours got away, the restaurant will prepare one of their fresh fish—blackened, grilled, or steamed. Onion-crusted Florida snapper with braised artichokes, black pepper–crusted shrimp with peppercorn tagliatelle, and grilled yellowfin tuna in a mango cilantro salsa are also excellent examples of the kitchen's capabilities.

MODERATE

Barracuda Bistro. Overseas Hwy., Mile Marker 49.5, Marathon. ☎ **305/743-3314.** Main courses $11–$23. AE, DISC, MC, V. Mon–Sat 6–10pm. BISTRO/SEAFOOD.

This relative newcomer to the Upper Keys dining world is a welcome addition. Owned by Lance Hill and his wife Jan, who used to cook at Little Palm Island as their day-time sous-chef, this casual-but-starched clean bistro serves excellent seafood and traditional bistro fare. Some of the best dishes are an old-fashioned meatloaf, classic beef stroganoff, rack of lamb, and seafood stew. In addition, this small barricuda-themed restaurant features a well-priced exclusively American wine list with a vast selection of California vintages.

✪ **Lazy Days Oceanfront Bar and Seafood Grill.** Overseas Hwy., Mile Marker 79.9 (P.O. Box 971), Islamorada. ☎ **305/664-5256.** Main courses $11–$20; lunch $5–$9. AE, DISC, MC, V. Tues–Sun 11:30am–10pm. AMERICAN/SEAFOOD.

Opened in 1992, Lazy Days quickly became one of the most popular restaurants around. It's architecturally interesting—a glass-enclosed rectangle on story-high stilts. You'll climb the stairs to a large and bright dining room that's surrounded by an outdoor terrace. Six-foot picture windows overlook the ocean. Meals are pricier than the dining room would suggest, but the food is very good and portions are large. Tempting appetizers include steamed clams with garlic and bell peppers, and nachos. Lunch selections include meaty chowders, salads, and a large selection of sandwiches, including charcoal-grilled fish and spicy Caribbean jerk chicken. Dinners rely heavily on seafood—and they really know how to cook fish here. Caribbean- and Italian-style foods are also served. Most main courses come with baked potatoes, vegetables, a tossed salad, and French bread.

Lazy Days is set slightly back from the road behind willowy palms. It's located on your left, when heading toward Key West.

Makoto Japanese Restaurant. 99470 Overseas Hwy., Mile Marker 101.5, Key Largo. ☎ **305/451-7083.** Reservations suggested on weekends in season. Main courses $8–$19. DC, DISC, MC, V. Mon–Fri 11:30am–2:30pm; Sun–Thurs 5–9:30pm, Fri–Sat 5–10pm. JAPANESE.

This Japanese restaurant run by a Laotian family is worth a stop for the unusual raw fish selections that are sometimes available. In addition to ample slices of standard Pacific Ocean fish like salmon and yellowtail, the restaurant serves local cuts that may include Florida snapper, tuna, black grouper, and wahoo. Cooked dinners include fish teriyaki, chicken curry, vegetable tempura, and sukiyaki. The dining room is not particularly cozy; its mounted-fish collection includes shark and swordfish, two varieties that seldom appear on the menu. The restaurant is located on the bayside of the Overseas Highway, at the Marina del Mar Resort.

✪ **Manny & Isa's Kitchen.** Overseas Hwy., Mile Marker 81.6 (P.O. Box 826), Islamorada. ☎ **305/664-5019.** Reservations not accepted. Main courses $9–$18; lunch $4–$9. AE, MC, V. Wed–Mon 11am–9pm. SPANISH-AMERICAN.

Opened over a dozen years ago as a small shop selling Key lime pie and conch chowder exclusively, this pint-size cafe-style restaurant has expanded its menu and become a very popular local hangout. It's a great little place, with fewer than 10 tables. The menu is filled with Florida-influenced Spanish-American specialties like pork chops with black beans and rice, lobster enchiladas, and sandwiches. And it's still a great place for conch chowder and Key lime pie.

Papa Joe's. Overseas Hwy., Mile Marker 79.7 (P.O. Box 109), Islamorada. ☎ **305/664-8109.** Main courses $10–$14; lunch $5–$8. AE, MC, V. Wed–Mon 11am–10pm. AMERICAN.

Opened in 1937, Papa Joe's is a veritable living museum of early Keys life. From the road, this two-story wooden landmark—under a big palm tree and yellow-and-white tiki-style sign—looks like the ultimate island eatery. It's well weathered and right on the water but, like so many eateries from this era, there are no outdoor tables and only mediocre views. Inside, it's so dark that it feels like night even on the brightest days. Whatever the fresh catch is, order it sautéed—either on a platter or a bun—and you won't be disappointed. The usual variety of burgers, salads, sandwiches, steaks, and chicken are also available. If you're arriving in the late afternoon, take advantage of their second-story tiki bar that's raised just high enough to see the sun set over the nearby mangrove islands. The raw bar is particularly appealing, and a full range of drinks is served. The restaurant is located across from Bud 'n' Mary's Fishing Marina, at the foot of Tea Table Bridge.

Sid & Roxie's Green Turtle Inn. Overseas Hwy., Mile Marker 81.5 (P.O. Box 585), Islamorada. ☎ **305/664-9031.** Main courses $12–$18; lunch $6–$12. AE, DC, DISC, MC, V. Tues–Sun noon–10pm. SEAFOOD/AMERICAN.

An Islamorada landmark since 1947, the Green Turtle comes from an age when dark interiors were equated with elegance. It's a family kind of place, where broiled American surf-and-turf dinners come with soup, potatoes, and a salad. Soups, breads, and pies are all made on the premises, and served by career waitresses who have been here for years. In addition to prime beef and fresh-caught fish, the restaurant offers alligator steak, shrimp, and chicken dishes. When driving south on the Overseas Highway, look for the giant turtle.

INEXPENSIVE

Mrs. Mac's Kitchen. 99336 Overseas Hwy., Mile Marker 99.4, Key Largo. ☎ **305/451-3722.** Reservations not accepted. Breakfast $3–$5; lunch $3–$7; dinner $6–$13. No credit cards. Daily 7am–9:30pm. AMERICAN.

Bypass Key Largo's swell of fast-food outlets and head for the "real Keys McCoy" of Mrs. Mac's, a roadside diner that, from the outside, looks suspiciously like an over-sized aluminum mobile home. The restaurant has wood-paneled walls decorated with the traditional license–plate–and–beer can clutter, and vinyl booths surround a circular bar that's crammed with stools. Breakfast, served until 11am, includes eggs, waffles, and crêpes. Lunch and dinner means meat- and cheese-stuffed pita sandwiches, cheese steak, burgers, and fresh fish specials. The Syrian Sub is particularly recommended.

Seven Mile Grill. 1240 Overseas Hwy., Mile Marker 47, Marathon. ☎ **305/743-4481.** Reservations not accepted. Dinner $8–$9; lunch $2–$5. No credit cards. Thurs–Tues 7am–8:30pm; off-season Fri–Tues. 7am–8:30pm. AMERICAN.

Everybody knows Seven Mile Grill. You'd have to be blind to miss their enormous red, white, and blue sign that's a masterpiece of 1950s roadside art. Of all the "authentic" downscale fry shacks that line the Overseas Highway, this home-style cookery is best. The restaurant is little more than a long J-shaped linoleum counter with 20 bar chairs. The entire dining counter is exposed to the highway by a "wall" made of garage doors that stay open during business hours, no matter the weather. Seven Mile Grill opened in 1954, but has changed with the times. The beer-can decor is augmented by a wall of aphoristic signs and bumper stickers that include WE DON'T CARE HOW YOU DO IT UP NORTH and UNARMED TOURIST ON BOARD.

Very good food, friendly waitresses, and three domestic beers on tap keep locals loyal. Appetizers include good chili, better shrimp bisque, and great conch chowder. Straightforward fry-house fare includes thickly battered fish, clam strips, sea scallops, shrimp, and oysters. Burgers, salads, and sandwiches are also served. Seven Mile Grill is also one of the few places where you can get authentic key lime pie. The restaurant is located at the foot of Seven Mile Bridge.

THE UPPER KEYS AFTER DARK

Nightlife in the Upper Keys tends to happen in the afternoon, because many fishermen and sports-minded folks go to bed early. It's not that they are a Puritanical lot; rather it's just that many have been drinking all day and crash before midnight in order to be able to get up and do it again. Here are a few good choices, particularly if you want to catch a spectacular sunset.

No trip is complete without a stop at the ✪ **Tiki Bar** at Holiday Isle, 84001 Overseas Hwy., Mile Marker 84, Islamorada (☎ 800/327-7070). Hundreds of partying types stop here for drinks and dancing any time of day, but in the evening, live rock music starts at 8:30pm. Still, the most fun is in the afternoons and early evenings when everyone is either sunburned, drunk, or just happy to be alive and dancing to reggae at **Kokomos's**, just next door to the thatched-roof Tiki Bar. They quit at 7:30pm on weekends, so get there early and then head over to the restaurant or Tiki Bar for more fun, food, and music that lasts past midnight every night.

The **Whale Harbor Inn,** Overseas Hwy., Mile Marker 83.5, Islamorada (☎ 305/664-4959), isn't exactly a nightspot, but it's a good place for a sunset drink and snack. Bypass the building with the imposing lighthouse exterior and cross the small marina to the second-story wood-beamed bungalow that's decked out with football pennants, photos of lucky fishermen, and a profusion of mounted monster fish. It's popular with locals (they're the ones who bring their own foam beer-can coolers to the old wooden bar). Good, greasy appetizers here include conch fritters, chicken wings, smoked fish, and fried mozzarella. The inn closes at 9 or 10pm.

The "hottest" local bar in the Upper Keys, **Woody's Saloon and Restaurant,** Overseas Hwy., Mile Marker 82, Islamorada (☎ 305/664-4335), is a lively, raunchy place serving up mediocre pizzas and live bands almost every night. The house band, Big Dick and the Extenders, features a 300-pound-plus Indian who does a lude, rude, and crude routine of jokes and songs. Don't think you're lucky if you walk in and are offered the front table, because it's the target seat for Big Dick's haranguing. He's been playing here for years to the joy of locals and visitors who can take it. You can get up and tell jokes on stage, but they better be good or you'll really get it. You can also play pool or video games.

4 The Lower Keys: Big Pine Key to Coppitt Key

110–140 miles SW of Miami

Big Pine, Sugarloaf, Summerland, and other Lower Keys are less developed and more tranquil than their Upper Key neighbors. If you're looking to commune with nature or adventures in solitude, you've come to the right place. Unlike their neighbors to the north and south, the Lower Keys are devoid of rowdy spring-break-style crowds, have few T-shirt and trinket shops, and almost no late-night bars. What they do offer are opportunities to hike, boat, bicycle, and camp. I suggest staying overnight in the Lower Keys, renting a boat, and exploring the reefs.

ESSENTIALS

VISITOR INFORMATION   The **Lower Keys Chamber of Commerce,** Overseas Hwy., Mile Marker 31 (P.O. Box 430511), Big Pine Key, FL 33043 (☎ 305/ 872-2411 or 800/872-3722), offers information on area sights, restaurants, and hotels.

GETTING THERE   See "The Upper Keys," above.

WHAT TO SEE & DO

Leda-Bruce Galleries. Overseas Hwy., Mile Marker 30.2 (Route 5, Box 130), Big Pine Key. ☎ 305/872-0212. Free admission. Tues–Sat 10am–6pm.

Owners Leda and Bruce Seigal are longtime residents of the Keys and famous in these parts for both their art and their eccentricities. In this concrete building, just past the island's only traffic light (when heading toward Key West), the couple displays some of the best works from the Keys' most important artists. In short, this is the finest gallery between Miami and Key West. Antiques and curios are sold in one adjacent room, while another contains top-quality antique clothing. Plays and classical-music concerts are sometimes staged in the attic theater. It's a great place to browse, and the friendly owners are usually on hand to chat.

National Key Deer Refuge. Key Deer Blvd., near Mile Marker 30 (P.O. Box 510), Big Pine Key. ☎ 305/872-2239. Free admission. Daily ¹/₂-hour before sunrise–¹/₂-hour before sunset.

You know you've reached Big Pine Key when the speed limit drops to 45 m.p.h. (35 m.p.h. at night) and road signs trumpet warnings to drivers to stay alert. Strict enforcement of driving rules is designed to protect the Key deer, twenty-eight-inch tall miniatures that are closely related to the common full-size Virginia white-tailed deer. Evolutionists believe that the diminutive deer are descendants of full-size animals that wandered south from the Florida mainland thousands of years ago. The reduced land, food, and fresh water available to the deer created environmental pressures that led to a prolonged "downsizing." They exist almost exclusively on Big Pine because this is the only key with fresh water year-round.

Once prized by trophy hunters, the dwindling population was protected by the U.S. government in 1957 with the establishment of this 8,000-acre refuge. The deer's rehabilitation is a qualified success in environmentalism. There are about 300 Key deer left and, given current conditions and resources, this is the maximum number of deer that can be expected to survive. In the last 25 years, the island has grown from about 700 residents to almost 5,000, and population pressure is causing some distress. Restrictions on development have hampered the construction of an elementary school, prompted protests, and led to a graffito on Key Deer Boulevard that reads KIDS BEFORE DEER.

Despite all the excitement, most people drive straight through Big Pine without spotting a single buck or doe. There can be no guarantees, but a visit to the refuge is your best chance of seeing a Key deer. The best place for observation is called the Blue Hole, a former rock quarry that is now filled with fresh water. When heading toward Key West, turn right at Big Pine Key's only traffic light onto Key Deer Boulevard (take the left fork immediately after the turn), and continue 1¹/₂ miles to the observation site parking lot, on your left. The half-mile Watson Hammock Trail, located about a third of a mile past the Blue Hole, is the refuge's only marked footpath. Deer can often be seen here during early morning and late evening.

Sugarloaf Bat Tower. Next to Sugarloaf Airport by Mile Marker 17.

It's really a peculiar sight—especially if you don't know what it is. Standing silently alone, surrounded by nothing but weeds, the large and stocky Sugarloaf Bat Tower was constructed in 1929 in an effort to attract bats that would, in turn, eat the ever-present mosquitoes that plague most of the Keys. Unfortunately, the bats have yet to come; the failed "bat motel" only attracts curious tourists. To reach the tower, turn right at the Sugarloaf Airport sign, then right again, onto the dirt road that begins just before the airport gate; the tower is about 100 yards ahead.

Bahia Honda State Park. 36550 Overseas Hwy., Mile Marker 37, Big Pine Key (☎ **305/872-2353**). Admission $3.75 per vehicle, $1.50 per pedestrian or bicyclist, free for children under 6; $2 boat-ramp fee. Daily 8am–sunset.

The Lower Keys has only one state park, but Bahia Honda has one of the most beautiful beaches in South Florida and certainly the most beautiful beach in the Keys. Meaning "deep bay" in Spanish, Bahia Honda is a great place for hiking, bird-watching, swimming, snorkeling, and fishing.

The 635-acre park encompasses a wide variety of ecosystems, including coastal mangroves, beach dunes, and tropical hammocks. There are also large stretches of white sandy beach and miles of trails packed with unusual plants and animals. Shaded beachside picnic areas are fitted with tables and grills. Bahia Honda is also a popular place to camp.

The park is true to its name, with deep waters close to shore that are perfect for snorkeling and diving. Daily snorkel and dive trips are operated to the nearby Looe Key coral reef. These depart daily March to September and cost $22 for adults and $18 for youths ages 6 to 16; under 6 free. Call 305/872-3210 for hours of departures and rentals.

Bahia Honda is as loaded with facilities and activities as it is with campers. Don't be discouraged by its popularity—this park encompasses more than 500 acres of land, and some very private beaches. There are 80 campsites and 6 cabin units. If you're lucky enough to get one, the park's cabins represent a very good value. Each holds up to eight guests, and comes complete with linens, kitchenettes, and utensils.

Camping costs $25.85 per site for one to four people with electricity, $21.69 without electricity. An additional person (over four) costs $2.23. Cabins range in cost depending on the season: From December 15 to September 14, it's $125 per cabin for one to four people; from September 15 to December 14 it's $97 per cabin. Additional people (over four) cost $5.58 each. MasterCard and Visa are accepted.

SPORTS & OUTDOOR ACTIVITIES

AIRPLANING   Fantasy Dan's Airplane Rides, Overseas Highway, Mile Marker 17, Sugarloaf Key Airport (☎ 305/745-2217), offers single-engine airplane rides over the reefs and Keys. Tours usually include a buzzing of Key West and the mangrove forests of uninhabited smaller islands. Flights require a two-person minimum and cost $30 per person for 15 minutes, $40 per person for a half-hour, and $50 per person for 45 minutes.

BOATING   Several shops rent powerboats for fishing and reef exploring. Most also rent tackle, sell bait, and have charter captains available. Rental shops include **Bud Boats,** at Old Wooden Bridge Fishing Camp & Marina, Overseas Highway, Mile Marker 59 (Route 1, Box 513), Big Pine Key (☎ 305/743-6316); **Jaybird's Powerboats,** Overseas Highway, Mile Marker 33 (P.O. Box 430513), Big Pine Key, (☎ 305/872-8500); and **T.J.'s Sugarshack,** at Sugarloaf Lodge Marina, Overseas Highway, Mile Marker 17 (P.O. Box 148), Sugarloaf Key (☎ 305/745-3135).

FISHING   Larry Threlkeld's **Strike Zone Charters,** Overseas Highway, Mile Marker 29.5 (Route 5, Box 89A), Big Pine Key (☎ 305/872-9863), offers captained boats in both the deep sea and the backcountry. Prices start at $250 to $375 for a half day. Reef-fishing trips are offered by **Scandia-Tomi,** Overseas Highway, Mile Marker 25 (P.O. Box 420623), Summerland Key (☎ 305/745-8633). There's a six-passenger maximum.

SKYDIVING   First-timers can jump almost immediately at **Sugarloaf Airport,** Overseas Highway, Mile Marker 17 (P.O. Box 290) (☎ 305/745-4386), in tandem with a certified instructor. Ten-thousand-foot jumps include a 40-second free fall and five-minute canopy ride using a steerable chute. Go for it! They're open daily from 10am to sunset by appointment only. Prices are $219 per jump with cash discounts available.

SNORKELING & DIVING   In addition to snorkeling or diving at Bahia Honda State Park, **Looe Key Dive Center,** Overseas Highway, Mile Marker 27.5 (P.O. Box 509), Ramrod Key (☎ 305/872-2215), transports snorkelers and divers to the reefs of the Looe Key National Marine Sanctuary.

WHERE TO STAY

Like the Upper Keys, there are pricey resorts in the Lower Keys, but in this area, it's not always the best bet to stay in one. A hotel room here is merely a place to lay your weary head after an invigorating day outdoors, so I'd suggest staying at a smaller motel, particularly because there are plenty of charming ones to choose from.

VERY EXPENSIVE

Little Palm Island. 28500 Overseas Hwy., Mile Marker 28.5, Little Torch Key, FL 33042. ☎ **305/872-2524** or 800/343-8567. Fax 305/872-4843. 30 suites. A/C MINIBAR. Winter $495–$645 suite for two. Off-season $330–$575 suite for two. Special honeymoon packages available. Additional person $52. No children under 12. AE, DC, DISC, MC, V.

Little Palm Island resort occupies the entire five acres of Little Munson Island, a former fishing camp that once accommodated presidents Roosevelt, Truman, Kennedy, and Nixon. The island is still popular among the power elite, but it's no longer a simple backcountry camp. Now a member of the exclusive Relais Châteaux group, the resort consists of 14 villas segregated by a profusion of foliage and flowering tropical plants. Set on stilts, the bamboo- and thatch-topped villas have been designed for absolute privacy. Each accommodates two casually elegant suites that enjoy ocean views and private sundecks fitted with rope hammocks. Inside are all the comforts and conveniences of a luxurious contemporary beach cottage, save telephones, TVs, and alarm clocks; cellularless guests can often be seen hovering around the single phone booth in the island's center.

Decorated in wicker and airy rattan, each suite is comprised of a comfortable sitting room accented with light floral fabrics, and an utterly romantic master bedroom with a king-size bed and thatched cathedral ceiling. The bathroom contains a spa tub and a bamboo-fenced outdoor shower.

There's a lagoonlike heated freshwater swimming pool with its own waterfall, and a small exercise room and spa offering therapeutic massages, facials, and body treatments. The resort also offers guests free use of sailboats, windsurfers, canoes, fishing rods, and snorkeling equipment.

Dining/Entertainment: The Little Palm Restaurant offers fine dining indoors or al fresco. The Palapa Pool Bar offers refreshments and light snacks all day.

Services: Room service, laundry, massage, airport transportation.

Facilities: Swimming pool, complimentary water-sports rentals, dive shop, boutique.

MODERATE

The Barnacle. 1557 Long Beach Dr., Big Pine Key, FL 33043. ☎ **305/872-3298.** 4 rms. A/C TV TEL. Winter $100–$110 double. Off-season $75–$85 double. Rates include breakfast. MC, V.

Joan Cornell, the Barnacle's owner, was once an innkeeper in Vermont; she knows what amenities travelers are looking for and goes out of her way to fulfill special requests. Her Big Pine Key home has only four bedrooms, each with its own character. Two are located upstairs in the main house—their doors open into the home's living room which contains a small Jacuzzi-style tub. For privacy, the remaining two rooms are best; each has its own entrance and is out of earshot of the common areas. The Cottage Room, a free-standing, peak-topped bedroom, is best, outfitted with a beautiful kitchenette and pretty furnishings. Accommodations are standard, not luxurious. All rooms have small refrigerators and private baths. The property has its own private sandy beach where you can float all day on the inn's rafts, rubber boat, or kayak. Beach towels, chairs, and coolers are provided for guests' use.

Deer Run Bed and Breakfast. Long Beach Dr. (P.O. Box 431), Big Pine Key, FL 33043. ☎ **305/872-2015.** 3 rms. Winter $85–$110 double. Off-season $75–$95 double. Rates include breakfast. No credit cards.

Located directly on the beach, Sue Abbott's small, homey, smoke-free B&B is a real find. One upstairs and two downstairs guest rooms are comfortably furnished with queen-size beds, good closets, and touch-sensitive lamps. Rattan and 1970s-style chairs and couches furnish the living room, along with 13 birds and 3 cats. Breakfast, which is served on a pretty, fenced-in porch, is cooked to order by Sue herself. The wooded area around the property is full of deer often spotted on the beach as well.

Parmer's Place Cottages. Barry Ave. (P.O. Box 445), near Mile Marker 28.5, Little Torch Key, FL 33043. ☎ **305/872-2157.** 19 rms, 22 efficiencies. Winter $70–$85 double, $85 efficiency. Off-season $60–$65 double, $75 efficiency. Festivals $70–$85 double, $85 efficiency. Additional person $12.50. Children under 12 stay free. AE, DISC, MC, V.

This downscale resort offers modest but comfortable cottages. Every unit is different: Some face the water, while others are a few steps away; some have small kitchenettes, and others are just a bedroom. Room number 26, a one-bedroom efficiency, is especially nice, with a small sitting area that faces the water. Room number 6, a small efficiency, has a little kitchenette and an especially large bathroom. Rooms are dated in style but are very clean, and many can be combined to accommodate large families. There's a horseshoe court and boat ramp, plus a heated swimming pool. Parmer's, a fixture here for almost 20 years, is well known for its charming hospitality and helpful staff.

Sugarloaf Lodge. Overseas Hwy., Mile Marker 17 (P.O. Box 148), Sugarloaf Key, FL 33044. ☎ **305/745-3211** or 800/553-6097. Fax 305/745-3389. 55 rms, 10 efficiencies. A/C TV TEL. Winter $85–$95 double, $100 efficiency. Off-season $65–$80 double, $85 efficiency. Additional person or pet $10. Children under 12 stay free. AE, CB, DC, DISC, MC, V.

On the one hand, this is just a two-story motel: plain rooms, good parking, swimming pool. But its ideal location, on the water in the heart of the Lower Keys, and its immediate proximity to the backcountry reefs, make the Sugarloaf Lodge special. There are two wings to this sprawling property, which surrounds a lagoon where the motel's mascot dolphin lives. Efficiency rooms outfitted with small, fully equipped kitchenettes are also available. The motel is close to tennis courts and a miniature golf course, and adjacent to T.J.'s Sugarshack, an excellent marina from which you can fish or sightsee on the reef (see "Boating" in "Sports and Outdoor Activities," above). There's a restaurant and lounge serving meals and drinks all day.

WHERE TO DINE

The restaurant scene is like that in the Upper Keys; there's decent food for the motorists passing through and the locals. Don't be afraid to try the little shacks selling food, however. You may very well be pleasantly surprised by the adequacy of the meal.

Island Reef Restaurant. Overseas Hwy., Mile Marker 31.3, (P.O. Box 430534), Big Pine Key. ☎ 305/872-2170. Reservations not accepted. Lunch $3.95–$7.95; dinner $9–$14. MC, V. Mon–Sat 11am–9:30pm. AMERICAN.

This colorful ramshackle restaurant seems almost as old as the Keys themselves. It's extremely popular with locals, and you'll overhear conversations about today's catch and tomorrow's weather. There are only about a dozen tables, as well as six stools at a small diner-style bar.

Breakfasts tend toward fresh-fruit platters and French toast, while lunches mean simple sandwiches and tasty island chowders. Dinner specials change nightly; sometimes it's roast chicken with stuffing or leg of lamb, and other times it's prime rib or baked dolphin fish. Specials are served with lots of fixings (soup of the day or salad, potatoes, vegetables, and dessert). Permanent menu items include English-style fish-and-chips with malt vinegar, veal sweetbreads, vegetarian stir-fry, and frogs' legs. Prime rib is served on Friday, Saturday, and Sunday and is particularly popular with locals.

Mangrove Mama's Restaurant. Overseas Hwy., Mile Marker 20, Sugarloaf Key. ☎ 305/745-3030. Reservations not required. Main courses $13–$19; lunch $2–$9; brunch $5–$7. MC, V. Daily 11:30am–3pm and 5:30–10pm. SEAFOOD.

One of the few structures to survive the infamous 1935 hurricane, Mangrove Mama's is a true Lower Keys institution and a dive in the best sense of the word. The restaurant is but a mere shack that used to have a gas pump as well as a grill. A handful of simple tables, both inside and out, are shaded by banana trees and often occupied by locals. It's not surprising that fish is the menu's mainstay, though chowders, salads, and large omelets (including one filled with shrimp, scallops, and crabmeat) are also served. Grilled teriyaki chicken and club sandwiches are available, as are meatless chef's salad and spicy barbecued baby back ribs. This is a great place to sample an authentic top-notch Key lime pie.

Monte's. Overseas Hwy., Mile Marker 25 (Route 6, Box 177), Summerland Key. ☎ 305/745-3731. Reservations not accepted. Main courses $10–$14; lunch $3–$8. No credit cards. Tues–Sat 9:30am–10pm, Sun 11am–9pm. SEAFOOD.

Nobody goes to this restaurant/fish market for its atmosphere: plastic place settings on plastic-covered picnic-style tables in a screen-enclosed dining patio. Monte's has been open for almost 20 years because the food is very good and incredibly fresh. The day's catch may include shark, tuna, lobster, stone crabs, and shrimp of various sizes. In addition, the restaurant prepares several dishes including clam chowder, spiced crayfish pie, and even barbecued spareribs.

The Sugarloaf Lodge. Overseas Hwy., Mile Marker 17 (P.O. Box 148), Sugarloaf Key. ☎ 305/745-3741. Reservations not accepted. Breakfast $2–$5; lunch $5–$8; dinner $7–$20. AE, DC, DISC, MC, V. Daily 7:30am–2:30pm; Sun–Thurs 5–9pm, Fri–Sat 5–10pm. AMERICAN.

This simple, small-town restaurant could be anywhere—if it weren't for the mounted marlin and view of the dolphin pool. It's a good place for the whole family since it serves a variety of entrees, and the staff is happy to accommodate children. It's hard to believe that this huge dining room ever fills to capacity, though the adjacent wood-paneled bar is often hopping with local fishermen. Breakfasts here include the usual variety of egg dishes, served with corned-beef hash, sausage, ham, or steak. At lunch and dinner, you can get hot and cold sandwiches including chicken and steak, fish, burgers, and other traditional American foods. In deference to their dolphin, which you can feed at appointed hours throughout the day, the diner never serves tuna. But the kitchen will happily cook anything you catch and serve it with a salad, vegetables, and bread for a small fee.

5 Key West

150 miles SW of Miami

This distant hideaway, famous for its relaxed atmosphere, is literally at the end of the road. Accessible only by boat until 1912, when Henry Flagler's railroad reached it, Key West's relative isolation from the North American mainland has everything to do with its charm. Home to Cuban, Caribbean, and American wanderers, writers, outlaws, and musicians, few islanders are actually "conchs" (pronounced "conk," the name for lifelong residents). The majority of Key West's residents have been ramblers who drifted south through the states until they could tramp no further.

In its colorful and complicated history, the island has long attracted luminaries, including Ernest Hemingway, John James Audubon, and Tennessee Williams. Due in part to pirating, salvaging, sponging, and shrimping, Key West was once one of the wealthiest towns in America. Hit hard by the double whammy of hurricane and recession, the city declared bankruptcy in 1934, then recovered by catering to mass tourism.

Key West's very tolerant live-and-let-live atmosphere is derived from its residents' die-hard individuality and independence. It is the same liberal philosophy that has made Key West especially welcoming to gays and fostered unchecked growth. Only recently has concern about the environment been building among Key West's residents. Increasing tourism and gentrification have sapped the once-funky fishing village of much of its charm. T-shirt shops are edging out smart boutiques and old gin-joints. The people strolling along the main streets are probably cruise-ship passengers on a few hours' leave, not longtime locals. But Key West is still a fun place, and consumerism is mostly fueled by hedonism.

ESSENTIALS

VISITOR INFORMATION   The **Florida Keys and Key West Visitors Bureau,** P.O. Box 1147, Key West, FL 33041 (☎ 305/296-2228 or 800/FLA-KEYS), offers a free vacation kit packed with visitor information. The **Key West Chamber of Commerce,** 402 Wall St., Key West, FL 33040 (☎ 305/294-2587 or 800/ 527-8539), also offers general and specialized information. It's open daily from 8:30am to 5pm.

GETTING THERE   Several regional airlines fly nonstop from Miami to Key West; fares range from $120 to $300 round-trip. American Eagle (☎ 800/443-7300) and USAir Express (☎ 800/428-4322) land at **Key West International Airport,** South Roosevelt Boulevard (☎ 305/296-5439), on the island's southeastern corner. Also, the new Pan Am Air Bridge (☎ 305/371-8628) flies from Miami and Fort Lauderdale to Key West for about $170 round-trip Friday to Monday.

If you're driving from Miami, take the Florida Turnpike south to the Homestead Turnpike Extension that meets U.S. 1 in Florida City. A much slower alternative is just to take traffic light–laden U.S. 1 the entire way from Miami to Florida City. From Florida City, the Overseas Highway will take you all the way to Key West. If you're driving from Florida's west coast, take Alligator Alley to the Miami exit, then turn south onto the Turnpike Extension. When entering Key West, stay in the far right lane onto North Roosevelt Boulevard, which leads to Duval Street.

Greyhound (☎ 800/231-2222) operates three buses daily, in each direction, between Miami and Key West. The four-hour trip costs $26 each way.

GETTING AROUND   Key West is just 4 miles long and 2 miles wide, so getting around is easy. The mile-square Old Town is centered around Duval Street, the island's most important commercial thoroughfare and collective watering hole.

EXPLORING KEY WEST

The best thing to do on this island is loosen your shirt, pocket your watch, and take a long stroll down Duval Street, the island's famously fun thoroughfare, which runs 13 blocks from the Gulf of Mexico to the Atlantic Ocean. Although Duval was tamed long ago by gourmet ice-cream parlors and tacky T-shirt shops, the street remains one of the world's best pub crawls. Stop in at some of the many open-air bars, have a few drinks, meet some locals, and end up at Mallory Docks by sunset, where street performers take a short break between shows to watch the sun disappear into the Gulf.

To see the "real" Key West, you'll need to get off Duval Street and wander (or bike) around the back roads of the island's compact Old Town. These smaller streets, lined with "conch" houses that are architecturally influenced by both England and the Caribbean, retain a charm that speaks volumes about the island's quixotic past. Along the way, you might visit some of the town's historical houses, museums, and other attractions.

Audubon House and Gardens. 205 Whitehead St. ☎ **305/294-2116.** Admission $7.50 adults, $6.50 seniors, $2 children 6–12, free for children under 6. Daily 9:30am–5pm.

Audubon House has a misleading name, as the naturalist John James Audubon never lived here; actually, the famous birder only visited in 1832. Yet this fantastically restored three-story house now features many of the master artist's original engravings and lithographs. Capt. John Geiger, the house's original 19th-century owner, was one of the wealthiest men in Key West. His former home is flawlessly restored and outfitted with his original furnishings. Key Westers do live differently from the rest of us, and this home, with its outdoor walkways and lush tropical gardens, proves how lucky they are. Admission includes a self-guided-tour brochure and an audio-tape tour, plus docents are available to answer questions.

Ernest Hemingway House Museum. 907 Whitehead St. ☎ **305/294-1575.** Admission $6.50 adults, $4 children. Daily 9am–5pm.

Key West's commercialization of Ernest Hemingway has turned this former local resident into a touristic icon, both figuratively and literally; the novelist's gruff image is emblazoned on T-shirts and mugs and used to sell everything from beer to suntan lotion. Hemingway's particularly handsome stone Spanish Colonial house was built in 1851, and was one of the first on the island to be fitted with indoor plumbing and a built-in fireplace. The author lived here, along with about 50 six-toed cats, from 1928 until 1940. During that period, Hemingway produced some of his most famous works, including *For Whom the Bell Tolls, A Farewell to Arms,* and *The Snows of Kilimanjaro.* Hemingway habitually awoke early and crossed the elevated walkway he

Key West

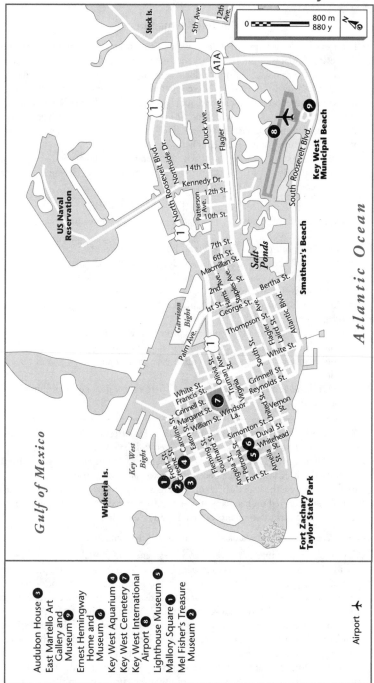

800 m
880 y

Stock Is.
5th Ave.
12th Ave.

A1A

US Naval Reservation

North Roosevelt Blvd.
Northside Dr.

Duck Ave.
Flagler Ave.

14th St.
Kennedy Dr.
12th St.
Patterson Ave.
10th St.

7th St.
6th St.
Macmillan St.
2nd Ave.
Harris Ave.
George St.
1st St. Ave.

Thompson St.

Palm Ave.

Garrison Bight

Key West Bight

Wiskeria Is.

Gulf of Mexico

White St.
Francis St.
Grinnell St.
Margaret St.
Caroline St.
Eaton St.
Fleming St.
Southard St.
William St.
Windsor La.
Virginia
Angela St.
Simonton St.
Petronia St.
Fort St.
Amelia St.
Front St.
Greene St.

Olivia St.
Truman Ave.

Grinnell St.
Reynolds St.
South St.
White St.
Flagler St.
Laird St.
Atlantic Blvd.

Vernon St.
United St.
Duval St.
Whitehead St.

Bertha St.

Salt Ponds

South Roosevelt Blvd.

Key West Municipal Beach

Smathers's Beach

Atlantic Ocean

Fort Zachary Taylor State Park

Audubon House ❸
East Martello Art Gallery and Museum ❾
Ernest Hemingway Home and Museum ❻
Key West Aquarium ❹
Key West Cemetery ❼
Key West International Airport ❽
Lighthouse Museum ❶
Mallory Square ❶
Mel Fisher's Treasure Museum ❷

Airport ✈

The Ten Keymanments

The Keys has long attracted independent spirits, from Ernest Hemingway and Tennessee Williams to Jimmy Buffett and Mel Fisher and Zane Grey. The writers, artists, and free-thinkers have drifted down to get away from society's rigid demands.

And standards do seem to be different here. In 1982, for example, when drug-enforcement agents blocked off the main highway leading into Key West, residents did what they do best—throw a party. The festivities marked the "independence" of the newly formed "Conch Republic." The distinctive flag with its conch insignia now flies throughout "the Republic."

While you'll still find a very laid-back and tolerant code of behavior in the Keys, *some* rules do exist. Be sure to respect the Ten Keymanments while you are here or suffer the consequences as proscribed below:

- Don't anchor on a reef. (Reefs are Alive. Alive. A-L-I-V-E.)
- Don't feed the animals. (They'll want to follow you home, and you can't keep them.)
- Don't trash our place. (Or we'll send Bubba to trash yours.)
- Don't touch the coral. (After all, you don't even know them.)
- Don't speed. (Especially on Big Pine Key where deer reside and tar-and-feathering is still practiced.)
- Don't catch more fish than you can eat. (Better yet, let them go. Some of them support schools.)
- Don't collect conch. (This species is protected. By Bubba.)
- Don't disturb the bird nests. (They find it very annoying.)
- Don't damage the seagrass. (And don't even think about making a skirt out of it.)
- Don't drink and drive on land or sea. (There's absolutely nothing funny about it.)

built from his bedroom to his writing studio. He often wrote all day, but "If the words are coming hard," he admitted, "I often quit before noon."

The Hemingway House Museum was opened to the public two years after the novelist's death. Knowledgeable docents guide you around the property, and then you are free to browse through displays of Hemingway's personal possessions and admire furnishings acquired on his many travels to Africa and Cuba. You can also pet dozens of six-toed cats, descendants of Hemingway's own pets.

The Key West Cemetery. Margaret and Angela Sts. Free admission.

Key West's quirky image is coveted by its residents and capitalized on by its tourist board. But no place on the island is wackier then this old and picturesque cemetery. This 21-acre graveyard is as irreverent as it is original. Key West's rocky geological makeup forced early residents to "bury" their dead above ground, in stone-encased caskets that are sometimes stacked several high, condominium style. And pets are often buried beside their owners. You will notice that many of the memorials are emblazoned with nicknames—a common Key West informality that is literally taken to the grave. Look for headstones labeled "The Tailor," "Bean," "Shorty," and "Bunny." Other headstones reflect residents' lighthearted attitudes toward life and death. "I Told You I Was Sick" is one of the more famous epitaphs, as is a tongue-in-cheek widow's inscription "At Least I Know Where He's Sleeping Tonight." The cemetery is open from dawn to dusk.

Mallory Square Sunset Celebration at the Mallory Square Docks.

Every evening, just before sunset, locals and visitors gather at the dock behind Mallory Square to celebrate the day gone by. It sounds like a quaint Caribbean tradition, and it once was, but sunsets have become big business in Key West. Don't miss this carnival of food vendors, portrait artists, acrobats, and dog acts. On the water, boatfuls of drunken sunset cruisers glide by in private and party yachts, while single-engine tour planes buzz overhead.

MORE MUSEUMS & AN AQUARIUM

East Martello Museum and Gallery. 3501 S. Roosevelt Blvd. ☎ **305/296-3913.** Admission $5 adults, $1 children 5–15, free for children under 7. Daily 9:30am–5pm.

If you can only stand to visit one museum in Key West, make this the one. Manageable in size and eclectic in variety, the East Martello Museum is located in an old brick Civil War–era fort that itself is worth a visit. The museum contains a bizarre variety of exhibits that together present a fairly thorough interpretation of the city's intriguing past. Historical artifacts include ship models, a deep-sea diver's wooden air pump, a crude raft from a Cuban "boatlift," and a horse-drawn hearse. Exhibits depict America's wars and illustrate the Keys' history of wrecking, sponging, and cigar making. And if all that's not enough, the museum also exhibits modern works by local artists. After visiting the galleries, you can climb a steep spiral staircase to the top of a lookout tower for good views over the island and ocean. The museum is located on the "far" side of the island, away from the Duval Street crowds.

Key West Aquarium. 1 Whitehead St., Key West. ☎ **305/296-2051.** Two-day pass $6.50 adults, $3.50 children ages 8–15. Daily 10am–6pm.

Built by the WPA as an open-air aquarium, this 1930s-era "fish zoo" has since been topped by a roof, but its interior is as antiquated as ever. The Key West Aquarium can't hold a candle to newer, glitzier ones, but it's not supposed to. This small and user-friendly aquarium is basically a single large room with fish tanks embedded in every wall and huge open touch tanks in the center. If you show up in time for one of the frequent show-and-tell tours, you'll learn about horseshoe and hermit crabs, starfish, sea rays, and queen conchs; feedings also coincide with the lectures. Three large outdoor pens in back of the aquarium house animals of the Atlantic shore, but are a snore.

Key West Lighthouse Museum. 938 Whitehead St. ☎ **305/294-0012.** Admission $5 adults, $1 children 7–12, free for children under 7. Daily 9:30am–5pm (last entry at 4:30pm).

When the Key West Lighthouse was opened in 1848, many locals mourned. Its bright warning to ships also signaled the end of a profitable era for wreckers, pirate salvagers who looted reef-stricken ships. The story of this, and other Keys' lighthouses, is illustrated in a small museum that was formerly the keeper's quarters. It's worth mustering the energy to climb the 88 claustrophobic stairs to the top, where you're rewarded with magnificent panoramic views of Key West and the ocean. The lighthouse used to be on the shore, but is now about a quarter mile inland, thanks to landfill.

Mel Fisher's Treasure Museum. 200 Greene St. ☎ **305/294-2633.** Admission $6 adults, $2 children 6–12, free for children under 6. Departures daily 9:30am–5pm.

Mel Fisher found a multimillion-dollar treasure trove when he discovered the wreck of the Spanish galleon *Nuestra Señora de Atocha* in 1985. And at this small museum, you'll see what he found: doubloons, emeralds, and solid gold bars. Some of the $400 million in gold and silver artifacts are displayed along with many copies. Cannons, ship parts, and other items of purely historical value are also exhibited. An aging, 20-minute video tells the story.

ORGANIZED TOURS

BY TROLLEY BUS   The city's whole story is packed into a neat, 90-minute package on the **Conch Train** tour, which comprehensively covers the island. The "train's" engine is a propane-powered truck disguised as a locomotive. Sitting in one of the little cars is more than a bit hokey, but worth the embarrassment. Tours depart from both Mallory Square and at the Welcome Center, near the intersection of U.S. 1 and North Roosevelt Boulevard, on the other side of the island. For more information, contact Conch Train at 1 Key Lime Square, Key West (☎ 305/294-5161). The tour costs $14 for adults, $6 for children ages 4 to 12; it's free for children under 4. Daily departures leave every half hour from 9am to 4:30pm.

It's remarkable that there are enough tourists in Key West to keep two competing trolley tours afloat. **Old Town Trolley's** open-air tram drivers maintain a running commentary as they loop around the island's streets past all the major (and many minor) sights. The main advantage of this 90-minute tour is that you can disembark at any of 14 stops on the tour route, explore a museum or visit a restaurant, then reboard at will. Trolleys depart from Mallory Square and other points around the island. For details, contact them at 1910 N. Roosevelt Blvd. (☎ 305/296-6688). Tours cost $15 for adults, $6 for children ages 4 to 12, free for children under 4. Departures leave from 9am to 4pm daily.

BY AIR   Proclaimed by the mayor as "the official air force of the Conch Republic," **Island Aeroplane Tours,** Key West Airport, 3469 S. Roosevelt Blvd., offers windy rides in their open-cockpit, 1940 Waco biplanes over the reefs and around the islands. Thrill-seekers, and thrill-seekers only, will enjoy a spin in the company's S2-B aerobatics airplane that loops, rolls, and makes sideways figure-eights. Company owner Fred Cabanas was "decorated" in 1991, after he spotted a Cuban airman defecting to the United States in a Russian-built MIG fighter. Flights last from 6 to 55 minutes. Sightseeing flights cost from $50 to $200, aerobatics flights are $150. For reservations, call 305/294-8687.

BY BOAT   **Pride of Key West,** at Ocean Key House, 0 Duval St., Key West (☎ 305/296-6293), is a 58-foot, glass-bottom catamaran that goes on coral-reef tours by day and sunset cruises by evening. Reef trips cost $18 per person; sunset cruises are $23 per person and include snacks, sodas, and a glass of champagne.

Wolf, at Schooner Wharf, Key West Seaport (☎ 305/296-9653), is a 44-passenger topsail schooner that sets sail daily for daytime and sunset cruises around the Keys. Key West Seaport is located at the end of Greene Street. Day tours cost $20 per person; sunset sails cost $29 per person and include champagne, wine, beer, or soda.

SPORTS & OUTDOOR ACTIVITIES

BICYCLING & MOPEDING   The best way to get around Key West is by bicycle. The island is relatively small, as flat as a board, and the streets are safe. Several shops rent one-speed cruisers for about $10 per day and ugly pink mopeds for about $30 per day. They include **The Bike Shop,** 1110 Truman Ave. (☎ 305/294-1073); the **Moped Hospital,** 601 Truman Ave. (☎ 305/296-3344); and **Tropical Bicycles & Scooter Rentals,** 1300 Duval St. (☎ 305/294-8136).

DIVING   One of the area's largest scuba schools, **Key West Pro Dive Shop,** 3128 N. Roosevelt Blvd. (☎ 305/296-3823 or 800/426-0707), offers instruction on all levels. Dive boats take participants to scuba and snorkel sites on nearby reefs.

Wreck dives and night dives are two offerings of **Lost Reef Adventures,** 261 Margaret St. (☎ 305/296-9737 or 800/952-2749). Regularly scheduled runs and private charters can be arranged. Call for departure information.

FISHING Many charter-fishing boats operate from Key West marinas. They include Captain Jim Brienza's 27-foot *Sea Breeze,* docked at 25 Arbutus Dr. (☎ 305/294-6027); Captain Henry Otto's 44-foot *Sunday,* docked at the Key West Hyatt (☎ 305/294-7052); and a host of deep-sea vessels docked at **Garrison Bight Marina,** Eaton Street and Roosevelt Boulevard (☎ 305/296-9969).

GOLF The **Key West Resort,** an 18-hole course, is located just before the island of Key West at Mile Marker 4.5 (turn on College Road to the course entrance). Designed by Rees Jones, the course features plenty of mangroves and water hazards on its 6,526 yards. It's open to the public. A driving range is open from 7am to sunset daily, and there's a pro shop. Tee-time reservations are required (☎ 305/294-5232).

SHOPPING

If you're looking for souvenir T-shirts or jewelry or art, Key West is a shopper's paradise. You'll find an eclectic selection of boutiques; one kiosk specializes in leather shoes with vivid impressions of the sunset or anything you might choose to have painted on them!

For anything else from bed linens to candlesticks to clothing, try downtown's most renowned and oldest department store, **Fast Buck Freddie's,** 500 Duval St. (☎ 305/294-2007). Open daily from 10am to 6pm, until 10pm most Saturdays, and some other evenings in season. For the same merchandise at much reduced prices, try **Half Buck Freddie's,** 726 Caroline St. (☎ 305/294-6799), where you can shop for out-of-season bargains and "rejects" from Fast Buck Freddie's that are anything but second-hand. Open Friday and Saturday only from 11am to 5pm.

Key West has a good number of art galleries and stores selling beautiful native art and even antiques for collectors. Many galleries are clustered on Whitehead Street, which runs parallel to Duval Street. You'll also find shops scattered along the side streets off Duval. One of particular note is the **Haitian Art Company,** 600 Frances St. (☎ 305/296-8932), where you can browse through rooms upon rooms of original paintings from well-known and obscure Haitian artists.

WHERE TO STAY

You'll find a wide variety of places to stay in Key West, from big resorts with all the amenities to smaller, quaint hotels that run the gamut from seaside motels to adorable bed-and-breakfasts. Shop around and take your pick.

Some big hotel chains that operate out of the Keys include Best Western (☎ 800/432-4315), Comfort Inn (☎ 800/695-5150), Econo Lodge (☎ 800/533-9378), Holiday Inn (☎ 800/465-4329), and Ramada Inn (☎ 800/330-5541).

VERY EXPENSIVE

Marriott's Casa Marina Resort. 1500 Reynolds St., Key West, FL 33040. ☎ **305/296-3535** or 800/228-9290. Fax 305/296-9960. 312 rms, 71 suites. A/C MINIBAR TV TEL. Winter $260–$325 double, $275–$710 suite. Off-season $180–$220 double, $275–$425 suite. Additional person $25. Children under 18 stay free in parents' room. No-smoking rooms available. AE, CB, DC, DISC, MC, V.

Built in the 1920s by railroad tycoon Henry Flagler, Casa Marina was Key West's first grand hotel, popular with movie stars and socialites. The hotel's fortunes waned after the 1935 hurricane and in the early 1940s was operated by the U.S. Navy for World War II military personnel. During the Cuban Missile Crisis in the early 1960s,

President Kennedy again moved troops into the hotel, and installed anti-aircraft missile launchers on its beach.

Today Casa Marina is far from being like a barracks. It's a nice place, encompassing several low-rise structures and a huge swath of oceanfront, but it's not grand on the scale of other Flagler-inspired projects created to lure film stars and land speculators. With saloon-style swinging doors, French doors, carved pillars, and dark woods, the lobby is the only room here designed to wow. Guest rooms, located in several three-story, Spanish Mediterranean–style wings, are comparatively modest and straight-forward. The most expensive accommodations have balconies overlooking the ocean, while those that are less expensive face inland. Most rooms are almost identical, making them popular with groups. The hotel is located adjacent to Higg's Beach, one of the widest strips of sand on the island.

Dining/Entertainment: Flagler's, the hotel's top restaurant, features Caribbean-inspired decor and fresh local seafood. There's a breakfast buffet and Sunday brunch served outdoors on the patio. The adjacent lounge offers regular live entertainment. The Sun Pavilion, a beachfront eatery, serves breakfast, lunch, dinner, late-night snacks, and drinks all day.

Facilities: Private beach with 80-foot swimming pier, two swimming pools, outdoor whirlpool, health club with sauna, three lighted tennis courts, water-sports center, beauty salon, gift shops.

Services: Room service, concierge, business center, evening turndown, laundry, overnight shoeshine, massage.

The Pier House. 1 Duval St., Key West, FL 33040. ☎ **305/296-4600** or 800/327-8340. Fax 305/296-7569. 142 rms, 13 suites. A/C MINIBAR TV TEL. Winter $275–$425 double, $535–$950 suite; additional person $35. Off-season $205–$355 double, $375–$750 suite; additional person $20. AE, CB, DC, DISC, MC, V.

The Pier House's excellent location at the foot of Duval Street, just steps from Mallory Docks and within stumbling distance of most every bar in town, is the envy of every hotel on the island. Set back from the busy street, on a short strip of beach, the hotel is a welcome oasis of calm, offering luxurious rooms, top-notch service, and even a full-service spa. Accommodations here vary tremendously, from relatively simple business-style rooms to romantic guest quarters complete with integrated stereo systems and whirlpool tubs. While every accommodation has either a balcony or a patio, some rooms in this sprawling hotel overlook the water, while others have views of the junglelike pool area. My favorite rooms in the two-story spa building don't have any view at all, but what they lack in scenery, they make up for in opulence. Each Spa Room features a huge Jacuzzi bathroom that's separated from the bedroom by a sliding wooden shutter. An adjacent sitting area is made up with a propped-open Ernest Hemingway novel.

Dining/Entertainment: The Pier House Restaurant has long been a part of Key West history. Its dark and depressing interior hardly makes up for great views of boats returning to harbor. Old Havana Docks is a good waterfront drinkery that becomes especially busy around sunset.

Services: Room service, concierge, laundry.

Facilities: Spa treatments, water-sports rentals, swimming pool, beach.

The Reach. 1435 Simonton St., Key West, FL 33040. ☎ **305/296-5000** or 800/228-9290. Fax 305/296-2830. 149 rms. A/C MINIBAR TV TEL. Winter $270–$450 double. Off-season $225–$350 double. AE, CB, DC, DISC, MC, V.

Painted the color of cooked shrimp and sporting white, gingerbread-style balconies, the colossal and labyrinthine Reach is one of the few hotels on the island with its own strip of sandy beach. Supported by stilts that leave the entire ground floor for parking, the hotel offers four floors of rooms designed around atriums. The large guest rooms are decorated in tropical colors. Each contains a small service bar with a sink, fridge, and tea/coffeemaker, and has a vanity area separate from the bathroom. Rooms are so nice you can easily forgive the small closets and diminutive dressers. All rooms have sliding-glass doors that open onto balconies, and some have ocean views.

Ample palm-planted grounds surround a small pool area with plenty of lounge chairs and a private pier for fishing and suntanning. The protected waters are tame and shallow. The hotel is located a short walk from the "far" end of Duval Street—15 minutes from the center of the action.

Dining/Entertainment: The forgettable Ocean Club serves fresh local seafood in an uninspiring dining room. The beachfront Sand Bar, a fish-and-burger place, serves mediocre food in a world-class location. For a quicker bite it's worth stopping at A Little Something, the resort's deli and French bakery. Nightfall, a low-rise rooftop bar, offers hotel-quality entertainment and obstructed sunset views.

Services: Room service, concierge, laundry.

Facilities: Heated swimming pool, sauna, health spa, steam room, sailboats, windsurfers.

Sheraton Suites. 2001 S. Roosevelt Blvd., Key West, FL 33040. ☎ **305/292-9800** or 800/325-3535. Fax 305/294-6009. 180 suites. A/C MINIBAR TV TEL. Winter $350–$420 double. Off-season $280–$300 double. Rates include breakfast. Additional person $15. Children under 18 stay free. AE, DC, DISC, EURO, JCB, MC, V.

Peach and purple with aqua accents on Bahamian hurricane shutters, Sheraton Suites stands out as literally as it does figuratively. The hotel's generously sized suites all contain separate living rooms with sofa beds, a comfortable dressing area, and terrific baths. Interiors are colorful, stylish, and well planned. Higher-priced suites include whirlpool baths, minibars, microwave ovens, coffeemakers, and two telephones. Unlike the outside, which looks more metallic and "prefab" than quaint turn-of-the-century "rehab," the beautifully designed interiors feel warm and private. The hotel is located on the beach side of Key West, just across the street from the island's best swimming and water-sports beach, but offers no water views.

Dining/Entertainment: The Crab House Restaurant, located on the lobby level, serves three meals daily, including a complimentary cooked buffet breakfast.

Services: Room service, concierge, overnight laundry, complimentary daily newspaper, airport transportation, free shuttle to Old Town.

Facilities: Gift shop, bicycle and scooter rentals.

EXPENSIVE

Banyan Resort. 323 Whitehead St., Key West, FL 33040. ☎ **305/296-7786** or 800/225-0639. Fax 305/294-1107. 5 studios, 33 suites. A/C TV TEL. Winter $185 studio, $220 one-bedroom suite, $245–$265 two-bedroom suite. Off-season $115 studio, $130 one-bedroom suite, $145–$165 two-bedroom suite. Additional person $20. AE, DC, DISC, MC, V. Parking $4.

Named for the many giant, sinuous banyan trees that give this property its character, Banyan Resort is a small cluster of petite historical apartment houses. The individually owned time-share apartments within are rented as hotel units with on-site management and daily maid service. Encompassing seven three-story, neo-Victorian-style houses and a former cigar factory, the resort offers good-quality accommodations. A large number of layouts can make booking bothersome, but it keeps groups at bay. Rooms are immaculately clean and designed for easy maintenance. Despite a standardized condo look, Banyan Resort has plenty of character. Most top-floor accommodations have high ceilings and some have small porches.

Studios have Murphy beds. Apartments include small bathrooms, medium-sized living rooms, and kitchens that range in size from breakfast to banquet.

There are two small pools, including one for kids, and plants and trees surrounding an outdoor tiki bar. The resort is situated on a moderately quiet street, within walking distance of Duval Street and Mallory Docks. Yet the excellent location can mean parking hassles.

Curry Mansion Inn. 511 Caroline St., Key West, FL 33040. ☎ **305/294-5349** or 800/253-3466. Fax 305/294-4093. 21 rms. A/C MINIBAR TV TEL. Winter $180–$220 double. Off-season $125–$175 double. Rates include breakfast. Additional person $25. No children under 16. AE, CB, DC, DISC, MC, V.

Built in 1855 by William Curry, Florida's first millionaire, the Curry Mansion Inn is now a private museum and hotel listed in the National Register of Historic Places. Restored and filled with innumerable antiques, the house is a lovely place, both inside and out. Unfortunately, all but three rooms are located in an adjacent annex that is not as luxurious as the inn's main building. Some rooms have four-poster beds and many have huge bathrooms. Unfortunately, many bathrooms lack toiletry space, lights and telephones are poorly placed, and TVs are missing their remotes.

Eight rooms in the restored James House annex, located across the street, are more recommendable. Most beds here have bowed wooden canopies, and upstairs rooms have private porches. Like accommodations across the street, room designs here are far from exciting; both houses are so intrinsically beautiful, one wishes the interior decorator had talent to complement the architects.

At James House, there's a hot tub on the back porch with a view of the parking lot. At Curry Mansion, there's a small swimming pool surrounded by a tiny sundeck. Guests are treated to complimentary afternoon cocktails and are entitled to use the facilities of the Pier House Beach Club, located just one block away.

Island City House Hotel. 411 William St., Key West, FL 33040. ☎ **305/294-5702** or 800/634-8230. Fax 305/294-1289. 24 suites. A/C TV TEL. Winter $165 studio, $185–$210 one-bedroom suite, $255–$275 two-bedroom suite. Off-season $95 studio, $115–$145 one-bedroom suite, $145–$175 two-bedroom suite. Rates include breakfast. Additional person $20. Children under 12 stay free in parents' room. DC, DISC, MC, V.

A little resort unto itself, Island City House is comprised of three separate buildings that share a common junglelike patio and pool. Island City House shares its property name with one of the buildings on it, making descriptions more complicated. The Island City House building is a historical three-story wooden structure with wraparound verandas that allow guests to walk around the entire structure on any floor. Old-fashioned interiors include antique furnishings. Many rooms have full-size kitchens. The clean tile bathrooms could use more counter space and room lighting isn't always perfect, but eccentricities are part of this hotel's charm. The unpainted wooden Cigar House's particularly large bedrooms are similar to those in Island City House. Most rooms enjoy big bathrooms that also suffer from a lack of counter space. As with the Island City House, rooms facing the property's interior courtyard are best. The hotel's Arch House is the least appealing of the three buildings, but still very recommendable. Built of Dade County pine, Arch House's cozy bedrooms come with small kitchens and baths.

The Marquesa Hotel. 600 Fleming St., Key West, FL 33040. ☎ **305/292-1919** or 800/869-4631. Fax 305/294-2121. 27 rms, 13 suites. A/C TV TEL. Winter $185–$225 double, $265–$280 suite. Off-season $150–$160 double, $160–$225 suite. Additional person $15. Children under 2 stay free. AE, DC, MC, V.

The Marquesa's owners are blessed with an enviable combination of great taste in interior design and enough money to execute it. With the 1994 addition of the properties next door, the Marquesa now encompasses four different buildings, two adjacent swimming pools, and a three-stage waterfall that cascades into a lily pond.

Two of the hotel's houses are luxuriously restored Victorian homes with beautifully appointed rooms outfitted with extra-plush antique and oversized contemporary furnishings. Rooms in the two newly constructed buildings are even richer, designed with contemporary furnishings that include four-poster wrought-iron beds. Green-marble baths with ultra-modern fittings have huge mirrors and thoughtful lighting. Some rooms have cathedral ceilings, and suites have majestic, carved wooden sleigh beds.

Dining/Entertainment: Cafe Marquesa is one of Key West's best restaurants (see "Where to Dine," below).

Services: Room service, concierge, evening turndown, morning newspaper.

Facilities: Two swimming pools.

Ocean Key House. Zero Duval St., Key West, FL 33040. ☎ **305/296-7701** or 800/328-9815. Fax 305/292-7685. 28 rms, 68 suites. A/C MINIBAR TV TEL. Winter $160 double, $340–$525 one-bedroom suite, $420–$700 two-bedroom suite. Off-season $135 double, $225–$495 one-bedroom suite, $320–$600 two-bedroom suite. Additional person $25. Children under 18 stay free. AE, DC, DISC, MC, V.

You can't get much more central than this modern hotel, located across from Pier House at the foot of Duval Street. Most guest rooms are suites, ample-sized accommodations fitted with built-in couches. Many rooms have sliding-glass doors that open onto small balconies, some of which enjoy unobstructed water views. All suites have Jacuzzi tubs in either the master bedroom or living room. Bathrooms are rather standard in quality, though many are fitted with double sinks.

Standard guest rooms are much less desirable, small and dark and without views. An intelligent design enables almost any suite to connect with a standard room to become a two-bedroom, two-bath suite.

Dining/Entertainment: The Sunset Pier Bar & Grill is located on the resort's 200-foot private dock, and serves lunch and dinner. Breakfast is served at the indoor/outdoor cafe, Zero's.

Services: Concierge, room service, laundry.

Facilities: Swimming pool, water-sports concession, private marina, tour boat, gift shop.

MODERATE

Chelsea House. 707 Truman Ave., Key West, FL 33040. ☎ **305/296-2211** or 800/845-8859. Fax 305/296-4822. 18 rms, 2 apts. A/C TV TEL. Winter $115–$165 double, $270 apt; additional person $20. Off-season $75–$125 double, $165–$190 apt; additional person $15. Rates include breakfast. No children under 15. Pets $5. AE, DISC, MC, V.

This lovely grey-and-white Queen Anne house, surrounded by a white picket fence and flying the American flag, seems like the quintessential American home. Despite its decidedly English name, Chelsea House *is* "all-American," a term that in Key West isn't code for conservative. Chelsea House caters to a mixed gay/straight clientele with a liberal philosophy that exhibits itself most demonstratively on the clothing-optional sundeck.

Ample-sized bedrooms are augmented by firm beds and TVs connected to VCRs. Apartments come with full kitchens and a separate living area, as well as a palm-shaded balcony in back. Baths and closets could be bigger, but both are adequate and serviceable. Like the beautiful floors and ceilings of the house, the pastel-colored wood walls are built from Dade County pine, a particularly fine termite-resistant tree that has been logged to extinction.

When weather permits, which means almost always, breakfast is served outside by the pool. There is private parking.

La Pensione. 809 Truman Ave., Key West, FL 33040. ☎ **305/292-9923.** Fax 305/296-6509. 7 rms. A/C. Winter $148–$158 double. Off-season $68–$88 double. Rates include breakfast. 10% discount for readers who mention this guide. Additional person $25. No children allowed. AE, DISC, MC, V.

Opened on Valentine's Day in 1991, the yellow-and-white two-story La Pensione is a lovely restoration of an 1891 Victorian home that, like so many on the island, is on the National Register of Historic Places. Guests enter the house via front steps that lead to a porch and a hallway with red floral carpeting. Rooms are colorful and airy. Bathrooms are serviceable, but far from plush. All in all, the new owners have done a good job creating a modestly priced charming inn. Breakfast, which includes Belgian waffles and fresh fruit, is served in a pleasing downstairs dining room.

South Beach Oceanfront Motel. 508 South St., Key West, FL 33040. ☎ **305/296-5611** or 800/354-4455. Fax 305/294-8272. 47 rms. Winter $99–$197 double. Off-season $67–$138 double. Additional person $10–$15. Children under 18 stay free. AE, MC, V.

This standard, two-story motel is located directly on the ocean, within walking distance of Duval Street. Because it is built perpendicular to the water, however, most rooms overlook a particularly pretty Olympic-size swimming pool, rather then a wide swath of beach. The best (and most expensive) rooms are those lucky two on the end—nos. 115 and 215—that are beachfront.

All rooms share similar aging tan-and-green motifs and include standard furnishings. Smallish bathrooms could also use a makeover, and include showers and no tubs. There's a private pier, an on-site water-sports concession, and a laundry room available for guests' use. When booking, ask for a room that's as close to the beach (and as far from the road) as possible.

INEXPENSIVE

Southernmost Point Guest House. 1327 Duval St., Key West, FL 33040. ☎ **305/294-0715.** Fax 305/296-0641. 3 rms, 3 suites. A/C TV TEL. Winter $80–$120 double, $130 suite. Off-season $55–$80 double, $95 suite. Rates include breakfast. Additional person $5–$10. AE, MC, V.

Built in 1885, this well-kept and architecturally stunning B&B pays tribute to the romantic charm of old Key West. The antiseptically clean rooms are not as fancy as the house's ornate exterior. Each has basic beds and couches and a hodgepodge of furnishings including futon couches and plenty of mismatched throw rugs. Room 5 is best; situated upstairs, it has a private porch and an ocean view, and windows that let in large quantities of light. Every room has a refrigerator and comes with a complimentary decanter of sherry. Mona Santiago, the hotel's kind owner, provides chairs and towels that can be brought to the beach, located just one block away.

Wicker Guesthouse. 913 Duval St., Key West, FL 33040. ☎ **305/296-4275** or 800/880-4275. Fax 305/294-7240. 21 rms. Winter $63–$125 double. Off-season $45–$95 double. Rates include breakfast. Additional person $15 ($10 low season). AE, DC, DISC, MC, V.

Occupying six separate buildings, one overlooking busy Duval Street, the Wicker offers some of the best-value accommodations in Key West. The cheapest rooms are in front of the complex. These have shared baths and are predictably sparse, with no telephones, TVs, or even closets. Guest rooms get nicer, quieter, and more expensive the farther back on the property you go. Way back, beyond a kidney-shaped, heated swimming pool, are the guest houses' top accommodations, each furnished with two double beds, cable TVs, and the ubiquitous wicker furnishings that give this house its name. Some have small kitchenettes. Three connected units share a living room and stoveless kitchen, and are particularly recommended for families and small parties. There is a communal kitchen for guests' use and a payphone by the pool.

A HOSTEL

Key West International Hostel. 718 South St., Key West, FL 33040. ☎ **305/296-5719.** Fax 305/296-0672. 80 beds. Winter $17 for IYHF members, $20 for nonmembers. Off-season $13 for IYHF members, $16 for nonmembers. DISC, MC, V.

It's not the Ritz, but it's cheap. Very busy with European backpackers, this place is just a hair above camping out. Facilities include a pool table under a tiki-hut top and bicycle rentals for $6 per day.

WHERE TO DINE

If you're tired of the roadside food you've eaten on your trip south, you'll enjoy the great places to eat in Key West. You won't have to search far for a good sit-down dinner. You'll find real "Key West" food, however, at the fish places and bars that line Duval Street and the side streets. That's where the locals congregate for a good time.

EXPENSIVE

Cafe Des Artistes. 1007 Simonton St. (near the corner of Truman Ave.). ☎ **305/294-7100.** Reservations recommended. Main courses $23–$25. AE, MC, V. Daily 6–11pm. FRENCH.

The dark woods, low arches, and 19th-century oil paintings that decorate Cafe des Artistes make these dining rooms—located in a small house that was built by Al Capone's bookkeeper—some of the most ornate in town. Open over a dozen years, Cafe des Artistes' impressive longevity is the result of its winning combination of food and atmosphere. Serious, traditional meals are served by aproned waiters whose uniforms include red towels slung over a single shoulder.

Start with the duck-liver pâté made with fresh truffles and old cognac, or Maryland crab meat served with an artichoke heart and herbed tomato confit. Nouvelle and traditional French entrees include lobster flambé with mango and basil, and wine-basted lamb chops rubbed with rosemary and ginger. A good wine selection includes several special wines served by the glass.

Cafe Marquesa. 600 Fleming St. (in the Marquesa Hotel). ☎ **305/292-1244.** Reservations recommended. Main courses $19–$26. AE, MC, V. Daily 6–11pm. SOUTH FLORIDA REGIONAL.

Attached to my favorite guesthouse in Florida, Cafe Marquesa's single smart dining room is a perfect extension of its well-run business. The food is the best in town and the service, unlike what you'll experience in the rest of the Keys, is professional and efficient.

Recipes are quite unusual, but waiters are well versed in each dish's ingredients. There's so much appealing fare to choose from that you might forgo ordering a single large entree in favor of "grazing" on several different appetizers. Particularly winning starters include grilled garlic-Dijon shrimp with sweet-potato andouille hash, pan-fried cracked conch with mango–black-bean relish and vanilla-bean–rum sauce, and Jamaican lentil gumbo with smoked chicken and brown rice. Entrees are similarly engaging if a little overwrought. Look for smoked pork chops with spicy apple relish, grilled citrus-marinated whole chicken with roasted garlic, and sesame-encrusted rack of lamb with coconut mint pesto.

Louie's Backyard. 700 Waddell Ave. ☎ **305/294-1061.** Reservations required. Main courses $25–$30; brunch and lunch $8–$15. AE, CB, DC, MC, V. Daily 11:30am–3pm and 6–10:30pm. CARIBBEAN CONTEMPORARY.

Louie's is a long-lived Key West institution, whose terraced rear deck, built directly over the water, is the picture of romance, particularly when there's a warm breeze and gentle surf. It's a great place for evening drinks. The contemporary inside dining room is far less desirable, but cozy, designed with pastel colors and large paddle fans that complement an authentic "conch" house feel. Unfortunately, when we dined there recently, the service was appallingly slow and unprofessional, and the dishes uneven at best.

Chef Doug Shook combines influences from around the world to create his own brand of contemporary Caribbean cuisine that sometimes works brilliantly and at others just falls flat. Grilled soy-marinated yellowfin tuna was tasty but the accompaniment, udon noodles with spiced peanuts, was bland and mushy. More reliable are the Sunday brunches, à la carte affairs that include an interesting and delicious selection of roast Cuban pork on black beans with sweet-potato pancakes, croissant French toast with Virginia ham, and poached eggs with mushroom hollandaise. For weekend dining, reserve up to a week in advance.

MODERATE

Bagatelle. 115 Duval St. ☎ **305/296-6609.** Reservations not required. Main courses $16–$24; lunch $5–$12. AE, CB, DC, DISC, MC, V. Daily 11:30am–3pm and 5:30–10pm. SEAFOOD/ TROPICAL.

Dining on the second-floor veranda of Bagatelle's historical grey-and-pink Queen Anne house is intimate while offering a bird's-eye view of the Duval madness below. It's even more fanciful when a keyboardist is at the grand piano. A nod away is a contemporary interior dining room; an entire wall has been removed for unrestricted access to the balcony. A massive mounted marlin and wooden schoolhouse chairs at white-clothed tables keep formality at bay. There's also a lively ground-floor bar in what was once the house's living room.

A large lunch selection includes a blackened chicken breast sandwich with crumbled blue cheese and a variety of grilled fish. Begin dinner with the herb-and-garlic-stuffed whole artichoke or the sashimilike seared tuna rolled in black peppercorns. The best entrees are the local Florida fish selections like shrimp-stuffed grouper crowned with shrimp-and-lobster-cream sauce, and garlic-herb pasta topped with Gulf shrimp, Florida lobster, local fish, and mushrooms. The best chicken and beef dishes are given a tropical treatment: grilled with papaya, ginger, and soy.

Kelly's Caribbean Bar & Grill. 301 Whitehead St. ☎ **305/293-8484.** Reservations accepted. Main courses $13–$20; lunch about half-price. AE, V. Sun–Thurs 11am–9:30pm, Fri–Sat noon–10:30pm. SOUTH FLORIDA CONTEMPORARY.

Kelly's is located in a large old Victorian home that was once the first office of Pan American Airways. An architecturally beautiful rehab removed so many major walls that today the line between inside and outside is obscured. The terrific design gives the dining room an airy, tropical feeling. The interior has an American-bistro look, with plain wooden tables and arty black-and-white prints of early airplanes. Two model 1929 Sikorski seaplane propellers spin overhead as ceiling fans. Out back, banyan trees shade a large brick patio topped with unfinished wood tables and white-metal chairs.

Kelly's food is gourmet in scope, if not in quality. Entrees include pasta with sautéed shrimp and buttery lime sauce, barbecued pork with fresh mango salsa, crispy roasted half duck with raspberry-orange glaze, and whole snapper with tomato-basil vinaigrette. Plus the restaurant has the Keys' only on-site microbrewery. Their 2,000-gallon's worth of stainless-steel tanks produce five varieties of beer that range from light to stout; Golden Ale is best. Kelly's is named for actress Kelly McGillis, who owns the restaurant with her husband.

Mangoes Restaurant. 700 Duval St. (corner of Angela St.). ☎ **305/292-4606.** Reservations recommended. Main courses $16–$20; pizzas $10–$12; lunch about half-price. AE, CB, DC, DISC, MC, V. Daily 11am–midnight. FLORIDA REGIONAL.

If the three most important components of a successful restaurant are location, location, and location, then Mangoes is the most prosperous eatery in town. The restaurant's large brick patio, directly on Duval, is so seductive to passersby that it is packed most every night of the week. Don't even think about eating in the drab dining room.

Mangoes enjoys a good buzz among locals, and even competitors envy the restaurant's servers, who are some of the best on Duval. Appetizers include conch chowder laced with sherry, lobster dumplings with tangy key lime sauce, and grilled shrimp cocktail with spicy mango chutney. Spicy sausage with black beans and rice, crispy curried chicken, and local snapper with passionfruit sauce are typical among entrees, but Mangoes's outstanding individual-sized designer pizzas are the best menu items by far. They're baked in a Neapolitan-style oven that's fired by buttonwood. Because of limited oven capacity, pizzas are only available on weekday evenings.

Turtle Kraals Wildlife Grill. 213 Margaret St. (corner of Caroline). ☎ **305/294-2640.** Main courses $12–$18. DISC, MC, V. Mon–Thurs 11am–1am; Fri–Sat 11am–2am. SOUTHWESTERN/ SEAFOOD.

You'll join lots of locals in this out-of-the-way converted warehouse that serves innovative seafood at great prices. Try the twin lobster tails stuffed with mango and crabmeat or any of the big quesadillas or fajitas. Kids will like the wildlife exhibits and the very cheesy menu. Blues bands play most nights; there's never a cover.

INEXPENSIVE

The Bangalore. 504 Petronia St. ☎ **305/292-2209.** Reservations not accepted. Main courses $3–$6. No credit cards. Tues–Sat 6pm–midnight. INDIAN.

Quite literally a hole-in-the-wall, the Bangalore is an all-vegetarian, Indian-inspired dining counter accommodating just four outdoor stools situated beneath a leaky awning. Both dirt-cheap and delicious, the restaurant is run by well-traveled owner/ waiter/chef/busboy Philip Simons, who's always up for some interesting chat. Start with a baked phyllo samosa, containing curried potatoes, peas, ginger, and cilantro. Main courses include tofu and peas in a coriander-based tomato sauce, cauliflower and potato sautéed with cumin and fennel, okra with roasted red peppers and onions, and mushrooms sautéed with garlic, onion, ginger, and spices. Located a half-block east of Duval Street, the Bangalore is open late.

Blue Heaven. 729 Thomas St. (in the heart of Bahama Village). ☎ **305/296-8666.** Main courses $7–$17. MC, V. Mon–Sat 8am–3pm and 6–10:30pm; Sun 8am–1pm and 6–10:30pm. AMERICAN/NATURAL.

You'll wait in line forever at this little hippy-run gallery and restaurant, which has become the place to be in Key West with good reason. This ramshackle Mediterranean Revival house serves up some of the best food anywhere in town, especially for breakfast. In this former bordello, where Hemingway was said to hang out watching cock fights, you can enjoy homemade granolas, fruit, huge tropical-fruit pancakes, and seafood Benedict. Dinners are just as good and run the gamut from just-caught fish dishes to Jamaican-style jerk chicken, curried soups, and vegetarian stews. While you wait, visit the galleries upstairs to see local work that ranges from the absurd to the incredible. Be sure to call and check that Blue Heaven is open, especially in the summer when it sometimes closes for weeks at a time.

Half Shell Raw Bar. At the foot of Margaret St. ☎ **305/294-7496.** Main courses $5–$10. No credit cards. Mon–Sat 11am–11pm, Sun noon–11pm. SEAFOOD.

If you want inexpensive, fresh-as-can-be seafood, in an authentic dockside setting, this is the place. Decorated with "vanity" license plates from every state in the union, the Half Shell features a wide variety of freshly shucked shellfish and daily-catch selections on styrofoam plates. The smoked fish is a great way to start your meal. Beer is the drink of choice here, although other beverages and a full bar are available, too. Though the locals tend to sit inside, ask for a seat on the small but pretty deck overlooking the piers.

Jimmy Buffett's Margaritaville Cafe. 500 Duval St. ☎ **305/292-1435.** Reservations not accepted. Sandwiches $5–$6; fresh-fish platter $10; margarita $5. AE, MC, V. Sun–Thurs 11am–2am, Fri–Sat 11am–4am. AMERICAN.

This easygoing restaurant/bar is heavy on soups, salads, sandwiches, and local catches. A long bar runs the length of the place, from which you can see the adjacent gift shop. Most people come here to eat (and drink), and the food is actually quite good. Don't get too ambitious, though. You and the rest of the tourists have just come for the myth. So have a margarita, enjoy watching the constant procession up and down Duval Street, and have fun. But don't ask the bar staff to play "Cheeseburger in Paradise."

Mangia, Mangia. 900 Southard St. (corner of Margaret St.). ☎ **305/294-2469.** Reservations recommended. Main courses $9–$13. MC, V. Daily 5:30–10pm. ITALIAN/AMERICAN.

This low-key Italian trattoria is one of Key West's best values and serves some of the best Italian food in the Keys. Locals appreciate that they can get inexpensive and good food here. You'll find this great Chicago-style pasta place off the beaten track, in a little corner storefront. The family-run restaurant offers superb homemade pastas of every description, including one of the tastiest marinaras around. Past the glossy glass front room is a fantastic little outdoor patio dotted with twinkling pepper lights and lots of plants. When the weather is nice, it's worth waiting for an outdoor table; relax out back with a glass of one of their excellent wines or homemade beer while you wait.

KEY WEST AFTER DARK
THEATER

The Red Barn Theater, 319 Duval St. (☎ 305/296-9911), was originally a carriage house connected to one of the island's oldest homes and now houses one of Key West's best stages. The 88-seat theater has gone through many changes since it was reborn in the 1940s as the home to the Key West Community Players. Local and visiting productions vary in quality, but are sometimes very good. Call for current performance information.

The Waterfront Playhouse, Mallory Docks (☎ 305/294-5015), is larger and prettier then the Red Barn and attracts a variety of theatrical performances, most often drama or musicals. Performances are usually held from December through May. Call for information and show times.

The **Eaton Street Theatre,** 524 Eaton St. (☎ 305/296-3030), a converted church that Harry S Truman used to attend, now runs "Flamingo Follies," a glitzy, fun-filled musical. The show runs most nights during the winter months at the theater's night-club, **Club Chameleon.** Call for more information and show times.

THE CLUB, MUSIC & BAR SCENE

Duval Street is the Bourbon Street of Florida. Between the T-shirt shops and cloth-ing boutiques is bar after bar, serving stiff drinks to revelers who usually bounce from one to another. Here's a rundown of the best.

Barefoot Bob's. 525 Duval St. ☎ 305/296-5858.

A local hangout for Deadheads, Barefoot Bob's attracts a multi-generational mix of tie-dye freaks and granola-types. Many patrons come barefoot, others wearing their Birkenstocks. Take a seat on the outside wooden deck where on Wednesdays and the weekends you'll hear classic rock with a heavy dose of the Grateful Dead, of course. An eclectic menu includes some excellent vegan choices and an array of seafood, pastas, and steaks, plus an Oreo chocolate cheesecake.

Captain Tony's Saloon. 428 Greene St. ☎ 305/294-1838.

Just around the corner from Duval's beaten path, Captain Tony's jealously retains its seasoned and quixotic pre-tourist ambience, complete with old-time regulars who remember the island before cruise ships docked here and who say Hemingway drank, caroused, and even wrote here. The smoky, small, and cozy bar is owned by Capt. Tony Tarracino, a former Key West mayor who is known in these parts for his acerbic wit and unorthodox ways.

Durty Harry's. 208 Duval St. ☎ 305/296-4890.

One of Duval's largest entertainment complexes, Durty Harry's features live rock bands almost every night (and most afternoons, too), and several outdoor bars. **Upstairs at Rick's** is an indoor/outdoor dance club that's very popular almost every night. **The Red Garter,** yet another related business on this property, is a pocket-size strip club popular with local bachelor parties and the few visitors who know about it.

Fat Tuesdays. 305 Duval St. ☎ 305/296-9373.

More than 20 colorful, slushy, slightly chemical alcoholic concoctions swirl in spe-cial see-through tanks behind this lively outdoor bar. Located on an elevated deck near the busiest end of Duval, the bar attracts a rowdy college-age crowd as well as rowdy any-age locals.

Hog's Breath Saloon. 400 Front St. ☎ 305/296-4222.

Except for the fact that they sell lots of T-shirts, this bar has no relationship with its namesake corporate chain with locations in California and around the country. It's an inviting, fun place to hang out, with several outdoor bars, good live music, a raw bar, and decent food. Daily happy-hour specials run from 5pm to 7pm.

Jimmy Buffett's Margaritaville Cafe. 500 Duval St. ☎ 305/292-1435.

This large, friendly, and easygoing restaurant/bar/gift shop features live bands most nights, and Mr. Buffett himself has even been known to take the stage. The touristy cafe is furnished with plenty of Buffett memorabilia, including gold records, photos, and drawings. The margaritas are generous in both quality and strength.

Sloppy Joe's. 201 Duval St. ☎ 305/294-5717.

Scholars and drunks debate whether this is the same Sloppy Joe's that Hemingway wrote about, but there's no argument that this classic bar's turn-of-the-century wooden ceiling and cracked tile floors are Key West originals. The popular and raucous bar is crowded with tourists almost 24 hours a day, and there's almost always live music.

Sunset Pier Bar. At Ocean Key House, Zero Duval St. ☎ **305/296-7040.**

It's on a pier, located behind Ocean Key House, at the end of Duval Street, with great views of the harbor and sunset. The bar offers a limited menu and a full range of tropical coolers. Live music begins as the sun goes down.

THE GAY SCENE

After the 1995 fire on Duval Street that destroyed the famous Copa, the gay scene has moved to various small, intimate bars around the city. The parties may not be on such a large scale as they once were at the Copa, but they are lively nonetheless. Here are a few of the more popular watering holes Key West has to offer.

Atlantic Shores Motel. 510 South St. ☎ **305/296-2491.**

Every Sunday night is "Tea by the Sea" on the pier at the Atlantic Shores Motel. Disco is the music of choice and who ever is in town usually comes to this well-known gathering place. Show up at dusk.

The Copa. 623 Duval St. ☎ **305/296-8521.**

At press time the Copa was in the midst of being rebuilt after their August 1995 fire; there's no set opening date as of yet, so call. Once the busiest and biggest nightclub in Key West, the Copa's main attraction was a large dance floor featuring disco music and nine rooms able to accommodate up to 1,200 patrons.

La Terraza. 1125 Duval St. ☎ **305/296-6706.**

Better known around town as La-Te-Da, La Terraza puts on themed poolside parties every Sunday that vary weekly at the discretion of the owners. The night spot is open daily from 10am to 4am, although the hours have also been known to change.

One Saloon. 524 Duval St. ☎ **305/296-8118.**

This popular gay dance bar features a male dancer strutting across the top of the bar nightly. The mostly male clientele frequents this spot with nondescript decor and an outdoor garden bar for those who want to get away from yet more disco music.

6 The Dry Tortugas

70 miles W of Key West

Because the Dry Tortugas are only accessible by boat or seaplane, few visitors realize that Florida's Keys don't end at Key West. Ponce de León, named them "las Tortugas" for their abundance of nesting sea turtles. Oceanic chats later carried the preface "dry" to warn mariners that fresh water was unavailable here. The seven keys that make up the Tortugas—Garden, Loggerhead, Bush, East, Middle, Hospital, and Long—are all very small; Loggerhead Key, the largest, is only 25 acres. The primary reason for visiting the Dry Tortugas is for bird-watching. The islands are nesting grounds and roosting sites for thousands of tropical and subtropical oceanic birds. There's also a historical fort, good fishing, and terrific snorkeling around shallow reefs.

ESSENTIALS

GETTING THERE   By Boat   Yankee Fleet, P.O. Box 5903, Key West (☎ 305/294-7009 or 800/634-0939), offers day trips from Key West for sightseeing, snorkeling, or both. Cruises leave from the Land's End Marina, at Margaret Street, Monday, Wednesday, and Saturday at 7:30am and breakfast is served on board. The journey takes three hours. Once on the island, you can join a guided tour, or explore Garden Key on your own. Boats return to Key West by 7pm. Tours cost $75 per person, including breakfast. Snorkeling equipment is available for rent, and costs $5. Phone for reservations.

By Seaplane   Key West Seaplane Service, 5603 W. College Rd., Key West (☎ 305/294-6978), flies daily from Key West to Garden Key in about one hour. Half-day trips depart Key West daily at both 8am and noon, include two hours of ground time, and cost $159 per person. Full-day trips last from 8am to 4pm and cost $275 per person. Reservations are required.

EXPLORING THE DRY TORTUGAS

Fort Jefferson, a huge six-sided 19th-century fortress, occupies the entire island of Garden Key and is the primary destination for most visitors. Begun in 1846, the stone fort was built with eight-foot-thick walls and parapets accommodating 450 guns. The invention of the rifled cannon during the 30 years of the fort's construction made masonry fortifications obsolete, and the building was never completed. For 10 years, from 1863 to 1873, Fort Jefferson served as a prison; a kind of "Alcatraz East." Among its prisoners were four of the "Lincoln Conspirators," including Samuel A. Mudd, the doctor who set the broken leg of fugitive assassin John Wilkes Booth. In January 1935, Fort Jefferson became a National Monument administered by the National Park Service.

OUTDOOR ACTIVITIES & SPORTS

BIRD WATCHING   Birding is the Dry Tortugas' main attraction; more than 100 species can be spotted here. The islands are located in the middle of the migration flyway between North and South America, and serve as an important rest stop. The birding season peaks from mid-March to mid-April, when thousands of birds including thrushes, orioles, and swallows show up. In season, a continuous procession of migrant birds fly over or rest at the islands. About 10,000 terns nest here each spring, and many other species from the West Indies can be found here year-round.

FISHING   Snapper, tarpon, grouper, and other fish are common, and fishing is popular. A saltwater license is required (see "Sporting in the Keys," above, for complete information). No bait or boating services are available in the Tortugas, but there are day docks on Garden Key as well as a cleaning table. Waters are roughest during winter, but fishing is excellent year-round.

Tortugas Unlimited, 6100 Griffin Rd., Suite 205, Davie, FL 33314 (☎ 305/791-1442 or 800/878-3474), takes anglers out for two- and three-day fishing trips to the Dry Tortugas. The boat leaves from Stock Island, Mile Marker 5, (about 5 miles north of Key West). Two-day trips leave Friday and return Sunday and cost $200 per person. The price includes sleeping accommodations on the boat, bait and tackle, but not food. Three-day trips leave the last Friday of every month and return the following Monday. They cost $240 per person. Phone for reservations.

SNORKELING & DIVING   The warm, clear, and shallow waters of the Dry Tortugas combine to produce optimum conditions for snorkeling and scuba diving. Four endangered species of sea turtles—the green, leatherback, Atlantic ridley, and hawksbill—can be found here, along with myriad marine life. The region just outside the sea wall of Garden Key's Fort Jefferson is excellent for underwater touring; an abundant variety of fish, corals, and more live in just three or four feet of water.

CAMPING

A more isolated spot can't be found anywhere else in Florida. The abundance of birds doesn't make it quiet, but camping here—a literal stone's throw from the water—is as picturesque as life gets. Campers are allowed to pitch tents on **Garden Key** exclusively. Picnic tables, cooking grills, and toilets are provided, but all supplies must be packed in, and out. Sites are free, and are available on a first-come, first-serve basis.

Appendix

Useful Toll-Free Numbers

AIRLINES

American	800/433-7300 or
	800/543-1586 TDD
Carnival	800/824-7386
Continental	800/525-0280 or
	800/343-9195 TDD
Delta	800/221-1212 or
	800/831-4488 TDD
Kiwi	800/538-5494
Northwest	800/225-2525
TWA	800/221-2000
United	800/241-6522
USAir	800/428-4322

CAR RENTAL COMPANIES

Alamo Rent A Car	800/327-9633
Avis	800/331-1212 or
	800/331-2323 TDD
Budget	800/527-0700 or
	800/826-5510 TDD
Dollar Rent A Car	800/800-4000
Enterprise	800/325-8007
Hertz	800/654-3131 or
	800/654-2280 TDD
National	800/CAR-RENT or
	800/328-6323 TDD
Payless Car Rental	800/PAYLESS
Thrifty	800/367-2277 or
	800/358-5856 TDD
Value	800/327-2501

LODGING: MAJOR CHAINS

Best Western International, Inc.	800/528-1234 or
	800/528-2222 TDD
Comfort Inns	800/228-5150 or
	800/228-3323 TDD

Days Inn	800/325-2525 or 800/325-3297 TDD
Econo Lodges	800/55-ECONO or 800/228-3323 TDD
Hampton Inns	800/HAMPTON or 800/451-HTDD TDD
Hilton	800/HILTONS or 800/368-1133 TDD
Holiday Inns	800/HOLIDAY or 800/238-5544 TDD
Howard Johnson	800/654-2000 or 800/654-8442 TDD
Hyatt	800/228-9000 or 800/228-9548 TDD
La Quinta Inns	800/531-5900 or 800/426-3101 TDD
Marriott	800/228-9290 or 800/228-7014 TDD
Marriott Residence Inn	800/331-3131 or 800/228-7014 TDD
Quality Inns	800/228-5151 or 800/228-3323 TDD
Radisson	800/333-3333
Ramada	800/2-RAMADA
Red Roof Inns	800/843-7663 or 800/843-9999 TDD
Rodeway Inns	800/228-2000 or 800/228-3323 TDD
Sheraton	800/325-3535 or 800/325-1717 TDD
Super 8 Motels	800/800-8000 or 800/533-6634 TDD
Travelodge	800/255-3050

Index

MIAMI

Accommodations, 43–76. *See also specific accommodations*
  best bets for, 45
  for children, 45, 63
  Coconut Grove, 72–74
  Coral Gables, 68–72
  Downtown, 63–66
  Key Biscayne, 62–63
  long-term, 75–76
  Miami Beach, 54–61, 74–75
  North Dade, 68
  reservations, 44–45
  South Beach, 45–54
  West Miami, 66–68
Acme Acting Company, 178
Actors' Playhouse, 177
Addresses, locating, 33
After dark, 176–86
Airboat tours, Everglades National Park, 198
Airport. *See* Miami International Airport
Air tours, 136–37
Air travel
  to Miami, 20–22
  to/within the U.S., 26–27
Alexander All-Suite Luxury Hotel, 56
  restaurant, 95
Amelia Earhart Park, 134–35, 136
American Express, 39
American Police Hall of Fame and Museum, 131
Anacapri, 118
Anhinga Trail (Everglades National Park), 195
Animal parks, 127–28
Annual events, festivals and fairs, 15–18
Antiques, shopping for, 164–65
Aquariums, 127–28, 136
Aragon Café, 112
Architecture, 9–10. *See also* Art Deco District

Area code, 39
Area Stage Company, 178
Arquitectonica, 10, 154
Art Deco District, 2, 7, 9–10, 33, 126–27, 152. *See also* South Beach
  Art Deco Weekend, 15
  bicycling tour, 127
  buildings of, 126, 152–53, 157–58, 160
  information sources, 12, 126, 157
  Lummus Park Beach, 123, 126–27
  organized tours, 127, 138
  walking tours, 157–60
    organized, 127
  Welcome Center, 126, 157
Art festivals, 15–18
Art galleries, 164–65
Art museums
  Bass Museum of Art, 128, 130
  Center for Fine Arts, 131
  Florida Museum of Hispanic and Latin American Art, 130–31
  Museum of Contemporary Art, 131–32
  The Wolfsonian, 130
Astor Hotel, 48
Atlantis Hotel, 154
Auto racing, 16, 17–18
Avalon Hotel, 50–51
Aventura Mall, 162–63

Bagel Factory, 92
Bahamas
  cruises to, 202–3
  weekend packages to, 203
Bal Harbour, 34
  accommodations, 57–58
  Beach, 123
  boating, 139
  shopping, 163, 173
Ballet, 179

Ballooning: Great Sunrise Balloon Race & Festival, 16–17
Barnacle, The, 133, 156
Baseball, 148
Basketball: Miami Heat, 3, 148
Bass Museum of Art, 128, 130
Bay Harbor Inn, 45, 59
Baymar Ocean Resort, 60
Bayside Marketplace, 137, 150, 153, 163, 168
  restaurants, 103
Bayside Seafood Restaurant and Hidden Cove Bar, 100
Beaches, 122–26
  best of, 123, 126
  Biscayne National Park, 189
  midnight swims, 2
  nudist, 126
  tanning on, 2, 126
Beachware, shopping for, 166
Best Western Gateway to the Keys (Florida City), 200–201
Beverly Hills Cafe, 78, 109, 110
Bicé Ristorante, 79, 84–85, 183
Bicycling, 39, 142–43
  Art Deco District tour, 127
  Everglades National Park, 194, 196–97
  Shark Valley, 142–43, 197
Bill Baggs Cape Florida State Park, 135
Biltmore Hotel Coral Gables, 45, 70, 138, 156
Bingo, 144
Birdwatching, Everglades National Park, 194, 197
Biscayne Bay, 153
  history of, 6, 7, 8
Biscayne Miracle Mile Cafeteria, 115

Biscayne National Park,
187–90
beaches, 189
boating, 188
boat tours, 140, 189
camping, 190
Elliott Key, 187, 188,
189
fishing, 188–89
recreational activities,
188–89
scuba diving/snorkeling,
3, 141, 188, 189
traveling to, 187–88
visitor information, 188
Bistro, The, 79, 112, 113
Blues Hotlines, 180
Boat cruises, to the Bahamas,
202–3
Boating and sailing, 2,
139–40
Biscayne National Park,
188
Columbus Day Regatta,
17
Everglades National Park,
191, 194, 197
houseboating, Everglades
National Park, 200
marinas, 144, 191
Miami International Boat
Show, 15
Boat tours, 137–38
Biscayne National Park,
140, 189
Everglades National Park,
198–99
Book Fair International,
Miami, 17
Bookstores, 166–67, 186
Botanical gardens.
See Gardens
Brigham Gardens, 53–54
Buses, 37
to Miami, 23
tours by, 138
within the U.S., 27–28

Cafe Hammock, 119
Cafe Prima Pasta, 96
Cafe Ragazzi, 96
Cafe Sci Sci, 116
Cafe Tu Tu Tango, 118
Caffe Abracci, 114
Calendar of events, 15–18

Camping, 74
Biscayne National Park,
190
Everglades National Park,
199–200
Canoeing, 140–41, 188
Everglades National Park,
194, 197–98
Caribbean Delite, 103
Caribbean Marketplace, 153
Cars and driving, 22, 37–38
automobile organizations,
28
driving tours, 150–56
parking, 38
rentals, 38
safety tips, 18–19, 26
Casa Grande Suite Hotel, 46
Casa Juancho, 79, 105
Cavalier, 51
Center for Fine Arts, 131
Centro Vasco, 105–6
Century, The, 51
Chef Allen's, 107–8
Children
accommodations, 45, 63
restaurants, 78, 109
sights and activities,
134–36. See also
specific parks
animal parks,
127–28, 136
Miami Museum of
Science, 132, 136
Miami Youth
Museum, 132, 136
Scott Rakow Youth
Center, 136
Space Transit
Planetarium, 132,
136
China Grill, 84
Chokoloskee Island Park, 197
Christy's, 111–12
Chrysanthemum, 88
Churchill's Hideaway, 180
Cigarettes and cigars,
shopping for, 167–68
Cinemas, 186
Classical music, 178
Clay Hotel & Youth Hostel,
74
Climate, 14–15
Clothes, shopping for,
162–64, 168–70

Coconut Grove, 36, 116, 153
accommodations, 72–74
Art Festival, 16
bicycling, 142
boating and sailing, 139,
140
dance clubs, 181–82
driving tour, 154–56
entertainment, 156
Goombay Festival, 17, 36
King Mango Strut, 18
performing arts, 156,
177, 180, 181
restaurants, 116–18
shopping, 162, 164, 167,
169, 170, 173
sightseeing, 132, 133
Coconut Grove Playhouse,
156, 177
Colonnade Building, 156
Colony Hotel, 158
Colony Theater, 177, 179
Columbus Day Regatta, 17
Compostela Motel, 60–61
Concert Association of
Florida (CAF), 178
Consulates, 28–29
Coral Castle, 133
Coral Gables, 36, 68, 70, 153
accommodations, 68–72
Art and Gallery tour,
139, 164
art galleries, 164–65
driving tour, 153, 156
Festival Miami, 17
golf, 156
health clubs, 145
history of, 7
nightlife, 184
Oktoberfest, 17
performing arts, 177–80
restaurants in or near,
111–16
shopping, 165, 166–67,
170, 172, 173, 174
Miracle Mile, 161,
162
sightseeing, 132, 133–34
tennis, 147
walking tours, organized,
138–39
Cost of everyday items, 13
Crandon Park Beach, 123,
147
Crepe Maker, The, 103

Crime. *See* Safety
Crowne Plaza Hotel, 64
    restaurant, 101–2
Cruises, to the Bahamas,
    202–3
Crystal Café, 78, 96, 98
Cuban Art and Books,
    167
Cuban cigars, shopping
    for, 167–68
Cuban music, 184–85
Cubans. *See also* Little Havana
    history of immigration,
    7–8
Cuisine, 10–11, 77. *See also*
    Restaurants
    food festivals, 15–16
    New World, 2, 10, 77, 112
    restaurants by, 80–82
    Spanish, 105. *See also*
        Little Havana,
        restaurants
Currency exchange, 28
Curry's, 98
Customs regulations, 25

Dade County Auditorium,
    179
Dadeland Mall, 163
Dance clubs, 2, 181–83
Dance companies, 179
Delano Hotel, 45, 46–47, 152
Department stores, 162–64
DeSoto Plaza and Fountain,
    156
Dezerland Surfside Beach
    Hotel, 59
    boating rentals, 139
Disabled travelers, 19
Doctors, 39
Dog racing, 148
Dominique's, 78, 79, 95
Don Shula's Hotel and
    Golf Club, 67
Doral Golf Resort and Spa,
    45, 66–67
Doral Ocean Beach Resort,
    56–57, 63
    boating rentals, 139
Doubletree Hotel at Coconut
    Grove, 74
Downtown Miami, 34, 101
    accommodations, 63–66
    performing arts, 179–80,
    181

restaurants, 101–4
shopping,
    Fashion District, 169
sightseeing, 130–31

Earhart, Amelia, 8
East Coast Fisheries, 102,
    163
Eden Roc Hotel and Marina,
    58, 153
Electronics, shopping for,
    168
Emergencies, 29, 39, 40, 41
Entertainment, 176–86
Entry into the U.S.,
    requirements for, 24
Essex House, 51–52, 157
Estate Wines & Gourmet
    Foods, The, 115
Estefan, Gloria, 8–9, 152
Everglades Hotel, 65
Everglades National Park,
    190–201
    access points, 191
    accommodations near,
        200–201
    airboat tours, 198
    bicycling, 194, 196–97
        Shark Valley,
        142–43, 197
    birdwatching, 194, 197
    boating, 191, 194, 197
    boat tours, 198–99
    camping, 199–200
    canoeing, 194, 197–98
    fishing, 198
    hiking, 194–96
    houseboating, 200
    Main Park Road, trails
        along, 194–96
    ranger programs, 192
        safety tips, 194
    tours, organized, 198–99
    tram tours, 199
    traveling to, 191
    visitor information,
        191–92
Everglades Tower Inn
    (Ochopee), 201

Factory outlets, 164
Fairchild Tropical Gardens,
    134
    The Ramble, 18
Fairmont Hotel, 157

Families. *See* Children
Farrel, Perry, 9
Fashions, shopping for,
    162–64, 168–70
Fast facts, 28–31, 39–42
Festivals, 15–18
Film(s)
    festivals, 16, 17, 186
    movie theaters, 186
    set in Miami, 8
Fishbone Grille, 79, 102
Fisher, Carl, 7
Fisher Island Club, 45,
    47–48
Fish Market, The, 101–2
Fishing, 134, 135, 144
    Biscayne National Park,
        188–89
    Everglades National Park,
        198
Fitness centers, 145–46
Flagler Greyhound Track,
    148
Flamingo Lodge Marina &
    Outpost Resort, 191, 197,
    198
    accommodations, 200
    boat tours, 198–99
    marina, 191, 197
    restaurant, 201
Florida City
    accommodations,
        200–201
    Alabama Jacks, 206, 208
    restaurants, 201
Florida Grand Opera,
    178–79
Florida Marlins, 148
Florida Museum of Hispanic
    and Latin American Art,
    130–31
Florida Philharmonic
    Orchestra, 178
Florida Shakespeare Theatre,
    177
Fontainebleau Hilton, 45, 57,
    63, 152
    Annual Chocolate
        Festival & Fair, 17
Food. *See* Cuisine
Food markets, 170–72
Football, 149
    Miami Dolphins, 3, 149
    Orange Bowl, 15
Foreign visitors, 24–31

Forge Restaurant, The, 78, 95–96
Freize, 80
Frommer's favorite experiences, 2–3
Fruit
 citrus, 11, 163
 fruit stand: Robert Is Here, 190
 shopping for, 163, 190
 strawberry farms, 143

Gables, The. *See* Coral Gables
Gallery, The, 75
Gardens
 Fairchild Tropical Gardens, 134
 Parrot Jungle and Gardens, 128
 Preston B. Bird and Mary Heinlein Fruit and Spice Park, 134
Gay men and lesbian travelers, 19–20, 183
George, Dr. Paul, walking tours with, 138
Golf, 144–45
 pro shops, 172
 tournaments, 16
Gourmet Diner, The, 108
Governor Hotel, The, 52
Grand Bay Hotel, 72–73, 154
Green Street Café, 117, 154
Greenwich Village, 102
Greynolds Park, 145, 147
Grillfish, 88
Grove Isle Club and Resort, 73
Gulfstream Park, 149
Gumbo-Limbo Trail (Everglades National Park), 195
Gusman Center for the Performing Arts, 179–80
Gusman Concert Hall, 180
Gyms, 145–46

Haulover Beach Park, 126, 144, 147
Health clubs, 145–46
Helicopter tours, 136
Here Comes the Sun, 110

Hialeah
 Amelia Earhart Park, 134–35, 136
 history of, 7
Hialeah Park, 149
Hibiscus Island, 152
Hiking, 189, 194–96
Hispanic and Latin American Art, Florida Museum of, 130–31
Historical and cultural museums
 American Police Hall of Fame and Museum, 131
 The Barnacle, 133, 156
 Historical Museum of Southern Florida, 131
 Holocaust Memorial, 130
 Sanford L. Ziff Jewish Museum of Florida, 130
 The Wolfsonian, 130
Historical Museum of Southern Florida, 131
Historic sites
 Coral Castle, 133
 Hialeah Park, 149
 Spanish Monastery Cloisters, 133
 Venetian Pool, 133–34, 156
 Villa Vizcaya, 132–33, 154
History, 6–8
Hobie Beach, 123
Holidays, 29
Hollywood Greyhound Track, 148
Holocaust Memorial, 130
Homestead
 restaurants, 201
 sightseeing, 133, 134
Honey, shopping for, 172
Horse racing, 149
Hospitals, 29
Hostels, in Miami Beach, 74–75
Hotel Continental Riande, 53
Hotel Inter-Continental Miami, 45, 63–64
 restaurant, 101
Hotel Place St. Michel, 45, 71–72

House of India, 115–16
Houseboating, Everglades National Park, 200
Hungry Sailor, The, 180
Hurricanes, 14
Hyatt Regency Coral Gables, 71
 nightlife, 184
Hy-Vong, 106

Imperial Hotel, 154, 158
Indian Creek Hotel, 60
Information sources, 12–13, 32. *See also* Telephone numbers, useful
In-line skating, 127, 146
Inn on the Bay, The, 61
Insurance, 18, 25
International Place, 154
Irie Isle, 110–11
Itineraries, 121–22

Jackie Gleason Theater of the Performing Arts, 180
Jai alai, 149
Jazz, 180–81
Jeffrey's, 88–89
Jetskis, 140
Jewelry stores, 173
Jewish Museum of Florida, Sanford L. Ziff, 130
Jimbo's, 171
Joe Robbie Stadium, 148
Joe's Stone Crab Restaurant, 85, 163
Jogging, 147
John Martin's, 80, 114–15
Johnson, Don, 9
Johnson, Jimmy, 3, 149
Judd, James, 178
Juice Bar, The, 111

Kaleidoscope, 79, 116–17
Kayaking, 140–41. *See also* Canoeing
Kent, The, 52–53
Key Biscayne, 34, 99
 accommodations, 62–63, 75–76
 Art Festival, 15
 beaches, 123, 135
 bicycling, 143
 boating and sailing, 139–40
 driving tour, 154
 fishing, 144

food markets, 171
golf, 145
jetskiing, 140
marinas, 144
restaurants, 99–101
scuba diving, 141
sights and activities,
    127–28, 135
tennis, 147
windsurfing, 142
Key Colony for Guests,
    75–76
King Orange Jamboree
    Parade, 18

La Boulangerie, 100–101
La Carreta, 106
La Sandwicherie, 92
Lagoon, The, 108–9
Languages, 29
    Spanish cuisine terms, 105
Larios on the Beach, 89
Larry and Penny Thompson
    Park, 135, 147
Las Tapas, 103
Latin nightclubs, 184–85
Laundry and dry cleaning, 40
Laurenzo's Cafe, 111
Layout of Miami, 32–33
Le Festival, 114
Le Pavillon, 101
Legal aid, 29
L'Entrecote de Paris, 89–90
Les Deux Fontaines, 79, 90
Libraries, 40
Lighthouse, in Bill Baggs
    Cape Florida State Park,
    135
Lingerie, shopping for, 173
Links at Key Biscayne, 145,
    147
Liquor laws, 40
Liquor stores, 174–75
Literary scene, 186
Little Haiti, 36, 153
Little Havana, 2, 36
    Calle Ocho, 2, 104
    Calle Ocho Festival, 16
    cigars, shopping for, 167
    nightlife, 184–85
    restaurants, 104–6, 186
    shopping, 173–74
    Three Kings Parade, 15
Locust Apartments, 158
Loews Miami Beach Hotel,
    152

Long Pine Key (Everglades
    National Park), 195
Lost property, 40
Lummus Park Beach, 123,
    126–27
Lyon Freres, 80, 92

Madonna, 9, 84, 133
    mansion of, 154
Magazines, 30, 40–41
Mahogany Hammock Trail
    (Everglades National Park),
    196
Mail, 29–30, 41
Main Park Road, Everglades
    National Park, 194–96
Majestic Hotel, 158
Malls, shopping, 162–64
Maps, street, 33
Marinas, 144, 191
Markets, food, 170–72
Mark's Place, 108
Marley, Bob, 9
Mayfair House Hotel, 73
Mediterranean Café, 79
Melting Pot, The, 109
Mercury, 90
Mermaid, The, 53
Merrick, George, 45, 70,
    153, 156
Metro-Dade Cultural Center,
    131
Metromover, 37
Metrorail, 37
Miami Ballet Company
    (MBC), 179
Miami Beach, 1, 34, 95. See
    also Art Deco District;
    South Beach
    accommodations, 54–61,
        74–75
    beaches, 122–23, 126–27
    bicycling, 142
    Boardwalk, 147
    boating, 2, 139
    driving tour, 152–53
    fishing, 144
    food markets, 170
    golf, 145
        pro shops, 172
    health clubs, 146
    history of, 7
    nightlife, 181–83
    performing arts, 180,
        181
    restaurants, 95–99

scuba diving, 141
shopping, 168–69, 174
sightseeing, 128–33
Miami Beach International
    Travellers Hostel, 74–75
Miami Beach Place, 98–99
Miami Beach Post Office,
    160
Miami Chamber Symphony,
    178
Miami City Ballet, 179
Miami City Hall, 154
Miami Dolphins, 3, 149
Miami Film Festival, 16, 186
Miami Heat, 3, 148
Miami International Airport,
    8, 20–22, 27
    traveling to/from, 21–22
Miami International Airport
    Hotel, 21, 67–68
Miami Lakes, restaurants,
    107
Miami Metrozoo, 127, 136
Miami Museum of Science
    and Space Transit
    Planetarium, 132, 136
Miami River Inn, 65–66
Miami Seaquarium, 127–28,
    136
Miami Youth Museum, 132,
    136
Miccosukee Indian Village,
    144, 198
    restaurants, 119
Mojazz Cafe, 180
Money, 13–14, 25
Monkey Jungle, 128
Monty's Bayshore Restaurant,
    117
Monty's Stone Crab/Seafood
    House, 85
Motorboating. See Boating
Movie theaters, 186
Mrs. Mendoza's Tacos al
    Carbon, 79, 92–93
Muhammad Ali, 8
Museum of Contemporary
    Art (MOCA), 131–32
Museums. See Art
    museums; Historical
    and cultural museums;
    and specific
    museums
Music
    classical, 178
    festivals, 15, 17, 18

Music *(cont.)*
  Latin, 184–85
  live and jazz, 180–81
  Miami Reggae Festival,
    17
  opera, 178–79
  salsa, 185
  shopping for, 173–74

National Hotel, 152
National parks. *See* Biscayne
  Bay National Park;
  Everglades National Park
Neighborhoods, 33–37. *See
  also specific neighborhoods*
Nemo Restaurant, The, 79,
  85–86
New Delhi Restaurant,
  109–10
New Theatre, 177
New World Symphony,
  178
News Café, 93, 152, 158,
  186
Newspapers, 30, 40–41
Nightlife, 176–86
Nixon, Richard M., 9
Normandy Isle, 153
Norman's, 112
Norma's, 86
North Bay Village, 153
North Dade, 107
  accommodations, 68
  restaurants, 107–11
Nude beaches, 126

Oasis, The, 101
Oceanarium, 127–28, 136
Ocean Front Hotel, 48, 50
  restaurant, 90
Oggi Caffe, 98
Omni Colonnade Hotel,
  70–71, 112
Omni International Mall,
  153
Opa-Locka, 7, 16
Opera, 178–79
Osteria del Teatro, 79,
  86–87

Pacific Time, 87
Pa-Hay-Okee Trail
  (Everglades National Park),
  196
Palm, The, 96
Palm Island, 152

Park Central, 157
Park Washington Hotel, 54
Parks, 134–36. *See also*
  Biscayne Bay National
  Park; Everglades National
  Park
    Amelia Earhart Park,
      134–35, 136
    Bill Baggs Cape Florida
      State Park, 135
    Larry and Penny
      Thompson Park, 135,
      147
    Preston B. Bird and Mary
      Heinlein Fruit and
      Spice Park, 134
    Tropical Park, 136
Parrot Jungle and Gardens,
  128
Pelican Island, 123
Peoples, 3
Performing arts, 177–80
Pets, shopping for, 174
Pharmacies, 41
Photographic needs, 41
Picknicking, 80, 123
Pinelands Trail (Everglades
  National Park), 196
Planetarium, Space Transit,
  132, 136
Planning your trip, 12–23
Police Hall of Fame and
  Museum, American, 131
Pollo Tropical, 79, 119–20
Port of Miami, 152
Post offices, 29–30, 41, 160
Preston B. Bird and Mary
  Heinlein Fruit and Spice
  Park, 134
Puerto Sagua, 93

Rainfall, average monthly, 14
Raja's, 103–4
Record stores, 173–74
Recreational activities,
  139–47. *See also* Parks;
  and specific activities
Red Lantern, The, 78, 117
Religious services, 41
Rental properties, 75
Resale stores, 169–70
Restaurants, 10–11, 77–120.
  See also specific restaurants
    best bets for, 78–80
    for children, 78, 109
    Coconut Grove, 116–18

Coral Gables and
  environs, 111–16
by cuisine, 80–82
Downtown, 101–4
Key Biscayne, 99–101
late-night, 79, 186
Little Havana, 104–6
Miami Beach, 95–99
North Dade, 107–11
South Beach, 82–95
South Miami, 118–20
West Dade, 107
Riande Continental Bayside,
  65
Riley, Pat, 3, 148
Ritz Plaza, The, 50
Robert Is Here, 190
Rollerblading, 127, 146
Roots, Rhythms, & Rituals,
  182
Rose's Bar and Lounge, 181
Rourke, Mickey, 9
Rusty Pelican, 99

Safety, 3, 18–19, 26, 42,
  194
Sailing. *See* Boating and
  sailing
Salsa, 185
Salvadore Park, 147
Sanford L. Ziff Jewish
  Museum of Florida, 130
Sawgrass Mills, 164
Science, Miami Museum of,
  132, 136
Scuba diving/snorkeling, 141
  Biscayne Bay
    National Park, 3, 141,
    188, 189
Seafood, 11
  shopping for, 163
Seasons, 14–15, 192
Senior citizen travelers, 20
Señor Frogs, 109, 117–18
Sergio's, 116
Shark Valley Entrance,
  Everglades National Park,
  191
Shelborne Hotel, 152
Sheldon's Drugs, 99
Shells, hunting for, on Bal
  Harbour Beach, 123
Sheraton Bal Harbour Beach
  Resort, 57–58
Sheraton Brickell Point
  Miami, 64–65

Sherbrooke Cooperative, 157
Shoe stores, 170
Shopping, 161–75
Shorty's, 119
Shula, Don, 67, 79, 107, 149
Shula's Steak House, 79, 107
Sightseeing, 121–36. *See also* Walking tours
Silver Sands Oceanfront Motel, 62
Simon, Kerry, 90
Smoke houses, 11, 171
Snorkeling. *See* Scuba diving/snorkeling
Sonesta Beach Resort Hotel Key Biscayne, 45, 62–63
South Beach, 33. *See also* Art Deco District
    accommodations, 45–54
    beaches, 123
    bicycling, 142
    dance clubs, 181–83
    driving tour, 152
    gay men and lesbian travelers, 183
    health clubs, 146
    history of, 7
    Lummus Park Beach, 123, 126–27
    performing arts, 178–81
    renovation of, 10
    restaurants, 82–95
        late-night, 79, 186
    shopping, 166, 168–69, 173
        Lincoln Road, 162
    sightseeing, 128–30
Southeast Financial Center, 154
South Miami, restaurants, 118–20
South Pointe Seafood House, 78, 87
Spa at the Doral, The, 45
Space Transit Planetarium, 132, 136
Spanish Monastery Cloisters, 133
Special events, 15–18. *See also specific events*
Sports, 139–49. *See also* Parks; *and specific sports*
Sports Cafe, 93–94
S & S Restaurant, 104

Stallone, Sylvester, 9, 133
    bayfront mansion of, 154
Star Island, 152
Starck, Philip, 45, 47
Stefano's, 99–100
Stephan's Gourmet Market & Cafe, 94
Strand, The, 90, 157
Strawberries, picking your own, 143
Student travelers, 20
Suez Oceanfront Resort, 61
Sundays on the Bay, 100
Sunny Isles, 34
    accommodations, 61
    bingo, 144
    restaurants, 99, 109
SuperShuttle, 22
Surfing, 123. *See also* Windsurfing
    shopping for boards, 166
Surfside, 34
    restaurants, 96, 99
Susser, Allen, 107
Swimming, 141. *See also* Beaches
    lessons, 141–42
    Venetian Pool, 133–34, 142
Symphonies, 178

Tap Tap, 90–91
Taxes, 30, 42, 161
Taxis, 38–39
    to/from airport, 22
Tea Room, The, 79, 119
Telephone, 30–31
Telephone numbers, useful
    accommodations, 13, 44–45
    Blues Hotline, 180
    emergencies, 29, 40
    hotels, chain, 44
    Jazz Hotline, 180
    tickets, 176–77
    transit information, 37, 42
    visitor information, 12, 32
    weather, 42
Television, 42
Temperatures, average monthly, 14
Tennis, 16, 147

Thai House South Beach, 91
Theater, 177–78
Thrift shops, 169–70
Tickets, 176–77
Tiffany Hotel, 157
Tobacco Road, 181
Toni's, 91
Tony Roma's, 107
Tourist information, 12–13, 32
Tours, 136–39. *See also* Walking tours
    by air, 136–37
    Art Deco District, 127
    by boat, 137–38, 140
    by bus, 138
    Everglades National Park, 198–99
Train travel
    to Miami, 22–23
    within the U.S., 27
Transportation, 37–39, 42
    to/from airport, 22
Traveler's Aid, 29
Traveling
    to Miami, 20–23
    to the U.S., 26–27
    within the U.S., 27–28
Tropical Park, 136
Tula, 118
Turnberry Isle Resort and Club, 68
Tuttle, Julia, 6

University of Miami
    baseball team, 148
    cinema, 186
    football team, 149
    jazz recitals, at School of Music, 180
    theater, at Jerry Herman Ring Theatre, 177
Uva Wine Bar & Eatery, 115

Van Aken, Norman, 112
Van Dyke Cafe, 94, 181
Venetian Pool, 133–34, 142, 156
Versailles, 78–79, 106, 109, 186
Victor's Cafe, 104
Villa Paradiso, 54
Villa Regina, 154
Villa Vizcaya, 132–33, 154
    Italian Renaissance Festival, 16

Visitor information, 12–13, 32. *See also* Telephone numbers, useful

Waldorf Towers, 158
Walking tours
    Art Deco District, 157–60
    organized, 127, 138–39
Walters, Barbara, 9
Water sports, 139–42. *See also specific sports*
Weather, 14–15, 42
West Lake Trail (Everglades National Park), 196
Wildlife. *See also* Biscayne Bay National Park; Everglades National Park
    animal parks, 127–28, 136
Windsurfing, 123, 142
Wines, shopping for, 174–75
Wolfie Cohen's Rascal House, 99
Wolfsonian, The, 130
World Resources, 95

Yuca, 79, 87–88, 114

Zoos, 127, 128, 136

THE KEYS

Accommodations. *See also specific accommodations*
    Key West, 235–41
    Lower Keys, 226–28
    Upper Keys, 215–20
Addresses, locating, 208
Air tours, 214, 225, 234
Airports
    Key West, 229
    Marathon, 210, 214
    Sugarloaf Key, 225, 226
Alabama Jacks (Homestead), 206, 208
Annual events, festivals and fairs, 205–6
Aquariums
    Dolphin Research Center, 212–13
    Key West Aquarium, 233
    Theater of the Sea (Islamorada), 212
Art gallery: Leda-Bruce Galleries, 224

Arts Expo Craft Show, 205
Atlantic's Edge (Islamorada), 220–21
Audubon House and Gardens (Key West), 230

Backcountry islands, 204, 210–11
    canoeing and kayaking, 209
Bagatelle (Key West), 242
Bahia Honda State Park, 209, 225, 226
Banana Bay Resort & Marina (Marathon), 217–18
Bangalore, The (Key West), 243
Banyan Resort (Key West), 237–38
Barnacle, The (Big Pine Key), 227
Barracuda Bistro (Marathon), 221
Bay Harbor Lodge (Key Largo), 219
Beaches, 208, 213, 225
Bicycling, 208, 234
Big Pine Key. *See also* National Key Deer Refuge
    accommodations, 227
    restaurants, 228
    sights and activities, 215, 224, 225, 226
Birdwatching, 208–9
    Dry Tortugas, 209, 246, 248
Blue Heaven, 243–44
Boating, 214, 225
    Super Boat Racing Series, 205
Boat tours
    Dry Tortugas, 246–47
    Key West, 234
Breezy Palms Resort (Islamorada), 219

Cafe des Artistes (Key West), 241
Cafe Marquesa (Key West), 241
Calendar of events, 205–6
Camping
    Bahia Honda State Park, 225
    Dry Tortugas, 248
    John Pennekamp Coral Reef State Park, 220

    Long Key State Recreation Area, 220
Canoeing, 209, 213, 214
Cars and driving, 206–8. *See also* Overseas Highway
Casa Marina Resort (Key West), 235–36
Cemetery, Key West, 232
Cheeca Lodge (Islamorada), 216, 220–21
Chelsea House (Key West), 239–40
Conch Key Cottages (Marathon), 218
Conch Republic Celebration, 205
Crane Point Hammock, 209, 211
Curry Mansion Inn (Key West), 238

Deer Run Bed and Breakfast (Big Pine Key), 227
Dolphin Research Center, 212–13
Dolphins, swimming with, 212–13
Dry Tortugas, 246–48
    birdwatching, 209, 246, 248
    camping, 248
    fishing, 247
    scuba diving/snorkeling, 247
    traveling to, 246–47
Duck Key, accommodations, 216
Duval Street, in Key West, 230, 234, 245, 246

Faro Blanco Marine Resort (Marathon), 218
Festivals, 205–6
Fisher's (Mel) Treasure Museum (Key West), 233–34
Fishing, 209
    Dry Tortugas, 247
    Key West, 235
    Lower Keys, 226
    tournaments, 205
    Upper Keys, 211, 213, 215
Flagler, Henry, 211, 213, 229, 235

Florida Keys Wild Bird
    Rehabilitation Center,
    212
Fort Jefferson (Garden Key),
    247

Garden Key, 247, 248
Gardens
    Annual House and
        Garden Tours, 205
    Audubon House and
        Gardens (Key West),
        230
    Key West Garden Club
        Flower Show, 205
Gay men and lesbian
    travelers, in Key West,
    229, 246
Golf, at Key West, 235
Goombay Festival, 206

Half Shell Raw Bar
    (Key West), 244
Hawk's Cay Resort
    (Duck Key), 216
Hemingway, Ernest, 243,
    245
    Ernest Hemingway
        House Museum
        (Key West), 230, 232
    Hemingway Days
        Festival, 206
Hiking, 209, 214
Holiday Isle Resort
    (Islamorada), 218–19,
    223
    Tiki Bar, 208, 223

Indian Key, 210–11
Islamorada, 210
    accommodations, 216,
        218–19
    nightlife, 208, 223
    restaurants, 220–22
    sights and activities, 208,
        212, 214, 215
Island City House Hotel
    (Key West), 238
Island Reef Restaurant
    (Big Pine Key), 228

Jimmy Buffett's
    Margaritaville Cafe
    (Key West), 244, 245
John Pennekamp Coral Reef
    State Park, 213, 214

camping, 220
scuba diving/snorkeling,
    209, 215
Jules' Undersea Lodge
    (Key Largo), 216–17
July Fourth Swim Around
    the Island, 206

Kayaking, 209, 214–15.
    See also Canoeing
Kelly's Caribbean Bar &
    Grill (Key West), 242–43
Key Largo, 210. See also
    John Pennekamp Coral
    Reef State Park
    accommodations,
        216–17, 219
    restaurants, 221, 222
    sights and activities, 214
Key lime pie, 221
Key West, 204–5, 229–46
    accommodations, 235–41
    after dark, 244–46
    airport, 229
    Aquarium, 233
    Audubon House and
        Gardens, 230
    bars, 245–46
    Cemetery, 232
    Conch Train, 234
    Duval Street, 230, 234,
        245, 246
    East Martello Museum
        and Gallery, 233
    Ernest Hemingway
        House Museum, 230,
        232
    fishing, 235
    gay men and lesbian
        travelers, 229, 246
    Lighthouse Museum,
        233
    Mallory Square Sunset
        Celebration, 233
    Mel Fisher's Treasure
        Museum, 233–34
    nightclubs, 245–46
    nightlife, 244–46
    Old Town Trolley, 234
    recreational activities,
        234–35
    restaurants, 241–44
    shopping, 235
    sights and attractions,
        230–34
    special events, 205–6

sunset at Mallory Square
    Docks, 233
theater, 244–45
tours, 234
transportation, 230
traveling to, 229–30
visitor information, 229
Key West International
    Hostel, 241
La Pensione (Key West),
    240
Lazy Days Oceanfront Bar
    and Seafood Grill
    (Islamorada), 221
Leda-Bruce Galleries
    (Big Pine Key), 224
Lighthouse Museum,
    Key West, 233
Lignumvitae Key, 210–11
Little Munson Island,
    226–27
Little Palm Island, 226–27
Little Torch Key,
    accommodations, 227
Loggerhead Key, 246
Long Key State Recreation
    Area, 209, 213–14
    camping, 220
Looe Key National Marine
    Sanctuary, 226
Louie's Backyard (Key West),
    242
Lower Keys, 204, 223–29
    accommodations, 226–28
    restaurants, 228–29
    sights and attractions,
        224–25
    visitor information, 224

Makoto Japanese Restaurant
    (Key Largo), 221
Mallory Square Sunset
    Celebration (Key West),
    233
Mangia, Mangia (Key West),
    244
Mangoes Restaurant
    (Key West), 243
Mangrove Mama's
    Restaurant (Sugarloaf Key),
    228
Manny & Isa's Kitchen
    (Islamorada), 221–22
Marathon, 210
    accommodations,
        217–18, 220

Music (cont.)
  airport, 210, 214
  restaurants, 221, 222–23
  sights and activities, 211,
    214, 215
Marquesa Hotel, The
  (Key West), 238–39, 241
Marriott's Casa Marina
  Resort (Key West),
  235–36
Mel Fisher's Treasure
  Museum (Key West),
  233–34
Monte's (Summerland Key),
  228
Mrs. Mac's Kitchen
  (Key Largo), 222
Museum of Crane Point
  Hammock (Marathon), 211
Museums
  East Martello Museum
    and Gallery
    (Key West), 233
  Ernest Hemingway
    House Museum
    (Key West), 230, 232
  Key West Lighthouse
    Museum, 233
  Mel Fisher's Treasure
    Museum (Key West),
    233–34
  Museum of Crane Point
    Hammock (Marathon),
    211
Music, 245–46
  Looe Key Underwater
    Music Fest, 205–6

National Key Deer Refuge,
  209, 224

Ocean Key House
  (Key West), 239
Old Island Days (Key West),
  205
Overseas Highway (U.S. 1),
  204, 206, 208
  Seven Mile Bridge, 211

Papa Joe's (Islamorada), 222
Parks, 209
  Bahia Honda State Park,
    209, 225, 226
  John Pennekamp Coral
    Reef State Park, 209,
    213, 214,215, 220

Long Key State
  Recreation Area, 209,
  213–14, 220
National Key Deer
  Refuge, 209, 224
Parmer's Place Cottages
  (Little Torch Key), 227
Pier House, The (Key West),
  236
Ponce de León, Juan, 204,
  246

Reach, The (Key West),
  236–37
Recreational activities,
  208–9. See also
  specific activities
Reef Relief's Cayo Festival,
  206
Regions, 204–5. See also
  Dry Tortugas; Key
  West; Lower Keys;
  Upper Keys
Restaurants. See also specific
  restaurants
  Key West, 241–44
  Lower Keys, 228–29
  Upper Keys, 220–23
Robbie's Pier, 212
Roosevelt, Franklin, 204

Scuba diving/snorkeling,
  209
  Dry Tortugas, 247
  John Pennekamp
    Coral Reef State Park,
    209, 215
  Key West, 234–35
  Lower Keys, 225, 226
  Upper Keys, 215
Sea Cove Motel (Marathon),
  220
Sea turtles, at Dry Tortugas,
  246
Seven Mile Bridge, 211
Seven Mile Grill (Marathon),
  222–23
Sheraton Key Largo Resort,
  217
Sheraton Suites (Key West),
  237
Sid & Roxie's Green Turtle
  Inn (Islamorada), 222
Skydiving, from t, 226
Sloppy Joe's (Key West),
  245–46

Snorkeling. See Scuba
  diving/snorkeling
South Beach Oceanfront
  Motel (Key West), 240
Southernmost Point Guest
  House (Key West),
  240
Special events, 205–6
Sports, 208–9. See also
  specific sports
Sugarloaf Bat Tower,
  225
Sugarloaf Key, 225
  accommodations,
    227–28
  airport, 225, 226
  restaurants, 228–29
Sugarloaf Lodge
  (Sugarloaf Key), 227–29
Summerland Key
  fishing, 226
  restaurant, 228

Ten Keymanments, 232
Theater, in Key West,
  244–45
Theater of the Sea
  (Islamorada), 212
Tiki Bar (Islamorada), 208,
  223
Turtle Kraals Wildlife Grill
  (Key West), 243

Upper Keys, 204, 210–23
  accommodations,
    215–20
  recreational activities,
    214–15
  restaurants, 220–23
  sights and attractions,
    210–14
  traveling to, 210
  visitor information,
    210
U.S. 1. See Overseas
  Highway

Wicker Guesthouse
  (Key West), 240–41
Wild Bird Rehabilitation
  Center, Florida Keys,
  212
Wildlife, 212–13. See also
  Parks
  Theater of the Sea
    (Islamorada), 212

FROMMER'S COMPLETE TRAVEL GUIDES

(Comprehensive guides to destinations around the world, with selections in all price ranges—from deluxe to budget)

Acapulco/Ixtapa/Taxco
Alaska
Amsterdam
Arizona
Atlanta
Australia
Austria
Bahamas
Bangkok
Barcelona, Madrid & Seville
Belgium, Holland & Luxembourg
Berlin
Bermuda
Boston
Budapest & the Best of Hungary
California
Canada
Cancún, Cozumel & the Yucatán
Caribbean
Caribbean Cruises & Ports of Call
Caribbean Ports of Call
Carolinas & Georgia
Chicago
Colorado
Costa Rica
Denver, Boulder & Colorado Springs
Dublin
England
Florida
France
Germany
Greece
Hawaii
Hong Kong
Honolulu/Waikiki/Oahu
Ireland
Italy
Jamaica/Barbados
Japan
Las Vegas
London
Los Angeles
Maryland & Delaware
Maui

Mexico
Mexico City
Miami & the Keys
Montana & Wyoming
Montréal & Québec City
Munich & the Bavarian Alps
Nashville & Memphis
Nepal
New England
New Mexico
New Orleans
New York City
Northern New England
Nova Scotia, New Brunswick & Prince Edward Island
Paris
Philadelphia & the Amish Country
Portugal
Prague & the Best of the Czech Republic
Puerto Rico
Puerto Vallarta, Manzanillo & Guadalajara
Rome
San Antonio & Austin
San Diego
San Francisco
Santa Fe, Taos & Albuquerque
Scandinavia
Scotland
Seattle & Portland
South Pacific
Spain
Switzerland
Thailand
Tokyo
Toronto
U.S.A.
Utah
Vancouver & Victoria
Vienna
Virgin Islands
Virginia
Walt Disney World & Orlando
Washington, D.C.
Washington & Oregon

FROMMER'S FRUGAL TRAVELER'S GUIDES

(The grown-up guides to budget travel, offering dream vacations at down-to-earth prices)

Australia from $45 a Day
Berlin from $50 a Day
California from $60 a Day
Caribbean from $60 a Day
Costa Rica & Belize from $35 a Day
Eastern Europe from $30 a Day
England from $50 a Day
Europe from $50 a Day
Florida from $50 a Day
Greece from $45 a Day
Hawaii from $60 a Day

India from $40 a Day
Ireland from $45 a Day
Italy from $50 a Day
Israel from $45 a Day
London from $60 a Day
Mexico from $35 a Day
New York from $70 a Day
New Zealand from $45 a Day
Paris from $65 a Day
Washington, D.C. from $50 a Day

FROMMER'S PORTABLE GUIDES

(Pocket-size guides for travelers who want everything in a nutshell)

Charleston & Savannah
Las Vegas

New Orleans
San Francisco

FROMMER'S IRREVERENT GUIDES

(Wickedly honest guides for sophisticated travelers)

Amsterdam
Chicago
London
Manhattan

Miami
New Orleans
Paris
San Francisco

Santa Fe
U.S. Virgin Islands
Walt Disney World
Washington, D.C.

FROMMER'S AMERICA ON WHEELS

(Everything you need for a successful road trip, including full-color road maps and ratings for every hotel)

California & Nevada
Florida
Mid-Atlantic
Midwest & the Great Lakes
New England & New York

Northwest & Great Plains
South Central &Texas
Southeast
Southwest

FROMMER'S BY NIGHT GUIDES

(The series for those who know that life begins after dark)

Amsterdam
Chicago
Las Vegas
London

Los Angeles
Miami
New Orleans

New York
Paris
San Francisco